Also by Meryle Secrest

Stephen Sondheim: A Life

Leonard Bernstein: A Life

Frank Lloyd Wright

Salvador Dalí

Kenneth Clark: A Biography

Being Bernard Berenson: A Biography

Between Me and Life: A Biography of Romaine Brooks

SOMEWHERE
FOR ME

SOMEWHERE
FOR ME

A Biography of Richard Rodgers

MERYLE SECREST

ALFRED A. KNOPF NEW YORK 2001

THIS IS A BORZOI BOOK
PUBLISHED BY ALFRED A. KNOPF

Knopf, Borzoi Books, and the colophon are registered trademarks of Random House, Inc.

Due to limitations of space, all permissions to reprint
previously published material may be found on pages 455–6.

Library of Congress Cataloging-in-Publication Data
Secrest, Meryle.
Somewhere for me: a biography of Richard Rodgers / Meryle Secrest.
p. cm.
Includes bibliographical references.
ISBN 0-375-40164-4 (alk. paper)
1. Rodgers, Richard, 1902–79. Composers—United States—Biography. I. Title.
ML410.R6315 S43 2001
782.1'4'092—dc21
[B]   2001029873

Manufactured in the United States of America
FIRST EDITION

For Martin

The sweetest sounds I'll ever hear

Are still inside my head.

The kindest words I'll ever know

Are waiting to be said.

The most entrancing sight of all

Is yet for me to see.

And the dearest love in all the world

Is waiting somewhere for me,

Is waiting somewhere, somewhere for me.

—*"The Sweetest Sounds," from* No Strings,
music and lyrics by Richard Rodgers

La vie: C'est la femme que l'on a;

L'art, C'est la femme que l'on désire.

—*Jean Dolent*

Contents

Acknowledgments

After more than two decades of writing biography my interest in the genre is as vivid as ever, but my approach increasingly selective. I am looking for the pertinent fact, one that will open up unsuspected insights. In my mind's eye I am walking over a beach covered with millions of pebbles, looking for those few remarkable stones that will begin to form a design. What makes the work even more exasperating is that I do not know what the pebble looks like until I have found it. This puts the idea of a research assistant out of the question, since no one can help me find something if I do not know what I am looking for yet. In much the same vein, there are aspects of Richard Rodgers's life, briefly outlined in my chronology, that did not get included for perhaps perverse reasons on my part. In the end what interests me is a subject's secret life, his struggles, his dreams, disappointments, loves and hates. I want to tell a true story that no one knows.

This book came about in an interesting way. In the course of writing a biography of Leonard Bernstein I met Mary Rodgers Guettel, who had worked with him on his famous television series of Young People's Concerts. I found her frank, funny, and very *sympathique,* with a special kind of strength that comes from surmounting the handicap of parents who do not necessarily see candor as a virtue. Then I met her sister, Linda Rodgers Emory, who was able to overcome her natural reluctance to discuss the emotional atmosphere of her own upbringing and offer observations based on a lifetime of careful listening. I was flattered and delighted to be asked by them to write a new biography of Richard Rodgers to coincide with the centenary of his birth in 2002. As Mary Rodgers Guettel observed, I would have to say as much about their mother, the extraordinary and complex Dorothy, as about their father. She turned out to be right. Richard Rodgers's daughters were generous in their decision not to ask for any kind of editorial control over the manuscript. So this is by no means an authorized biography, and any omissions or erroneous conclusions are entirely my own. Just the same, they gave me every possible help and put up with my innumerable tiresome questions. I owe them my deepest thanks.

I am indebted to Theodore S. Chapin, president and executive director of the Rodgers & Hammerstein Organization; Bert Fink, its director of special projects and public relations; and Bruce Pomahac, its music director. They took the brunt of my inquiry with endless patience and good humor. Thanks to their ministrations I spent weeks going through their Rodgers and Hammerstein archive, which begins in the late 1950s and continues to the end of his life in 1979. Most of the files are business related, since Dorothy Rodgers removed many personal items before she died. The whereabouts of that part of the archive is unknown. Dorothy Rodgers kept a detailed diary, which, sadly, she destroyed. However, there were enough clues to Rodgers's state of mind to reward my efforts, and I am so grateful to the Rodgers & Hammerstein Organization for allowing me this privilege. I have seldom met a warmer or more friendly group of people.

I am also indebted to Robert Marx, director; Susan Sommer, chief of the music division; and George Boziwick, curator, of the New York Public Library for the Performing Arts at Lincoln Center. Before she died Dorothy Rodgers deposited fifty-eight scrapbooks about her husband's career, from his earliest achievements to the end of his life. After persistent badgering from me, Susan Sommer overcame her natural curatorial reluctance to allow me some photocopies from the originals, for which I am much in her debt. This branch of the New York Public Library also contains letters from Richard Rodgers to his wife, particularly rich in the early years before and after their marriage, when they were often apart. The library has published most of these letters in a limited edition, *Letters to Dorothy,* and I was delighted to have the opportunity of comparing the originals with the published versions. As any wife would do, Dorothy Rodgers removed some references that she found too personal. As any biographer knows, those were the ones that are particularly interesting.

Although she did not go to Radcliffe College (she attended Wellesley), Dorothy Rodgers chose to leave her own archive to Radcliffe's Schlesinger Library, several boxes of scrapbooks, clippings, photos, and letters, which I was able to study. My thanks go to the curator of manuscripts, Eva Moseley, and staff of the library, who were uniformly helpful and forthcoming. Perhaps the library's most valuable holding is its oral history of Dorothy

Rodgers, made late in her life (in 1987), which was a serendipitous discovery. Her published memoir, *A Personal Book,* which appeared in 1977, while her husband was still alive, was not very personal and barely a book. Its curiously stilted air is in marked contrast to the relaxed and confiding tone of the Radcliffe transcript. Like many husbands, Rodgers invested in his wife the responsibility, perhaps even the duty, of taking charge of their joint emotional life. For a parallel one thinks of the relationship between Mary Berenson and her husband, Bernard; her gossipy, amused and devastating letters make up in tone for everything her husband does not say in his own. Dorothy Rodgers certainly knew every nuance of the way her husband thought, felt, and reacted. Much of that has disappeared with the loss of her own diaries, but enough is contained in her Radcliffe account to make it a valuable guide.

Family—husbands, children, cousins, nieces and nephews—are on the fringes of any biographical work; and the task of a biographer, it seems to me, is to give due weight to their opinions while avoiding the danger that their lives will become entangled in the narrative. I hope I have eschewed that trap by keeping the focus on what they remembered about Richard and Dorothy Rodgers and otherwise keeping their private lives private. One of the people I have depended on the most has been Henry Guettel, whose manner is unruffled and whose judgments unerring. Another has been Julian ("Jerry") Beaty, Mary Rodgers Guettel's first husband and father of her children Tod, Nina, and Kim Beaty. Jerry Beaty has a priceless memory and a gift for the insightful anecdote that biographers dream of. His children have inherited his wit and warmth; to them all, and also to Adam and Alec Guettel, I extend my thanks and appreciation.

Dorothy Rodgers's nieces, Judith Crichton and Margot Conte, have given me a special perspective. They were far enough away from the drama to see its broader outlines; close enough to value the qualities, as well as the problems, of the major characters. Margot Conte has taken a special interest in the histories of the Rodgers and Feiner families and treated me to a wonderful overnight stay in the country as well as the benefits of her hard-earned knowledge. Daniel Melnick, Linda Rodgers Emory's first husband, entertained me in his Hollywood house while reminiscing about his former in-laws. Their son, Peter Rodgers Melnick, himself a successful composer, was equally helpful. The late William Hammerstein and the late Jamie Hammerstein were immensely kind in helping me to understand the relationship between their father and Richard Rodgers. The late Dorothy Hart and I spoke by phone but, unfortunately, never met. Her son Larry, named for his uncle Lorenz, answered many of my questions and has been particularly helpful in explaining the intricacies of his parents' lawsuit over the Lorenz Hart will. I am most grateful to him.

Biographers make wonderful colleagues and willing listeners at moments when the eyes of one's husbands, wives, and friends start to glaze over. So I have to thank my dear friend Patricia Bosworth, who is always there when I need her, and some new friends I've made. They include Steven Bach, who offered much help, particularly about the Hollywood years; Dr. William Hyland, author of a previous Rodgers biography, who generously passed along a number of files; Max Wilk, who cheered me on; Robert Kimball, who watched with a benevolent eye as I navigated the intricacies of American musical theatre history; and Frederick Nolan, whose own biography of Lorenz Hart is invaluable.

I particularly want to thank Jeffrey Lunden, whose collection of oral histories of this period is quite amazing, for his kindness in copying many of the interviews and making them available for this study. The biography of Lew Fields, *From the Bowery to Broadway,* by Armond Fields and L. Marc Fields, is a monumental work and has been an indispensable guide in this search. I also want to cordially thank Jason Rubin for the loan of his Ph.D. thesis, *Lew Fields and the Development of the Broadway Musical;* the staff of the Shubert Theatre archive, for many helpful suggestions; David Thompson of the BBC, producer of the Great Performances television documentary on Rodgers and Hart, *Thou Swell, Thou Witty;* and Walter Willison, one of the stars of *Two by Two,* who was particularly helpful about this and many other aspects of Rodgers's life and work. Many other people lent articles, photographs, books, and memorabilia. Among them I must mention the actor Bill Hayes, who played a principal role in *Me and Juliet* and lent me his unpublished memoir, giving an unexpected view into the inner workings of that ill-starred venture.

For those who offered advice, encouragement, and help and/or allowed themselves to be interviewed, I want to extend further thanks: Joy Abbott, Shelley Ackerman, Bill Anderson, Barbara Andres, Milton Babbitt, Ben Bagley, Isabel Bigley Barnet, Leigh Beery, Roger Berlind, Anne Bernays, Theodore Bikel, Paul Blake, Eddie Blum, Dwight Blocker Bowers, Ralph Burns, Billie Worth Burr, Stephen Douglas Burton, Jonathan Bush, Schuyler G. Chapin, Martin Charnin, Alexander H. Cohen, Barbara Cook, Alvin Cooperman, Joan Copeland, Anna Crouse, Gemze de Lappe, Irene Diamond, Nancy Dolan, Barry J. Drogin, Duane Garrison Elliott, Eleanor Elliott, Don Fellows, Professor George Ferencz, Cy Feuer, Hugh Fordin, Bill Frohlich, Myrna Katz Frommer, Penny Fuller, Julie Goldsmith Gilbert, Professor Jonathan Gill, Herbert G. Goldman, William Goldman, Lisa Vaill (librarian, Goodspeed Opera House), John Steele Gordon, Robert Gottlieb,

Linda Gras, Kay Green, Edward Hall, Sheldon Harnick, Kitty Carlisle Hart, Robert Hartmann, David Hays, Amy Henderson, Florence Henderson, Molly Henderson, Peter Howard, Lois Hunt, Zoë Hyde-Thomson, Jane A. Johnston, Shirley Jones, Milton J. Kain, Al Keith, Jane Klain, Miles Kreuger, Bill Krokyn, Shirley Rich Kron, Dania Krupska, Arthur Laurents, Jerome Lawrence, Dick Lewine, Craig Lucas, Pete McGovern, Cathy McKeany, Hugh Martin, Alice Mathias, Barbara Meister, Sheldon Meyer, Nina and Irwin Miness, David Bushman (curator, Museum of Television and Radio), Trevor Nunn, Victor Oristano, Laurie Peters, John Raitt, David Raksin, Jonathan Reed, Frank Rich, Trude Rittmann, Joan Roberts, John Rodgers, Ned Rorem, Richard Sabellico, Rita Salzman, Anne Kaufman Schneider, Canon Louis C. Schueddig, Dr. Victor Sendax, Edwin Sherin, Max Showalter, Joanna Simon, Joan Sitwell, Stephen Sondheim, Harry Miller (reference archivist, State Historical Society of Wisconsin), Elaine Steinbeck, Gary Stevens, Peter Stone, Samuel Taylor, Pat Suzuki, Joseph Trigoboff, Jon Voight, Anita V. Waksman, George D. Wallace, Marie Nash Walling, Fiona Walsh (head of press, Royal National Theatre), Anthony Ward, Alix B. Williamson, Julie Wilson, Martha Wright, Robert Wright, Sherman Yellen, and William Baldwin Young.

Victoria Wilson, my incomparable editor at Knopf, was quick to appreciate this subject's possibilities as a biography. My agents, Lynn Nesbit in New York and Bruce Hunter in London, gave me the benefit of their expertise and help at every stage. I am indebted to that incomparable historian of musical theatre, Robert Kimball, who has saved me from many egregious errors. I must also thank John and Caroline Macomber, who, hearing of my plight, generously made their apartment in New York available while I worked for a month on the Rodgers archives, for which I shall be forever in their debt. As always, my husband, Thomas Beveridge, has been my advisor, confidant, and friend, the best companion a writer ever had.

SOMEWHERE
FOR ME

Chapter One

BLUE ROOM

H ERE COMES Jacob Levy trotting along the street, a tiny little man in a neat black suit and fussy bow tie, carrying a cane and sporting a white panama with a surprisingly rakish brim. It is 1926, and Richard Rodgers's grandfather on his mother's side is spending the summer in Long Beach, New York, walking down an expanse of sidewalk bordered by identical lawns, a single Model T Ford parked behind him on that ramrod-straight, deserted street. Now here is Will, Dick's physician father, in the home movies Richard Rodgers began to take with his fancy new film camera, the one you wound up by hand. Will, too, is spending his summer in Long Beach, and stands on the steps of their cottage, red-haired, handsome, and blue-eyed, a smudge of moustache on his upper lip, in his starched-collar shirt and his suit with matching waistcoat, laughing uproariously at some forgotten joke. And here is Mamie, Dick's mother, with her flat, blunt nose, close-set eyes, pince-nez, and distinct gap between her front teeth. Even in those days of blurry and faded film one somehow knows it is a dusty afternoon in high summer, and only city folk get dressed up in hats and gloves to have their pictures taken.

Now the golden boy himself appears, towering (even though of modest height) over his tiny mother, his hair glistening in the sunlight, his lips parted in a curving smile, with his beautifully modeled forehead and the slight cleft in his chin, the kind of face to be found in magazine illustrations of the period advertising cigars, cognacs, Cadillacs, and crossings on the Cunard Line. His suit is something formal and dark and the shirt collar is fashionably stiff and confining, but his tie tells another story: it is daringly patterned with dots and can only be bright red. He leans solicitously over his mother and the

3

tree under which they are posing throws a pattern of light on his cheekbones and the edge of his lapel.

Soon they are on the boardwalk in Atlantic City, whither they have come for the tryout of a new show. Here is Dick, the brim of his hat pulled down snappily over one eye, with his mother on his arm. She is in mourning for her father, lately dead, and looks, in her mountainous black hat, as solemn as an owl. Next to them, in a line advancing toward the camera, are Lew Fields, the famous comedian-turned-producer who backed so many of Rodgers's first shows, and Lew's son Herbert, Rodgers's collaborator on the books. At the far right is the impeccably dressed Lorenz Hart, Rodgers's brilliant lyricist, whose Homburg hat and perfectly tailored double-breasted coat only serve to underline the contrast between his manly head and stunted body. Now we are at the tennis courts, where the agile form of Richard Rodgers, in faultless white flannels, can be seen serving and volleying with the rapidity of a drag-onfly. Next we are on a lake and he is lounging in a canoe, wearing a fashion-able two-piece swimsuit (striped, sleeveless top, white belt, dark trunks), with his half-smile, his widow's peak of immaculate dark hair parted just off-center, the ever-present cigarette between his fingers. Or he is standing on the dock beside Bobbie Perkins, who sang "Mountain Greenery" in the *Garrick Gaieties* of 1926, his arm around her waist, a charming scene disrupted by his handsome older brother Mortimer. Morty interposes himself between them and triumphantly carries off the girl.

Next he is on a picnic in Canada, wearing a beret, eating sandwiches and drinking from a thermos flask, then proudly displaying the fish he has just caught. Or he is in Cannes, coming around the corner with a beauty on each arm. On one side is Corinne Griffith and on the other, Kendall Lee, then married to Jules Glaenzer, vice-president of Cartier's. Rodgers is on the Rivi-era to attend some kind of lavish party at the invitation of Glaenzer, youngish and handsome and wearing what looks like a silk kimono. For Richard Rodgers, ambitious young composer-about-town, has been taken up by café society and invited everywhere. And no wonder, since although he is only in his mid-twenties, he has had several hit musicals and has taken bachelor's quarters, three rooms on the nineteenth floor with a wrap-around terrace, in a deluxe apartment hotel called the Lombardy at 11 East Fifty-sixth Street, with its two-story-high Spanish Renaissance lobby and hand-modeled stucco walls with travertine quoins and jambs. There he has decorated his study as befits his status: light red draperies, cork walls (a daring touch), Moderne furniture, and the latest in Art Deco built-in bookcases. Writing to his future wife, Dorothy Feiner, he said that a divan and bookcase had just arrived and he was biting his nails with anxiety. "I suspect it's rather successful, but you'll

Young and famous: Richard Rodgers in the 1920s

know!" he wrote. Charles, his valet, who insisted on the French pronunciation of his name, did everything without being told. One night Rodgers brought home a congenial group after a prizefight, and they sat around singing songs and strolled about on his spacious terrace. Charles made sandwiches, scrambled eggs, and sausages and served champagne. He left the gathering at 4:30 a.m. and "showed up again at nine-thirty to give me breakfast, with the same smile," Rodgers wrote. "Dot, what a way to live! Expensive, but *so* nice."

The year was 1929, and a decade had gone by since that hot summer day when he and Larry Hart had traveled out to Rockaway to play some of their first tunes for Lew Fields. That same summer the two of them stood in the back of the Casino Theatre at Broadway and Thirty-ninth Street to hear Eve Lynn and Alan Hale sing "Any Old Place with You." It was 1919, the musical was *A Lonely Romeo,* and Rodgers's first song had been heard on Broadway; he was just seventeen. Years of struggle followed until the big chance came with *The Garrick Gaieties* of 1925, and the writing team of Rodgers and Hart was launched. By the late 1920s newspapers were publishing drawings of Rodgers, the composer of such musicals as *Peggy-Ann* and *A Connecticut Yankee* and such songs as "My Heart Stood Still," "Manhattan," "Here in My Arms," "The Girl Friend," "Thou Swell," and "This Funny World." The headline was "The Young Master of Melody." A short film had even been made, with Rodgers and Hart as the stars, celebrating their rapid rise. And everyone was singing their songs.

> We'll have a blue room,
> A new room,
> For two room,
> Where ev'ry day's a holiday
> Because you're married to me.
>
> *("The Blue Room")*

Spring of 1929 began, appropriately enough, with a February tryout for *Spring Is Here* at the Shubert Theatre, Philadelphia; it moved to the Alvin Theatre, New York, the following month. The musical was based on a book by Owen Davis, which he had adapted from his play *Shotgun Wedding,* and, like most confections of the period, told a forgettable story about a boy in love with a girl in love with somebody else until the last act. It ran for 104 performances, not a very prepossessing number, although the reviewers had been kind, and was notable for at least one wonderful melody, "With a Song in My Heart." It was also notable for its bevy of pretty girls, called "Ladies of the Ensemble" in the program, every one vivacious and charming and with perfect thighs. Rodgers lovingly photographed them all in their silk negligées or their garden outfits of white cloche hats and polka-dot dresses, or their Pierrette costumes—it was the moment for puffed sleeves and tiers of frills on skirts—in which they pouted, pirouetted, and drooped charmingly against doorways. The early home movies are full of such pretty girls, and Dorothy Rodgers, who later provided the commentary, was forbearing. "This is Bobbie Perkins," she announced as that particularly trim and lively girl appeared

Inez Courtney as a despondent heroine in
Spring Is Here, with, from left, Dick Keene,
Glenn Hunter, and John Hundley, spring 1929

to take her bow. "Dick used to take her out a lot, and she and I became great friends."

Dorothy herself appeared in the films, her long brown hair loose around her face, swimming in the pool of the house in Tarrytown, New York, that her parents had rented for a year, or riding horseback with Herbert Fields, her ponytail bouncing along behind her, or posing against the doorway of the house in something clinging and low-cut, a dress one would have thought too sultry for a girl of seventeen. Or she is getting into Dick's chauffeur-driven Stutz Bearcat convertible, in an amazingly chic outfit, a belted two-piece with contrasting trim, and, in those days of the universal cloche hat, wearing what looks like a very becoming turban. There is an air of maturity about this young and pretty admirer, whose youthfulness is betrayed occasionally by a tremulous uncertainty in her smile. And, indeed, she was something of a sophisticate, the much-indulged daughter of wealthy parents, who had made the yearly pilgrimage to Europe since childhood. She knew, for instance, that one went to Egypt for perfume, to Turkey for star sapphires, to Naples for coral and tortoiseshell, to Rome for antiques, and to Florence for leather goods.

In Paris, she and her mother spent countless hours being fitted for clothes. It was, she wrote later, "an era of almost unimaginable luxury . . . French underwear, for example, was made of the sheerest pure silk ninon and trimmed with hand-run Alençon lace. Combinations called 'teddies,' slips, petticoats and nightgowns were designed to be knife-pleated—a process that had to be repeated by hand each time they were washed." Since American laundries would not perform this time-consuming work, Dorothy Feiner would take her dirty underwear to France on each transatlantic trip to be painstakingly repleated. Such close knowledge of the fine points of haute couture would stand her in good stead when she came to buy her trousseau, a year's worth of hats, coats, dresses, evening clothes, furs, shoes, and underwear—everything, right down to the hand-pleated silk chiffon handkerchiefs.

By June of 1929 Rodgers was working on a new show, *Me for You*, later called *Heads Up!*, all about rum runners in yachts and true love winning through in the end. Rodgers had written a song, "A Ship Without a Sail," and thought it sounded "pretty hot." He had spent the weekend at the painter and illustrator Neysa McMein's and was touched by the flowers Dot had wired from Paris for his twenty-seventh birthday. As she traveled on to Vittel and Biarritz, his letters followed: optimistic predictions for the success of the show, a few lame jokes, and sporadic references to weekend parties in Westhampton (to celebrate Glaenzer's forty-seventh birthday), deep-sea fishing with friends off Montauk, telephone calls from Florenz Ziegfeld about his next show, *Simple Simon,* and offers from Paramount. "This is going to be a big year," he wrote with some prescience in the summer of 1929. They went through the tryouts of *Heads Up!* together. They got engaged during the New York run. Meanwhile, in that winter of the Depression, *Simple Simon,* starring Ed Wynn as the proprietor of a newspaper shop in Coney Island more at home with fairy tales than with newspaper headlines, made its way through a Boston tryout to the Ziegfeld Theatre early in 1930. When Dick married

Dorothy Belle Feiner, the future
Mrs. Richard Rodgers, about 1930

Dorothy, on March 5, he and Larry Hart had two shows on Broadway, but reviews had been mixed in both cases: *Heads Up!* closed ten days later and *Simple Simon* in mid-June.

Theirs was one of the weddings of the season, and Mrs. Richard Rodgers's photograph appeared a day later in the Social News section of the *New York Times*. She was married in her parents' home, the paper reported, at 270 Park Avenue. The apartment had been transformed into an outdoor garden with quantities of flowers and fruit blossoms. The bride chose a medieval gown of ivory-colored satin without any adornment, a simple tulle veil, mittens of old rose-point lace, and carried a sheaf of calla lilies. Her bride's book records one hundred and fifty gifts, neatly catalogued and described, checked to show that they had been acknowledged: a custom-made crystal bowl and plate; several traveling clocks of green leather; silver, crystal, and agate ashtrays; towels decorated with Milanese lace; a silver smoking set; silver bonbon dishes; crystal decanters; a breakfast set from Tiffany's; a silver bowl from Cartier's; a Lalique vase; an antique cigarette box; Wedgwood china from

Tiffany's; bronze candelabra; ditto; rock crystal champagne glasses; lamps, vases, bowls, ornaments, tiles, earrings, silverware, and other miscellany, some returned. Dorothy's new mother- and father-in-law contributed a diamond bracelet. Her own parents gave her a baguette diamond watch bracelet.

There was a dinner for the wedding party at 270 Park Avenue, and the happy couple boarded the SS *Roma* that very evening, bound for Naples. "It was a lovely dinner," she recalled later, "but we ate nothing, we were so excited and nervous." By the time they were settled in their spacious suite— there was a cabin just to hold their trunks and hand luggage—it was close to midnight and Dorothy was finally hungry enough to eat a few dried-up sandwiches. Rodgers wrote, "That night we . . . retired with the heady thought of how romantic it would be to awaken . . . far out to sea. When we got up the next morning we found we were still tied up at the North River dock," because of engine problems. Dorothy's main memory of that morning was of being asked by the Italian stewardess what her husband would like for breakfast and being embarrassed that she did not know.

A honeymoon trip to Europe would be the least one could expect from a young husband with the income of a Richard Rodgers—one family story has it that when he got married at the age of twenty-seven, he was making $75,000 a year—but in a display of that practicality which would become a marked aspect of his character, he was combining business with pleasure. He and Larry Hart had been having discussions with the London producer Charles B. Cochran about an idea they had for a musical to be called *Ever Green;* it would star an exquisite young singer and dancer named Jessie Matthews. Rodgers and his bride would spend a few weeks in the Mediterranean and then join Larry Hart in London to begin work.

Rodgers and Hart were familiar names in London, having had several productions there, including the British version of *A Connecticut Yankee,* retitled *A Yankee at the Court of King Arthur,* in 1929. In those days he and Hart had shared quarters cheerfully enough in a series of service flats, i.e., apartments with meals and maid service. But when Dick took Dorothy to inspect the flat on St. James's Street where they usually stayed, she was horrified: "It was run down, depressing and none too clean." Before she could think of a tactful objection, her husband quickly decided it would not do. They looked all over London, but everything seemed too dark, too grubby, and certainly too small, since most of the flats could not even hold their three large Oshkosh trunks, not to mention her trousseau and Dick's own sizable wardrobe: suits, white tie and tails, sports jackets, slacks, dinner jackets, and cutaways for going to the races.

Dorothy went to explain their dilemma to a new friend, Beatrice Guinness, and that lady had an immediate solution. Why didn't they take her daughter's town house, at 11 York Terrace, while her daughter was away? It was fully furnished, and in the very best neighborhood, right on Regent's Park. Dorothy was enchanted with it. "The house was charmingly furnished with eighteenth-century pieces, delightful chintz in all the rooms and everything done in light, gay colors. It had modern bathrooms—ours had pink marble fixtures and a cork floor—and, miracle of miracles, there was an electric refrigerator in a respectable up-to-date kitchen. Most important of all, there was a good piano in the living room."

One of the advantages of 11 York Terrace was that it had a large top floor. Larry Hart could move in and have the whole place to himself; and after more than a decade of their partnership Rodgers welcomed the idea of having his mercurial librettist on the premises when there was work to be done. This infinitely charming, disorderly, gifted man, who was capable of sitting down with a book and forgetting about the bathtub water he had left running—as he did almost as soon as he moved in—had only the sketchiest notions of day and night or, for that matter, the needs of others. He worked when the spirit moved him and when he could be found, and his erratic schedule inevitably dictated that of his partner. Coping with Larry's peccadillos would become an unwelcome necessity, almost a trial by fire in the first weeks of Dorothy's marriage to Dick. She said later, "He really was a darling but he was quite difficult. He loved to drink. Because we wouldn't let him pay rent or anything, he insisted on taking care of the liquor. He would buy it and see that we had everything we needed. When we had guests to dinner, he would go into the kitchen and make the cocktails. He'd give one to the cook, and he'd have one, and the cook would have one, and he'd have one. And pretty soon, no dinner. So it was trying."

There was further unwelcome news. A few weeks after they moved into York Terrace she had some "suspicious symptoms," and went to see an obstetrician with the preposterous name of Dr. Ovary. He confirmed that she was pregnant, and while they paid lip service to the idea that "of course we were happy," the fact remained that they had hardly expected to become parents with such dispatch. The more she thought about it, the more resentful Dorothy became. Dick's three-room apartment in New York was barely big enough for them and a baby, even with that spacious terrace. He had just signed a contract to do three pictures in Hollywood. He had to return to London in the autumn to attend rehearsals for *Ever Green*. How were they going to fit into the Lombardy? Could she travel to the West Coast and back again and then take a transatlantic voyage when she was six or seven months pregnant? And if she had to stay behind, how would she feel? Her unwillingness to put up with long absences had made itself felt almost as soon as they got engaged, when Dick had to go to Boston for the tryouts for *Simple Simon*. Writing in his usual rapid, sloping hand, he complained, "Have I been impatient with your impatience? Sweet, I'm sorry. You're anxious to see me, and I don't want you to be so anxious because I can't come to you sooner; and because I can't, I feel guilty, and resenting that, I become impatient."

As Dorothy Rodgers observed, by the time they married, her husband was "the darling of the Mayfair set": an exaggeration, but perhaps not much of one. Among his first friends in London was Myrtle Farquharson, then married to Robin d'Erlanger, who moved in exalted circles and introduced him everywhere. Such personages as Lord and Lady Mountbatten and Prince George, Duke of Kent, were already admirers of his. People seemed drawn to his easy, unassuming manner, his evident talent, his fund of jokes, puns, and quips, and his willingness to enliven any party at the piano, playing all the popular music of the day as well as his own. It was as if, as F. Scott Fitzgerald wrote in *The Great Gatsby,* "there was something gorgeous about him, some heightened sensitivity to the promises of life," that had nothing to do with the creative temperament as commonly explained. "It was an extraordinary gift for hope, a romantic readiness such as I have never found in any other person . . ." Even the sought-after Prince of Wales responded to this irresistible quality in Rodgers's work. One of the Rodgers and Hart songs he took up with alacrity was "My Heart Stood Still," from the London revue *One Dam Thing After Another* of 1927. His Royal Highness had memorized the verse and chorus then and there and left the theatre humming the song. The next time he went to a dance he asked that the song be played. When he discovered that the bandleader had never heard of it, he obligingly sang it all the way through until the musicians were able to improvise the tune. The next day, words and music to "My Heart Stood Still" were on the front pages of the newspapers and the song's success was assured.

Shortly after arriving at York Terrace, Dorothy Rodgers made plans for her first dinner party. She and Dick then received an invitation from Sir Philip Sassoon, a wealthy, prominent, and art-loving bachelor who owned an estate near Hythe in Kent, to attend a golf match the prince was to play with Bobbie Jones, the famous professional, and then stay for dinner. Sir Henry ("Chips") Channon, whose diaries of the period make essential reading, called Sassoon "the strangest of sinister men," and his house "a triumph of beautiful bad taste," a verdict shared by Kenneth Clark, the aesthete and administrator. Be that as it may, Sassoon was on close terms with the prince and his invitation was most pressing. Still, the date was that of her own dinner party, and Mrs. Rodgers was obliged to decline.

All too late she learned that, faced with this open-sesame onto the pinnacle of social aspiration in Britain, she should have postponed her party and canceled everything to meet the prince; and her guests would have understood. Her society friends would have given her this advice, but it had not occurred to her to ask. Nor would her husband have known that the invitation was tantamount to a royal command; perhaps he trusted her apparent expertise in such matters. Even when the host made a second phone call, hoping, no doubt, that she had come to her senses, she did not waver. All too late she discovered her gaffe. (Her dinner party was not much of a success, either, but that is another story.)

In those days Rodgers took his rapid rise with commendable modesty, but also a certain sangfroid. His wife might see the value of cultivating the right people—and that she had turned down the Prince of Wales from a misguided sense of obligation was something forever imprinted on her memory—but her husband was too absorbed in his work to spend much time contemplating her social faux pas. What mattered most to him just then was earning a living. Broadway was in a slump; Hollywood, which had just discovered the talkies, was an attractive alternative and, if he was to continue earning money, he had to be open to every possibility. So when Larry Hart arrived one evening in the company of Jed Harris, then the most successful producer and director in the United States, Rodgers was ready to keep him there all night if necessary. Two years earlier Harris had four of the biggest hits on Broadway running simultaneously. Perhaps Rodgers knew that, although Harris was barely thirty, he had already acquired a reputation for being, as Edna Ferber described him, "a strange, paradoxical creature, fated to destroy everything he loves": certainly the kind of person one does not want to antagonize. So when Dorothy, pleading a headache, went to bed, Dick was probably delighted to have her leave so that the three of them could get down to business.

There must have been several rounds of drinks. The hours slipped away, chattering, talking about ideas, swapping jokes, and roaring with laughter—Harris had a wicked wit, Dorothy Rodgers recalled. Finally, it was four in the morning. Rodgers heard an upstairs bedroom door slam and guessed at once what had happened. He raced upstairs. Dorothy said, "I'm terribly sorry, darling, and I know I shouldn't have done it, but I couldn't get to sleep, and I was just getting so frustrated." Rodgers said, "They're just about to leave. I'll be right up."

She remembered: "Well, he came up in a few minutes. He got undressed, folded everything very neatly, and sat down on a chair to take off his shoes." All this was done in complete silence. It transpired that Harris had agreed to produce a show with them, but now that she had interrupted this fruitful conversation, of course, he would not do so. (Harris did not.) That was awful enough, but her husband's icy disapproval was the final blow. She cried herself to sleep.

Chapter Two

ONLY MAKE BELIEVE

T HERE WERE, during Richard Rodgers's childhood, so many long silences. Weeks would go by when his father would refuse to speak and would communicate his needs in dumb show as when, slicing his fingers together, he signaled his desire for a pair of scissors. For William Abraham Rodgers, the oldest son who had surmounted so many obstacles to become the family's first doctor, its pride and joy, had pocketed that pride and moved in with his wife's family. To be in their debt infuriated him, yet he never left.

His father-in-law, Jacob Levy, Richard Rodgers's maternal grandfather, was a Russian immigrant who had made a fortune in the silk business. Rodgers recalls seeing him go to his office in his bowler hat, highly polished shoes, and immaculate linens, looking every inch the patriarch of the family as he stepped heedlessly into the street. Brakes would screech and insults fill the air as Jacob meandered to the other side of the road, for, as he reminded his wife, Rachel, it was up to the drivers to watch for him, not the reverse. Rodgers's chief memory of him is of a man who would swear violently when he asked him for the morning paper, then appear minutes later in his room, hand him the paper, and pat his cheek fondly. As for Rachel, descriptions are sparse, but since she and her husband fought loudly and often, the implication is that she was equally unpredictable. Children of such unions tend to value peace at any price. Their daughter Mamie was a pleasant, retiring sort of person who liked nothing better than to sit at her beloved piano, pouring forth, in those days before radio, an inexhaustible flow of soothing melodies.

Richard Rodgers's daughter Mary recalled that as a grandmother, Mamie was completely indulgent. "The famous story about her is when I, like all little girls, was going through her pocketbook, my mother heard her say, 'Mary dear, you mustn't do that. I don't mind but your mother does.' She was completely benevolent, while not being much of a presence, a very fearful person." In the days when tuberculosis ravaged the tenements and diphtheria was still a child killer (even into the 1920s, despite the introduction of serum in 1894) and Jewish children were regularly attacked by gangs, a modicum of fears would seem to be justified. Mary and her sister, Linda, agreed that their grandmother was completely "under the thumb of" her own mother. So when Rachel Levy required that the newlyweds come and live with them, Mamie meekly complied.

Morris Rogozinsky, the father of Dr. William Rodgers, came from Russia as a young man with his parents and brother in 1860, well in advance of the mass immigrations of the 1880s. In those days before Ellis Island, incoming aliens were received in what had actually been a theatre a few years earlier, an odd coincidence in light of Richard Rodgers's choice of career. The theatre was located on Castle Garden, an island joined by a landfill to the southern tip of Manhattan, and had seen performances by the dancer Lola Montez and the American debut of Jenny Lind, the "Swedish Nightingale." It was pressed into service as an immigration depot so hastily that most of its original features were retained, and what were once ticket and refreshment booths now sold postage stamps or exchanged money.

Unlike most new arrivals the Rogozinsky family did not settle in New York but made the unlikely choice of Holden, a small town in Missouri. No one knows why. Perhaps the Rogozinskys had relatives there. Perhaps a *landsman,* i.e., a friend from the same town in the old country, had recommended it. In those days a family with adolescent sons would want to get as far away as possible from the reach of czarist conscription. During the terrible years of Nicholas I's reign (1825–55), Jewish boys as young as twelve had been eligible for military service for periods of up to twenty-five years; most of them never returned. Parents lived in terror of losing their sons, and even the relatively benign rule of Alexander II, beginning in 1855 (in which the period of military service was reduced to only five years), would not have seemed much of an improvement. A tiny hamlet in Missouri, so far away as to be unimaginable, would have seemed the right distance.

Soon after their arrival the name Rogozinsky was casually discarded—perhaps it was considered unpronounceable—in favor of the easier surname of Abraham, sometimes shortened to Abrams. Morris married Sarah, of Alsatian Jewish extraction, and their firstborn, the oldest of eight children, was born in 1871, the future Dr. Rodgers. After moving to New York, Morris Abrams worked as a barber at Delmonico's. Then, in 1889, when his son was just eighteen, Morris died, leaving Will as the family's chief breadwinner.

Photographs of the period show a youthful, handsome, luxuriantly bearded Will, with the ramrod bearing of one who has military ambitions, and in fact he tried and failed to enter West Point, to his eternal chagrin. In later years he would become an Army medical examiner. A year after his father's death Will was working for the Manhattan Cloak and Suit Company at 548 Broadway. When he left in 1890 to become a customs officer on the New York docks, his employers provided him with a glowing letter of recommendation along with a medal, and the pious hope that it would accompany him as he climbed the ladder of success. It must have been evident to everyone that he was bound to succeed. While working, he put himself through City College and graduated with a degree in medicine when he was just twenty-two. Moreover, he was capable of great wit and charm. Linda Rodgers Emory said, "One evening when our parents were away he came to dinner and had us in hysterical laughter telling us about life as an intern; I remember he said that one time he gave a cadaver's hand at a tollbooth instead of his own. This was the first time I realized that this person could be fun."

Mary Rodgers Guettel believed her grandfather had "tried to get into a Presbyterian medical school and they wouldn't let him in because he was a Jew, so he changed his name." The name change actually took place a year before his graduation from Bellevue. William Abraham was given leave to become William Abraham Rodgers by the Court of Common Pleas in the summer of 1892. When his son was interviewed by Edward R. Murrow for one of his *See It Now* programs, one of the items on prominent display was a framed telegram from his father to his grandmother Sarah: "DEAR MOTHER, I AM A DOCTOR NOW. AFFECTIONATELY WILL." The date was March 29, 1893.

By the time Will met Mamie Levy in 1896, he was living at 146 East 115th Street, his home and office; she was living with her parents at 816 Lexington Avenue. It is possible that his mother and one or more siblings were living with Will, because when he was on his honeymoon in London and Paris in the autumn of 1896, his mother was writing to the newlyweds on his business stationery. Exactly when Will moved in with his relatives is not known, but the likelihood is that it was on returning from their honeymoon. It is possible that Mamie did not relish the idea of moving into a house already fully occupied by her husband's family. Living and working under one roof, sharing the household expenses: this must have seemed a tempting idea to the young Dr. Rodgers, particularly if, as seems likely, he was supporting his mother and younger siblings. And the well-to-do Levys had plenty of space. Sam, Mamie's brother, lived with them—he worked for an importer of ostrich feathers—but he was at his club most of the time. Summers were spent in the sleepy Long Island town of Arverne, where Will also practiced medicine, and there Richard Rodgers was born on June 28, 1902.

A year after his arrival the Levys took an even larger house at 3 West 120th Street, on the southwest corner of Mount Morris Park West, a handsome address in Harlem, then "the aristocratic Jewish neighborhood of New York." The doctor's office and waiting rooms were on the main floor and the family lived upstairs. By then the joint household was apparently functioning smoothly, but only on the surface. Will and his mother-in-law had taken a permanent dislike to each other. Rodgers wrote, "Both were stubborn and opinionated but their clashes stemmed primarily from my father's financial dependence . . . on the Levys, and also from his unhappiness at his mother-in-law's domination of his wife." As for Jacob Levy, that disciplinarian with a fiery temper, which could be counted on to erupt when baited by his wife or anyone else who crossed his path, he dominated the household with "his rough voice and his demanding nature and his unwillingness to compromise," wrote Rodgers, who loved him nonetheless. Sharp words, flaring tempers, people rushing from the dinner table, doors slamming, malign silences: such was the family battleground. "Even today a loud voice makes me uncomfortable," Rodgers wrote, and he spent much of his early years with "a deep feeling of tension and insecurity." One of the marked traits of his character in later years, according to his daughters, was his refusal to be drawn into an argument unless goaded beyond endurance, when his remarks could be as cutting as any he had once heard.

RICHARD RODGERS'S ACCOUNTS of his early childhood hardly varied. He sometimes said he was weaned on music, and the remark was not much of an exaggeration. For the reason why, there is first of all the sarcastic Rachel Levy, part of whose frustration stemmed from the fact that she had been brought up in an atmosphere of culture and refinement and had married a vulgarian. Who knows how much persuasion it took to get Jacob to go to a concert with her, but go he did, and they even had a season subscription to the Metropolitan Opera. Once she saw musical talent in her daughter Mamie, private tutors were summoned, and Mamie no doubt practiced her scales on a baby grand. A consuming love of music was the passion that brought Mamie and Will together, and the whole family went to the musical comedies and operettas of the day. After each performance, Mamie and Will bought the printed sheet music for sale in the lobby and played it the minute they got home. If daily life took place in no-man's-land, the piano, and a sizable area around it, was the demilitarized zone. As Mamie played on and on,

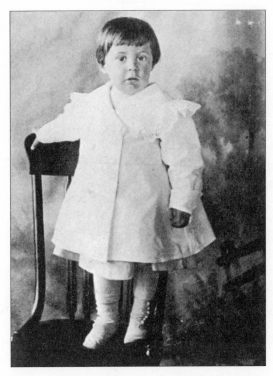

Richard Rodgers, 1904, at the age of a year and a half

the handsome, red-haired Will, perhaps with hands on his lapels, roared out the latest songs, while Rachel nodded and smiled.

All those tiny green silk tassels around the edge of the piano stool fascinated the infant Rodgers, and perhaps they were at eye level, because he had to be lifted up whenever he wanted to play. That was often; he would sit down and energetically bang away. Pretty soon, threads of something more were appearing in the cacophony. People noticed that he was repeating sounds he had heard his mother play. He was finding melodies, and at a very young age. He does not remember the moment when he began playing by ear, but he knows it was soon. That marked ability was being channeled in the direction of music for the theatre, and the sounds that filled the Rodgers household came mostly from Vienna. From 1907 until 1914, when the war intervened, Viennese operetta was the rage, thanks to the discovery, or rediscovery, of the Viennese waltz as interpreted by Franz Lehár, whose *The Merry Widow* was the sensation of 1907, in large part because of the eponymous waltz that ended the second act. The new idea of the waltz was as a ballroom dance, the epitome of modern romance, and the Viennese concept of the

The Rodgers family in about 1905, Dr. "Will" Rodgers sporting a
luxuriant moustache, with
his wife, Mamie; older son, Mortimer; and
three-year-old Richard

waltz, with its three/four meter, its languorous hesitations and impulsive forward movement, its invitation to steps that swirl, glide, and skim along, drew
audiences irresistibly. Johann Strauss II had perfected the form; Lehár,
Rudolf Friml, and Oskar Straus channeled its lineal descendants into
operetta. *Merry Widow* hats, dresses, and drinks became the rage, and it was
claimed that more than a hundred *Merry Widow* companies were performing
simultaneously. Rodgers said that without ever having seen it, he knew *The
Merry Widow* by heart, and his marked responsiveness to, and feeling for, the
waltz form must have had something to do with this indoctrination when he
was five years old.

When he was six, the daughter of one of his friends taught him to play "Chopsticks," and once he had learned the bass accompaniment he adapted it, experimenting with chords and rhythms until it was made to fit whatever song he wanted to play. "A few years later, when I could play pretty well, I started extemporizing, which is really composition," he said. "So I was composing by the time I was nine or eleven." Sitting at the piano and playing, with people clustered around: films exist of such a Rodgers as a young man, and his face is always aglow. Whenever he sat down at the piano he was showered with compliments and affection, so that is what he wanted to do: "There was a star danced, and under that was I born."

Their first teacher was an aunt, Will's sister Tillie, whose plodding approach would have deterred anyone less committed than Rodgers; accompanied by his brother, he trotted off to a local music school and was enrolled. Mortimer was going to take lessons, too; no pipsqueak brother would get the better of him. He worked and studied and practiced and ground out the obligatory pieces. The adults murmured politely. Then Dick took the stage. Most of the time he had not bothered to practice. "My ear was so acute, and I was able to do so much without studying that going through an ordinary pianistic routine was a bore." He did not need a score in order to perform his miracles, but there was a price to be paid when Morty, four and a half years his senior, took it upon himself to redress the balance. As Rodgers put it, he "didn't hesitate to use his strength on me." How many of these hopelessly ill-matched fights took place without being stopped by adults is not known.

He saw Diaghilev's Ballets Russes make its celebrated debut in New York and, a few years later, stood in the back of Carnegie Hall to hear Tchaikovsky's Piano Concerto No. 1 played by Josef Hofmann. His grandparents had regular weekly seats in the third row of the Metropolitan Opera, and one night Rachel gave her seat to Dick. Enrico Caruso and Geraldine Farrar were singing *Carmen,* and the conductor was Giorgio Polacco. "Not being able to see the musicians in the pit, and never having heard a large orchestra before, I had no idea what to expect," he wrote, "but when Polacco brought his baton down on those first crashing figurations of the introduction it was so overpowering that I thought I was going to faint."

He saw his first live theatre in 1908, when he was only six. It was a children's show, *The Pied Piper,* about the legendary thirteenth-century figure who was said to have charmed all the rats of Hamelin into the river Weser. He remembered that less well than *Little Nemo,* based on the comic strip, with a score by Victor Herbert. When he knew that he was being taken to a matinée of this musical at the New Amsterdam, "I was tremendously excited about it for weeks beforehand," he said. "I remember sitting in a left-hand upper box;

the whole family went, including my brother." It was thrilling to see real musicians in the pit and real singers on the stage.

From the age of nine he was allowed to attend the theatre by himself, and would go to the old Standard Theatre at Broadway and Ninety-first Street "as regular as a clock" every Saturday afternoon. The Standard in those days was part of a suburban circuit where one could see top Broadway shows in local neighborhoods, presumably at reduced prices; and since there were often thirty or forty shows running downtown simultaneously, there was plenty of choice. He would take a first-balcony seat at fifty cents and sometimes bribed the usher with a quarter to sneak down to the second balcony. There he would sit in solitary bliss, missing nothing, from the sets and lighting to the costumes and props and, of course, the songs. He said later, "When I get an idea for a song I can hear it in the orchestra; I can smell the scenery; I can see the kind of actor who'll sing the song and the audience sitting there listening to it."

Music conjured up roseate dreams of happiness; and the stage, the musical-comedy stage in particular, was a place where such visions could be realized. He said years later that he had only to walk into a theatre to find himself in a good mood. "If I'm unhappy," he said, "it takes my unhappiness away; if I'm happy, I get happier." His granddaughter Nina Beaty said, "He invented a special world. In anything to do with musicals, he lived in full color; the grass was green, the sky was blue, the birds sang and the butterflies flitted about. The real world was black and white to him, and not pretty at all."

MOUNT MORRIS PARK remained his principal playground even after the family moved when he was nine years old to a large fifth-floor apartment in a new building on West Eighty-sixth Street. For the first time home and office were separate: Dr. Rodgers took quarters on the ground floor of the same building. It was a pleasant middle-class neighborhood, one in which Oscar Hammerstein and Lorenz Hart also lived, although the three of them did not meet until years later. Rodgers had the usual childhood, "baseball, running around and having fights," he told an interviewer. During the long summers on Long Island one of his ways of idling away the hours was to roam around the outskirts of Arverne with friends, looking for empty houses. "Our pleasures were simple and direct in those days. All we wanted to do was break some windows," he wrote. After the family moved to a bigger house in Long Beach, he learned to swim and fish there and shot his first rifle behind the sand dunes. His first school was P.S. 10, at 117th Street and St. Nicholas Avenue, chiefly memorable for a gentle homeroom teacher named Marion

Schlang, who taught every subject. His memories of her kindness remained so vivid that when he spotted her years later in the audience at one of his concerts with the New York Philharmonic in Lewisohn Stadium, he threw his arms around her. His teacher recalled a certain student, the son of a doctor, who showed great aptitude in music but was so shy that it took all her powers of persuasion to get him on the stage.

Photographs of the young Dick Rodgers show a precociously grown-up, wise-looking little face beneath the correct attire of a middle-class boy. Feet planted well apart, he looks every inch the little soldier, which may not be a coincidence, given his father's love for uniforms, ribbons, and medals. Bennett Cerf, who formed a lifelong friendship with brother Morty, recalled a weekend he spent with Rodgers in Long Beach when, late one night, there was a violent thunderstorm. He wrote, "One particularly vivid flash of lightning revealed a trembling, white-faced little boy inside our bedroom. It was Richard. 'I j-j-just came by to see if you f-f-fellows were all right,' he explained. Mortimer . . . replied with that quiet charm that has won him the nickname of Sunshine: 'Gittouta here before I cream ya!' " If boys had fears they learned to ignore them; and if they were beaten up and left with a black eye and a bloody nose, what was important was the question one's father asked: "What did you do to the other guy?"

Dick's indoctrination in stoicism came at an early age. Rodgers recalls that he awoke one night when he was eight years old, screaming with pain. His right index finger was "flame-red and swollen almost to the thickness of my wrist." Since his parents were at the theatre, he had to lie there in agony until they returned. What happened then was traumatic: his father took a scalpel and made a single terrifying slash in his finger to allow the pus to escape. He had contracted osteomyelitis, an infection of the bone marrow, with an abscess at the site. It was exquisitely painful, and in those days before antibiotics, serious bone damage was a real possibility. His father's chief concern was that his finger or even his hand might have to be amputated. The wound had to be kept open so that it would drain. "Local anesthetic was seldom used in those days and so what followed were eight months of torture." John Rodgers, Morty's son, said that his grandfather was notoriously impatient and irascible. "My father, who became a doctor, used to say that when the patient was in pain grandfather's first impulse was to blame the patient! He had a low fuse."

During those eight months Rodgers had to have his right arm in a sling and all piano playing stopped. "All I could do was wait in terror for the next visit to the doctor." After a series of operations Rodgers was eventually taken to Mount Sinai Hospital to be operated on by a famous surgeon, Dr. A. A. Berg. He was given cocaine (the predecessor to novocaine) and his finger went numb. After a few minutes Berg withdrew a piece of bone from the middle of his finger, just a quarter of an inch square, with a pitted surface: the result of the osteomyelitis. The wound was finally allowed to heal and he could dispense with the sling, but he ended up with a badly deformed index finger which, in an early experiment in plastic surgery, was given a new tip. From then on he could fit this finger into the space between the black keys on almost every kind of piano except a Knabe. Because of it, however, any thoughts he might have had of a concert career were at an end.

The fact that the wound could not be allowed to heal, the pain involved, the torture of doctors' visits, the fruitless operations, and the lack of painkillers had lifelong repercussions. On the one hand Rodgers became adept at hiding his feelings. He presented an impassive face to the world and dealt with illness with a self-control that seemed almost superhuman. On the other hand he was, by his own account, morbidly fearful. His daughters described some of his many phobias: fear of flying, dislike of tall buildings and elevators, panic when required to go over bridges or under tunnels. He was a particularly poor passenger in a car; feeling himself at someone else's mercy seemed to revive all the terrors of the original trauma. Rodgers himself wondered whether his hypochondria had its origins in the night his father suddenly appeared "to cut me savagely with a knife."

ONCE RELEASED to the piano again, he attacked it with renewed vigor. The move to West Eighty-sixth Street meant he was transferred to a new school, P.S. 166, on West Eighty-ninth. There he had the good luck to become a student of Elsa Katz, head of the music department, who recognized his talent and gave him the task of playing all the music for the daily assemblies, from traditional hymns and "The Star-Spangled Banner" to the marches that accompanied the arrival and departure of the student body. Those he usually wrote himself. His sense of humor was already well developed. When the principal told the students to sit, he would play the familiar musical doggerel of "Shave and a haircut . . ." Then, once they were seated, he would finish it off with ". . . two bits." Miss Katz, who, he noted approvingly, was young, slim, and attractive, always obliged him with a giggle. That was the year (1911) that he started falling in love with actresses. Ina Claire was the first. He saw her in *The Quaker Girl,* and when they met years later he was never able to utter the "most crushing sentence" an actress can hear, i.e., that he had seen her when he was a child. Then he became enamored of Marguerite Clark, who appeared in *Snow White and the Seven Dwarfs*—she would become a star in silent pictures—and she kept him awake for nights. "My prepubescent fantasies were restricted by my innocence, but as I look back on them I realize I was doing very well mentally for a ten-year-old and was clearly heading in the right direction."

From the age of ten, until he was confirmed, Rodgers went to Temple Israel (120th Street, near Lenox Avenue) for religious instruction. His parents were Reform, but not particularly observant; his grandmother Rachel was an atheist, and only Jacob Levy believed his grandsons should have some awareness of their ancient heritage. Dick and Mortimer both had their bar mitzvahs and received the usual gifts of fountain pens, books, and gold coins. Will Rodgers, with his passionate patriotism, his Anglicized surname, and what he must have heard about the exodus from his parents, thought only in terms of the New World. He naturally wanted every advantage for his sons, unhampered by social prejudice, and his father-in-law's insistence on the old religion must have struck him as old-fashioned, if not recidivist. The whole family venerated its adopted tongue. Mary Rodgers Guettel recalled that Will Rodgers taught her to parse sentences years before she learned the same subject in school. The cultured Rachel's English was, of course, perfect, and Dick showed no tolerance, as an adult, for careless usage; his daughter said, "Daddy was militant about grammar at home and had a more sensitive awareness of language than my mother did. When I was beginning to write he would give me little pieces of information, like, don't use exclamation points unless absolutely necessary." She also said, "I learned more from him about words by far than I ever learned . . . about music." Poor English was, perhaps, a symbol; it was connected with immigrant status and all that this implied: poverty, rough manners, injustice—the lack of everything that made life agreeable and civilized. The world of immigrant Jews "had no symphonies or operas, no ballets or museums; its approach to the treasures of the West was decidedly tentative." To be cultured, accepted; to have social status: this was the goal, and if that meant jettisoning the past, it was a small price to pay, as Rodgers himself must have thought. One could perhaps say of him what has been said of Irving Berlin, that he was "a classic outsider intuiting the mood of the culture into which he longed to assimilate, and earning inclusion by portraying that culture's rosier dreams of itself in his songs."

A CERTAIN SCHOLASTIC PATTERN was beginning to evolve. Rodgers had breezed his way through P.S. 166 with an admixture of talent and musical jokes, relying on his native abilities and enthusiasm to keep afloat while avoiding as much as possible the tedium of learning. When the moment came to decide on a high school, he blithely applied to Townsend Harris

Hall, known as THH, which was affiliated with the College of the City of New York and known for its intellectual rigor; THH crammed into three years what took four years everywhere else. It was early in 1917; Rodgers was fourteen and, by his own admission, more interested in what took place after hours than in anything THH had to teach. He loved to play tennis and was a champion swimmer. He won first prize in a novice meet at the New York Athletic Club, so his election to secretary of the athletic association was a logical one. He then campaigned with characteristic zest for the post of treasurer of the student government and was elected. Quite soon thereafter his grades were so disastrous that "I decided to quit before I flunked out." He transferred to DeWitt Clinton High School in the autumn of 1917. Its charm, he wrote, "started at the front door and pervaded the entire building . . . the faint but unmistakeable scent of men's room." Schoolwork was even more dull and boring and he could not find any agreeable companions to "raise a little hell with."

Rodgers was going to concerts of Bach, Beethoven, Mozart, and Brahms, but the music that informed his ear originated from another direction entirely. Just as American architects of the late nineteenth century yearned to create buildings untainted by European influences so, too, native composers, whether writing for the concert hall or the stage, believed they had an obligation to create music that was distinctly American. Although Victor Herbert, an adopted American of Anglo-Irish and German background, was highly popular, he remained a writer of European-style operetta. The honor of being one of the first truly American writers of theatre music went to Jerome Kern.

Writers have grappled with the quality that made Kern's music so fresh, so American in feeling. He did not, after all, as Aaron Copland would do with his ballet music, make reference to ballads and folk songs that had arrived with the first settlers and acquired their own regional flavor. With Kern, while there was something "wonderfully new and clear" in his work, Rodgers wrote, he did not seem to know what. Alec Wilder described Kern's "pure, uncontrived melodic line." Stephen Sondheim wrote, "Antoine de St. Exupéry pointed out in *Wind, Sand, and Stars* that the history of the airplane . . . was the gradual development of its shape into a cigar. The more knowledge gained, the more additions required . . . the simpler the shape. Complexity leads paradoxically to simplicity. And this hard-won simplicity is, I think, the keynote of Jerome Kern's style. His melodies are as smooth, rounded, streamlined, simplified and undecorated as a cigar." To recognize the freshness, complexity, and sophistication of Kern's music was far easier than identifying its indigenous roots. The best that could be said was that it

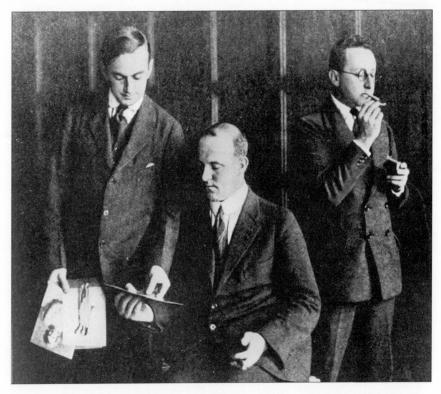

Guy Bolton, P. G. Wodehouse, and Jerome Kern (right), collaborators on a series of successful musicals for the Princess Theatre between 1915 and 1918

was a new form of melodic writing unlike that of his predecessors, and that made it American.

The Viennese operetta left the life of Richard Rodgers, and the music of Jerome Kern took its place when he was just fourteen. He went to see *Very Good Eddie* at the Standard Theatre on upper Broadway; it was one of the turning points of his life. He said later, "I remember my mother asking me, when I was very young in the theatre, a question about some show we were doing. She said, 'Who's going to be the comedian?' Now that question is loaded because it gives you a complete rundown in the way shows were built in those days. I remember a firm of producers who were very successful for about five years and then they went out of business because they would take the program of the last show they had done and duplicate the list of musical numbers—with different titles, of course, but you had an opening chorus, then sometimes called an icebreaker. This was obligatory. You had to have a fast 2/4 opening number . . . then you had a number between the soubrette, in those days she was called the second girl, and the young comedian called the funny boy, not the top banana, then you had your first sentimental song, a romantic ballad between the ingénue and the leading man. It was a 1-2-3-4 order and you didn't break that sequence because if it had been successful once before it was assumed it would be again. Then you had the comedian, the top banana. He got laughs by just coming on. He didn't have to do anything to get laughs. Sometimes he would use a slight gag to establish himself as a funny fellow. Then, and only then, would he do dialogue. Shows were put on along an iron-bound formula."

Into this cartoonish formula came *Very Good Eddie*, one of the "Princess Theatre Shows," which took their cue from the theatre's intimate setting, experimenting with small casts, unpretentious sets and lighting, and an air of verisimilitude. *Very Good Eddie*, with its music by Jerome Kern and words mostly by Schuyler Greene and Herbert Reynolds, was something new in American musical theatre. Its songs were fitted into a romantic comedy of errors in which the participants were neither one-dimensional nor clichéd; these were human failings and aspirations, told with amused tolerance. *Very Good Eddie*, Bordman wrote, was the mold "out of which poured a half-century of American Musical Comedy." Sensing the transforming nature of what he was seeing and hearing, Rodgers went back again and again. If he was weaned on Viennese operetta, his finishing school was the work of Jerome Kern.

Given the lure of musical theatre, his academic labors were bound to be perfunctory. In the summer of 1916 he wrote "Camp-Fire Days," an innocuous little ditty celebrating the virtues of life at Camp Wigwam in Harrison, Maine, where he was spending the summer. He then experimented with a song called "The Auto Show Girl," which he thought was bound to sell because of its catchy title, but nothing came of that. Meanwhile, Morty had enrolled at Columbia University and was studying hard for a medical career. About the only thing his fourteen-year-old brother knew about Columbia was the annual Varsity Show, and in the spring of 1917 Morty took him to see *Home James* in the Astor Hotel ballroom. Oscar Hammerstein, who happened to be a fraternity brother of Morty's, and who had written the lyrics for the show, recalled that Lorenz Hart, another Columbia University student, had written a burlesque of silent movies. This was somehow incorporated into the play, and, his black eyebrows waggling, Hart played Mary Pickford in a curly blond wig. "Imitating the way movie ingénues were chased around trees by playful but purehearted heroes, Larry skipped and bounced around the stage like an electrified gnome," Hammerstein wrote. After the performance, while the room was being cleared for dancing, Morty introduced

Hammerstein to his brother, a smaller and darker version of himself. Hammerstein thought Dick looked about twelve, and remembered him as wearing short pants—a detail Rodgers hotly disputed forever afterwards. Rodgers saw "a very tall, skinny fellow with a sweet smile, clear blue eyes and an unfortunately mottled complexion," who was graciousness itself. The set, the plot, the personalities, and the music suddenly sprang to vivid life in Rodgers's imagination. He was going to attend Columbia University and write a Varsity Show.

Chapter Three

"MY FUNNY VALENTINE"

RICHARD RODGERS'S FIRST real song, "The Auto Show Girl," had been set to the words of a young lyricist, David Dyrenforth, but the association was to be short-lived. Brother Morty, who retained his habit of putting his little brother in his place at home, became the soul of benevolence once in the world at large. He was the one who had taken Dick to the Varsity Show and introduced him to Oscar Hammerstein, and he was the one who engineered Dick's first attempt at a complete musical-comedy score. Mortimer Rodgers belonged to a neighborhood boys' athletic club, the Akron; the American Expeditionary Forces were fighting in World War I, and every patriotic nerve was being exercised to support them. The least the boys in the Akron Club could do was raise some money for the boys over there; the carcinomatous bounty would be cigarettes, or "smokes," in the current slang. A musical show was just the thing, but who would write it? Morty had a brother. When members found out just how old Dick was at the time (fifteen), rebellion set in, but Morty was more than equal to that and Richard sat down to write his very first score. It was the autumn of 1917.

One Minute Please was a musical farce in three acts with a book by Ralph G. Engelsman, who also wrote the lyrics, with some help from Rodgers, according to the program. The ballroom of the Plaza Hotel was decorated with flags, cigar boxes, and hundreds of cigarettes festooned overhead. The absurdist plot involved a vampire, Nijinsky, Pavlova, George Sand, and something called a "Yogi burlesque," and was decorated with six sprightly tunes by the baby composer, who managed to slide in "The Auto Show Girl" somewhere. Even before opening night young Richard had waltzed off to Max and Louis Dreyfus, heads of the pre-eminent publishing house, T. B.

Harms, Inc., with his sheaf of songs and the hopeful idea that at least one Dreyfus would recognize his spectacular promise. Louis Dreyfus asked what he did besides composing and, told he was in school, expressed the earnest hope that he would go back to school and stay there. That might have deterred anyone less single-minded than Rodgers, who only redoubled his efforts. The press called the show "a clever work, splendidly produced."

To save money, young Richard played the piano himself and conducted an orchestra of five professional musicians. He had been rehearsing for months and spent hours wondering why ideas that looked irresistible in theory had a way of falling flat in front of audiences, and the equally mysterious process by which ordinary bits of business turned out to be miraculously effective onstage. How to know in advance became a conundrum he pondered weightily; and perhaps it was then, during the long gestation period of *One Minute Please,* that he began his habit of scowling during rehearsals, which would prove so unsettling to everyone else.

There are numerous references to the moral and financial support Rodgers was given in those early years, not just by Morty but by their father as well. His reminiscences emphasize the fact that, unlike the paths of some composers, his was unclouded. His mother and father approved of his choice of career and unhesitatingly supported him. This appears to have been only partly true, to judge from a letter one of Dick's cousins wrote years later. How well she remembered, Lillian Landay recalled, sitting in the music room at the Rodgers house on Long Island listening to him play. She recalled that just as the concert was in full flood, his father's car could be heard turning into the garage. Then, she wrote, his mother came in and said, "Dick, dear here comes your dad, so get away from the piano." Dr. Rodgers always wanted him to become a doctor like his brother, she observed.

All three men shared a kind of genius for making the right contacts. Rodgers had a way, without being told, it would seem, of knowing how to introduce himself into an advantageous situation. Even girlfriends would turn out to have widowed mothers whose great friends were the brothers Dreyfus. Convincing somebody's mother to make the right introduction was the work of a moment, and it is clear that the plain little boy with the prematurely wise face had become a compactly built adolescent with an irresistible grin and looks to match. There was a strategist at work, plotting his career as methodically as if it were a military campaign, and in fact he saw it as a battle. "I've heard it said and read that in attempting to break through the line, tanks move parallel to the line nosing in for a soft spot," he observed. "This process is likely to be found in the theatre as well. Even the spots are misleading . . . In my own case I ran parallel to the line of battle for many years . . ."

Having demonstrated his versatility with *One Minute Please* and modestly added to his height (as an adult he stood five feet eight inches tall), the young composer felt prepared, early in March 1919, to tackle another amateur show. This one, in aid of the Infants' Relief Society, was called *Up Stage and Down,* involved a theatrical manager, a playwright, and a chorus girl, and played at the Waldorf Astoria for one night. Again, brother Morty stepped in to smooth the path of the family prodigy. He persuaded Oscar Hammerstein to contribute lyrics for three of the songs, no mean feat, since that scion of a famous theatrical family was launched on his own career and working as a stage manager to his uncle Arthur. Morty persuaded one of his father's patients, Benjamin Kaye, who happened to be a theatrical lawyer, to contribute lyrics to another nineteen songs. This choice proved to be less sanguine, to judge from the titles: "Love Me By Parcel Post," "Wild Woman's Wiles," "Prisms, Plumes and Prunes," "Love Is Not in Vain," and "Japanese Jazz." Morty intervened again during rehearsals. As Rodgers told it, dissatisfaction with his amateur efforts as a conductor was about to boil over until Morty quelled it with his customary dispatch. Rodgers wrote, "The show marked the first publication of my songs, an event hardly as impressive as it may sound, since my father paid the printing costs and I published them myself." Once again the Rodgers men had formed their own tactical unit and circumvented enemy lines, but despite the fusillade of songs produced, or because of it (the show was six hours long) the result was not a success. A new friend said he knew just what to do.

One of Rodgers's admirers was another classmate of Morty's at Columbia. Philip Leavitt was a singer and sometime author who happened to know that an extremely accomplished lyricist was looking for a composer. One Sunday afternoon shortly before *Up Stage and Down* was performed, in the early spring of 1919, Leavitt took Rodgers to Lorenz Hart's brownstone on West 119th Street in Harlem. Rodgers said, "We climbed the stoop and Larry came to the door in house slippers, a pair of tuxedo trousers and some kind of shirt, and he needed a shave. He always needed a shave except on rare state occasions. Larry ushered Philip and me into the parlor of his parents' house." Hart was then twenty-three and Rodgers had not yet reached seventeen. "I was not so naive that I didn't know I was in the presence of talent, because what Larry Hart had to say about lyrics and the relationship of lyrics to the theatre was exciting and tremendously stimulating."

Lorenz Hart was born in New York on May 2, 1895, the firstborn son of German-Jewish immigrants from Hamburg who claimed descent from the poet Heinrich Heine. Their second son, Theodore Van Wyck Hart, was named for one of New York's mayors; Max Hart had been involved in

Tammany Hall politics and helped to get Van Wyck elected. Hart, like his modest, cultured wife, Frieda, was no taller than his son Larry and perfectly round—it was said he weighed three hundred pounds—with chins that descended without interruption to the massive undulations of his stomach. He was incredibly vulgar—Rodgers recalled one time when he said of some thick lentil soup, "it lookth like ———," and his wife screamed in protest. It was claimed that neighbors had witnessed him urinating from his dining-room window when he was too lazy to go to the bathroom. Along with such coarseness went the suspicion that he was something of a confidence man, if not an actual crook. Rodgers recalled that Hart was always founding new companies which just as mysteriously disappeared, and then Frieda's expensive old-fashioned jewelry would go back to the pawnshop. When in the money, Hart was the soul of liberality and would tuck a one-hundred-dollar bill into his son's pocket with the smiling admonition that he go out and enjoy himself. Suddenly there would be servants in the house again (Max dearly loved having a butler), three cars would be back in the garage, and the house would be filled with a bohemian crowd of singers and actors, along with whatever celebrities could be persuaded to overlook Max's improprieties.

Teddy, who had a high, squeaky voice and became a successful comedian, was his father's child; Larry, more sensitive and introspective, his mother's. She was the one who taught him German, and perhaps it was her passion for literature that kindled something in Larry. In any event his facility with words was soon so marked that his father would invite his friends to witness the verbal pyrotechnics of his child versifier. Larry went to private schools and enrolled in Columbia University's School of Journalism despite, he later claimed, his disinclination to go into newspaper work. His own version of events is that he "majored in Varsity shows." When Rodgers met him he had graduated and was eking out a living translating German operettas. He began with Gustave Amberg, who was producing them at the Irving Place Theatre and had an arrangement with the theatrical impresarios and owners Lee and J. J. Shubert to transfer the operettas to Broadway if they showed promise. Hart was soon working for the Shuberts, writing English lyrics for Jacques Offenbach's *La Belle Hélène* and making translations of successful operettas such as *The Lady in Ermine*. Then another Broadway producer paid Hart two hundred dollars to translate *Liliom*, by Ferenc Molnár, into English. When it was produced by the Theater Guild in 1921 it starred Eva Le Gallienne and Joseph Schildkraut, but Hart, who was at least partly responsible for the play's huge success, received none of the profits.

Philip Leavitt recalled that in 1919, Hart was dedicated to the perfection of meter and rhyme and shared Rodgers's devotion to Kern and Wodehouse.

"His shrine was a phonograph that continuously spilled out the music of the Princess Theatre shows. He listened to them for hours in rapt, critical silence. He was sure that, in certain respects, he could do better than Wodehouse." At the time Hart was working on a lyric he called "Venus," the first line of which was, "Venus, there's no difference between us!" Leavitt continued, "He was a pixie! An extrovert! . . . When he spoke of lyrics, he could be very convincing. He was sure 'Venus' would be a hit song."

Rodgers listened in respectful silence as Hart, from the majestic heights of his twenty-three-year-old learning, talked about such esoterica as exterior and interior, male and female rhymes. (A male rhyme is generally exterior and has its accent on the final syllable, while a female rhyme has the accent on the penultimate syllable and is usually interior.) Rodgers was initially so much on edge that he nearly jumped out of his chair at the sound of a clock striking, but he was put at his ease by the appearance of the family cat. Larry introduced them. "This is Bridget," he said. "She's an old fence-walker," chuckling and rubbing his hands together, a nervous tic. Oscar Hammerstein wrote, "In all the time I knew him I never saw him walk slowly. I never saw his face in repose. I never heard him chuckle quietly. He laughed loudly and easily at other people's jokes and at his own too. His large eyes danced and his head would wag."

Quite soon thereafter Rodgers was asking Hart's advice about *Up Stage and Down*. That was easy, Hart said: cut out three hours. Rodgers did as he was told and the new show, obtusely renamed *Twinkling Eyes* and benefiting the Soldiers' and Sailors' Welfare, was presented at the Forty-fourth Street Theatre in May 1919. The performance was directed by Lorenz M. Hart, the beginning of a collaboration that would last for almost a quarter of a century.

Hart's single major drawback manifested itself at an early stage. Rodgers, who was wide awake and ready for work after breakfast, discovered that Hart was useless before noon. This was because he "loved carousing" until all hours of the night, Rodgers wrote. In the morning he would be trying to pull himself together and would have to have a drink before lunch; "by early afternoon he needed more help, and by late afternoon, the working day was over." Soon after meeting Hart, Mamie Rodgers sadly observed, "That boy will never see twenty-five." Hart was to live another twenty-three years, but the warning signs were already clear enough; even at that young age he was forgetting faces, and actually had to be reintroduced to Rodgers at one point. Rodgers would arrive at the house and, while waiting in the Harts' overstuffed living room, spend long hours listening to the phonograph and playing two records over and over again: parts of Tchaikovsky's Fourth Symphony and Rimsky-Korsakov's *Scheherazade*. Then Hart would groggily appear and they would be off and running; once stimulated, he worked with a facility that equaled that of his young partner.

Theirs was the perfect match of opposites. Hart's exuberance, impulsiveness, and unpredictability appealed to the side of Rodgers that admired such seeming inner freedom and that chafed under restrictions that had been self-imposed. In those days there was never any doubt about who was leading whom. Hart was the teacher and Rodgers the eager pupil, one who shared his goals and accepted his foibles as part of the general scheme of things. For Hart was so often lovable; under the wisecracking manner and boisterous conviviality there was a childlike sweetness. He was like his father, in that whatever money he earned went to make others happy.

He showered his friends with expensive gifts and had nonstop parties where he drank whatever was left. If Hart were rebelling against what could be seen as some stringent inner demands, he appreciated Rodgers's reliability and every appearance he gave of being in control. Hart was aware he was squandering his talents on translations when he should be writing lyrics, lyrics that he knew would transform a cynical trade into a respectable craft, if not a new art form. Here was an amazingly talented youngster who was providing him with an ideal opportunity. And when a submerged melancholy threatened to overwhelm him, Rodgers was the one who rescued him from the depths, although there was a price to be paid, as is hinted at in Rodgers's famous remark that Hart became "a permanent source of irritation." Hart the pixie, the sprite, the Lilliputian, was the same height as Dick's own mother. Any fellow would be bound to feel quite tall in comparison.

IT IS AN AXIOM of theatrical lore that Lorenz Hart had such a phobia about writing that Rodgers had to come up with the music first to spark his interest. That may have been true in later years, but was not true at the beginning, to judge from an interview Hart gave a few years after they had begun their partnership. If they were working on a comic song, the lyrics came first, since, he explained, many of them were just musical dialogue, in which case the sense was more important than the sound. However, when a "melodic" song was called for, Hart let his composer write the music first. Then, he said, "I take the most distinctive melodic phrase in his tune and work on that. What I choose is not necessarily the theme or first line, but the phrase that stands out. Next I try to find the meaning of that phrase and to develop a euphonic set of words to fit it. For example, in one of my songs just published the first line runs like this: 'Here in my arms it's adorable.' The distinct melodic phrase came on the word 'adorable,' and the

The successful writing team of Richard Rodgers and Lorenz Hart
in about 1925

word 'adorable' is the first word that occurred to me, so I used it as my pivotal musical idea. And as the melodic phrase recurs often in the chorus it determined my rhyme scheme. Of course, in a song of this sort, the melody and the euphonics of the words themselves are really more important than the sense."

During the spring and summer of 1919 in the big house in Harlem, Rodgers and Hart worked around the piano, which was always covered with musical scores, scores of operettas and musical comedies from every country in the world. While Rodgers played, Hart darted about the room, snatching at ideas which he scribbled down on whatever paper was handy—usually the backs of envelopes. Finally, they decided they had some songs worth showing. Presumably, they could have approached the formidable Dreyfus brothers, but another prospect looked more inviting. In the summer of 1919 the Leavitt family had rented a house in Far Rockaway next door to the family of the great Lew Fields, and Phil Leavitt, ever resourceful, promised to introduce them.

Lew Fields was in the great tradition of actor-managers, a comedian turned actor and producer. He had made his reputation at the turn of the century performing slapstick comedy with his partner, Joe Weber, with whom he built a theatrical empire. The Weber and Fields Music Hall was the place where one went to see the most famous stars of the time, including Lillian Russell, Fay Templeton, and DeWolf Hopper, and after Weber and Fields parted company, Fields became an innovative producer of revues and musicals.

When Rodgers and Hart met him, Fields was playing the leading role in *A Lonely Romeo,* a featherweight comedy he co-authored and produced and in which he starred, about Augustus Tripp, a man who made hats by day and danced the night away in cabarets. The plot, such as it was, centered around the hero's frantic efforts to find innocent explanations for his nocturnal frolics to allay his wife's suspicions. The play opened in June, and by the summer

Lew Fields and Joe Weber, the slapstick
comedy team

Fields, who turned handsprings every night at the end of the second act, was too tired to argue when Leavitt, and Fields's son Herbert, urged him to meet Rodgers and Hart.

Leavitt recalled that they all walked from the railway station to the summer cottage, which was near the beach. "It was a pretty long walk, but not too long for Larry. In his nervous, jerky way he drew up a line of strategy for the meeting. He was sure that 'Venus' would be immediately interpolated into *A Lonely Romeo* . . ." The whole Fields family had been assembled to act as an audience: Lew and Herbert; fourteen-year-old Dorothy, "with the most dazzling eyes I had ever seen," Rodgers wrote; the older son, Joseph; and Frances, the only child who would not have a theatrical career. "Venus" came and went with only polite applause. But after hearing "Any Old Place with You," Fields let it be known that this was the one he wanted. Rodgers could hardly believe that he would have his first song on Broadway at the age of seventeen.

Rodgers remembered that the song was introduced on August 26, a Wednesday matinée. That date was queried by Armond and L. Marc Fields in their comprehensive biography of Lew Fields, *From the Bowery to Broadway,* which established that an actors' strike—it led to the formation of Actors' Equity—had by then shut down *A Lonely Romeo.* The show did not reopen for a month, but the day finally arrived in September when the song about a couple on their honeymoon had its premiere, along with the bouncy melody Rodgers wrote "to simulate the carefree chug-chugging of a honeymoon express," he explained. He added, "It wasn't much of a splash, but to Larry and me Niagara Falls never made such a roar as the sound of those nice matinée ladies patting their gloved hands together . . ."

A YOUNG COMPOSER who already has a song in a Broadway show may be forgiven for wanting to dispense with high school as fast as possible. After persuading his parents that he could not bear DeWitt Clinton a minute longer, Rodgers was enrolled in extension courses at Columbia University, which meant he could attend freshman classes even though he had not finished high school. The real reason behind the maneuvering was that he would be eligible to write the Varsity Show, his lifelong ambition. He entered the freshman class in fine style. Hardly had he arrived on campus when he learned that each of the four classes was invited to compose a song, the best of which would win a prize. Now a member of the Class of 1923, Rodgers sat down and whipped up the music and lyrics for a rousing panegyric to his graduating class and his university and won hands down. It was an auspicious beginning for what would become a wreath of extracurricular academic honors.

There was plenty of work to be done, although, as usual, it was not in class. He was working on a new musical for the Akron Club of Harlem, *You'd Be Surprised*, with Dorothy Fields playing Carmen, a florist. He was writing twenty new songs with lyrics by Larry Hart and a book by Milton G. Bender. Hart even allowed Bender to contribute some lyrics, although he regretted it later.

For all of his theatrical ambition, "Doc" Bender, who had been a classmate of Hart's, had little or no talent except that of ingratiating himself with Hart. When Bender and Hart met, he was studying to become a dentist. There are few details about the life of this shadowy figure, and Rodgers never mentions him once in his autobiography, *Musical Stages*. However, everyone seems to agree he was a very bad dentist, as well as being openly homosexual. Orville Prescott, who met him in the thirties, called him "an anomalous gentleman." He wrote, "A tall, bald, bespectacled person, he looks like a stooge, discourses volubly and insists he 'represents Mr. Hart.' " The gossip, even in those early days, was that the ubiquitous "Doc" Bender survived on the scraps that were swept off Hart's table whenever the latter made one of his expansive gestures. Something about him filled people with misgiving, an emotion that the legions of Hart's friends tried to suppress.

Philip Leavitt painted a vivid picture of the Rodgers and Hart collaboration as he saw it develop during rehearsals for *You'd Be Surprised.* There was Dick at the piano, coaching the singers, playing the same notes over and over, rehearsing with a five-piece combo and, on the rare occasions when there was nothing for him to do, tinkling away with new ideas. There was Hart with a cigar—he seemed to like them very large and very black—watching the rehearsals closely and occasionally scribbling something on one of his scraps of paper that would become a new line of dialogue. *You'd Be Surprised* had started with the sketchiest of scripts; each scene grew and took shape in rehearsal. Leavitt said, "If Dick happened to improvise a good melody Larry would turn like a pointer and rush to the piano to hear it played again. If they both liked it, Dick would sketch out the notes on a staff sheet, and Larry would make his own lead sheet. Sometimes Dick would say, 'I think we need a waltz here,' and then sit at the piano and play one. Instantly, Larry would start to build a lyric for it."

It would become characteristic of them to begin a new project even before the previous one had proved itself, either because of the exuberance of their imaginations or, more likely, because in a world where most ideas are still-born it does not do to care too much about any of them. This pattern was already in effect when *You'd Be Surprised* reached an audience in the spring of 1920; two weeks later, Rodgers and Hart opened their first Varsity Show.

With his usual dispatch Rodgers had gone looking for an author at Columbia and found a script by another student, someone named Milton Kroopf, "who promptly disappeared out of my life," he wrote. For revisions he turned to his writer friend Leavitt, who had graduated two years before. In that entering class of 1919 were young men whose college careers had been postponed by the Great War; older, more mature, and prepared to make up for lost time—a potential pool of talent. This was also a class with a wider awareness of the great political movements then sweeping across Europe, which may account for the choice of subject matter: a fantasy about an island (Manhattan) fifty years later, when communism had triumphed. The references might be topical but the mood was strictly farcical; and after adding all the "gags" the team could think of, they submitted their script to three judges. One of them happened to be Hammerstein, who was no longer stage-managing for his uncle but wrote the book and lyrics for his first musical on Broadway, *Always You*. Since there were four other entries, the mood was tense, but *Fly with Me* won.

Rodgers made sure that there were plenty of sons and daughters of influential theatre men in the cast. Dorothy Fields was again in the cast; so was Etta Leblang, daughter of Joe Leblang, a prominent ticket broker, and so was Ethel Rogers, daughter of the actress Maud Raymond and the late Gus Rogers, of the comedy team of Gus and Max Rogers. And, to ensure his father's presence, Herbert Fields was chosen to stage the dance and musical numbers. In pursuit of control over his work, Rodgers made himself the orchestra's conductor. To do that he had to join the musicians' union and became the youngest conductor in the city.

It seemed a shame to waste songs that had barely had a hearing, so Rodgers and Hart prudently revived two songs from *Up Stage and Down*—"Twinkling Eyes," here called "There's Always Room for One More," and "Weaknesses"—both of them, by a strange coincidence, with lyrics by Hammerstein. Rodgers and Hart had great fun spoofing Bolshevism, as it was called, in their song "Gone Are the Days":

> Down with all ecclesiastics,
> Moral teaching by bombastics,
> We've our own iconoclastics,
> Teaching plastics, by gymnastics.

There were new songs called "Working for the Government," "Peek in Pekin," "A College on Broadway," and something called "The Third Degree of Love":

> You feel the fever,
> You can't deceive her
> When first she looks into your eyes;
> You think you're wise—
> You're otherwise!

The actors and singers had been well rehearsed, there were some genuinely funny performances and unusually good voices, but the main charm of the evening was the bevy of chorus girls, their powdered and rouged faces set with smiles, "distinctly masculine chins, points where there should have been rounded flesh, bones and muscles where there should have been gentle curves . . . They were precision trained in the dance steps but when they kicked, their feet looked grotesquely large . . . Even if you were fooled by the padded-out shapes and makeup, it all fell apart when they joined in the chorus of a song," Leavitt said. "You expected a high treble chorus, and instead, booming bass voices came out. Well, a lot of people fell right out of their seats." After the limited run at the Astor Grand Ballroom, the reviews predicted a glowing future for the team of Rodgers and Hart, and they were promptly hired by Lew Fields to write the score for a new musical. "Rodgers has real talent," Fields said. "I think that within a few years he will be in a class by himself."

IN ONE OF HIS Jeeves–Bertie Wooster stories, P. G. Wodehouse tells the tale of an aristocratic uncle whom a nephew wants to soften up so that he will approve of the latter's marriage to a waitress and not, as he fears, dock his allowance. By means of complicated shenanigans the uncle is persuaded to read a raft of romance novels by Rosie M. Banks. After finishing *Only a Factory Girl,* the rich uncle, genuinely moved, wipes away a tear and marries his cook, thereby depriving his nephew of any allowance at all. Wodehouse must have been thinking of *Irene,* a musical comedy that was the toast of Broadway during the 1919–20 season. It told the story of a shopgirl from the tenements whose shining virtue softened all hearts, including that of the wealthy New Yorker she eventually married. Cinderellas besieged Broadway for the next three or four seasons; there were musicals about salesgirls, secretaries, orphans, waitresses, and even dishwashers. Lew Fields, seizing his opportu-

Richard Rodgers, age eighteen, reviewing the script
for *Poor Little Ritz Girl*

nity, chose a chorus girl as his ideal Cinderella and titled his new musical
Poor Little Ritz Girl.

It ought to have been a surefire idea. The script, by Harry B. Stillman and
William J. O'Neil, was influenced by the "intimate" musicals of the Princess
Theatre genre, used only two sets (a Riverside Drive apartment and a theatre
stage), and relied on situation and character development rather than prat-
falls and gags. Herbert Fields had already added numerous revisions to the
book and was about to dispense with the services of his original composing team, the lyricist Vincent Bryan and the composer Joseph Meyer. New
lyrics were needed for five or six of the songs; Rodgers and Hart had to contribute the rest of the songs and do so fast, since Boston tryouts were scheduled for the end of May. Fields was not averse to the idea of recycling some of
their earlier songs, with appropriately revised lyrics. "Peek in Pekin"
became "Love's Intense in Tents," "Dreaming True" became "Love Will

Call," and "Don't Love Me Like Othello" became "You Can't Fool Your Dreams." Rodgers and Hart also trotted out "Mary, Queen of Scots," the biggest success of *You'd Be Surprised,* with lyrics by Herbert Fields. As might have been expected, the pair met their deadline, and when the Boston opening came, they took the night train up from New York with the rest of the company. Rodgers wrote that they got off the train in the morning only to discover that they had lost Larry. "It seems that he was so small that the porter couldn't find him in his upper berth to wake him in time, so he slept his way out to the train yards. He didn't make it to the theatre until the afternoon." Then began the countdown hours that would come to typify their opening nights:

> Hart . . . assaults a telephone with excited orders to have his suit pressed. He dashes into a barber shop demanding that the frightened attendant do things with his razor in five minutes . . .
>
> Hart is . . . doing two things at once, continuing to telephone and pursuing a floating cake of soap in the bathtub. He recalls twenty clever wires he had intended sending twenty members of the cast and associates, but the hands of the clock warn him that fleeting minutes play havoc with the best-laid plans and he abandons his intention . . . Dinner consists of one long and two short gulps. Three drinks give him sufficient strength to make the final lap to the theatre . . .

Meanwhile Rodgers is methodically chewing food he cannot bear to look at. Arriving at the theatre, he paces around backstage, determined to "renew heart on the one hand and avoid Hart on the other." Hart has taken a seat in the first row with a fixed grin on his face. Rodgers slips into a seat in the darkened balcony. As the orchestra strikes up he goes into a sweat and, the minute the first act is over, he plunges downstairs into the nearest dressing room, where he begins to smoke furiously. Hart's solution is to find the nearest bar: "Bartender enquires about the play. Drinks ruined." Eventually the curtain comes down and the two head out, looking for reviews in the late editions. As darkness fades into dawn, they fling the papers away.

The Boston reviews for *Poor Little Ritz Girl* were kind, even though, Hart said later, "the timing was all wrong and the second-act curtain rose too soon. Instead of the chorus on the stage there were forty stage hands milling about in their overalls." That was because the musical had grown physically cumbersome; Herbert Fields had insisted that they buy some complicated equipment that facilitated one aspect of the scene changes, but at a price. What still had to be moved by hand were all the accoutrements of the Riverside Drive apartment: real bookcases full of real books and a real grand piano. During the first-night curtain call the stagehands came on in their shirtsleeves and took a bow. The escalating cost of the production was not the only part of the problem. The principal actors were unknown, the script still did not please, and something seemed to be wrong with the music. Fields was in financial trouble and looking for a scapegoat; there would be five credited writers, three directors, three sets of romantic leads, and three songwriting teams in the space of a few months. The situation was not helped by the review in *Variety:* "It is said that both [Rodgers and Hart] are close friends of Fields's son, Herbert, and whether 'Daddy' dug down and put the show on to give his son's friends an opportunity and to put Herbert into the producing business . . . is a question."

The much-revised *Poor Little Ritz Girl* opened to glowing reviews in the summer of 1920 and almost everyone was delighted, except Rodgers and Hart. When Rodgers returned from Camp Paradox in Maine, where he had been working as a counselor, he discovered that half of their songs had been cut, replaced by eight songs from that reliable writer of Viennese schmaltz Sigmund Romberg. No one had bothered to tell them. Rodgers wrote in 1975: "More than fifty years later, I can still feel the grinding pain of bitter disappointment and depression. I didn't want my parents at the opening, but since there was no way to keep them out, we sat and suffered together until they took me to the train to go back to camp—one badly bruised unconquering hero."

Chapter Four

"WAR IS WAR"

B ROADWAY, THEN AS NOW exquisitely sensitive to the temperature
of the business climate, was having one of its booms in the autumn of
1920. Theatres were being built everywhere and an average of $50,000 would
launch a musical comedy that, with a little luck, would turn a profit, as it
would seem, since more than fifty producers took chances on that genre during that season. Everyone knew that *Irene,* the hit of the previous season,
which had cost $41,000 to produce, had paid off its entire investment and was
showing a profit of $20,000 after just six weeks; and this was in the Vanderbilt,
a theatre with limited seating. If a musical or play lasted for a hundred performances, its financial success was practically guaranteed, and even those that
did not last could often cover their production costs by going on tour. In the
first two weeks of October, *Poor Little Ritz Girl* was playing to packed houses;
there would be 119 performances on Broadway. But the conventional wisdom
could not always be relied upon. In his determination to bring in a first-rate
production, the extra rehearsal time, the expensive new machinery, and all the
hirings and firings had driven up Lew Fields's costs past the point of easy
returns. When Lee Shubert, owner of the Central Theatre, where the musical
was playing, decided a feature-length film would bring in more money and
closed the show, the fate of *Poor Little Ritz Girl* was all but sealed, even though
Lew Fields arranged for a road tour. And by the spring of 1921 Broadway was
experiencing one of its periodic busts, a bad time "for an aging actor with a
high-living family to be broke and out of work," Fields's biographers wrote.

In their continuing campaign to find a way to insinuate themselves onto
Broadway, Lew Fields had been Rodgers and Hart's mentor and patron, a
benign and generous presence. But *Poor Little Ritz Girl*'s problems were

absorbing all his time, and Rodgers was back where he started, a sophomore at Columbia, struggling with geometry and French and wondering why he was there. True, he and Hart had been given a nice mention or two. One critic praised their "hard, brisk tunes" and another wrote that Rodgers "writes uniformly with a light hand; now and then with neat modulations or pretty turns of ornament; here and there with a clear sensibility to instrumental voices; and once again with a hint of grace and fancy." There was a new Varsity Show to prepare for, and in the winter of 1920–21 he and Hart wrote eleven new songs for *You'll Never Know.* Herbert Fields did the choreography; Oscar Hammerstein II, who had a new musical on Broadway, *Tickle Me,* obligingly directed; and the musical had a respectable run in the Grand Ballroom of the Astor Hotel—but Rodgers did not remember a thing about it. By then, he was looking elsewhere.

Friends had convinced him that he was misplaced at Columbia. After all, music was the only thing in his life, so why was he wasting his time on academic subjects? This was the argument, and in the late spring of 1921, the most prestigious music school in the city, the Institute of Musical Art (now the Juilliard School), was willing to take him. Still, Rodgers hesitated. His father, for whom a well-rounded education was essential, would be bound to disapprove. Rodgers prepared his arguments carefully. His father listened without commenting and finally told him the decision was up to him. The only opposition he received was from his grandfather, Jacob Levy, who was convinced that "even if you are successful, they'll never pay you."

In years to come Rodgers would see his two years at the Institute of Musical Art as the best decision he could have made. The fact that a Broadway-bound musician had been accepted by an institute devoted to classical music made a deep impression on Rodgers, who was at first self-conscious about being with people "whose aims in life were, at least by tradition, considered loftier." But that feeling disappeared in the atmosphere of friendliness and respect that he found, "and I'm sure that's why, for the first time in my life, I was actually learning something in a school," he wrote. Sheer talent had taken him this far, but now he was ready to benefit from the discipline of, for instance, a class in harmony, taught by Percy Goetschius, "who was to harmony what Gray was to anatomy." Rodgers added, "Whenever Goetschius talked about ending a phrase with a straight-out tonic chord (the first, third and fifth step of any key), he would call it a 'pig,' his term for anything that was too easy or obvious. Once I heard the scorn in Goetschius's voice I knew that I'd avoid that 'pig' as if my life depended on it."

With George Wedge, ear training was fun; with Franklin W. Robinson, theory was transformed into something much more like musical aesthetics;

and a lecture by Henry Krehbiel, music critic of the *New York Tribune,* might reveal riches undreamed-of in a Beethoven symphony or sonata. Every morning his anticipation began as soon as he got onto the subway at Eighty-sixth Street and Broadway, and by the time he was at the end of his journey, "I could scarcely keep from running." Each day he came home full of stories about what he had learned. The one discipline he did not study, one essential to a serious musician, was orchestration. In a world where music has to be tailored to the demands of the production, and often does not take final shape until the eleventh hour, orchestration is a waste of effort. Like others before him and since, Rodgers always worked with a talented orchestrator and copyists.

He was fortunate in that the school's founder and director, Frank Damrosch, was an admirer of musical theatre and encouraged his ambitions. As soon as he arrived Rodgers was pressed into service to write the music for *Say It with Jazz,* a spoof on Rimsky-Korsakov's *Le Coq d'or,* in which jazz and classical music battle it out. It was so successful that Rodgers believed he was awarded scholarships at the institute "just to make sure I'd be on hand to write the shows." He and Larry wrote some new songs and recycled a few others from earlier shows. By then the team had been joined by Herbert Fields, who had helped contribute to the financial problems of *Poor Little Ritz Girl.* Fields was five years older than Rodgers, and his original ambition had been to act. But one night in 1919, Rodgers had asked him bluntly, "Why do you want to be an actor? You can't sing and you aren't too handsome. You'll end up as you began—in bit parts. Now if you were to write a book for a musical comedy . . ." The fact that Fields had never done that hardly crossed Rodgers's mind; he was one more link to a family Rodgers and Hart had no intention of allowing to forget they existed. Fields proved to be a competent author, if not a particularly inspired one. He contributed the book for one more in a string of amateur efforts, *Say Mama,* the last Rodgers would write for the Akron Club, in the spring of 1921. What that one was about has slid into obscurity, but there were at least three songs, "Chorus Girl Blues," "Watch Yourself," and "Wake Up, Priscilla," that showed a new self-assurance and sophistication. *Theatre World* of March 1921 predicted that Rodgers would someday be "among our great composers."

ALTHOUGH LARRY HART was the only lyricist Rodgers wanted to work with during this period the same could not be said for Hart. Rodgers was, after all, still just a student. Hart was now in his mid-twenties and beginning to be haunted by the idea that time was slipping away. For all he knew,

Rodgers might be moving in the direction of classical music—certainly, that was what he was being trained for. Through another young composer, Arthur Schwartz, Hart had met Elliott Shapiro, head of the well-known publishing firm of Shapiro, Bernstein & Co., and played him some of the songs from *Fly with Me*. Shapiro listened and shook his head. "It's too collegiate. You fellows . . . will never get anywhere unless you change your style. These songs are great for amateur shows. I've got to tell you the truth, fellas. Change your style or give up."

The truth, however painful, was salutary. Hart was too shrewd an observer of the Broadway scene not to know that the musical was going through one of its periodic slumps (one that would end only with the onset of the 1924–25 season). The time was ripe for the kind of fresh vision Hart could bring to it, but how was that to come about? Perhaps he should turn to producing plays—in fact, he even launched a couple of them himself. Or perhaps he needed to distance himself from Rodgers and come up with a whole new way of looking at the contemporary scene.

A few years later he was talking confidently about the changes in public taste:

> The old song of the "Kiss Me Again" type, the song based on a direct statement of affection, was written for the girl who played the piano when her young man came to call.
>
> The romantic scene at the piano used to play an important part in courtships. Then girls didn't have "sex appeal"; they had "allure," and they all knew this allure could be displayed to the best advantage at the piano. When the beau called on Sunday night and presented his bouquet or box of bonbons, the girl spoke of a new song which was "simply divine" . . . They sang it together, maybe. After a few verses of one of those tender, romantic lyrics beneath rose-shaded lights his sales resistance was shattered completely and he was sure that his devotion would last until the sands of the desert grew cold.

But now, Henry Ford had changed all of that:

> You can't sing "Kiss Me Again" to the sound of a slapping tire-chain . . . Now the direct declaration of affection in a song is passé . . . If the girl plays the piano, she plays jazz. The piano tête-à-tête has gone and now the song writer is thinking of the boy and girl dancing . . . Words must have a lighter ring to them, but must appeal to the emotions of the dancing couple.

Hart had identified some surefire themes: the southern song, which dealt with cotton-picking time, watermelons and peaches; the kind of song, according to Will Rogers, "that makes people born in New York tenements yearn for their Negro mammies in Alabama." Then there were the songs about the girl in the moonlight; the one about building a love nest, "the cottage small by the waterfall"; and, finally, the mother-and-child song. No one was more heartily sick of that last hackneyed theme than he was; but there was no getting around it, that one was probably the most popular of all.

While this revolution in Hart's thinking was taking place and he was experimenting with lyrics for music by Schwartz, Mel Shauer, and a couple of others, Rodgers was still stuck in the college mold, as it would have seemed to Hart. Rodgers had written some of his songs for *Say It with Jazz* with Frank Hunter, a fellow student, and one of them, "Every Girlie Wants to Be a Sally," was a reference to a new hit musical: *Sally,* which had opened just before Christmas of 1920 and was the latest rage. Seeking to recoup his losses Lew Fields had turned to the popular revue form and produced *Snapshots of 1921,* and Rodgers persuaded him to include "Every Girlie Wants to Be a Sally." The song was a success, and by way of reward, Fields offered Rodgers the job of replacing the music director while the show was on the road. Rodgers was granted a leave of absence from the Institute of Musical Art, opened in Detroit in December 1921 and stayed with the show until it closed the following spring. Meanwhile, according to the headlines, BROADWAY THEATRES HIT BY WORST BUSINESS SLUMP IN YEARS. Fields was broke again and in no mood to help anyone; he filed for bankruptcy. It was small consolation to read that a number of other Broadway producing companies, including Oscar Hammerstein, Inc., were in similar straits. Rodgers went back to writing amateur shows.

AMID THE FLOTSAM of musicals with such sophomoric titles as *A Danish Yankee at King Tut's Court* that occupied his time for the next two or three years, there were some that showed real promise. Mrs. Benjamin, founder of the Benjamin School for girls, where Dorothy Fields was a pupil, wanted a musical in the spring of 1923. There was no money in it for him, as usual, but the budget was surprisingly attractive—three thousand dollars—and the musical would be performed at the Thirty-ninth Street Theatre. That was enough to convince Hart to write the lyrics; Herbert Fields would provide the book. They decided upon a musical version of *If I Were King,* Justin Huntly McCarthy's novel about the poet François Villon, who becomes king for a day but will lose his head if he does not woo and win Catherine de Vaucelles. There was an all-girl cast with Dorothy Fields playing Villon, complete with beard. Thanks to Lew Fields, Russell Janney, a producer, took an interest in the project and Rodgers was sent for. He went by himself—the chore of auditioning being one Hart disliked intensely—and played several numbers. Janney was enthusiastic, and visions of a Broadway production began to take shape. No actual contract changed hands, but Janney seemed so sincere that Rodgers was sure something magical was about to happen. Janney would telephone him. He waited and waited. Finally, he contacted Janney. It seemed that the financial backers were unwilling to risk their money on untried talent. This may have been the moment when Rodgers was asked whether he and his partners owned the musical adaptation rights. They did not. Two years later, Janney mounted his own version of *If I Were King*. Now called *The Vagabond King*, with Dennis King as Villon and music by Rudolf Friml—such songs as "Only a Rose," "Love Me Tonight," and "Song of the Vagabonds"—it was an enormous success.

When, a year later, the trio again adapted a novel as a musical for the Benjamin School for Girls, they must have known the risk they were taking. This time it was Anthony Hope's *The Prisoner of Zenda,* and, once more, the fact that the Rodgers and Hart musical was performed in a Broadway theatre (the Selwyn) gave it almost too much prominence. But no producer was willing to entertain such numbers as "My King Can Do No Wrong," "Farewell to Rudolph," and "Song of Russia" when they could have songs by Sigmund Romberg instead. And so in due course *The Prisoner of Zenda* made a new appearance on Broadway, retitled *Princess Flavia.* This time Romberg seemed to have lost his touch; the operetta was considered derivative and closed after nineteen weeks. In the meantime Rodgers had learned some painful lessons about protecting his intellectual property, ones that would stand him in good stead.

A note of panic begins to enter his memories of this period, perhaps a reflection of Hart's even more desperate mood. It seemed to Rodgers that he had more than proved his worth and that while he was still struggling, others with no more talent were being offered opportunities on a platter. Was it fair that a piano pounder (Rodgers's term) named George Gershwin should have been offered a show to write, *La-La-Lucille!,* when he was only twenty? What about Vincent Youmans, aged twenty-four, who had written music for *Wildflower,* one of the biggest successes in town? Even Oscar Hammerstein was well launched, with six productions—not that he resented Hammerstein's success, of course. As he was about to graduate from the Institute of Musical Art, the question of his future was beginning to loom large. How long could he afford to go on turning out these modest amateur efforts? At some point or other he had to earn a living.

Hart, Fields, and Rodgers had been working on a full-length musical, *Winkle Town,* about a man who invents a new electrical system that dispenses with the need for power lines. Given the unpromising nature of such subject matter, it seems inconceivable that the three of them should have spent so much time and effort trying to make the idea work. But try they did. Dorothy Fields, who would write lyrics herself, recalled that they were "working like mad upstairs on the top floor of our house on Ninetieth Street. They had fresh, bright, wonderful ideas," which included a jaunty, irreverent paean to the joys of living in New York called "Manhattan." It ought to have been a musical for Lew Fields, but he was either short of funds or not in the mood, or both. Dorothy Fields explained, "Pop came from an earlier era in which musical comedy meant just that—music and comedy. He didn't want a coherent libretto or a book show. He wanted music, yes, but the rest should just be gags, blackouts, and belly laughs, whereas Herb, Dick and Larry were obsessed with the necessity of having a strong story." They began to make the dispiriting rounds of producers "who liked the tunes but not the words, or the words but not the book, or the book but not the tunes," Orville Prescott wrote. Having Lew Fields in the background did nothing to improve their chances, because, Dorothy Fields explained, "they'd take their wares to diverse producers, who'd fix a baleful eye on my brother Herb and say, 'If you guys are as good as you think you are, how come your father isn't willing to produce your show?' "

Finally, in sheer desperation, Rodgers asked Oscar Hammerstein for advice. The latter was basking in the success of *Wildflower,* the libretto and lyrics of which he had co-authored with Otto Harbach, and was beginning to talk about the novel concept of a musical play. Hammerstein came to read and stayed to collaborate, but even he could not conjure up a way to turn an essentially intractable story into the bright and shining hit they had to have. They rewrote *Winkle Town* thirty times before abandoning it.

At the end of the day all they had left were a libretto no one wanted and some sprightly tunes, including "One a Day" and that little song called "Manhattan." Perhaps the songs could be sold to someone? Rodgers knew a young producer named Laurence Schwab who was about to go into production with a new musical and had not yet chosen a composer and lyricist. Could the *Winkle Town* score become the basis for his new show? Schwab thought it might, but first wanted the approval of his good friend Max Dreyfus, of T. B. Harms.

Oscar Hammerstein during his college days
at Columbia University

Rodgers reluctantly agreed—he had not forgotten his teeth-jarring encounter with Max and his brother, Louis—and he and Schwab were duly admitted into the great man's presence. After listening to the score, including "Manhattan," Dreyfus turned to Schwab. There was nothing of any interest, and he thought Schwab would be making a great mistake. Now if Schwab wanted a really *good* composer, that young prodigy Vincent Youmans just happened to be under contract with T. B. Harms . . . Rodgers wrote, "I was so stunned that I couldn't say a word. My heart began to pound violently and I felt the blood rush to my face. Nothing of value? He didn't hear any music? . . . With two sentences, the verdict was being handed down that I had no talent."

AS ONE DISAPPOINTMENT followed another, Rodgers further refined his tactical skills, nosing his way along the enemy lines. He had left his student days behind, and with them went those lighthearted, evanescent melodies that had charmed his Varsity and club audiences, but which steel-eyed men in music publishing offices dismissed with a snort of contempt. As it happened, Lew Fields was back on the stage again, having abandoned, for the time being, his disappointing adventures as a producer of musical comedies. His son Herbert happened to know that his father was looking for a play, so the trio decided to write a straight comedy with a leading role for Lew Fields.

However, it was not to be just any comedy. It would be based on *The Music Master*, a melodrama that had marked the transformation of David Warfield, once known only as a famous comic, into a serious actor. Herb Fields knew how much his father wanted to make the same transformation, that he considered it to be "the paradigm of professional achievement." So the team craftily set about appealing to his ambition of a lifetime. *The Music Master* was about an old German musician who comes to America looking for his daughter. Their version would be about an old Austrian composer who comes to America, is forced to make his living as an arranger for a Tin Pan Alley music publisher, and suffers the ultimate indignity of having his own compositions turned into popular hits. This gave Rodgers and Hart an opportunity to insert a couple of satirical songs into the proceedings: "Moonlight Mama" and "I'd Like to Poison Ivy." The team, who billed themselves for the first and last time as Herbert Richard Lorenz, knew their man. Lew Fields loved the idea, produced the show, and, after the usual last-minute crises, succeeded in bringing *The Melody Man* to New York. The reviewers had kind words for Lew Fields even if the play had not quite given him the stature as a tragedian that he had hoped for. But, Rodgers noted, there were no kind words for Herbert Richard Lorenz. George Jean Nathan wrote, "The plot is not only enough to ruin the play; it is enough—and I feel that I may say it without fear of contradiction—to ruin even *Hamlet*."

THE TWO FRIENDS who had urged him to enter the Institute of Musical Art when he was eighteen were both girls; Rodgers developed an early weakness for a girl on each arm. One was Dorith Bamberger, whose mother had introduced him to Louis Dreyfus, and the other was Helen Ford.

Just when he and Helen Ford met is not clear, but it could have been through Larry Hart. She appears in Rodgers's autobiography as simply "Helen," perhaps in deference to her privacy, since she was still alive when his book was published in 1975 and because, when they began seeing each other, she was already married. She was petite (about the size of his mother), a singer and comedienne who had been a child star, and had met and married George Ford, nephew of the Ford who had built the theatre in Washington in

The young Helen Ford

which President Lincoln was assassinated. Ford was considerably older than his wife when they married in 1918 (he was almost forty and she was just twenty-one), a producer of Shakespearean festivals. Almost as soon as they married he left on another of his interminable coast-to-coast tours, and they did not see each other for months at a time.

Meanwhile Helen was looking for work wherever she could find it, so both she and Dick were eager and hopeful when they started taking walks in Central Park, "discussing our two favorite topics—ourselves and music," he wrote. In an early version of his autobiography (later omitted) he said that the affair was never consummated, but he was more than a little in love with her and she with him. For, apart from their mutual attraction, it is clear that they could help each other: she had a producer for a husband, and one day he was going to need a leading lady. In the meantime they listened to Brahms, read books, talked interminably, and probably experimented, given the arrival of Prohibition, with their generation's drug of choice. One of the mock-serious articles Rodgers wrote for the Institute of Musical Art's magazine had to do with the effect on his life of his first taste of alcohol. "Uncle

Hiram," the family practical joker, brought a bottle of vintage Scotch to a Christmas party; Mother, scandalized, banished the bottle to the kitchen pantry. After wrestling with the temptation in vain, the author and his girl-friend, Cora, who might have been Helen, quietly left the gathering. They tiptoed out to the kitchen, found a corkscrew, some glasses, and ginger ale, and proceeded to sample the bottle. "The time passed; the amber fluid went soothingly and pleasantly on its course of joy. Mellowness pervaded the room. What was once a cold ugly kitchen had softened . . . Pretty colors paneled the walls . . ." They both had a hangover the next day.

As Dick went through school and launched himself on a dispiriting series of amateur musicals, Helen Ford was making rapid strides. In 1922 she appeared in the title role of *The Gingham Girl,* playing the part of a country bumpkin who follows her boyfriend to New York and launches herself in the cookie-making business; the show's "simple charm" made it one of the successes of the season. She followed that with the role of a poor Irish heroine who, faced with losing her man, comes up with another surefire business ploy in *Helen of Troy, New York.* The libretto, by George S. Kaufman and Marc Connelly, was praised as "a bright travesty" but the critics did not think much of the score, by Bert Kalmar and Harry Ruby. So by the time the team of Rodgers, Hart, and Fields were ready to work on their next project in 1924, Helen Ford was more than just an eager ingenue; she was established in musical comedy with two leading roles. Two sets of producers would appear to have seen her as a pretty singer with an iron determination, a role she would play in earnest in the lives of Rodgers, Hart, and Fields.

Their next subject came about serendipitously. Passing by the corner of Lexington Avenue and Thirty-seventh Street in 1924, they had noticed a small plaque on an eighteenth-century house commemorating an event that took place there a hundred and fifty years before, when that area of Manhattan was in the middle of a forest. A division of American soldiers under General Israel Putnam had been trapped in lower Manhattan by the invasion of British troops in September 1776. A certain Mrs. Robert Murray invited the English generals to her house that same afternoon. There was cake and plenty of wine, and one way or another the officers dallied for a good two hours. That was long enough for Putnam's division of four thousand men to make their escape from the city and join General George Washington's army on the Harlem heights, where they reassembled with the loss of only a few men; it was a turning point in the American Revolution. Larry Hart was the first to see the plot's delicious possibilities. Herbert Fields came up with the idea of a love interest between a British captain and an Irish-American girl named Betsy Burke. Frederick Nolan, Hart's biographer, wrote, "Herb may have written it that way because spunky Irish heroines were all the rage—his ideas were never startlingly original—or, more likely, because he thought it would be perfect for Helen Ford (Helen's recollection was that Herb wrote it with her in mind)." *Sweet Rebel,* which would become *Dearest Enemy,* had an irresistible opening scene for a forward-thinking actress: Betsy Burke is caught skinny-dipping in Kips Bay by a British officer, who requisitions her clothes to prevent her from sounding the alarm, so she arrives onstage wearing nothing but a barrel. Helen Ford said, "It was a wonderful entrance, and it was cute and . . . funny, with this English redcoat . . . chasing me with one of my slippers in his hand, and obviously I have no clothes . . ."

Since Rodgers established the fiction that "Helen" was not Helen Ford, he rather disingenuously describes the latter's introduction to *Dearest Enemy* in the early autumn of 1924 as if it were her first appearance in his life. Helen Ford recalled it slightly differently. She had been acting in "a kind of flop," another musical with a Kalmar-Ruby score, *No Other Girl,* and was living at the Algonquin Hotel. She already knew about the problems the trio had been having, and as she stepped out of the elevator one day Herbert Fields was waiting to hand her a copy of the script. She immediately wanted to play the role of Betsy Burke, which was gratifying, but did not immediately offer her husband as the producer, which was deflating. However, she promised to do everything she could to help. Her first stratagem was to set up an appointment with the producers of *No Other Girl,* but since that musical had just closed at a loss, they were not particularly anxious to take a chance on another.

They then turned to Lew Fields, but unfortunately that perennial performer had just completed a film with his partner called *Friendly Enemies,* with the same kind of plot. So he did not want to repeat himself, and in any event he distrusted costume musicals. His biographers wrote, "The old showman's overwhelming fear of yet another flop and his lack of confidence in its young authors blinded him to the show's obvious merits." That autumn and winter of 1924 was to be immortalized by Rodgers and Hart a few years later when they starred in a pseudo-documentary, *Makers of Melody,* recounting their experiences as one door after another was slammed against them. In the film they file out of a door emblazoned with the name "Peerless Music Publishers Inc.," looking dejected. Rodgers is impeccably dressed, as is Hart, and they are wearing matching boaters. Hart exclaims that he is "sick of this racket." Rodgers, unkindly: "Now you'll *have* to go into the real-estate business with your father," and then, with an impatient gesture, "Come on!" They are thinking of murder, suicide, robbery, or blackmail. "Which one are you gonna do?" Hart asks. Rodgers: "The way I feel I'd like to do 'em all."

The acting is stiff and mannered, but it is clear that the experience had left scars. In his single-minded campaign to take Broadway by storm, Rodgers had not been able to find one vulnerable spot in the enemy lines.

One of the stories told at the time was that Rodgers and Hart planned an assault upon a certain publisher who specialized in production numbers rather than just popular songs. "Someone had tipped them off that this publisher's opinion carried great weight with the musical comedy entrepreneurs. The two collaborators made several visits to his office where, after being made to wait for hours upon each occasion, they were told to return the following day. This publisher was their last trump, and they were determined to harass him until he consented to hear the score. Finally their opportunity came . . ." Unfortunately for Rodgers and Hart, the opening song of *Dearest Enemy* accompanies a scene in which ladies of the ensemble, who are sitting in Mrs. Murray's parlor, quietly sewing, are bewailing the fact that their boyfriends have gone off to war. So the first line of the lyric is, "Heigh-ho! Heigh-ho! Lackaday!" The nameless producer burst out laughing and then gave them a stiff lecture for wasting his time.

They went looking for backers to finance the proper sets, costumes, and furnishings: the sum of $50,000. The prospective angel was invariably a businessman who had fifteen minutes for them while he was dressing for dinner, or waiting for his wife to come down, or interviewing his accountant. They enlisted the help of Hugo Romberg, brother of the famous Sigmund, who took them all over the city, into "speakeasies, clip joints, bagnios and penthouses. At two in the morning he cornered a rich and guileless prospect at a drunken party. Propping him up he commanded the composer to play and the lyricist to sing. But the general hilarity drowned out both music and the bullfrog voice and nobody listened . . ." At the end of the day it is not quite true, as was claimed, that they only had enough money left for carfare, some doughnuts, and coffee, but it could have been. They were psychologically threadbare, at the end of their rope.

Or perhaps that was not quite true of Larry Hart, since, Rodgers recalled, he was perennially hopeful and always sure that something would turn up soon. The problem was with Dick. He began to suffer from insomnia, tossing and turning as he examined the possibilities. Should he become a conductor? Could he bear to spend the rest of his life playing someone else's music? What about the concert stage? Well, no, because of his finger. Perhaps teaching? Did he know enough about any aspect of music to be able to teach it? What was he good for, besides tinkling away on a piano?

He wrote, "Life in the Rodgers household when I was a kid had been hell chiefly because of the friction between my father and my grandmother." Now the formidable Rachel was gone—she had died four years before—but life was "still hell. There was no bickering, no yelling, no tight-faced silence. Now it was hell because I hated myself for sponging off my parents, and I hated myself for the lies I would rattle off about this producer or that publisher being so impressed with my work that it wouldn't be long before everything was just dandy." When he published his autobiography he could not remember having heard a single reproach from either parent about his inability to support himself. But David Ewen, who published a biography of Rodgers in 1957, based on numerous interviews with his subject, wrote that Will Rodgers was "increasingly impatient," torn between the feeling that Dick must do what he wanted to do and his desire to see him started on a career—after all, he himself had been practicing as a physician at the age of twenty-three. Perhaps he did not have to say much; silences in the Rodgers household spoke volumes.

Rodgers was in debt. His father's allowance did not extend to taking girls out dancing, so Rodgers had been borrowing money, five dollars at a time, from a friend, a young businessman named Earl Katzenstein, and now something had to be done because he owed Earl one hundred and five dollars. Margaret Case Harriman wrote, "In something of a panic, he went to his friend's office and said, 'I'm through trying to get anywhere in music. I want a job.' "

Chapter Five

"WE'LL HAVE MANHATTAN"

As it happened, Earl Katzenstein knew of a job. He led Rodgers across the hall to meet a Mr. Marvin who had a small business in children's underwear, buying, selling, and traveling on the road. Although he was not yet ready to retire, Marvin was looking for a likely youngster whom he could train to replace him. He listened to Rodgers's qualifications and, apparently impressed by the fact that he had attended Columbia University, and finding him polite and well groomed, offered him a job on the spot. The salary was the "fantastic" sum, for Rodgers, of fifty dollars a week. Rodgers knew it was a handsome offer, perhaps the best he could ever hope for, and was tempted, but something made him hesitate. He asked for time to think it over.

He was having dinner that night when a phone call came from Benjamin Kaye, the theatrical lawyer whom brother Morty had persuaded to contribute lyrics to the songs for *Up Stage and Down* some five or six years before. Kaye, who liked to dabble with sketches and plays in his spare time, had been consulted by Dr. Will Rodgers, who had taken to worrying out loud to his friends about Dick's future. Although Kaye was reassuring, Dr. Rodgers was not altogether convinced, and it is likely that Kaye was actively looking for a way to help this talented youngster get his start. At any rate, he rang to say there was yet another amateur musical in need of a composer. After listening to the groans at the other end of the phone, Kaye hastened to add that this was no ordinary benefit show. This was in aid of the Theatre Guild, which, in its seventh season, had acquired a reputation on Broadway for its high-minded productions of such playwrights as Strindberg, Tolstoy, Molnár, Shaw, and Andreyev. In fact the Theatre Guild had never had a musical but needed one now, since it intended to move from its charming but cramped home at the Garrick Theatre on West Thirty-fifth Street to handsome new quarters that were being built on West Fifty-second Street; a group of its apprentices had decided to put on a show to help raise money for tapestries for the new theatre. Kaye was writing most of the skits—this would be a revue—and a young actress named Edith Meiser was writing the lyrics. But they needed a composer. How about it? Rodgers was about to say no again when Kaye threw in the names of Lawrence Langner and Theresa "Terry" Helburn. They would be so disappointed after the glowing advance notice Rodgers had received from Kaye. Rodgers did an abrupt about-face. The opportunity to audition before such influential producers was too good to ignore. Mr. Marvin could wait.

Edith Meiser recalled that early in February 1925 she borrowed her mother's fur coat, so as to make an impression, left her tiny East Side apartment, and went to West End Avenue, where the Rodgers family lived in style. "We were having a February thaw," she said.

> Everything was dripping. The air was soft, but there was still snow on the ground, and I could see across the river, which was very hazy, kind of dreamlike.
>
> This elegant apartment had an enormous foyer and an enormous grand piano. Dick was waiting and said, "I'll play you a few of the things I've done for the Varsity Shows up at Columbia." So he did, and told me, "I did these with Larry Hart, who is a friend of mine."
>
> I said, "Well, you know, I have the ideas for all the songs, so I will naturally be doing some."
>
> He played some songs from other shows he had done. I wasn't terribly impressed. Then he played "Manhattan."
>
> I flipped!
>
> . . . And . . . so . . . I pulled myself together and said, "I think you're going to be our boy. Can you do the whole show or do you just want to—?"
>
> No. He wanted to do the whole show!

There was no money of course, but Rodgers managed to work out an arrangement by which he and Larry would receive a small percentage of the gross, plus a weekly salary, if the musical was to run. This was not likely, since it was slated for only two performances, a matinée and an evening on May 17, a Sunday, the day the theatre was dark. The rest of the week the Garrick's tenants were Alfred Lunt and Lynn Fontanne, in an extremely successful

Philip Loeb, Sterling Holloway, and Neal Caldwell as the
Three Musketeers in *The Garrick Gaieties*, 1925

production of Ferenc Molnár's *The Guardsman*. At the time the play opened
the Guild was dangerously overextended financially because of construc-
tion on the new theatre and in desperate need of a hit. *The Guardsman*
more than lived up to expectations; it was the greatest success the husband-
and-wife acting team had had so far, and was later made into a film. It was
still drawing a capacity audience when *The Garrick Gaieties* was scheduled
to make its debut. The chances of ever dislodging Lunt and Fontanne
seemed slim.

There was a further complication: after Rodgers had convinced Langner
and Helburn and even Edith Meiser that Lorenz Hart had to be the lyricist
for the revue, Hart himself balked. He was not impressed by the chance

to rub elbows with Theatre Guild producers and especially unimpressed by the lack of money involved. He disliked the idea of writing unrelated songs rather than songs that were an integral part of the plot, as was becoming his passion. That, perhaps, was Rodgers's finest hour. He knew that Meiser, clever as she was, was no match for Hart, and he knew that, in a revue, everything hinged on the brilliance of the minds behind the jokes. He argued and argued, and finally convinced Larry that they would invent their own chance to shine. They would write a mini–book musical and present it as the first-act finale. They called it a "jazz opera." Hart grumbled but finally agreed. Then there was Herbert Fields—what were they going to do with him? Someone finally remembered that Fields had had experience with dance numbers, a desirable skill since the crowd of young apprentices were fledgling actors, not singers and dancers. So Herb was given a job and the trio went to work.

Although they could not know it, the cast assembling for *The Garrick Gaieties* included some important future stars of the Broadway stage. The future director Harold Clurman was stage manager—he had recently been hired as a play reader. Lee Strasberg, future director of the Actors Studio, had a minor role. Sterling Holloway, tall, skinny, and agile, who would play a vital role in the proceedings, had already acquired a reputation as a mimic at Guild parties for his impersonation of Emily Stevens, who had starred in its recent production of *Fata Morgana*. Holloway was then only twenty years old and lacked a leading man's looks, but he more than compensated for that with his high spirits and wicked sense of timing. He would go on to play hillbillies, soda jerks, delivery boys, and country bumpkins in a hundred films, and his gifts of mimicry would make him an indispensable voice in Walt Disney cartoons.

Libby Holman, another young hopeful with a bright future, was at the start of her singing career when *The Garrick Gaieties* was being cast. She arrived wearing a pink wool suit and auditioned with "Jealousy." The young director, Philip Loeb, thought she looked far too knowing for a show that was introducing fresh young faces, but was persuaded to let her audition for Rodgers, who had assumed the role of the revue's music director and conductor. Holman, a contralto with a huge voice, kept asking for lower and lower keys, which did not endear her to the music director. And besides, he said, she sang out of tune. At the eleventh hour it was decided that her legs were the main attraction, and she was allowed to remain—in the chorus.

Since most of the actors were college-educated, Rodgers fitted comfortably into the crowd. And just as he began to feel almost too indispensable— he was supervising the musical numbers, accompanying the singers and dancers, and writing new songs—someone dropped into his life at the best possible moment. She was Margot Hopkins, then Margot Milham, "a plump, pretty girl," who walked into the theatre one day and offered to play the piano at rehearsals. Rodgers wanted to know how well she could play, so she sat down without a score and repeated a note-perfect copy of the song he had just finished playing, down to the "exact harmonies and rhythmic nuances." In short, she was a treasure, and stayed on to become his rehearsal pianist for decades. She later told him, "Dick, I'd never heard of you when I played your first songs." He said, "Even my own mother hadn't heard of me at the time."

Everyone liked Dick, but they immediately adored Larry Hart and felt protective of him. Edith Meiser said, "I always thought he was the American Toulouse-Lautrec . . . an enchanting man. He had such appeal. He was already balding. He had this enormous head and a very heavy beard that had to be shaved twice a day. And of course that big cigar that always stuck out of his mouth. And he was always rubbing his hands together. This was his great gesture when he was pleased."

There was a great deal to be pleased about. *The Garrick Gaieties* was taking shape as a topical revue, far funnier and more spirited than had, perhaps, been anticipated. Beginning with the Theatre Guild's high-minded choice of Art over Commerce, the songs and skits took on Lunt, Fontanne, and *The Guardsman;* Emily Stevens in *Fata Morgana;* the fate of young understudies (ever ignored and cast aside); the anonymous drudgery of the stage managers; and what was likely to become of the heroines of Theatre Guild plays once they arrived at the heavenly gates. But the canvas was much larger, and modern life itself was the target. There was a reference to the recent play *Rain,* with Sadie Thompson singing:

> I'm the sexy play that makes the clergymen censorious.
> My leading lady must subtract
> Her virtue in the second act
> But when the curtain falls her sacrifice is glorious.

There was a ruthless sketch titled "Mr. and Mrs.," depicting President Calvin Coolidge being scolded by Mrs. Coolidge because he had stayed out until the ungodly hour of ten o'clock. Rodgers wrote, "The audience roared at the sight of Coolidge taking off his coat to reveal both red suspenders and a thick red belt." Their jazz opera was ostensibly about a shipping clerk and a salesgirl who are locked into a department store all night and are fired by the owner, but in fact described the long hours and miserable pay of such workers; as the opera ends, the owner faces a near-riot. The mixture of saucy sexuality and nonstop ribbing seemed to exactly mirror the irreverent mood of the bright young things of the postwar world. And above all, there was "Manhattan" itself, with its lighthearted, skittering melody and rose-colored lyrics. Rodgers, conducting the orchestra, turned around after the finale to look at the audience "standing and clapping, cheering, yelling, stomping, waving and whistling. I turned back to the orchestra and had the boys strike up 'Manhattan.' The cast sang it. The musicians sang it. Even the audience sang it. After about ten curtain calls, the house lights went on, but still no one wanted to go." It had been extraordinary, magnificent, an unbelievable success.

In the euphoria and confusion of the opening performance, the hugging and kissing, hands sweating and eyes blurring, Rodgers remembered Hart "jumping up and down, rubbing his hands together and screaming, 'This show's gonna run a year! It's gonna run a year!' " That was the moment when he realized that the show was not going to run a year or even a week; they had one more performance that night before it closed. Rodgers, who was rapidly assuming the role of spokesman, went to see Terry Helburn. Would she consider some extra performances? She would. Four matinées were announced for June and all of them sold out, even though it was the middle of a heat wave, which was almost worse than a blizzard in the days before air conditioning. So Rodgers returned with yet another suggestion. He had taken the trouble to find out that *The Guardsman's* weekly gross had dwindled to about five thousand dollars. Rodgers boldly suggested that *The Garrick Gaieties* could do twice that business, so how about it? Helburn consulted Lunt and Fontanne, who, having given eight performances a week since the previous October, were ready for a rest. *The Garrick Gaieties* began its regular run on June 8 and stayed for twenty-five weeks, a total of 211 performances. Rodgers and Hart each received about $50 a week from their percentage of the gross; in addition, Rodgers was earning the handsome sum of $83 a week, union scale, for being the show's conductor. It was the first actual wages either of them had earned from their work on musicals since the day they joined forces nine years before.

Robert Benchley called *The Garrick Gaieties* "by miles the . . . most civilized show in town." Richard Watts Jr. had nothing but praise for its "gaiety, high spirits and cleverness, combined with a certain quality that makes the spectator feel that he is a guest at a party." Bernard Simon, in the *New York Morning Telegraph,* called it "as spontaneous and quick moving a show as is to be found in town." E. W. Osborn, in the *New York Evening World,* found it "absolutely fresh in word, song, dance, skit and bit of skittishness." Alexander Woollcott wrote, "All of it is fresh, spirited and engaging; some of it is bright with the brightness of something newly minted . . . the elders of the Guild

Reliving the moment when they wrote "Manhattan" for *Makers of Melody,* filmed in 1928

must know now the acute discomfort of parenthood when one finds that one's prodigy are almost embarrassingly bright." The team's eleven songs came in for particular praise. Their work clicked, Robert F. Sisk of *Variety* wrote, "like a colonel's heels at attention." In short, they had arrived.

RODGERS AND HART were already old hands at intuiting the attention span of an audience; of deducing, by the minutest of signs, those moments when a wavering of interest spelled disaster. For unlike some other forms of theatre, a play for instance, which can afford to develop by degrees, its best moments arriving in the second or third act, a revue must start out with a flash of excitement and then get better. Each segment has to be, if possible, more amusing, surprising, and wittier than the one before. In a world where insecurity is rife, Rodgers and Hart were not the only professionals to fret over every trifling hint of indifference; and they, like their colleagues in *The Garrick Gaieties,* could cut with a ruthless hand. Still, it was something of a shock to Rodgers to learn that their jazz opera, their proud experiment demonstrating, he thought, how to set a story entirely to music, had to go. It was not bright enough or snappy enough; the audience's attention was wandering. He accepted defeat but was stung by it. As for Larry Hart, who had insisted that they write something of value for this frivolous undertaking, he did not mind a bit. Whatever he had just finished had lost all interest for him. As Edith Meiser said, "Larry lived always just for today."

There were, however, compensations. "Manhattan," that little ditty nobody wanted until the public roared its approval, promptly found a publisher in Edward Marks, who also took six of their other songs, including "April Fool," "Do You Love Me?," "On with the Dance," and "Sentimental Me," giving promise of a steady source of income.

That was an unforgettable summer. On very hot nights Rodgers took the late train to Long Beach, spent the next day with his parents, swimming, playing tennis, and lazing on the beach, and would get back to Manhattan in time for work. The rest of the week he was hardly at a loss for amusement. The cast of *The Garrick Gaieties* had become the pets of New York society. There were Sunday-evening parties at the home of George Gershwin, parties given by Gertrude Lawrence and Bea Lillie in the duplex apartment they shared on the West Side, parties at the Algonquin with Dorothy Parker and Robert Benchley, parties at which Rodgers played the piano and Larry Hart did Al Jolson imitations. Or Hart would hire a chauffeured limousine and take members of the cast out for all-night drives in the cool air, laughing and singing. Edith Meiser said, "We'd take a dawn dip in the ocean somewhere out on Long Island, and having cooled off, we'd go back to the city freshened for the night's show."

Rodgers and Hart were inseparable in those days. If Larry wanted a poker game or a trip to the newest speakeasy, or tickets for a prizefight, Rodgers was a willing partner. As men of the theatre they went to every opening, taking copious notes. Both were capable of working with extraordinary rapidity and concentration, and neither needed to be told the crucial importance of the other's contribution to their success. That summer of 1925 made up, to Rodgers, for all the rejection and misery of the past few years. Night after night he exulted as audiences "laughed, clapped, cheered," sending waves of warmth that made the back of his neck tingle, there in the orchestra pit. He could hardly believe he was the same man who, only two months before, had been resigned to the life of a traveling salesman. When he thought about what would have happened if "some kids" had not decided to put on a revue, and Ben Kaye had not thought of him, he shivered. Some years later he and Hart were at an opening of a play at the Guild's new theatre and admired the tapestries hanging beside the boxes. Hart nudged him. "See those tapestries?

he said. "We're responsible for them." Rodgers corrected him. Hart had it backward. "They're responsible for us."

Despite the impression Rodgers gave in later years that he rejected Mr. Marvin's offer to become a children's underwear salesman as soon as he received the fateful phone call from Ben Kaye, such does not seem to have been the case. It would be unlike him to cut all ties before he was quite sure he would not need that steady, well-paying job, even if the thought of it made him wince. He seems to have temporized, even after *The Garrick Gaieties* became a success. After so many failures, the real test of their abilities would only come when they had shown what they could do with a musical. Following the success of his Princess Theatre shows, Jerome Kern had retreated to safer, more conventional formulae with *Sally* (about a dishwasher who becomes a leading lady), the year's biggest hit in 1920, and *Sunny* (1925), set in a circus; his masterpiece, *Show Boat,* was still to come. The operetta tradition, in which impossibly perfect heroes and heroines lived happily ever after against scrumptious backgrounds, fairy stories for grown-ups, persisted in such Romberg triumphs as *The Student Prince* (1924) and in Friml's *Vagabond King* (1925). The typical musical comedy was as ossified as was the operetta; stock characters went through their boy-meets-girl, boy-loses-girl, boy-gets-girl formulae; chorus lines opened and closed the show; comedians parroted fatuous jokes; and the action ground to a halt at predictable moments for songs that had only the most tenuous of links to the plot. Rodgers and Hart had contemptuously rejected such claptrap, but whether they could improve upon it had yet to be demonstrated.

On the other hand, although they could not know it at the time, the 1920s were a glorious decade for the Broadway musical, the years 1926–29 in particular. A seasoned writing team might have several shows running simultaneously, and even a series of disasters could be offset by a successful show. Theatres were being built wherever a plot of land could be cobbled together in the Times Square area, because running a theatre in those days was a profitable proposition. During the twenties an entrepreneur could build a theatre on Broadway for about $1 million, an amount that hit shows running for a year could gross. "The theatre owner's share was forty percent of the gross receipts, or around four hundred thousand dollars, out of which he had to pay overhead expenses," but none of the production costs, Mary C. Henderson wrote. An owner could close any show when revenues fell below a set amount. "It became a near impossibility for a theatre owner *not* to make money."

A number of the theatres in which Rodgers and Hart musicals would run in the years before the Depression were brand new, or had been built within the past decade. Lew Fields, who would own six theatres, took over the Mansfield on West Forty-seventh Street when it was just a year old (it opened in 1926) and renamed it Lew Fields's Mansfield Theatre; Rodgers and Hart's *Present Arms* played there in 1928, as did their *Chee-Chee*. Three of their most successful shows of the time, *The Girl Friend* (1926), *Peggy-Ann* (1926), and *A Connecticut Yankee* (1927), played at the Vanderbilt on West Forty-eighth Street. This handsome theatre had opened in 1918 with a musical titled *Oh, Look*. But Rodgers and Hart's crowning achievement would be to have their musical *Simple Simon* playing at the Ziegfeld at Sixth Avenue and Fifty-fourth Street, one of the most magnificent theatres ever to be built on Broadway. Architect Thomas Lamb and Joseph Urban, designer of Ziegfeld's famous *Follies,* combined forces for the concept, which might have been called a palace for art. (Urban, who was Hungarian, had actually designed castles for Hungarian noblemen.)

The Ziegfeld's novelty stemmed as much from its radical design as from its lavish appointments, its five-hundred-pound brass auditorium doors, its free-flowing lounge ceiling dappled with flowers, its velvets, satins, and gold veneers. The usual fan-shaped auditorium was abandoned in favor of an almost perfect dome-ceilinged ellipse, with the stage opening at the narrow end. Sight lines were ideal, and the whole interior, walls and ceiling, was covered with a polychromed mural, a mosaic of color laced with gold leaf. *The Joy of Life,* it was called. "Under a roof of flowers and foliage, among castles and hamlets . . . [are] human beings in a mad happy medley,—no deep meaning, no serious thoughts or feelings,—only joy, happiness,—a veritable trance of color." Richard Rodgers might have written the description himself. Here *Show Boat* opened in 1927 for a run of 572 performances, and here audiences had flocked, willing to pay the exorbitant price of $27.50, the top price in the city on opening nights, to see Noël Coward's *Bitter Sweet,* Gershwin's *Show Girl,* Fred Astaire, Bert Lahr, Jimmy Durante, and a host of others. To have a show in the Ziegfeld was to have attained all that Broadway had to offer.

For the city's longest street—it stretched eighteen miles from its origins in Battery Park to the Broadway Bridge at its northernmost point—Broadway was an infinite charivari of sights, sounds, smells, and all the celebrations that the human imagination could devise. The unintended consequence of Prohibition, i.e., a flourishing business in illegal liquor, had spawned a plethora of "blind pigs, gin joints, and beer flats," along with a rise in organized crime, networks to purchase, distribute, and market the merchandise, no questions asked. On the strip that ran from just south of Forty-second Street to Fifty-ninth Street and centered around Times Square, mobsters rubbed elbows with "journalists, gamblers, sportsmen and bootleggers, all joining the show people who were already there." Legitimate theatres in stone and marble stood back to back with flophouses, dance halls, and speakeasies. For, as Neal Gabler pointed out in his biography of Walter Winchell, Broadway was more than just a theatre district: "it was as much a mythical city as Hollywood, and made nearly as strong a claim on the national imagination." It was a raffish mix of the genuine and the counterfeit, of elegant façades and gimcrack realities. As Richard Rodgers said later, "When I started [Broadway] was crooked, opportunistic, sordid and sharpshooting." He added, "I've seen it at its worst."

Even Walter Winchell used to say of Broadway that it was hard and unforgiving, even for those who were successful. "What you accomplished last season doesn't matter. 'What have you got now?' is the incessant query." He might have been talking about Rodgers or, at any rate, Rodgers's fears for the future, which were precariously balanced on the edge of his equally fervent hopes. It was true that crowds were roaring their approval, but he already knew how fickle the public's taste could be, and all his life he hated to gamble. Fortunately for him, Hart's calm acceptance of success or failure, his willingness to wager everything on one last, munificent gesture, his stubborn confidence, all the buoyant aspects of his nature, acted as the ideal antidote. Once he had committed himself, Rodgers was not an easy man to dissuade.

The next logical step was to launch *Dearest Enemy,* the score that had caused nothing but derision when they had tried to audition "Heigh-ho! Lackaday!" a year before. They still needed a budget of $50,000 and had been offered half by "some gangster," Helen Ford recalled. She had "fallen completely in love with Betsy," so she rashly offered to raise the remaining $25,000 even though she knew almost nothing about finding a backer. "In my naïveté I asked everyone I knew, or met, connected with our business." But she raised no money.

One day, as she was coming out of the elevator of her hotel, she was met by a businessman who, it turned out, was the brother of her husband's roommate at Dartmouth. Robert Jackson had made a fortune in the butter-and-egg business in northern New York State and owned a chain of stores in Canada. By a curious coincidence George S. Kaufman had just opened a comedy called *The Butter and Egg Man,* about a dairy farmer who is duped into backing a Broadway show. It transpired that Jackson, who was ardently stagestruck, was willing to put up the remaining $25,000. The moment they heard that Jackson wanted to see *The Butter and Egg Man,* Ford, Rodgers, and Hart had turned on the full force of their dissuasive charms.

" 'It's no good; you wouldn't like it at all,' said the composer.

" 'Perfectly terrible,' said Miss Ford.

" 'Lousy,' said the lyricist.

"But the prospective angel escaped from his chaperones one night and saw the play anyway. 'Say,' he said the next morning, 'that's a swell show. Isn't that guy who backs the play an awful fool?' "

Nothing daunted, Jackson came up with the money, but then the anonymous gangster dropped out. Helen Ford said, "Nobody argued with him, and maybe it was just as well for me, because, in those days, when a gangster backed a show, he usually had some cutie he wanted to play the leading role."

Just as things began to look completely hopeless George Ford, who had returned from a road trip, was given a *Dearest Enemy* audition of his own. Ford said, "Dick Rodgers said to me, 'I've been at work on this two years, and I haven't made hardly a cent. I put two songs into a show for Lew Fields, and I'm going to quit music. I've got a job, I can go on the road selling children's clothes. If something doesn't happen, I'm going to do it.' That's when I decided to put it on, right there." At that juncture, Jackson came up with the rest of the money, and they were finally on their way.

George Ford's brother Harry was running a stock company at the Colonial Theatre in Akron, Ohio, which was willing to give *Dearest Enemy* a trial that summer of 1925. So early in July Rodgers relinquished his conducting chores at *The Garrick Gaieties* and took the train to Akron. Harry Ford directed the show, which only rehearsed for a week, and gave a single performance. But the decision to try it out far from the scrutiny of Broadway was prudent. There had only been one other Broadway musical that dealt with the American Revolution, *A Daughter of the Revolution* in 1893, and despite its reenactment of Washington crossing the Delaware, it had not been a success. Lew Fields could be right that Broadway audiences would not stand for a costume musical, and if so, there was no point taking it any further. But the signs were promising. A bright young director who had studied with Beerbohm Tree and worked with Sir Herbert Tree for two years was next to be contacted. John Murray Anderson, "a saturnine, elegant Englishman with sad eyes and a prominent jaw," who had previously agreed to direct if backing could be found, was still agreeable. He took complete charge of the production, headed by Helen Ford and Charles Purcell, as the English redcoat who requisitions her clothes, and rehearsals began in earnest. The producers astutely chose Reginald Marsh, a young painter, illustrator, and scene designer who would become well known for his lively evocations of Manhattan street life, to design an intermission curtain in the shape of a map of old

Lovers are reunited in the final scene of *Dearest Enemy,* 1925.

New York. The scenes for the three acts were up to the same standard, in particular an interior of Mrs. Murray's house with a central curving staircase that allowed for some impressive entrances. Costumes were executed with an equal eye to style and dash. Even as the Art Deco movement was sweeping away the final vestiges of High Victorian taste, such brilliant English muralists as Rex Whistler were experimenting with scenes in eighteenth-century rococo; others were imitating the fin-de-siècle decadence of Aubrey Beardsley, with his powdered and bewigged eighteenth-century beauties; and crinolined figures with gallant attendants were all the rage as china ornaments. Although *Dearest Enemy* might appear to be calling forth a vanished age, its mood was up-to-the-minute, if not ahead of it. So was the script.

During their famous encounter, when Betsy Burke is discovered in the nude, the captain says, "At first glance I thought you were a boy." Betsy replies, "Well, you should have taken a second look," very daring for 1925. "Sweet Peter," a song about Governor Peter Stuyvesant, teasingly suggests that his efforts to cheat his wife were doomed to failure because the sound of his wooden leg pounding up the stairs late at night would always give him away. And in "War Is War," a galaxy of maidens contemplates the arrival of foreign troops by sighing that they are bound to be "compromised": a delicious thought. Such sexual double-entendres, which managed to be naughty without being shocking, did not hurt the musical's chances. As for the score, that included a charming gavotte in the eighteenth-century style and ran the gamut of duets, trios, and choral numbers. There were at least two hits, "Bye and Bye" and "Here in My Arms." Rightly deciding that this was going to be one of the hits of the show, Rodgers set about giving it two more hearings, ones that would fit the logic of the story, while allowing the melody to imprint itself on the audience's memory, a trick he was to use later with equal success. In the first hearing the English redcoat is attempting to seduce the young American. In the second version Rodgers reverses the order and, having fallen for him, Betsy Burke sings, "Here in *your* arms . . ." Finally, at the obligatory happy ending, the war is over, the lovers are reunited and will always be—in each other's arms. Taking their cue from *A Daughter of the Revolution,* the authors added an appearance by General George Washington at the patriotic finale. They were taking no chances.

In a further display of caution, George Ford, as producer, took the musical to the familial Ford's Theatre in Baltimore for a week of intensive rehearsals and performances early in September of 1925; it would open at the Knickerbocker on the eighteenth. The show was too long and needed cutting and rewriting, but Rodgers allowed himself to hope, and Hart was ever ready with a new solution. Orchestra rehearsals, which Rodgers was conducting, were across the street in a burlesque house, and Ford was chagrined to see that ticket queues were much longer over there than they were at Ford's. Nevertheless, audiences seemed to like the show, especially the part where Betsy Burke arrives wearing nothing but a barrel, and laughed at the jokes. Having spent so much time and energy finding their "angel," Helen Ford ought to have been happy, but she was not. Most popular songs were in too low a key for her coloratura soprano, so she kept asking the composer for rewrites, with no success. "Whether he knew it or not," she said, "Dick wrote his songs for Larry to sing, and if it were in another key, it sounded wrong to him, I swear." She added, "Dick hates sopranos, you know," perhaps meant as a final verdict on a once close relationship.

The heat that week was frightful. Helen Ford perspired so much in the heavy costumes that she dreaded wearing them. She also had an accident. There is a moment in the plot when Betsy is signaling American troops with a light but is discovered by Captain Copeland. He shoots out the light and she is supposed to take a tumble. One night she caught her foot in her negligée, tripped, and fell in earnest. Had it not been for the heavy wig she was wearing, she would have been knocked out. That, in fact, did happen to Rodgers. It was a freak accident; he was quietly minding his own business, eating in a café twenty minutes before he was due to conduct the orchestra for a matinée. A huge icebox was right behind him, and a gallon can of peaches unaccountably fell off the top of it and hit him on the head. Somehow he staggered back to the theatre and picked up his baton, the only time, he wrote, when he failed to enjoy conducting his own music.

Even Helen Ford had to concede that the sets and costumes were perfection. For the opening number of the second act she wore a black dress with a close white wig behind a dozen showgirls wearing lemon-yellow taffeta dresses and white wigs decorated with cherry-red ribbon bows. "And with that Colonial set, and the staircase that came down in a circle to the platform on the stage, it looked just so delightful, so pretty." When the show finally opened in New York, Alexander Woollcott agreed that "the parades of damsels clad in Reynolds costumes past the fine, white balustrades of the old Murray staircase . . . this alone is worth the price of admission." The charm of the period and elegance of the decor went some distance to compensate for what most critics seemed to think was the failure of the book: polite and sentimental, but dull.

All the critics liked the score, some enthusiastically. Frank Vreeland thought Rodgers was improving with every score, "and he has such a fecund store of catchy tunes . . . that he will go far as a composer . . . He seems ideally teamed with Lorenz Hart and Herbert Fields . . . We have a glimmering notion that someday they will form the American counterpart of the oncegreat triumvirate of Bolton, Wodehouse and Kern . . ." It was clear that Rodgers's score owed a great deal to the operetta he had loved as a child, just as Hart's endlessly inventive lyrics reflected his adoration for W. S. Gilbert. Operetta historian Richard Traubner wrote, "Just as Sullivan's sweet, tuneful music sweetened and made irresistibly tuneful Gilbert's irony, Rodgers's music did much the same thing for Hart's words." His work had a freshness and spontaneity that lifted it far above the usual formulaic Broadway fare. "Moreover, in their range the melodies occasionally touched . . . on arioso effects. 'Here in My Arms' stretches to an octave and a fifth in the nineteenth bar of its chorus, still pleasantly and easily singable, but a departure from the tightly knit melodies of most musical comedy songs," theatre historian Gerald Bordman observed. The *New York Herald Tribune* called it "a baby-grand opera." Even those who did not like *Dearest Enemy* had words of praise for

Hart's contribution. A man who could rhyme "radiant" with "lady aunt" was to be cherished, Gilbert W. Gabriel concluded in the *New York Sun*.

In short, *Dearest Enemy* was a success, no mean achievement in a week during which the musical by Vincent Youmans, *No, No, Nanette*, arrived in New York after a record run in Chicago, and Marilyn Miller starred in *Sunny*, with books and lyrics by Otto Harbach and Oscar Hammerstein II and a score by Rodgers's idol, Jerome Kern. Rudolf Friml's operetta *The Vagabond King*, the idea that was stolen from Rodgers and Hart, also opened that week, and all three went on to have record runs. *Dearest Enemy* did not quite fall into their category, but Rodgers was on Broadway with his adored Kern, if he could manage to stay there.

That was far from certain. Business was very slow for several weeks after the opening. That was when Jackson, who had laughed so hard at the gullibility of the butter-and-egg man, came through with flying colors. He kept covering the losses week after week and slowly, business picked up. This would not be the last time in the careers of Rodgers and Hart that the popularity of one or two songs would carry a show along with them. "Here in My Arms" and "Bye and Bye" became so well known that *Dearest Enemy* stayed on and on, for a total of 286 performances. A touring company—their first—opened in Columbus, Ohio, and went on the road to eleven other cities. Meantime, Rodgers was still living at home and was expected to let his mother know whether he would be late for dinner. Things were much better there, too. Praise and encouragement were his daily fare, and his father took to assembling articles about him and pasting them in a series of scrapbooks which would faithfully record his career. After refusing to have anything to do with Rodgers and Hart, Max Dreyfus called them in and peevishly wanted to know why they had never offered him "Manhattan." Showing an almost superhuman restraint, Rodgers refrained from telling him that they already had. This time, Dreyfus was the soul of liberality. He took their songs from *Dearest Enemy* and even put them on his payroll—a common practice of music publishers at the time—giving them his permission to draw anywhere from $50 to $200 a week against royalties. Suddenly there was quite a bit of money coming in, and Rodgers went out and bought a car.

One of his good friends was Ben Feiner, son of a prominent New York lawyer. One night during the run of *Dearest Enemy*, Feiner's parents came to the show and were sitting in the first row to the left of the orchestra, that is to say, just behind him as, baton in hand, he struck up the overture. He noticed Ben's sister Dorothy sitting there. She looked quite pretty, but definitely too young. (She was just sixteen.) Some time after that, when Rodgers had given up his job as music director, he made a date with Ben to go to the movies.

When he walked into the Feiner living room he found Andrew Goodman, son of the founder of Bergdorf Goodman, already waiting. He and Dorothy were going to see *Sunny.* Then Dorothy appeared, wearing an evening dress. "Although I had seen her at the theatre only a short time before, she no longer looked like just a young kid; in fact, she looked like the prettiest girl I had ever seen." That night he decided he would wait until Dorothy was a year older and then ask her out.

Chapter Six

"MY HEART STOOD STILL"

H AVING MADE A TRIUMPHANT breach of the enemy lines, Rodgers was quick to press his tactical advantage. Almost as soon as *Dearest Enemy* opened he and Larry Hart were at work on the next idea. Their play *The Melody Man,* which had closed after fifty-six performances, had had the merit of introducing them to a handsome newcomer named Frederick Bickel, who had rapidly changed his name to Fredric March; he and Rodgers would become lifelong friends. The play was also enlivened by a husband-and-wife team of vaudevillians, Eva Puck and Sammy White, who gave such spirited renderings of Rodgers and Hart's two songs, "Moonlight Mama" and "I'd Like to Poison Ivy," that the songwriting team promised to write a musical just for them. After the successes of *The Garrick Gaieties* and *Dearest Enemy,* the time was right. Lew Fields needed no persuading, and he immediately signed a contract for their next show.

Rodgers and Hart had succeeded with a costume drama; now they wanted to show what they could do with something topical and light-hearted. Bicycle races at Madison Square Garden were all the rage, and so was the Charleston, named for the city in which it was conceived. This symbol of the jazz age arrived on Broadway with the start of the 1923–24 season, and within weeks everyone from exhibition dancers to flappers and patrons of the Silver Slipper and Texas Guinan's El Fay Club were jogging elbows and bumping knees. So Herbert Fields concocted this plot about a country bumpkin with ambitions to become a champion bicycle racer (played by Sammy White), the girl who is his trainer (Eva Puck), a siren, and some gangsters who are trying to fix the race. The title song of the musical, *The Girl Friend,* made pragmatic use of the Charleston theme. During the frantic

Sammy White and Eva Puck in *The Girl Friend,* 1926

weeks of tryouts—the scenery had to be cut down and refitted when it was found to be too large for the minuscule Vanderbilt stage—Rodgers recalled seeing Hart write a verse for "The Girl Friend" in "a hot, smelly rehearsal hall, with the chorus girls pounding out jazz time and principals shouting out their lines," fashioning his idiosyncratic juxtapositions of non sequiturs and ingenious rhymes. For instance, in the first refrain, which begins, "Isn't she cute? / Isn't she sweet? / She's gentle / And mentally nearly complete," there are two further rhymes: "A look at this vision / Will cause a collision," followed by "An eyeful you'd die full / Of pleasure to meet." The writer and composer whipped up a saucy tune for Eva Puck to introduce, "The Damsel Who Done All the Dirt," on the well-worn theme that behind every historical crisis was a girl.

The biggest hit was what Alec Wilder called Rodgers's "first wholly distinctive . . . song." Wilder wrote: " 'The Blue Room' is a strong, uncluttered, direct statement. In it is the first instance of a Rodgers stylistic device which he continued to use throughout his career, that of returning to a series of notes, usually two, while building a design with other notes . . . Here he keeps returning to b and a while ascending from d to e, to f sharp, to g, and a." Rodgers said that his decision to begin the second, third, and fourth bars on a C natural and end each bar by rising a half-tone each time gave Hart the idea of using "a triple rhyme on the repeated C note, and then, for emphasis, repeating the word 'room' on the rising half tones." Repeated rhymes added to the effect as the melody culminated in the final thought: "Because you're married to me." It sounded so simple, but it was, as Stephen Sondheim observed, the kind of simplicity that evolved from a highly developed talent. It was also more than that; there was a mood of genuine longing behind the trite sentiment that transcended the limitations of the genre and kindled a certain emotion in the listener, a catch and tug at the heart. And the depth of the feeling, its direct, unguarded quality, was a demonstration, if such was needed, that the emotions Rodgers had learned to hide during his stoical childhood had found their logical outlet.

Reviewers took *The Girl Friend*'s deficiencies of plot in their stride—musical-comedy plots were always trite and implausible—concentrating on the virtues of the humor, the dancing, and, particularly, the captivating music. Alan Dale of the *New York American* wrote, "This WAS music, instead of molasses. There was a ditty called 'The Blue Room' which should be sung to exhaustion, whilst 'The Girl Friend' has melody, quaint orchestration and decided lilt." The praise was general and should have brought in a steady stream of customers, so it was dispiriting when after the first week, the crowd dwindled and even in the intimate space of the Vanderbilt—which seated just 655 people—there were too many empty seats. Rodgers wrote, "Drastic steps were needed . . . Herb, Larry, and I agreed to a plan that I think was then unprecedented in the theatre: we offered to suspend our royalties if Lew Fields would keep the show running." He did, and, once more, word of mouth and the growing popularity of "The Girl Friend" and "The Blue Room" turned the corner. The show, which opened in March 1926, when *Dearest Enemy* was still running, stayed on until December, for a total of 301 performances, their longest-running show to date. Here Rodgers was on Broadway with two shows at the age of twenty-three.

By the autumn of 1926 "The Girl Friend" had become Rodgers's top-selling song in sheet music, having sold close to half a million copies; and his other songs, including "Here in My Arms," "Bye and Bye," "Manhattan," and "The Blue Room," together sold more than one and a half million copies. His songs had been recorded by almost every phonograph company and played by almost every band, and was also available on piano rolls. In the spring of 1926 *Variety* intimated that Rodgers and Hart were making five thousand dollars a week, an astonishing sum for those days, which put them in the same league with Vincent Youmans and George

Gershwin. Victory had become theirs in a lightning flash; the capitulation was complete.

That winter and spring of 1925–26 were as busy as any they had ever spent. Larry Hart, whose friendships inclined more and more to the disreputable Broadway fringe, had written lyrics for the future entrepreneur Billy Rose, who was then making a living peddling other people's songs to publishers and exacting exorbitant commissions. A few years after that Rose was running a speakeasy on West Fifty-sixth Street and had conceived the ambition to open an even grander establishment on Fifth Avenue at Fifty-fourth Street. He had invested a thousand dollars in *The Melody Man* and, having lost it, felt something was owed. At any rate, Rodgers and Hart spent some weeks working on nine songs for *The Fifth Avenue Follies,* which opened the supper club in January 1926. The reviews were passable, but the club, which had a dance floor and a minute stage, served no liquor and did not attract much of a clientele. Rose promptly sold it to a bootlegger. Rodgers and Hart were supposed to receive a percentage of the five-dollar cover charge but were never paid. Then, just as *The Girl Friend* opened, Rodgers had a call from Terry Helburn. She and Langner wanted to produce a second *Garrick Gaieties.* Would they do it? Rodgers agreed, with some reservations. The first one had seemed like a fluke. With hardly any money or advance expectations, the team had come up with something fresh, engaging, and original; but now there were demands to be met and a standard to equal, if not improve upon. Still, it was a chance to work with the old gang, including Ben Kaye, Philip Loeb, Lee Strasberg (who had graduated to stage manager), Edith Meiser, Betty Starbuck, Sterling Holloway, and a very pert and pretty newcomer named Bobbie Perkins. It was her first appearance in a Rodgers and Hart show. He was smitten.

As usual, Rodgers and Hart went to work with a will; the tighter the deadline, the more they enjoyed the challenge. Hart said that most of *The Garrick Gaieties* was written in rehearsal and their modus operandi was to keep a day or so ahead of everyone else. For instance, this year's counterpart to their "jazz opera," a sort of operetta that they called a "comedy burlesque," was written in half an hour. They free-associated, beginning with a spoof of "The Vagabond Song" from *The Vagabond King.* Hart said, "We liked 'To hell with Mexico!' for a refrain and started off with that . . . I scribbled off the lyrics while Herb wrote the lines and Dick didn't even sit down at the piano—he just wrote off the notes." One song was written on a Thursday, rehearsed on Friday, and performed on Saturday. They called the songs "happy travesties."

The result, "Rose of Arizona," was called "capital" when the show opened at the Garrick Theatre in May of 1926. Brooks Atkinson wrote, "The book, written by Herbert Fields, forgets none of the old banalities—the stalwart hero, the fragile heroine, the insinuating temptress, the stout-hearted lads of the indomitable American Army, the glorious flag itself, and the barefaced devices for breaking out into song." One of their parodies involved the sentiment about how if the sky was gray it might rain and how, if it stopped raining, the sun would shine ("It May Rain"). There were so many easy targets, irresistible ones, including the song about an "American Beauty Rose," superior to all other botanical species, and celebrated with excruciating rhymes: "no land" with "Holland," and "under the drizzle" with "falling in Brazil." There were ballets: Nijinsky was given the once-over in a ballet called *L'Après-Midi d'un Papillon*. Some plays that had come and gone rather briskly at the Theatre Guild were celebrated ("Six Little Plays"):

> Each little play has passed away—
> Some died because the public scorned 'em.
> They met their fate
> And got the gate
> Though all the learned critics mourned 'em.

The Knights of the Round Table were thoroughly roasted and even Queen Elizabeth I was spoofed for her amorous proclivities. Instead of the joys of city life ("Manhattan"), this year's emphasis was on more bucolic delights: "While you love your lover, let / Blue skies be your coverlet," and "How we love sequestering / Where no pests are pestering— / No dear mama holds us in tether!" ("Mountain Greenery"). Sterling Holloway and Bobbie Perkins introduced this one, to admiring comments. Rodgers and Hart had, they admitted, a rollicking good time even if, as they all sang, "We Can't Be as Good as Last Year." They were right about that. None of the critics believed the cast had lived up to their own standards, which did not seem to deter audiences in the slightest. "The audience at the opening applauded everything but the hat-holders under the seats," grumbled George Jean Nathan in the *Judge*. *The Garrick Gaieties of 1926* settled in for another comfortable run and 174 performances. Richard Rodgers, who had conducted the first, was in the pit to conduct the second, but only on opening night. After that he was far too busy.

DESPITE, OR PERHAPS BECAUSE OF, the volume of music they undertook to produce during the next few years, Rodgers and Hart prudently recycled whenever they thought they had a useful song that deserved a second hearing. "Manhattan," originally written for *Winkle Town,* was a deserved success in the first *Garrick Gaieties;* "Maybe It's Me" from *The Fifth Avenue Follies* would be revived for *Peggy-Ann* later that year; "Where's That Little Girl?," also from *Follies,* would have a new life as "What's the Use?" in *Lido Lady,* also of 1926; and "I Want a Man" from *Winkle Town* would appear twice more: it was given new lyrics for *Lido Lady* and again for *America's Sweetheart* of 1931. Perhaps it was just a coincidence that, as Rodgers and Hart sat down to write their first spoofs on British themes, "Idles of the King" and "Queen Elizabeth" for the *Garrick Gaieties* of 1926, they had already decided to write a musical for the British stage.

The musical-comedy team of Jack Hulbert and Cicely Courtneidge were appearing on Broadway with a sprightly British revue called *By the Way.* Since American musicals, with their unfamiliar themes and high energy levels, were all the rage in London, Hulbert and Courtneidge were actively scouting around for bright young Americans to import. *No, No, Nanette* had been a huge success in London, and Gershwin's musical of 1924, *Lady, Be Good!,* with its mesmerizing jazz rhythms, had taken London by storm. The hunt was on for other writers, and Hulbert and Courtneidge thought "Here in My Arms" showed promise of even better things to come. It looked, however, as if the American Revolution was not quite the right theme, and a bicycle race in Madison Square Garden seemed equally unpromising. A new book would have to be written, and Hulbert, and his partner Paul Murray, thought they had the right one in *Dancing Time,* by Guy Bolton, when they signed up Rodgers and Hart in the spring of 1926. That was soon abandoned in favor of yet another libretto, *Lido Lady,* all about a girl (Courtneidge) whose father sells sports equipment and her unsuccessful efforts to turn a languid man-about-town (Hulbert) into an athlete. The title referred to the musical's setting, the Lido in Venice. That was an almost engraved invitation to visit Italy and, as it happened, brother Morty and his bride, Ethel, were about to go to Venice on their honeymoon.

So that summer of 1926, Rodgers and Hart embarked on the SS *Conte Biancamano* for Naples. They met up with Morty and Ethel in Venice, and also encountered Noël Coward, whom Rodgers knew slightly. Coward introduced them to Cole Porter, then staying with his wife in extremely elegant surroundings, the Palazzo Rezzonico, where Robert Browning had died. They had a dull time in Paris and arrived in London with relief. Hart said later, "It occurred to us that we might not be able to reach the British audience with no more than a rudimentary knowledge of what that audience cares to see. We had about five weeks in which to work. Part of that time was devoted to finding out where we were, familiarizing ourselves with places, names, colloquialisms, the popular news topics of the day . . ."

Once in London they discovered that Hulbert and Murray had booked them into a fancy hotel, the Savoy, but had managed to find the two smallest and darkest rooms in the house. Then, according to Rodgers, they were left to their own devices even though they knew no one in London. Hulbert, who had seemed so friendly in New York, had become distant and cold. Nevertheless, Hart commented politely on "the extreme friendliness of those with whom we were associated." He also described the difference between a London musical-comedy company and an American: "Rehearsals are quite the most leisurely affairs in the world. They are halted each afternoon for tea, and the vibrating energy which distinguishes American preparations for the fateful first night is missing. At first we missed this scurrying to and fro, the uncertainty about details, the maddening stretching of working hours into early morning day after day." What they did like was the difference in preparation time; *Lido Lady* was trying out in several provincial cities for nine weeks, in contrast to the two or at most three weeks they got at home.

Hart might have guessed that the tone of his remarks, i.e., that one could learn all there was to know about England in five weeks, would elicit adverse comment in the national papers. Some of the critics were severe about Hart's insouciant disregard for precision in rhyming; the *Sunday Times* complained about "such English [as] 'Here in my arms it's adorabull; / It's deplorabull that you were never there!'" The writer explained: "The melodic accent falling on the last syllable of these dreadful words, the singer has to take the choice of pronouncing them properly and ineffectively or effectively and ridiculously." That there were unseen quagmires to be surmounted in the differences in pronunciation was clear, and the gulf was hardly to be bridged by the addition of a few "What, ho!" remarks straight out of P. G. Wodehouse.

Still, given their crash course in British manners and mores, Rodgers and Hart acquitted themselves creditably. There was "A Tiny Flat Near Soho," and "A Cup of Tea":

> The Briton must have his cup of tea.
> He takes it wherever he may be.
> He drank it in the land that once was known as no-man's.
> When he's in Rome he doesn't imitate the Romans.
> The Briton in Pekin or in Nome
> Remembers it's five o'clock at home.
> On Red or Yellow Sea,

Oh, can't any fellow see
The sun never sets on a cup of tea!

In sentiment, if not in theme, the song seems to be allied with Noël Coward's better-known "Mad Dogs and Englishmen."

Rodgers recalled that he and Hart were so bored with *Lido Lady* that they left England during the tryouts. (The show opened that December.) They were amazed when it turned out to be a huge success. (It would play 259 performances at the Gaiety.) The principals, Phyllis Dare, Cicely Courtneidge, and Jack Hulbert, were the main attractions, Hulbert's performance being particularly admired: the *Sunday Times* critic wrote, "Can any man so put on the rapture of an invoice clerk? Or the despondency of a plumber who, calling to mend a leak, finds that he can stop it on the same day? Can any light comedian so simulate the Cyrano who is at the heart of every humble lover, take rebuffs with so high a spirit, or so gallantly return unto the breach? Mr. Hulbert is optimist par excellence, or you might put it that he is all silver-lining and no cloud." The plot was trivial and the music almost irrelevant; one critic thought it commonplace. In short, the London experiment was hardly the critical triumph they had hoped for, but, true to form, they dusted themselves off and escaped on the first boat from Southampton bound for New York.

That happened to be the *Majestic,* a superb ocean liner which, as was the custom in those days, made a stop on the other side of the Channel to pick up visitors to the Continent. The port was Cherbourg, and as luck would have it, among the first-class passengers coming aboard were Mr. and Mrs. Benjamin Feiner and their daughter, Dorothy. Dorothy Rodgers recalled, "A tender took the passengers . . . from France out to the ship. So all the luggage and the passengers were on the tender, and my mother was looking at all the passengers on the *Majestic,* who were looking at us, and she said to me, 'Isn't that Dick Rodgers up there waving?' I looked and I said, 'Yes, I think it is. . . . It never occurred to me that he was waving at us . . .'"

But he was.

A PHOTOGRAPH OF MARY "May" Adelson, Dorothy Rodgers's mother, shows her dressed for an amateur musicale while she, her mother, and her sister were living in San Francisco. She has an elaborate velvet hat trimmed with ostrich feathers on her abundant curls, and a white lace dress almost buried under ribbons, but the most arresting aspect of the picture is her eyes. Perfectly formed, widely spaced, they look out with the faintly bemused expres-

Mary "May" Adelson, the
Belle of San Francisco

sion of a beautiful girl—as indeed she was—who cannot quite understand why so much attention is being lavished upon her. For there is no doubt that she took the city by storm; at the age of eighteen she was being admired and courted as an aspiring actress and coloratura soprano. She made such a success of her stay there that, when she later became engaged in New York, the West Coast papers referred to her as "the Belle of San Francisco." She was spirited, mercurial, and very adventurous. The family story is that she was in China in the 1930s after the war with Japan began and flew over the front lines, lying flat on her stomach in the plane, looking through the cracks at the fighting below.

The women in that family were known for their independence. May's mother, Jennie Rubin, was, Dorothy Rodgers remembered, "a wonderful looking woman" who wore "beautiful clothes. She was enchantingly feminine and I can still see the bottle of Houbigant's 'Quelques Fleurs' toilet water she always used, with its flowered label and the milles-fleurs purple and yellow silk box it came in, sitting on her dressing table." May used to talk about the terrible temper of her father, Philip Adelson, a Polish Jew—he came from Sulwalki and her mother from the town of Vilna—who made a comfortable living as an importer of flowers and feathers. Dorothy Rodgers remembered him as a handsome man with "a neatly trimmed Vandyke beard and impeccably turned out," who would draw pictures for her by the hour. But May disliked him, partly because if either of her two sisters, Belle and Eva, got into trouble, all three of them were punished. May was stagestruck and always claimed that Philip had locked her up in a room for three days to prevent her from going to rehearsals when she announced she had won a part in a show. His major flaw, in his wife's eyes, was his insistence that four of his sisters (there were ten in his family) live with them. "They were referred to as the evil sisters," Margot Conte, Dorothy Rodgers's niece, recalled, because they tried to run Jennie's life. At some point or other she had had enough. Taking her two younger daughters, May and Eva, with her, she boarded the train for California. Judy Crichton, Dorothy Rodgers's other niece, said, "She could only afford to go by coach, meaning that they cooked at the end of the train and bought food at stops along the way, and saw buffaloes and Indians; it established in May an independent and adventurous streak." There Jennie Adelson became either a milliner or a seamstress (accounts differ) to support her family.

There is no agreement about when this rebellion took place. Dorothy Rodgers wrote that it happened when her mother was about five, which would have been in 1883. However, May was certainly in San Francisco as a teenager, and she could not have been there before 1895, since she noted in her bride's book that this was when she met her future husband, placing her in New York at that time.

The differing accounts agree, however, that the rebellion was a success. Judy Crichton said, "The family was reunited under remarkable and romantic circumstances. Jennie Adelson was walking down a street in San Francisco one day when she ran into a brother of her husband's, who had been up in the Klondike during the Gold Rush. This is all family lore. She was so lonely for her husband that she packed everyone up and went back to New York. She won out that time and the sisters left." A slightly different version is given by her sister, Margot, who believes that Philip Adelson went out to San Francisco to claim his wife and remained there for a time. What is evident is that by the 1890s the family was back in New York and reunited. Belle, the oldest and most fragile of the three daughters, died there in 1897, at the age of twenty-two.

Before she left on her San Francisco jaunt, May Adelson had met a young man from an impoverished working-class Jewish family from the Lower East Side, "which, in the class-ridden world in which the Rodgerses eventually found themselves, never entirely jibed," Judy Crichton said. Benjamin

Franklin Feiner was the fourth of five surviving children of a Polish-born Jew who became a New York tailor. Dorothy Rodgers has no happy memories of her father's side of the family. Her grandmother had died before she was born and her grandfather, Solomon Feiner, was "an uncommunicative man who retired when he was about fifty and, so far as I knew, spent the rest of his life sitting in front of a window in his apartment." He had married his house-keeper, "with whom we had nothing in common." Whether he approved of his son Ben is not known, although it is evident that this was a brilliant boy. When Ben met May late in 1895 he, two years her senior, had just entered New York University Law School, where he distinguished himself so emphat-ically that by the end of his second year, in October 1897, he was admitted to the bar and immediately set up a law firm with Isaac Moss (Moss and Feiner). Despite this display of erudition Feiner continued his courses at the univer-sity until he graduated, holding half a dozen prominent positions in the stu-dent body. A subsequent article noted, "He had been examined in seventeen subjects in three years, and had passed with sixteen A's and one B, out of a possible seventeen A's, thus establishing (a) record." By February of 1900 Maurice B. Blumenthal, then an assistant district attorney in New York City under Asa Bird Gardiner, joined Moss and Feiner, and the three partners spe-cialized in corporate and mercantile law.

Some time after May Adelson returned to New York she met the up-and-coming young lawyer again, and in the autumn of 1902 they became engaged. She kept the program of her husband's bachelor dinner, which included some entertainment, one of them a lady wearing a hat and a skirt and not much else. The program's caption said, "Next time I will ask my wife." The marriage took place in Synagogue Shearith at Central Park West and Seventieth Street on June 16, 1903, and Blumenthal was best man. At the age of twenty-seven, Benjamin Feiner had arrived.

FIRST CAME BEN FEINER JR., born a year after the marriage, who lived in a home in which another nanny took over when his nanny had her day off, so that his mother never had to change a diaper. The apartment on Riverside Drive had a handsome parlor, formal dining room, library, numer-ous bedrooms, and he was attended by a governess, various domestic servants and driven around town by a chauffeur. His sister, Dorothy Belle Feiner, arrived on the scene on May 4, 1909, when he was almost five. Her gay, impetuous, high-living mother had regarded her son benevolently, in the fashion of well-to-do parents who can admire their offspring from a safe dis-tance, but she took a more active role in her daughter's upbringing, particularly her dress. There is a picture of the young Dorothy in a white coat and leggings with a huge ermine collar and muff. She has a tiny look of protest on her face because, as she recalled later, the outfit was so constricting that she could hardly move. Her mother loved "all kinds of beautiful things—linens, porcelain, fine furniture, jewelry, furs . . ."—and dressed Dorothy in custom-made, hand-smocked dresses from the most expensive shops. Clothes (what she wore, what her mother wore) formed some of Dorothy's very earliest memories. As with her description of the case in which her grandmother's Houbigant toilet water was contained, one can perceive behind the words a precise and exquisite possessiveness. Unlike some girls who begin with features of doll-like symmetry and grow plain later, Dorothy began as a beauty and grew ever more beautiful. There were the calm, broad forehead; the delicately pointed chin; the full mouth, always ready to curve into a smile; and most of all, her mother's wide-spaced and perfectly modeled eyes, with something of the same grave and vulnerable look.

Ben was strong, fair, and handsome and went to Horace Mann, but for some reason could not please his father. Benjamin Feiner Sr., who had reached eminence with such brutal speed, had, perhaps, the usual expectations for a firstborn son, but he seems to have been driven by more than impatience when confronted with a dreamier temperament; his attitude approached poisonous dislike. Ben Jr.'s daughters recalled that their grandfather took a picture of his son peering out from behind the iron bars of a dog cage. Everyone thought that was very funny except the butt of the joke. Judy Crichton said, "The classic story is that one day a grand piano was being delivered, and my father had done something mischievous, certainly not bad, and he was locked in the maid's room so he wouldn't see it being pulled up the side of the building and brought in through the window, an adventure he had been looking forward to for months." One of the problems was that he was physically not strong. Margot Conte said, "His weakness was considered a deficit because this is an over-achieving family; they are not tolerant of perceived deficiencies." The summer of his sister's arrival, 1909, Ben Jr. contracted typhoid fever; his attending physician was Dr. Will Rodgers. Dorothy Rodgers said, "As he recovered Dr. Rodgers brought his two sons, Mortimer and Richard, over to play with my brother. Dick was seven years old and his brother was eleven. I was in the carriage. Dick said he remembered seeing me; he didn't have any babies in his family so that made an impression on him. Then he and my brother became friends, and he would visit and they'd go out to the movies together or have dinner. And I would be there, but I might just as well not have been because they would look right through me."

Benjamin Feiner's dislike of his son was in marked contrast to the tender indulgence with which he treated his daughter. "Daddy's darling? Yes," Judy Crichton said. "Part of the lore was that she had three ermine coats before she was eighteen. Dorothy was known both sarcastically and affectionately as 'The Princess,' a term used behind her back more often than to her face." Ben was being held up to demanding scholastic standards, but it was enough if Dorothy was charming, tender, sweet, and beautiful. How Dorothy looked and what she wore became increasingly important. Of their trips to Paris to buy clothes, Dorothy Rodgers wrote, "Mother and I would leave the hotel at about nine thirty in the morning and except for time out to give my father the privilege of taking us to lunch, we would shop until the stores closed . . . Father never went shopping with us . . . but he was incredibly patient about all this nonsense. (Nothing pleased him more than seeing us dressed in beautiful clothes, and he never objected to paying for them. If something didn't please him, however, he could be quite critical, and his authority over me was such that once—and only once—when he suggested that I had put on too much weight, I went on a diet immediately.)"

However lightly she tried to dismiss that particular incident, her daughters believed Dorothy Rodgers became severely anorexic. Mary Rodgers Guettel said, "My view is that this whole generation was told they had to go to the bathroom every single day right after breakfast." Because of it perhaps, Linda Rodgers Emory thought their mother became dependent on laxatives "to flush herself out," rather than, for instance, teaching herself to vomit. Judy Crichton said, "Dorothy had acute physical problems for much of her life. Some of them were mysterious but I think they were real. She was terribly constipated and developed adhesions. These things were embarrassing, difficult and complicated and had to be faked out socially in a million different ways. She was an extraordinary anal neurotic, as was the entire family. People in my family would talk about sex but they didn't defecate. That was for the lower classes." As for Ben Feiner Sr., Linda Rodgers Emory said, "I didn't know him but what I heard about him from my mother made me dislike him intensely because of the mean, cruel things he did to Ben, and he sounded insufferable with my mother as well, very fussy about how she looked and what she wore and whether she was gaining weight. She thought she was saying nice things about him. I never heard it."

OF ALL THOSE TRIPS to Europe taken when she was small, Dorothy Rodgers explained that her parents went to take "the cure." She added, "I never knew what they were being cured of. There was a mania to be very, very thin in those days, but it wasn't just to take off weight. I think people did over-eat a lot . . . and they over-drank, too," so she went to a lot of "very boring places." As soon as he was old enough to travel alone, Ben Jr. almost always went separately, with his friends, on a low budget while she and her parents traveled first-class. She said, "College kids took their dinner jackets with them so they would be allowed up to first class after dinner. They could dance with us and it was fun. It was like a houseboat party. It was a glorious thing on those transatlantic ships in those days, just wonderful! You could play games all day. There were movies. There was a swimming pool on the ship. There was shuffleboard and all kinds of things to do." She made her first trip in 1910, when she was only a year old, and learned to walk in Germany. They went again when she was five, in 1914, lost their luggage, and almost got stranded during the outbreak of war; her father wrote a long account.

She attended Horace Mann (there was a separate high school for girls in those days), and when she graduated in the summer of 1926 was business manager for the yearbook, the *Horace Mannikin.* There she appears in profile, her hair drawn back to the nape of her neck, above the comment, "If eyes were made for seeing, then 'Beauty' has its own excuse for being." This was no doubt a reference to the fact that she had played the part of "the Beauty," wife of "the Ogre," in the senior play, *The Prince Who Learned Everything Out of Books,* and also perhaps a reference to her middle name of Belle. Elsewhere in the yearbook she was deemed to have "the Perfect 26," evidently referring to her waistline and judged to have the best figure. Her nickname was "Dot." She did not entirely escape a ribbing. "The Horace Maniac Asylum" noted that she was suffering from "her role in the senior play"; that her "main trait of insanity" was "spike heels"; and that "she thinks she is . . . a joy forever."

The undemanding future planned for Dorothy was a Swiss finishing school, but she had decided otherwise. A friend had been accepted at Wellesley and Dorothy thought it might be fun to live away from home for the first time in her life, so she applied and was also admitted. But before that happened, she deserved an extra-special treat, and got one. Since May had made up her mind that going to college required the equivalent of a trousseau, they shopped in Paris that summer with more tenacity and zeal than ever. There were the haute-couture fashion shows, which Dorothy loved, the haggling over prices, the decisions over fabric, line, and color, and the interminable fittings. Later there would be the exquisite chore of packing "the carefully folded underwear, the hundred-gauge sixty-denier sandal-foot stockings, clocked stockings, enamel- and jade-framed evening bags of antique brocade, sweaters, scarves, antelope gloves, shagreen compacts, marcasite monograms, stationery, perfumes packaged in bottles of Lalique glass and boxed to look

twice their size," everything except shoes and furs, since the best were made
in New York. Each of the dresses, jackets, and coats had to be swathed in
quantities of tissue and packed in wardrobe trunks, the kind that opened up
and functioned as impromptu closets complete with drawers. All of which
made settling into her first-class cabin on the *Majestic* a lengthy chore, since
there were so many functions to attend and nuanced decisions to be made
about exactly which dress was to be worn when. Finally, she was ready to
leave the cabin, which she shared with her mother. Entering the hall, she was
surprised to find Dick sitting on a little settee. He had been waiting for her.

She wrote, "Larry Hart was travelling with Dick, and my closest friend,
Rosemary Klee, and Andrew Goodman of Bergdorf-Goodman fame, Bob
Jacobs, a young architect, as well as several other kids I had grown up with
were also on board. But as far as Dick and I were concerned, we were alone
on that vast ship."

The day after they set sail from Cherbourg, Dick asked if she had a book
he could borrow. She said she would go and find one. While in Paris she had
bought a couple of books at a French bookshop that a young salesman had
recommended: *The Diary of a Masseuse* and the *Kama Sutra,* the latter the
classic Indian treatise on the hundreds of possible positions for sexual intercourse. Dorothy Rodgers claimed that at the age of seventeen, she was "as
innocent as could be" and had no idea what she had been mischievously
duped into buying. Since her mother had picked up *The Diary of a Masseuse*
and was reading it with interest, Dorothy took the *Kama Sutra* up on deck
and dropped it on her chair while she went for a stroll, unaware, if she is to be
believed, of the not very subtle invitation she was about to make to the recipient. When she returned, her father, who had the chair next to hers, was sitting with the book in his hand. Was it hers? he wanted to know. When he
learned she had brought it up to give to Dick, "that did it," she said, and he
ordered her to take it back to her cabin. So she left it in the room. A few
hours later, when she went looking for the book, it was gone. She suddenly
had the awful suspicion that her father had thrown it overboard. Had this
happened? It was clear from the look on her mother's face that he had. Far
from being embarrassed and grateful that she had been spared a mortifying
faux pas, Dorothy erupted in a fury. These books had been bought with her
own allowance. He had no right . . . She even made threats, turning on her
mother all the resentment she felt. Then she snatched *The Diary of a Masseuse*
out of her mother's hands and threw it out of the porthole.

Chapter Seven

"HE'S A WINNER"

S WEETHEART," Ben Feiner Sr. wrote to his daughter in December 1926, "Believe it or not, I have been stunned into silence by an overpowering anxiety at the mere prospect of having my love with me again in a few days—and I mean every word of it!" Dorothy was spending her first semester at Wellesley, but she was unhappy. That shipboard flirtation with Richard Rodgers had developed into a grand passion and she was "shamelessly in love." Before they disembarked Dick had torn off the corner of a magazine page and written his phone number on it, Schuyler 8181, and she placed it carefully among her most precious possessions. They had dated a few times before she left for college. The fact that her exile had been self-imposed made it no easier to bear. If only he had asked her to stay! She would have given up Wellesley, her future, everything, just to be near him. But since he seemed to be having far too gay a time to want to pin himself down, she left, "resentful and jealous—not of any girl in particular, but of the good times Dick and I weren't sharing," she wrote.

Richard Rodgers was very attracted, no doubt about it, and had spent every waking moment on the boat with this charming girl, this "child," "baby," he would call her, this "sweet kid." But he could hardly be expected to spend much time mooning over a college girl when so many others were immediately available and he was being feted and courted all over New York. He recalled that as the *Majestic* drew into New York harbor, with its escort of tugboats nudging it into dock, there were sounds of band music and singing coming from the starboard side. One of the tugboats sported a banner, WEL-COME HOME DICK AND LARRY, and the cast of *The Garrick Gaieties* was on the dock, singing, dancing, and waving. It might have been just a press agent's bright idea, but it was pretty flattering all the same. One can imagine the confusion on the dock, the kisses and hugs, a delighted Bobbie Perkins, and another girl watching as her shipboard suitor is borne away, shrugging and smiling.

Meanwhile there were Wellesley and Daddy, who had sent her a pair of flannel pajamas and then, it would seem, made a joke about it. He wrote, "Now don't get alarmed about my telling your admirers that you have fallen so low, because I realize only too well that, at their age, I, too, believed 'my lady' spurned anything so utilitarian and, in her slumbers, was swathed in swandown, as it were, sheeted in silks and warmed with fluff . . ." He was overjoyed to know how anxious she was to get home, although he must have sensed the real reason why. In the meantime she had to be satisfied with letters.

THERE WAS A FURTHER REASON why all thoughts of a serious relationship would have receded into the background just then for Richard Rodgers: he was working night and day on the fifth and sixth productions that he and his partner would launch in 1926, and they were due to open a day apart: *Peggy-Ann* on December 27 and *Betsy* on December 28. In the process of becoming established and in choosing to display their work against a formulaic backdrop, Rodgers and Hart were simply being pragmatic. As they were well aware, when faced with a choice, backers would always prefer a commercial idea from an established hack rather than an imaginative one from talented unknowns. That did not mean that they had abandoned their principles; they had already made use of as many Princess Theatre innovations as they dared. Now they and Fields felt ready to make the gamble offered by what they would call their first musical play.

Peggy-Ann came about almost by accident. In looking around for a new subject, Herbert Fields had decided to rework an old production of his father's, *Tillie's Nightmare,* a musical of 1910 that had starred the comedienne Marie Dressler. The plot line remained basically the same. Tillie became Peggy-Ann, who slaves in her mother's boardinghouse and, like Cinderella, dreams of the larger world she will never see. "But while the story was the same, the tone was drastically altered. The broad, rough-and-tumble musical hall fun of the earlier show gave way to finely tuned words . . ." Gerald Bordman wrote. At its start, the reworked *Tillie's Nightmare* followed the path of a dozen other shows with luckless heroines bewailing their fate as the curtain rises. However, instead of a fairy godmother conjuring up a handsome prince, Peggy-Ann is visited by a vivid dream in which she arrives at her own wedding in a state of undress, takes her vows on a telephone book, and then

Helen Ford, Patrick Rafferty, and Lulu McConnell in *Peggy-Ann,* 1926

has a series of adventures of Lewis Carroll complexity in which policemen wear pink uniforms, a yacht is manned by pirates, fish talk, and she bets on a talking horse named Peggy. The idea of an extended dream sequence had never been tried before and may have had its germination in a song Rodgers and Hart wrote for *Poor Little Ritz Girl,* "You Can't Fool Your Dreams." However, its Freudian references were very much of the moment; terms first coined by that master of the unconscious, such as "repression," "fixation," and "slips of the subconscious," were beginning to make their way into the vernacular.

To introduce psychological fantasy into a musical comedy would have seemed the height of daring in 1926, and in fact it was not tried again until Moss Hart, Kurt Weill, and Ira Gershwin wrote *Lady in the Dark* for Gertrude Lawrence in 1940. To succeed, such a libretto had to have a certain sophistication, and Herbert Fields, whose work had seldom been more than workmanlike, rose to the challenge. True to the Princess Theatre example, there would be no fairy-tale ending. Peggy-Ann's story would begin in a drab boardinghouse and end there, the heroine's subconscious bid for freedom having changed her only to the extent that she was now willing to defy her mother and marry her small-town boyfriend, a clerk at the A&P. To use a musical as a vehicle for the exploration of inner fantasies, to show a heroine of real flesh and blood (the path first marked out by *Very Good Eddie* a decade earlier), was still a large step in 1926. Herbert Fields hedged his bets by splitting the Marie Dressler role into two parts. He gave the buffoonery to Mrs. Frost, a broadly drawn comic character, and her adventures to Peggy-Ann, played by Helen Ford at her spunkiest. If he could somehow reconcile all the elements, Herbert knew his father would be willing to produce and, to his credit, Lew Fields agreed, even though there was no opening chorus, and the finale, always designed to bring an audience to its feet, was equally dispensed with. Instead, Peggy-Ann returns to reality and finds it as she left it; she is once more alone.

None of the songs Rodgers and Hart wrote for *Peggy-Ann* has stood the test of time, with the possible exception of "Where's That Rainbow?" Perhaps, as Armond and L. Marc Fields observed in their biography of Lew Fields, this is why *Peggy-Ann* is not remembered as one of the outstanding musicals of the 1920s, along with *No, No, Nanette* and *Lady, Be Good!* "In the end, it is always the hit songs in the score that determine the fate of a musical comedy . . ." Nevertheless, the fact that its team had created such a sprightly and coherent production was cited admiringly: "Aided by Gilbertian satire, Broadway slapstick, attractive dancers, the pepper of quick wisecracks, the charm of music, it skipped right up to the head of the class in current musical diversions . . ." *Time* wrote. Alan Dale in the *New York American* called it "the daintiest, most whimsical, unusualest and captivatingly concise and imaginative little musical play we've had for some time," and Robert Coleman in the *New York Daily Mirror* was willing to place "this triumvirate in the foremost ranks of our youthful and talented show builders." Critics began to refer to Rodgers and Hart as "the modern Gilbert and Sullivan."

All this would help compensate Rodgers for the staggering disappointment of *Betsy,* their final venture for 1926. He had no business agreeing to work on another musical which was going to open the same night as did *Peggy-Ann*—as he and Hart thought for a while, though in the end they were given a day's grace. But, as Mary Rodgers Guettel observed, in those days he was "joyously into absolutely everything," and the offer seemed irresistible, since it came from the great Florenz Ziegfeld himself. He and Larry signed a contract to do two shows, the first to star Belle Baker, "a tiny woman with a huge voice," Rodgers wrote, and had to create a score in a matter of weeks.

Betsy's plot, such as it was, concerned a girl named Betsy Kitzel, living on the Lower East Side, who cannot find a husband and whose Jewish mother decrees that none of her remaining children will marry until Betsy does. There was quite a nice part for Bobbie Perkins, playing Betsy, while Baker played her younger sister Ruth. It was the kind of trivia Rodgers and Hart had spent years trying to escape from, but, well, it was Ziegfeld. So they told each other as they struggled desperately to do two things at once. Rodgers wrote that although he had been doing "a terrific amount" of composing for several days, even so there were twenty-five songs to write. "Of course . . . when both shows are seriously in rehearsal I expect to give up eating and sleeping entirely," he told Dorothy.

He and Hart had expected negotiations with Ziegfeld to be protracted and for the great man to be preoccupied by other matters—he was then building his great Ziegfeld Theatre, which would open with *Rio Rita* in February 1927. They were not prepared for him to be as difficult as he increasingly became. Matters were not helped by the fact that Rodgers adored *Peggy-Ann.* He told Dorothy it was "such a daring idea and is being done to the limit," whereas *Betsy* was "so much applesauce." (But in 1962 he told musical-theatre historian Robert Kimball that *Peggy-Ann* was his favorite among all his 1920s shows.) It could not have taken Ziegfeld long to discern where Richard Rodgers's true interests lay. Early in December there was "a terrific blow-up" when Ziegfeld and the general manager "bawled me out for not appearing at enough rehearsals. Z. said some rotten things and I told him I was 'through with his lousy show.' " The general manager and Max Dreyfus smoothed over the rupture, and "last night Z. and I were walking around rehearsal with our arms about each other's waists. That's that," Rodgers told Dorothy. But he was being optimistic. The opening night could not have been worse. Ziegfeld had hired Irving Berlin to contribute the sure-fire hit for Belle Baker he evidently felt he had not received from Rodgers and Hart. Berlin came up with "Blue Skies," which stopped the show; the composer, who was in the audience, stood up and took a bow. Like Lew Fields inserting Romberg into *Poor Little Ritz Girl,* Ziegfeld had not bothered to tell them. It was just Rodgers and Hart's bad luck that the song should turn out to be one of the enduring classics of Berlin's oeuvre. They must have taken some comfort from the fact that *Betsy* closed after thirty-nine performances and *Peggy-Ann* went on and on for 333, and then had a London production.

Although the songs they wrote for *Betsy* do not approach "Blue Skies" in distinction, one of them, "This Funny World," has lingered down the decades. The lyrics are in part:

This funny world
Makes fun of the things that you strive for.
This funny world
Can laugh at the dreams you're alive for.
If you're beaten, conceal it!
There's no pity for you.
For the world cannot feel it.
Just keep to yourself.
Weep to yourself.

Although often cited as evidence of Lorenz Hart's submerged melancholy, his words "It's all a joke, for you will find / This funny world is making fun of you" would have found an answering chord in his composer's childhood experiences.

WITH HIS USUAL rapid assessment of situations, Dick could not understand why Dot kept writing about how unhappy she was. After all, Wellesley was a famous college, she had maids in the dorms, there were plenty of extracurricular activities like swimming and horseback riding, and so what could be wrong with it? He wished she would cheer up. He was sure things would get better, but if not, she should tell him and he would do something. He was also worried about the news that she was not eating. If she was trying to lose weight, he wished she wouldn't; she could get ill.

There were frequent misunderstandings. She thought he was angry about something and he could not understand why. He was just trying to be funny, he assured her. "Wouldn't I be a fool to start trouble over a little thing like that when what we have is worth so much more to me? You don't understand me, that's all, Baby!" He was writing often but not enough to please her that autumn. He said, "I wonder if you think I am entirely neglectful not ever to phone, no less send some little thing that does mean so much. Or maybe you realize with some extra sense that I can't help myself; that when I am not at home working I am rushing a taxi driver to reach some place before it's too late." By early December he was beginning to resent the pressure from her. Of course she could have seats for the openings, he wrote; but even if she were "in town," he would be too busy to see her. But they did meet during Christmas vacation, and he wrote to apologize for not getting to the train to see her off early in January of 1927. He had gone to a wedding, and then on to the Club Richmond with Jack Rumsey and his wife, so he "couldn't very

well leave them." He was about to leave town himself. To their enormous surprise, *Lido Lady* had turned out to be a great success, so Rodgers and Hart
decided to go to London and see what miracles had been wrought.

IN THOSE YEARS BEFORE the Great Depression Rodgers and Hart were
constantly on the high seas, since six of their shows were produced in London, either works, like *Lido Lady,* specifically for the British market or reis-
sues deemed to be exportable, like *Peggy-Ann.* Rodgers, who disliked
traveling on land, had no qualms about an ocean voyage and was never seasick. The excitement of something happening always stimulated him: the
packing, the last-minute flurry of phone calls, the telegrams and bon-voyage
parties, then the crossing itself, full of opportunities to make new contacts,
and in the background the comfortable knowledge that he was wanted
immediately in London. Even if travel was for business reasons, by sea it had
a festive air, and so many luxurious liners were ferrying passengers back and
forth that it was not unusual for the New York docks to be jammed with
those arriving and departing; on a typical day in 1925, for instance, eleven
ships sailed out of New York harbor, eight of the liners bound for Europe.

The choices were splendid. One could take the *Rotterdam* on the Holland
America Line, the *California* on the Anchor Line, the Royal Mail liner
Orduna, the *Cedric* or the *Majestic* on the White Star Line, and the *America*
or the *Leviathon* on the U.S. Lines. He frequently took the Cunard Line,
which operated an express service to Southampton, shuttling the *Berengaria,*
the *Mauretania,* and the *Aquitania* back and forth. That trip took a brisk
seven days; and when the Queens *Mary* and *Elizabeth* came into service, the
time was cut to a snappy five days, for which the traveler paid a premium. On
this particular January of 1927, he was sailing on the *Aquitania,* then one of
the largest (44,000 tons) boats afloat if not the fastest; it had been built in
1914 and proved so durable that it ferried troops in World War II and immigrants to Canada and the United States in the years that followed. Perhaps it
was on one of the *Aquitania's* upper decks that Rodgers and Hart had a photograph taken, Rodgers in a faultless pinstripe, Hart in a gray flannel and on
his knee the wire-haired terrier named John they bought in England.

Rodgers had particular reason to be happy as he left New York. He told
Dorothy, "Once again do I sleep like a babe; I eat my food with understanding, I snap not at my parents, and I feel a lovely glow of health as I waken
toward noon." He had no worries. *Peggy-Ann* was playing to a capacity
crowd, and even on a slow night like Monday there was standing room only.

Betsy, for the moment, was selling, and he had made the charming discovery that box-office receipts now flowing in from their various enterprises for the past ten days had "contributed enough to pay for my entire European excursion." Added to that, *Lido Lady* was breaking all records at the Gaiety Theatre, T. B. Harms had bought the British rights to *Peggy-Ann* on satisfying terms, and Arthur Hammerstein was tempting them with the idea of writing a musical which would open his new Hammerstein Theatre. (That one was never written.)

Larry Hart was in an equally good mood; he, too, reveled in the fun to be had on board, beginning with a minute exploration of the cabin they usually shared. "Look, Dick," he announced one time after he had climbed onto the upper berth, "I can stand up!" That was typical of his humor. That impish quality had a special appeal for children. Mary Rodgers Guettel said, "One of the things that fascinated me about him was my realization when I was about six that he was older than my father, because the way children see people, if you're smaller, you're younger . . . Then he had this strange habit: he would rub his hands together and sort of give this . . . catarrhal throat-clearing sound. He would go 'Kkhhkkhh!' And then he was always smoking big black cigars, and he never, it seemed to me, ever came to the house without presents for everybody." These were usually expensive; one time he gave them all watches. Judy Crichton saw him as "an enormously entertaining elf, taller than we, who left dirty lyrics lying in the cracks of couches." (It was said that Hart would "pay any price" for a rare edition of a salacious story, and that he had a library of erotica.) Judy Crichton continued, "And he used to hide in Mary's treehouse when he didn't want to go back to work."

That childlike quality was becoming more marked, it would seem. Rodgers was beginning to take charge, marching him off to the children's department to get new outfits whenever Hart began to look particularly rumpled. By degrees he was becoming a parent figure and Hart a disreputable and irresponsible adolescent. On the days when Hart did not show up, Lucius Beebe wrote,

> Mr. Rodgers is morally certain that he could be found, attired in outrageous and florid linen, in the back room of Tony's Fifty-second Street fun soup parlors.
>
> On such occasions Mr. Hart prefers not to apprise Mr. Rodgers of his disinclination for labor in person, but the spectral voice of a waiter announces over the phone, "Mr. Hart is running a temperature again," and Mr. Rodgers knows that he may as well go back to Port Washington for the day and water the begonias.

Lorenz Hart and Richard Rodgers in a tense moment in *Makers of Melody,* 1928

Once Hart was found, one can be certain, there would be black looks from Rodgers and possibly a lecture as well. One of the scenes from the short film *Makers of Melody* has to do with an evening when they had been invited to the White House and were in a hotel room dressing. Dick was ready and Hart, partially hidden behind a wardrobe trunk, appeared to be in complete evening attire but explained that he could not go after all. Why not? his partner demanded to know. Well, Hart said, stepping out from behind the trunk, he had forgotten his pants. Now neither of us can go! Rodgers scolded. They would have to go back to New York. "Yes, Papa," Hart said in a resigned sort of way. The fact that Hart would allow the scene to be filmed is curious, since it had almost nothing to do with the matter at hand and seems to have been inserted simply to make him the butt of a joke. The "Yes, Papa" spoke volumes.

In his ability to appear and disappear Hart resembled a character in a Feydeau farce. Rodgers wrote that they would be walking down the street; Hart would be there one minute and gone the next. "Not a vestige of the man can be seen until, having been abandoned for lost, he bobs up serenely, without explanation, some five blocks from the scene of evaporation." It was a strain to have to keep making transparently hollow excuses when everyone knew only too well that Hart was off on another of his binges. Gary Stevens, columnist, publicist, and TV producer, who knew Hart well, said, "Larry wasn't easy to work with and Rodgers, who by that time had become a technician, a dedicated, disciplined man about such things, treated it as a business. Hart didn't treat it as a business. Hart didn't even have lyrics finished at times when he was supposed to make presentations." Hart would not be bound by Rodgers's expectations, because, he would say, "I am an artist." Rodgers was wise in the ways of the world; "Hart was light years removed from anything like that. He never knew what he had, or what was going on; a total scatterbrain. The difference between Oscar Hammerstein and Larry Hart was that Hammerstein was concerned with the dot, the sentence, the thought in a lyric. He wanted the material understood and appreciated in forty-eight states. Larry Hart was happy if two guys in Sardi's understood it." Rodgers said:

When he got into trouble your instinct was to get angry because it interfered with work. And you got angry but not for very long . . . I had an appointment to meet Larry for lunch one day and he called it off, had his maid phone to say he couldn't make it, and I couldn't establish contact with him for a week. And then one day he showed up. He met me at Tony's on Fifty-second Street for lunch. He needed a shave. He looked terrible.

His face was bruised and one side of his jaw was swollen so badly it looked as if he had a golf ball in it . . . He ordered scrambled eggs, ice cream, things that were easy to eat. Then I said, "Tell me what happened." He said a man arrived at his apartment late one afternoon with a letter of introduction from a mutual friend of the cast. They started talking and Larry invited him to stay for dinner. The man had some cocktails and wine with dinner and along about ten o'clock Larry thought the man ought to go home . . . He wouldn't go and Larry, wanting to get him out of the apartment because his mother was there, said, "Let's go downtown some place and have a drink." They got down to the sidewalk in front of Larry's house and Larry said, "Now don't you think you'd better go home and sleep this off?" and the fellow called Larry a very dirty name and took a swing at him, hit him on the chin. Larry went down and the taxi drivers who were standing around waiting for fares formed a circle and watched. He didn't have a chance. Finally someone broke it up and the man disappeared. A friend of Larry's who happened to be there took him to his house, afraid to take him back to his apartment because Larry didn't want his mother to see all the blood . . . I had hoped somebody called the police and put this fellow in jail, and said so. Larry said, "As a matter of fact, I feel sorry for him." I asked why. Larry: "I broke his wrist, knocked out three teeth, kicked him where it hurt the most and he won't be out of the hospital for three weeks."

Rodgers knew Hart wore a wicked pair of elevator shoes and admired his fighting spirit. "That was Larry's sense of drama, you see. He would make me feel awfully sorry for him and then tell me what he did to the other guy."

Hart still lived at home, sharing a bedroom with his brother Teddy in an apartment on Central Park West, and teasingly called his mother "a sweet, menacing old lady." He loved impromptu parties; "he scowls at white ties, gives manners-be-damned, whiskey-by-the-case, all-night free-for-alls, gets bored with people and keeps picking up new ones," *Time* magazine reported. Milton G. ("Doc") Bender was always somewhere in the background: "a very devious, nefarious, strange man who preyed on the weaknesses of men basically homosexual," as Stevens said of him. Claiming to be their manager, he procured booze and boys. "He did it to Hart and he did it to another man, Harry Revel, who was a big songwriter, of the [Mack] Gordon and Revel team, supplying him with boys for money. Harry Revel had to go to ASCAP [the American Society of Composers, Authors, and Publishers] to get advance money" to pay Bender off. Public knowledge of his private life was a threat Bender could use to maintain his hold on Hart, too. But there is some evidence that Hart's greater fear was having his mother find out, as the composer Larry Adler believed. There is even a hint that she might have suspected as much. Peter Garey, who began life as a circus barker, toured with the Lunts, and appeared with Noël Coward, recalled that Hart brought him back to the family apartment one evening and his mother stood on the couch by the window and said, "If you go out with my son I am going to jump." But they did leave together. The evening ended at Hart's private hideaway at the Ritz. When Garey realized that Hart wanted sex, he refused and left. Hart was quite rude about it, but he apologized in the morning and sent Garey a necktie.

There is a general impression that Hart was a homosexual faute de mieux, because of repeated rejections by women. Daniel Melnick, Rodgers's son-in-law, said that the composer knew Hart had male lovers, "but would say it was not because Larry was a homosexual, but because he was so short he thought he was ugly. It was sweet, but it was also so naïve." Hart certainly had a knack for choosing women who were likely to reject him. Musical-comedy star

Nanette Guilford was one of his women friends and so was Vivienne Segal; he proposed to the latter at least once, but she said that marriage was out of the question. "I mean, I never even *kissed* Larry." Still, Hart's mother fondly believed the right girl would come along and was always urging her son to marry and settle down. Whatever he thought privately, Rodgers loyally rose to defend his partner against what would have seemed a scurrilous accusation in those days. He told his interviewer, Ken Leish, when he was being taped for a Columbia Oral History, that one night at a Hollywood party (perhaps in the early thirties) a publisher for a trade magazine came up to him on the lawn and asked if Larry Hart was "a fairy." Rodgers said, "I grabbed him by the coat collar and I said, 'I've never heard that. And if you print it I'll kill you.'" That ended the matter. Hart managed to maintain the same kind of double-image view of the issue throughout his short life. Melnick said, "Dick told one story about once when they were in rehearsal for a show and the director was hitting on one of the young boys in the chorus who was not gay. [The boy] complained to Hart one day in the theatre. Hart called the director over and things got to be very heated. So Larry put down a theatre seat, stood up on it and punched the director in the nose."

If the public never knew about Hart, everyone knew about Bender, including Walter Winchell. Stevens, who occasionally came up with the kinds of double entendres that the columnist loved, invented a name for Bender. "I combined the evilness and his procuring faculties and described him in one word as 'Assputin.' I said, 'Walter, this is for your private file.' He sent me back a note saying, 'It's a pip.'" Stevens thought one of the biggest sources of irritation, for Rodgers, was Bender. "He was embarrassed by Hart's conduct but he hated violently his association with Bender."

THE SONG THE PRINCE OF WALES liked so much, "My Heart Stood Still," has a curious history. After their triumphant return to London ("You can imagine what fun it is to be in London when the biggest hit is yours"), they had traveled to Paris, where an extremely talented American orchestrator and arranger for the theatre, Robert Russell Bennett, was living. The object was to persuade Bennett to orchestrate songs for *One Dam Thing After Another*, a new revue being produced by Charles B. Cochran, the preeminent producer of musicals for the London stage. They were successful, as it turned out, and Bennett was to play a major role in the development of Rodgers's work for decades. Rodgers told Dorothy, "Charles B. Cochran, who's too big to turn down, signed [us] to write an ultra-smart 9:30 p.m. revue at the largest royalty we've ever gotten. *Peggy-Ann* goes into rehearsal in May, so by August we'll have four shows running in London! . . . For one month's work away from home we ought to get an income from England easily as large as our American revenue." When he thought about what life had been like such a short time before, he had to "laugh like Hell!" (The two other shows were *Lido Lady* and *The Girl Friend.*)

Paris had turned out to be much more fun this time, mostly because they "ran into" two girls they had known in New York, who knew their way around the city. One of them was Rita Kempner, a friend of Larry Hart's, and when Rodgers's letters were published in 1988 Dorothy Rodgers, who edited the volume, believed she was the one involved in the story about "My Heart Stood Still," but Rodgers wrote that the two girls were a Rita Hayden (sometimes spelled Heiden) and Ruth Warner. "We made a happy foursome, taking in all the expected sights . . ." Rodgers wrote. Finally, Hart insisted that they could not leave without seeing Versailles. After spending the day there, the two couples were on their way back to Paris in a taxi in the early evening, in a race to get to their hotels and change for the opera. Hart kept encouraging the driver to drive faster: a superfluous command if one knew Paris taxi drivers, Hayden observed.

Rodgers always said that a taxi suddenly darted out of a side street, but Hayden, who claimed that he and Hart were "sitting on the jump seats riding backwards" and therefore could not see exactly what happened, described a truck coming straight towards them. "My friend and I in the back seats of the cab saw it loom up at terrific speed. It missed us by inches—there weren't more than *inches* between us. After it went by, I let out a deep breath and said, 'Oh! My heart stood still!' " All accounts agree that Hart immediately thought that would be a wonderful title for a song. Rodgers was shocked that he should be thinking about work at a time like that, but he got out his address book and scribbled down the words. Some time later, when they were back in London, he was looking up a phone number and came across the remark. "Then I remembered the night in Paris. It was early and Larry was still asleep, so I simply sat down at the piano and wrote a melody that seemed to express the feeling of one so emotionally moved that his heart has stopped beating." By then Hart had quite forgotten the incident, but after he heard the melody, he "finished the lyric in no time at all."

Rodgers believed it was the only time in his career when a specific incident gave rise to a song, and he was particularly fond of it. Alec Wilder thought he knew why. He wrote that "My Heart Stood Still" was a perfect example of Rodgers's mastery of step writing, that sequence of rising cadences designed to take the listener to the song's dramatic high point. This effect was executed so deftly and unobtrusively that, as always with Rodgers's best work, it caught one off guard. Coupled with the composer's demonstrable skill with unusual releases and unpredictable harmonies, this made "My Heart Stood Still" a certain moneymaker, as everyone connected with the show realized. Cochran gave the ballad a prominent place in his revue, where it was sung by Jessie Matthews, London's bright young musical comedy star, and her partner Richard Dolman. The opening night at the London Pavilion in May 1927 was a very grand affair, attended by the Prince of Wales. First-night audiences paid the astonishing sum of a guinea and a half (plus tax), and box office receipts were a handsome 643 pounds, 12 shillings, and 6 pence. Hart said:

> The Prince is the busiest person in the world. He had ten places to go to that night, but he came to ours. As a result, the audience looked at the Prince all night—and we never got a laugh.
>
> It was raining. I ran away—I didn't want Cochran to see me. Dick, too, hurried out of the theatre. We were both feeling wretched—for we had only recently learned that Cochran was now broke.
>
> But Cochran ran after us, "Come here! Larry—don't go out without a topcoat!" he called. That's the kind of a fellow he is.
>
> But next day, the show got brilliant reviews.

Then, after the Prince taught the song to a bandleader, Hart recalled, "over here that would just rate column space. Over there, a big paper printed the whole piece on the front page! And the show ran for five years!" (It actually ran for seven months.)

American producers immediately wanted "My Heart Stood Still." One of them was Charles Dillingham, who had won Rodgers and Hart's agreement to write the score for *She's My Baby*, a musical comedy starring Beatrice Lillie. Dillingham thought the song would be perfect for his leading lady, but Rodgers, convinced that Lillie "simply didn't have the voice" to introduce the song, begged off. He, Larry, and Herb had decided to make a musical from Mark Twain's *A Connecticut Yankee in King Arthur's Court,* and, he said, they wanted the song for that show. That meant they had to get permission to use it from Cochran, since his revue was still running. Cochran, who, as they knew, needed the money, drove a hard bargain. They could have it on condition that they accepted a cut in royalties. The exact price was never made public, but since an offer from Flo Ziegfeld for $10,000 was on the table, there is little doubt that Rodgers and Hart were obliged to match it. So "we found ourselves paying for the right to use our own song." But at least "My Heart Stood Still" did not go to Ziegfeld.

The team had been fascinated by Mark Twain's classic ever since, years before, they had seen a silent movie adaptation of it. They had thought the story "wonderfully funny, with an irresistible combination of fantasy and social commentary," and to their immense surprise they had been given a free hand to adapt it for a stage musical by the lawyer for the Mark Twain estate. The musical never emerged, but a weak parody of it, *A Danish Yankee at King Tut's Court,* had been the result. Now they were ready to tackle the real thing, but they were no longer poor and unknown and the terms were stiff. Nothing daunted, the Herbert Fields-Richard Rodgers-Lorenz Hart team set to work. Their first choice of producer was, of course, Lew Fields; but if he did not see the book's possibilities (as at first he did not), they were quite confident someone else would. *A Connecticut Yankee,* like *Peggy-Ann,* was framed as a dream play. As the musical begins, Martin, an ambitious young businessman, is having a bachelor party to celebrate his coming marriage to a socialite. Since Martin's hobby is medieval England, his friends give him a suit of armor. But there is trouble ahead, and after his fiancée breaks a champagne bottle over his head, Martin obligingly goes to sleep and wakes up in Camelot, A.D. 528. Herb Fields had a fine time juxtaposing so-called archaic English with modern slang; meeting Sir Kay in full regalia, Martin asks, "How long can you stay fresh in that can?" He compares Camelot with the inside of the Paramount Theatre and terrifies the natives by producing a cigarette lighter. After similar displays of sangfroid the natives begin to imitate the exotic language of the newcomer, spouting such remarks as "Methinks yon damsel is a lovely broad" although the joke is pursued so relentlessly that, as Alexander Woollcott observed, it begins to wear thin. But most audiences found the humor uproarious. A magazine called *Judge* actually commissioned a full-page comic strip illustrating some of the more hilarious remarks. "And what music!" the headline added. Rodgers, who conducted the opening-night performance, struck up "Thou Swell," which includes a burst of inspired doggerel from Hart:

> Both thine eyes are cute, too—
> What they do to me.
> Hear me holler
> I choose a
> Sweet lolla
> Palooza
> In thee.

The successful writing team of Herb Fields, Richard Rodgers, and
Lorenz Hart during *A Connecticut Yankee,* 1927

Rodgers recalled that William Gaxton, playing Martin, was not "more than
eight bars into the refrain when I began to feel that something on the back of
my neck. It wasn't the steady, growing sensation I'd felt during the first *Garrick Gaieties,* nor was it the more subdued, all-is-well feeling I had during
Dearest Enemy. This time the audience reaction was so strong that it was like
an actual blow ... The applause at the end of the number was deafen-

ing . . . That did it; from then on, the show was in. Nothing, I knew, could stop it from being a smash."

Ironically, tryout audiences had been cool to "Thou Swell," and Lew Fields had almost succeeded in removing it, but was persuaded by Rodgers to give first-night audiences in New York the chance to pass their unanimous verdict. "Thou Swell" is a shining example of the freewheeling inventiveness which is such a marked aspect of Rodgers's best work. Having absorbed the rhythms of the jazz age, he had not been content merely to imitate but wanted to elaborate upon them, twist them into new and provocative shapes. Referring to the eighth–dotted quarter figure that occurs at the end of the first stanza, Allen Forte noted that not only had Rodgers set two-syllable words amusingly ("pretty," "witty," "kitchen"), but he had aptly articulated some word pairs ("cute too," "do to," "rich in," plot of," and "lot of") to droll effect. He wrote, "This figure derives from the Charleston rhythm that had become so popular four years earlier." The pattern consisted of a dotted quarter note followed by an eighth note tied to a quarter or half note. In "Thou Swell," Rodgers reversed the Charleston figure and made it an eighth note followed by a dotted quarter tied to a quarter. "Syncopations of this kind, which are so prominent in the refrain, first appear in its verse, which is taken at a faster tempo than the refrain, suggesting a dance number. Indeed the refrain of 'Thou Swell' is often performed at a relatively fast tempo, even though the performance instruction reads 'slowly, with grace.' " Its melody rose and fell so unexpectedly, just the way a dancer liked, that Wilder thought "Thou Swell" might have been written for Fred Astaire.

"Thou Swell" joined "My Heart Stood Still" in perennial popularity. Two other songs from the show, a patter song, "On a Desert Island with Thee," and a dance tune, "I Feel at Home with You," enjoyed a transient vogue. It helped that *A Connecticut Yankee* had cast Constance Carpenter, who had appeared in *Charlot's Revue* and was Gertrude Lawrence's understudy in *Oh, Kay!,* in a prominent role. The dances were created by the young Busby Berkeley, who before going on to Hollywood would make his name on Broadway for "introducing complicated and offbeat syncopations, executing broken rhythms, and employing two or three different rhythms simultaneously," Martin Rubin wrote in *Showstoppers. A Connecticut Yankee,* which ran for 418 performances, would be the longest-running show of Lew Fields's career, and by far Rodgers and Hart's biggest hit in the twenties.

WHAT IS INTERESTING about the first night of *A Connecticut Yankee* as Rodgers stood there in the orchestra pit is not only his sensation that he could perceive with the back of his neck but the *degree* of that sensation. Such a precise rendering of the emotional atmosphere in the room ought to put paid, once and for all, to the superficial view of Rodgers as a man with the soul of a banker. If he were only practical, methodical in his habits, exacting, undeviating, able to write to order—and all this was true—then it would be impossible to explain the depth of feeling that can be perceived in his work. But a man who is also singularly sensitive to nuances of feeling and can precisely describe the atmosphere of a room is a man with a highly developed artistic sensibility, however difficult this may be to detect on the surface. Someone so attuned to the work as it develops will pick up signs and portents long before they reach conscious awareness.

If Rodgers was supremely confident of *A Connecticut Yankee's* brilliant future, he could not say the same for *She's My Baby,* even though, as he wrote, it *ought* to have succeeded. Bea Lillie, at the height of her powers as a comedienne, could hardly be faulted in anything she did. The farce had been devised by Guy Bolton and the songwriting team of Bert Kalmar and Harry Ruby, and the cast included the young Irene Dunne playing the ingenue and Clifton Webb, who would go on to have a long Hollywood career playing, essentially, the same role, "suave, soigné and unflappable," as Rodgers wrote. Yet something was wrong. Good or bad, Rodgers would invariably have a nervous stomach and some sleepless nights as the date for rehearsals drew near. *She's My Baby* was due to open in Washington for tryouts on December 12, 1927, just over a month after *A Connecticut Yankee* had opened, and there was no score. Rodgers set to work with his usual frenzied determination but was only halfway through when he developed a bad case of influenza and went to bed. Hart would have vanished at this juncture. Rodgers, true to his training, struggled out of bed and shakily presented himself at the first rehearsal. His producer took one look at him and sent him home with the stern admonition to take five days off in Atlantic City as his guest. Rodgers, conceding that he was "a nut," declined Dillingham's generous offer. Still, he did go home and finished the work there. Behind the hopeful tone of his progress reports to Dorothy it is clear he thought the show should never have been written—Hart was urging him, he said, to give it up, but he could not leave them "in a hole"—and the reviews bore him out. Beatrice Lillie's performance saved what critics felt was an inconsequential effort with a few pleasant, below-par Rodgers and Hart songs. *She's My Baby* opened at the Globe early in January 1928 and closed after 71 performances.

Rodgers was writing once or twice a month to "Dearest Dot" and seeing her on her holidays, but the tone of his letters had changed. After reporting

Richard Rodgers with, from left, Larry Hart, Beatrice Lillie, and
Joan Clement just after the opening of *She's My Baby,* 1928

the success of *A Connecticut Yankee* he wrote, "And when may we expect to
see you?," a significant use of the plural. He and his cousin Eddie Lee were
going to Cambridge for the Harvard-Yale game, and he also planned to drive
up to Boston later for the road-tour opening of *Peggy-Ann,* and he hoped to
see her at one or the other of those times. He sounded distinctly cool. As soon
as *She's My Baby* opened, he and his parents were sailing on the *France* for
London and points south. It had crossed his mind that he would be en route
to New York just as she, with her parents, was on the high seas bound for

Europe. He suggested they might exchange radiograms as they passed each other by.

If Rodgers was sensitive to rejection, so was Dearest Dot. Since she was effectively removed from the one person she wanted to see, nothing Wellesley had to offer could possibly compensate, and although she did competently at her studies—her amour propre would not allow her to do otherwise—she was becoming increasingly rebellious. When she first broached the idea of leaving college, her father told her the decision was hers entirely, and he reiterated that in later letters. Personally he had never seen any great need for a college education for her, weighed against "the disadvantages of missing out socially," he wrote. After all, she did live in an educational and cultural center, "and it is a comparatively simple thing for you to formulate a new program right here at home which I am sure will give you that mental stimulant which you now so sorely need." There was a further factor, to which he confessed. "I want my sweet daughter to keep as close and as warm, in her heart and soul, all our lives as it is humanly possible. So make every effort, and I hope that but little effort will be necessary, to be one of us at all times, in spirit if not in body, so that we shall never feel that we all paid too high a price for your attendance at College."

Early in 1928 she was on her way home to her new dog and her new car. Once she had collected herself, she and her parents were off on a nice long trip to Europe.

She said later that she and Dick had agreed "maybe we should not see each other quite so much for a while": perhaps a diplomatic version of the situation. One would have thought from the tone of Rodgers's letters that he was actively romancing someone else, although this has to be speculation. He seemed in no particular hurry to see Dearest Dot, if ever again. In her misery she wanted to get away. She said later, referring to her abandonment of a college education, "Well, my parents sort of lured me. I think they had a few motives. They wanted me to have the experience of a wonderful trip they were planning, and I think they also thought it would be good to get me away from Dick for a while . . ."

Did they, and perhaps did Benjamin Feiner Sr., not approve of a songwriter as a future son-in-law? Was Feiner, with his heartfelt appeal to his darling to stay "close and . . . warm" to him all her life, bound to be resentful, consciously or unconsciously, of any man who captured her affections? It is impossible to know, but what is clear is that Rodgers's increasing psychic distance caused a major upheaval in Dorothy's life. "I was miserably unhappy. I remember listening to the radio one night while one of my favorites among

Dick's songs was being played . . . and the tears ran down my cheeks." When he was on the high seas returning from his Mediterranean trip in March of 1928, Rodgers sent a radiogram saying "Hello"—"just 'Hello,' " she said. "And I didn't know that was meant to be the beginning of a conversation." So she sent another one-word radiogram back. It said, "Goodbye."

Chapter Eight

"WITH A SONG IN MY HEART"

I N THE EARLY PART of 1928 Rodgers was in a state of dissatisfaction and self-doubt and, not surprisingly, hard to please. The stress of composing while ill with flu had delayed his recovery; while attending tryouts for *She's My Baby* in Washington the previous month, he had been hopeful that "I don't get tired any more," but he did add that he was "not quite up to throwing pianos about." He had written to Dot during his trip before receiving her devastating telegram, although, to be truthful, the tone of his first few letters was hardly encouraging. He made a point of telling her about "a young lady on board" he had been seeing, who was en route to Paris to buy her trousseau. He wrote, "In spite of her open declaration of a consuming passion for her fiancé, I believe she could be made to listen to reason, but who gives a good Godam?"

It was true that he enjoyed himself once they arrived in London in January. "Maw and Paw scored what the papers call an instantaneous success and we went out to parties and made whoopee for five nights and four days." *The Girl Friend* was doing well financially, news that always cheered him up. But now he was in Paris, visiting the same boringly expensive shops, taking the same sightseeing tours, and wondering again why the revues were so inept. Paris would always seem like "a stupid, over-dressed blonde," and he would never get to like it. But Algiers, once they arrived, was worse. They had had a bad night on the train and a terrible trip on the boat, but the city was unspeakable; he could not believe that "people actually exist this way." Knowing Dot was planning to visit it, he suggested she take a walk through the native quarter, "and thenceforth you'll love your life."

Even before he received her "radio," as he called it, the door between them was closed, if he wanted it closed. Paradoxically, knowing that she was on her way to who knows where, and might be gone for months, had a softening effect on his mood. From Algiers at the end of January, he wrote, "I wish I could talk to you. Three times now since I've left home I've experienced something I've never known before [not explained], and tonight is the third. I have an active and intense feeling of depression, which is absolutely impossible to shake off." He could not understand why, but then immediately began to write about feeling nostalgic for home, which he could not understand because his parents were right there with him. They were the best traveling companions in the world. It was not that; "I need something very badly and I don't know what it is." He hoped she would not think he was crazy.

That he would be writing to her about a black mood, and the confession of his need, illustrates the extent to which he confided in her. She had become important in his life after all, one of the few people (perhaps the only person) to whom he could give voice to his doubts and fears. Here, he must have thought—and with reason—was a careful listener with a sympathetic ear. To have her on a boat going in the opposite direction gave him some glimpse of the empty feeling she left behind. And the coupling of a depressed state with thoughts of home is a provocative connection; who was Dorothy, anyway, in his mind's eye? Just another pretty girl, or a special girl, someone he had grown up knowing, who had always been in the background of his life? In matters of hearth and home Rodgers would always be the most sentimental and conservative of men. Faced with the mind-numbing uncertainties, last-minute crises, and violent disappointments of his world, what he needed were predictable comforts: pot roast every Monday, fish every Wednesday, the atmosphere he had grown up knowing, exact and unvarying. Certainly, with respect to close relationships, the least tremor under his feet would shake him to the core. But it would be many months before his attraction to and need for Dorothy would overcome an awareness, as one reads his letters, that to be intimate with her would exact a high price.

The state of his work, always in the forefront of his thoughts, was another cause for unease. Despite the successes of *The Garrick Gaieties, Dearest Enemy, Peggy-Ann,* and *A Connecticut Yankee,* he had allowed himself to turn out another potboiler, *She's My Baby,* and had the perverse satisfaction of seeing that it was just as bad as he had expected. His work for it had been mediocre and he knew it. As soon as he returned to New York, he and Larry would begin a new show for Lew Fields that hardly looked any better.

Present Arms, as it would eventually be called, would inaugurate the sixth and last of that extraordinary impresario's theatres to bear his name. Irwin and Henry Chanin, who built five distinguished theatres in the Times Square area, had opened their Mansfield Theatre on West Forty-seventh Street a year before. Anticipating a long run for *A Connecticut Yankee* at the Vanderbilt, Lew Fields was casting around for a new theatre in which to launch his spring production. He took over the Mansfield's lease on the first of January 1928, and after renaming it Lew Fields' Mansfield Theatre, announced his intention of turning it into "an American Savoy." Armond and L. Marc Fields wrote, "He now believed the critics who, show after show, compared Herbert, Rodgers and Hart to Gilbert and Sullivan." A further cause for inner reproach, in Rodgers's mind, could have been that Herbert Fields had joined with his rival, Vincent Youmans, and also Clifford Grey and Leo Robin, to write a musical about men in uniform, *Hit the Deck,* which had been a huge success. Herb was now suggesting that he, Dick, and Larry write another musical about men and uniforms. Dick and Larry made the obvious objection, but Herb was ready for them. *Hit the Deck* had been about sailors; this one would be about marines. In *Hit the Deck,* the heroine, who owned a small coffee shop, chased the hero; in this one it would be the other way around. And instead of a heroine who casts aside rags for riches, *Present Arms* would have a humble hero, son of a Brooklyn plumber, who marries a member of the British aristocracy; in other words, "only the most threadbare of Broadway clichés would do." There are no clues in Richard Rodgers's letters or autobiography to indicate why he and Hart would take on yet one more dispiriting piece of nonsense. It is possible, although there is no evidence, that Lew Fields brought them around by pointing out the glories of the new theatre and the handsome sums he was willing to spend on special effects. He must have told them about his dream to build a repertory company to rival the Savoyards. Perhaps he even promised them a "serious" production once the theatre was launched.

It was true that the old showman spared no expense to launch the production. In the second act a yacht broke apart in full view of the audience and its passengers were cast adrift on a raft. As they approached land, palm trees on the horizon gradually increased in size, an island hove into view, and the castaways tumbled through the waves to reach its shore—miraculous effects for the day and age. *Present Arms,* generally considered "a summer show," not only paralleled *Hit the Deck,* as critics noted, but even made the elementary error of hiring one of the same leading actors, Charlie King, as its hero, risking even more invidious comparisons. But *Present Arms* did have the antic participation of Busby Berkeley, who, besides playing second male lead, led his marine dance team on "the kind of tricky formations that [he] later perfected in Hollywood." Along with Joyce Barbour, "a juicy little grape of a

Dorothy and Lew Fields, 1928

girl," as Rodgers described her, Berkeley also introduced the song "You Took Advantage of Me," which became an instant hit. Perhaps in an effort to make up for his lackluster score for *She's My Baby,* Rodgers took particular pains with *Present Arms* and was rewarded when Brooks Atkinson called his music "the most beautiful element in the production" when the show opened on April 26. (After receiving pleasant notices, it ran until September 1.) There was also the song "Tell It to the Marines," which foreshadowed "There Is Nothing Like a Dame" in a similar context in *South Pacific.* But the one song for which they had the highest hopes, and to which they gave generous prominence, "Do I Hear You Saying 'I Love You'?," refused to become a commercial success. That proved, Rodgers observed, that you never could tell about a song.

As the show was taking shape, Rodgers's mood had been improving, even though he had had a tooth out and an ear operated on. There was no anesthesia "and a hell of a lot of pain," he wrote to Dorothy at the end of March. His grandfather Jacob Levy had had a "nasty collapse and nearly left the scene." However, Grandfather was much better and sitting up for a couple of hours a day, he was glad to say. It was an improvement that was fated not to last. After an emergency operation soon afterwards, he died, and Rodgers was devastated; "I adored the old man." That spring he was being taken up by society and, in his curiosity to see "how the upper crust carries on," he had been accepting numerous invitations. He was grateful when, "strangely enough," he was not expected to sit down and play yet another rendition of "My Heart Stood Still." The first orchestra reading of *Present Arms* was coming up, and "I'm already having the usual tummy-ache in anticipation thereof. Twenty-eight men in the pit this time, and a chorus of sixty-two. Oh well, lots of money can be played away this time too . . ."

He ended that letter by saying he would like it much better if Dorothy were home and, although she spent most of that year and the next abroad, she did return in the summer of 1928. By then she was responding to his letters, and they began seeing each other again. One August night they went to a performance of *Present Arms* together. It was an evening Dorothy Rodgers would never forget.

One of the actresses, who had adopted the preposterous name of Hotsy-Totsy, was in the middle of her solo number, "Crazy Elbows," when the drummer made a mistake; her words of displeasure would have made a marine blush. Since this was not the first such incident, and she had already been warned, Rodgers shot backstage and told the stage manager she was fired. The stage manager got in touch with the agent Louis Schurr, whom Dorothy described as a little man famous for owning a single ermine coat. (He presented it every time he took a girl out on a date, and at the end of the evening took it back at the door.) Schurr came up with "a cute little kid" as a replacement, but, unfortunately, in those days before microphones her voice did not carry, and she was not hired, something Rodgers did not know.

Next night they went to see Marilyn Miller in *Rosalie,* the new Ziegfeld hit at the New Amsterdam and, while they were standing on the sidewalk during intermission, "this agent, white-faced and trembling, came up to Dick and he said he didn't know what to do," Dorothy said. Rodgers's version was that the girl he had rejected was a "particularly close friend" of an unnamed Brooklyn gangster and that this gangster was out for revenge. As Dorothy remembered it, the message came directly from Owney ("the Killer") Madden, "who was *our* Al Capone, not as famous or as vicious, but he was a tough guy, that this agent was not to send any other girls for this part because he had a girl in Texas Guinan's nightclub show and he wanted her to have the part."

As Dorothy knew, nightclubs were "mob joints," owned by gangsters but fronted by partners who ran the clubs. Dutch Schultz was the proprietor of the Embassy Club, where Helen Morgan sang, according to Armond and L. Marc Fields. Larry Fay, who was a bootlegger, was a partner of Texas

Guinan's at the El Fay Club and of Frankie Marlow's at the Ambassadeurs. Owney Madden owned several nightclubs in part, including the famous Cotton Club in Harlem. Dorothy believed that gangsters had made fewer inroads into the theatre. Perhaps she knew they sometimes backed musicals, and Madden could have had some money, either in *Present Arms,* or in the Mansfield Theatre itself. In any event, Lew Fields knew him because his daughter Dorothy, then a youthful lyricist, had written some songs that had been performed at the Cotton Club; he had a confrontation with Madden when he discovered that her lyrics had been spiced up without her approval. If Madden did have some kind of investment in *Present Arms,* and if Rodgers knew it, he chose not to mention it, but the hypothesis is plausible since, as Helen Ford observed in the case of *Dearest Enemy,* if a gangster backed a show it was usually because he had some cutie whose career he was promoting. That quiet little fact would have gone some distance to accounting for Dick Rodgers's reaction after listening to Schurr's message. He would go to see the girl perform. Dorothy was terrified, but agreed to go with him.

Dorothy was soon to have some further experience with gangsters. In 1929, having decided to become a sculptor, she was studying in New York with Alexander Archipenko. Her parents rented a studio for her at Fifty-sixth Street and Sixth Avenue, one room with skylights and a bathroom. "One day a young man called on me and he said that for five dollars a month he would protect my studio. I said, 'Well, you know, I don't live here and I don't have anything worth anything.' He said, 'Well, you wouldn't want somebody to come in and break up your plaster casts, would you?' " So she paid him the five dollars every month. Extortion was as much a fact of life as knowing which gangster sold reliable Scotch or vodka.

If Rodgers never had any direct dealings with the New York mob, he knew plenty of people who did. "Doc" Bender's links to the underworld were already common knowledge, as were those of Billy Rose. When Rodgers got to Hollywood, he would socialize with Fanny Brice and Jimmy Durante, both of whom were known to have mob ties, according to Stephen Fox in *Blood and Power.* "Legs" Diamond, who Dorothy said acted as their contact with Madden once they arrived at Texas Guinan's, was a friend of a showgirl named Marion Roberts, who would appear in *Simple Simon,* the Rodgers and Hart musical of 1930. Hart recalled, "Marion was one of the toughest kids I have come across on the stage." In Hart's hearing, she said she was going to "get" Diamond, and she was, in fact, later implicated in his shooting death in the autumn of 1930. Whatever Rodgers knew about that world, and particularly if money was involved, would have made him tight-lipped. Dorothy was sure it was "Legs" Diamond. As Rodgers told it, they met Guinan's partner

"Legs" Diamond

Larry Fay, "a tall, black-haired, gray-faced man with a sagging jaw who looked like an undertaker—which, in a way, he was." Dorothy's impression of Diamond, or Fay, was that "he looked like somebody's chauffeur and obviously . . . was not a man of great education." Texas Guinan came over to chat and once she had left, the Fay-Diamond character said, "She's a son of a bitch." Dorothy went bright red. Rodgers's tactful solution was to ask for a ringside table, since those would only seat two people. The girl duly appeared and was terrible, but Fay-Diamond was very persuasive. He turned to Rodgers, squeezed his wrist, "and in a voice of gravel said, 'As a special favor to me, Dick, wouldja let the girl go on for one performance?' " So the girl made her debut.

Rodgers wrote, "As I left the theatre during the intermission, Fay was waiting for me at the curb. Uh-oh, I thought, here it comes. Now he's going to tell me she's another Marilyn Miller and as a special favor to him I'll have to give her the leading part and put her name in lights." Dorothy continued the story: "And Mr. Diamond came up to Dick and said, 'She stinks. I'll fire her.' And he was so grateful to Dick for having given him a chance to prove to his boss and gotten the girl her chance. They saw the fairness of that. Every time he saw us, at a place like Reuben's, which was a very good delicatessen on Fifty-eighth Street . . . People would go there after the theatre to have something to eat, and one night 'Legs' Diamond was there. When I saw him, I started to shiver, I was so frightened of him. He wanted to repay this favor. He said to Dick, 'If there's ever anything I can do for you . . . If you want to get rid of a car, I could get rid of it so you can collect the insurance. You can get somebody roughed up a little bit, maybe some legs broken.' He was very nervous-making." Rodgers's comment was that he never took advantage of that offer, but he sometimes wished he had.

JACOB LEVY'S DEATH threw Rodgers into a predictable emotional turmoil. He felt he had to get away and went to Colorado Springs for several days. While there he took up a new interest, golf: "I vary nicely between beautiful 200 yard drives and five-foot dubs, and the fact that I never know which it's going to be keeps me constantly amused," he wrote to Dorothy. He felt tremendously well and had gone for long rides through the mountains; "You can imagine the lift it gives me after the life I've been leading the past four months." She had sent him a wonderful letter (unfortunately, hers to him of this period have not survived), one that amazed and delighted him. It had set him to thinking. He wrote, "Dot, there are changes to be made. It's going to take all summer to figure out one or two problems, but there'll be a difference. You're concerned more than you think."

Present Arms was another failure as far as Rodgers was concerned. (Actually, it had a respectable run of 155 performances, although it may not have made much money.) He was back again in the old dilemma of how to be commercially safe while also satisfying his own standards, or, as a writer for the *Evening Post* phrased it in the spring of 1928, how to be "clever without being too clever." Hart, as usual, had an answer to that:

We have never tried to be clever in the sense that polysyllabic and intricate rhyme schemes were a goal. We have tried to adjust our technique to the requirements of the situation in the play and the characters who sing the songs. If the songs were sung by a chorus of aesthetes, such as the Little Theatre Group in the first *Garrick Gaieties,* we were consciously and intentionally extreme and provided music and lyrics to fit the situation. If, however, our characters are simple, such as the Marines in *Present Arms,* . . . we let them use the vernacular . . .

Of course, as we grow older we learn. And we have tried to be simpler in what we hope to make song hits. The music in our biggest sell-
ers is becoming more melodic and more definite in rhythm, the lyrics
less complex . . .

They were, he insisted, "striving to write for the public consumption."

That polite wish veiled the unpopular idea that they were also trying to
write intelligently and imaginatively and lift the musical out of the stultifying
formulae that dogged the genre and threatened to drive them mad with bore-
dom. Privately, they had agreed very early in their careers that the only safe
way to exist in the theatre was to take chances, as Rodgers put it. Or, borrowing from the art historian Bernard Berenson, they would have offered the
silent prayer: "Give us this day our daily idea and forgive us all we thought
yesterday!" The notion of taking off in a new direction after every show
would become axiomatic for Rodgers and would buoy him up in the early
years, although it would become something of a handicap later in life. Having seen what a mistake it had been to repeat *Hit the Deck,* he could hardly be
faulted for wanting to try something new. What he wanted was a musical
play, and Lew Fields seemed benignly prepared to let his boys have their way.
But even Rodgers was taken aback with the idea Hart proposed.

While Rodgers was in Colorado Springs he began to get "frantic" phone
calls from Larry Hart and Herb Fields. They were wild with enthusiasm over
a 1927 novel by Charles Petit called *The Son of the Grand·Eunuch,* and so
Rodgers bought a copy. Set in ancient China, the plot concerned a young
man who was willing to inherit his father's exalted position but trying to
avoid the terms that went with it. According to Frederick Nolan, Hart's biographer, what probably set the lyricist into ecstasies were the possibilities for all
those wonderful double entendres. The subject matter was certainly offbeat
enough to satisfy the composer. One could say with complete safety that no
musical comedy had ever taken castration as its main theme before, and even
in a time of increasingly daring subject matter, that seemed to be the limit. To
Rodgers it was a one-joke plot, and he did not see how it could be made to
work. That put him at odds not only with Larry and Herb but with Herb's
old man. Through some miracle, Lew Fields liked the idea. It would be their
serious work, all those sexual innuendos guaranteeing popular success, went
the reasoning; and while the audience was roaring with laughter the team
would be introducing their experimental ideas.

Rodgers kept demurring and Herb and Larry urging him on. He wrote,
"They were all so sure of themselves that I didn't want to be the one to tor-
pedo a project . . . While I found the story distasteful, I had to admit that it

Helen Ford and William Williams in *Chee-Chee,* 1928

was a daring departure from the average . . . Maybe we could shock people into liking it." And while *Present Arms* had suffered from comparison with its more successful predecessor there was no danger of *Chee-Chee,* as it came to be called, being compared with anything. What won him over was the fun he could have with a new musical form. "To avoid the eternal problem of the story coming to a halt as the songs take over, we decided to use a number of short pieces of from four to sixteen bars each, with no more than six songs of traditional form . . . In this way the music would be an essential part of the structure of the story rather than an appendage to the action." Cutting a song from the usual thirty-two bars to sixteen was daring enough, but to insert snippets of melody that came and went in four bars seemed like madness. It guaranteed that nobody in the audience would remember anything, as if Rodgers and Hart had forgotten the first rule of musical writing, i.e., to send them out humming and whistling.

In other words, *Chee-Chee* would be through-composed, in imitation of an opera, already a fashionably avant-garde idea. The musical play, their *beau idéal,* was making its debut with a vengeance. They set whole scenes in music and verse, using extended recitative and experimenting with rhyming dialogue, a conceit they liked so much that they used it when they began making films. Rodgers threw in a few private jokes and was delighted when audiences recognized a quotation from Tchaikovsky's *Nutcracker,* slyly inserted as the hero is led away to his apparent emasculation.

To be given such a musical challenge had the predictable effect on Rodgers's mood. He was writing to Dearest Dot: "You're liable to get the idea that I'm raving about the show, but honestly, Dot, it all sounds marvellous. I never realized how deeply I'd gone into it from a musical standpoint until I heard the orchestrations . . ." Now he was almost afraid that he had taken things too far but too excited to care. Meantime he pulled "my usual pre-opening stunt" of becoming sick with a heavy cold just before the orchestral rehearsals. There was always Helen Ford to contend with. Somehow they had managed to persuade her to play the leading role of Chee-Chee, the resourceful wife of the son of the Grand Eunuch, even though she disliked the plot, had not liked the role, and had been advised to have nothing to do with it by her husband and his brother, Harry. Perhaps because she had been so reluctant, nothing seemed to please her, and the keys the composer had given her were a predictable bone of contention. How could she project all those low notes into the back of the balcony when her vocal strength was in her upper range? Why couldn't Dick rewrite the songs for her? She was "a bitch of the first water, and is causing us our only trouble," he told Dearest Dot. "She's so fine in the part, however, that almost anything is worth it." His elation lasted through the Philadelphia tryouts, when he was getting to bed between five and six every morning and getting up again at eleven. No matter what the New York critics thought, the Philadelphia papers agreed they had managed "to produce that difficult thing—a unit. Dot, it really is swell! There are doubts as to its financial future and its reception by the New York press . . . but I know we've done something fine at last."

As Robert Coleman of the *Daily Mirror* observed when the show opened at the Mansfield Theatre at the end of September, the problem with the show was that the theme was tragic, rather than comic. It was funny, Percy Hammond of the *Herald Tribune* supposed, only if one found humor in mutilation and the transformation of a baritone into a falsetto tenor. He commended the opera "to those who love unprintable situations." St. John Ervine, in the *New York World,* was even more forthright. "NASTY! NASTY! . . . There can rarely have been a play so ornately produced to so little effect." So, in spite of beautiful costumes, sets by Norman Bel Geddes, and deft orchestrations by their dependable music director Roy Webb—i.e., all that art and money could achieve—*Chee-Chee* demonstrated that even men as seasoned and astute as Rodgers, Hart, and Lew and Herbert Fields could make a gross miscalculation. The musical closed after thirty-one performances and would be the last Rodgers and Hart show Lew Fields would produce.

As for Rodgers, it was a case of finding forgiveness for yesterday's idea. His partner was otherwise occupied, since his father, Max, who had been in failing health for several years, suffering from a weak heart and arteriosclerosis, was slowly dying. Max Hart had continued to involve himself in hopeless business deals, and although his son gave him a weekly stipend of $250 as "spending money," a lavish sum in those days, he was forced into bankruptcy. Dorothy Hart, Larry's sister-in-law, wrote, "During the rest of Larry's lifetime Larry was hounded and pursued by his father's creditors." Hart died with his two sons beside his bed early in October, saying, "Don't grieve for me. I didn't miss anything." As for Rodgers, he was beginning to think increasingly about Dorothy, who had returned to Europe with her mother, writing, "Please come home. All is forgiven and I miss you so much!"

DOROTHY WAS HAVING a fine time in Paris. She studied for a while "in a studio with an American boy, whose parents were friends of my parents'. He was very nice, Dick Davis. It was on the rue de Châtillon, just off the avenue de Châtillon." They used to have professional sculptors come in and give them critiques. She also went to croquis (sketching) classes at the Grande Chaumière, a popular art school in which foreign students like herself were surprised to discover that male models were quite naked. She also made drawings of an old lady who had been Rodin's model for one of his most famous sculptures, *Eve*.

In the meantime Rodgers was having what, as was said in another context about those bright young things in London Kenneth and Jane Clark, his "swimgloat" (a term coined by Berenson's erudite brother-in-law, Logan Pearsall Smith). His nineteenth-floor apartment in the Lombardy on East Fifty-sixth Street was one that shared a balcony with Edna Ferber, whose novel had formed the basis for *Show Boat,* then playing to sold-out houses. He went to Elsa Maxwell's costume ball as Zeppo Marx. He threw a party at the Park Lane Hotel in mid-December for one hundred select guests from the worlds of the theatre, the arts, and society which was attended by Mayor Jimmy Walker. He was taken up by Jules Glaenzer, Cartier's vice-president, and was one of the weekend guests at the latter's country house in Westhampton, where other guests were likely to include Gertrude Lawrence and George

The sheet music for "A Ship Without a Sail," for
the musical *Me for You,* renamed
Heads Up!, 1929

Gershwin. And he had found new friends and admirers in the producing team
of Alex Aarons and Vinton Freedley, who had presented a succession of
Gershwin hits during the previous five years. Their theatre, the Alvin on West
Fifty-second Street, would serve as the setting for Rodgers and Hart's next
show, *Spring Is Here,* which opened in March 1929. That was the musical that
introduced the song "With a Song in My Heart."

The song was written after Rodgers took his first plane flight with Dick
Hoyt, another member of the Glaenzer set, who lived near Westhampton.
Rodgers went up into the air, came down, and went back home and wrote it.
All his life he fought against the idea of inspiration. Songs never came out of
actual events but arose, he argued, out of the sum total of personality, experience, and theatrical craft. Just the same, there is no doubt that the experience
left an indelible impression and that the elation of the moment found its way

into the rhythm and full-hearted expressiveness of the writing. Then Hart came up, as he so often did, with the perfect words.

It is difficult to know why Vinton Freedley should have taken a dislike to "With a Song in My Heart," but dislike it he did, and he and Alex Aarons, who was just as enthusiastically pro, almost came to a parting of the ways as a result. Freedley finally conceded defeat, and public acceptance did the rest.

"With a Song in My Heart" was always one of Dorothy Rodgers's favorites, perhaps because of its special timing. They had corresponded during her lengthy absences and saw each other whenever she returned to New York. Still she lingered in Europe, and in the summer of 1929 he was writing *Me for You,* or *Heads Up!,* a spoof of life on a yacht and another "mess" for "Vinton and Freedley," as he lightheartedly put it. That soon forgotten musical did, however, contain a piece of writing that would show Rodgers in a rare mood of introspection, one that would find an echo in "Little Girl Blue," a song for *Jumbo,* six years later. He and Larry conceived the idea of comparing the isolation of a loveless state—a recurring theme for Hart—and a ship adrift, calling the song "A Ship Without a Sail." Taking up the theme of emotional isolation and comparing it to being adrift at sea was perhaps more than a coincidence for Rodgers just then, given Dorothy's persistent absence. The song was also unusual for the complex experimentation it represented. Not

Janet Velie, Barbara Newberry, and admirers in *Heads Up!,* 1929

only had Rodgers broken away from the standard ABA form to some degree (dividing the refrain into twelve-, eight- and twelve-bar sections), but he used dissonant chords to paint a mood of unease, even despair, all the more heart-felt for being understated. As an example of the subtlety and finesse with which Rodgers embellished his work, "A Ship Without a Sail" has hardly been surpassed.

In mid-July, Dorothy decided to return for good. Writing to her had been better than nothing, he said, but it would be so much nicer to have her there in person so that he could tell her just how he felt. Soon after her return they were having dinner one night at Montmartre, a fashionable nightclub, when "we found ourselves discussing our future together as if it were the most inevitable thing in the world. I don't think there was even a formal proposal," he recalled. They then went to tell their parents. That was not quite the way Dorothy remembered it. She said that, after they decided to get married, they chose not to tell their parents for a few days. As she returned home, "absolutely on cloud nine," her mother handed her a letter from Ronald Colman that had just arrived—she recognized the address. She put it aside to read later and her mother could hardly believe her eyes: "Any girl would give her eye teeth to get a letter from Ronald Colman!" When they finally told their parents, his, of course, were delighted. So was her mother. As for her father, "he didn't look unhappy," Rodgers commented cautiously. He must have sensed how Benjamin Feiner would take such news.

RODGERS ALWAYS BELIEVED he had agreed to write his second musical for Ziegfeld, *Simple Simon,* after he and Dorothy got engaged, after the stock market crash and because, despite his misgivings, he needed the money and could see that Broadway was going to be badly buffeted. His letters while Dorothy was still in Europe in the summer of 1929 show that the agreement was reached then, long before anyone suspected the arrival of the Great Depression. He needed money, all right; he wrote, "I need a hit now as I need food," but that was because earnings had been thin that summer. He now had a big apartment to pay for, not to mention wages for his man Charles and his chauffeur, and the bills for parties like the one at the Park Lane Hotel. He had had great hopes for *Heads Up!,* but when this show proved disappointing he transferred them to *Simple Simon.* He was banking on the popularity of Ed Wynn in the central role, whose perfect timing he had admired for years; and indeed Wynn had co-authored the book with Guy Bolton. It was bad luck perhaps that Ziegfeld, who was already over-extended when the show opened in Boston in January of 1930, was bankrupt shortly thereafter—he lost $50,000 in the market. Ziegfeld had refused to pay George and Ira Gershwin the royalties he owed them for *Show Girl,* which had opened and closed shortly before the crash, and, predictably, now refused to pay Rodgers and Hart what he owed them for *Simple Simon*'s run of 135 performances. (Rodgers wrote that he finally paid up.) But the writing team was rewarded handsomely in an unexpected way. Their song "Ten Cents a Dance" was written for that show, a poignant lament about a dance-hall hostess that came to symbolize the misery of the Depression years:

> Sometimes I think
> I've found my hero,
> But it's a queer romance.
> All that you need is a ticket.
> Come on, big boy, ten cents a dance!

They also wrote "Dancing on the Ceiling," which Ziegfeld disliked so much that he succeeded in having it dropped before the New York opening at the end of February. That was another piece of luck for Rodgers and Hart, who promptly transferred the song to *Ever Green,* the show they were writing for Jessie Matthews in London. It would become a huge success and launch her on a decade-long career as the preeminent star of British film musicals. The plot, which had been dreamed up by Rodgers and Hart, was set in Paris. It had to do with a woman who, thanks to the miracles of modern science, never loses her looks. Jessie Matthews was to play herself and also her grandmother, an idea she did not relish; she "pronounced it corny and the character she played a mess." Part of *Ever Green*'s charms for her, however, had to do with the fact that her lover, Sonnie Hale, who had appeared with her in *One Dam Thing After Another,* would star opposite her in the new one. There was a slight problem: Hale happened to be married to the British musical star Evelyn Laye, a divorce was in the offing; and circumstances completely outside the control of Rodgers, Hart, or anyone else would delay the opening of *Ever Green* and seriously complicate Rodgers's first year of marriage. None of this was apparent when he and Dorothy set sail on their honeymoon. In fact, despite ominous signs of box-office disasters on Broadway, he had reason to be optimistic. Cochran was promising a big production, and he and Larry had just signed a three-picture deal with Warner Bros.; they were due to start in June. Talking pictures had arrived, and every studio wanted a musical. Even Rodgers and Hart shows with middling success on Broadway, such as

Present Arms, Spring Is Here, and *Heads Up!,* were being made into films. Now Hollywood wanted them in person.

IN MARCH 1930, the newlyweds were on the SS *Roma* bound for Naples and Richard Rodgers was writing his first, placating letter to his father-in-law, whom he nicknamed "Dadina." They had experienced a rough crossing. At one point the whole boat reared up into the air and landed with a terrible plopping noise. To his amazement his bride had not been seasick, and "you can't help loving a girl [like that]," he wrote. In fact, "I can probably sit here all day looking at this sheet of paper without finding proper words to tell you about your little girl. Fortunately, you know she's sweet and good and fun to have around. But unfortunately, there's no way for me to tell you about the strange magic that these well-known qualities assume when a well-founded love asserts itself and thrives. In other words, sweet people, we're terribly in love. I have to thank your child . . . for the first real, unspoiled happiness I've ever had." The sea was calm again, and "the Baby sits in a deck chair on my left reading a book" and nibbling on a cake a stewardess had just given her. "My God, we're happy."

Arriving in Naples, they went straight to Rome, where Elsa Maxwell, the columnist and party giver, had "plunged into the Roman season," as she described it. She had given them a big party at the Ritz just after they became engaged. They encountered her one evening at the opera, where she was in the company of the elderly Princess of San Faustino, the former Jane Campbell of New Jersey and a prominent socialite. Rodgers told his "dearest Dadina," "They had us join them for supper at the Ambassador and Her Nibs made us promise to come for tea the next afternoon at the Palazzo Barbarini, where she lives. We went. Counts, Barons and Princes kept running around loose and we had an intimate glimpse of Roman nobility at its noblest . . ." His wife was quite a success. She had been asked to dance by the ex–Crown Prince of Germany, and all went well until His Royal Highness asked her why on earth the United States had entered World War I. Dorothy, who was only five in 1914, thought it had "something to do with the sinking of the *Lusitania.*" HRH dismissed that international incident as the work of "some stupid U-Boat captain," ending any hope of an entente cordiale. She and Dick made a stormy crossing over the Straits of Messina to Taormina—Dick was moaning, she recalled, convinced he was having an attack of appendicitis—but after two days of tea and toast in a Sicilian monastery-turned-hotel, he recovered. On the French Riviera, Dorothy discovered an appetite for gambling, something that made her husband shudder; he hated losing money and felt

Elsa Maxwell, 1930

guilty about winning it. Then Larry Hart appeared; he was wandering around Europe, too. He had a friend with him whom Dorothy cordially disliked, she said. She never got over her revulsion when obliged to be in the company of Milton Bender.

Elsa Maxwell was already in Paris by the time they arrived there, ready to introduce them to another round of her aristocratic pals. Dorothy was used to being with older people and had deserved confidence in her well-developed clothes sense. Even so she was totally unnerved when, thanks to Elsa, they were invited to a formal dinner at the home of a Rothschild. She wore an exquisite white evening dress by Molyneux, which did not help at all; she felt "terribly young and devastatingly insecure . . . It took me years to get over thinking of myself only as Dick's wife."

RETURNING TO NEW YORK in June, they had every reason to expect that *Ever Green* was about to be launched in London; but publicity about the

Matthews-Hale-Laye triangle was at its height, with sympathies on the side of the abandoned wife. This was no moment, Cochran decided, to bring in a big musical starring Matthews and Hale. After trying, and failing, to get them out of the show—their contracts were too good for that—Cochran proposed a delay. He would wait until the autumn and then begin the tryouts as far away as possible; Glasgow looked about right. For Rodgers and Hart, it would mean another trip to London later that year, but there was nothing else for it. Meantime they had to make a cross-continental train trip to Los Angeles. With luck they could be at the First National studios in Burbank by the end of June.

There is a glimpse of Dorothy Rodgers on the Hotel Lombardy terrace in the brief period after they returned from their honeymoon and before Dick left for California. She is sitting in a wicker chaise longue, wearing a loose, sleeveless blouse and pants, brushing her hair in the sunlight and smiling while a nurse, all in white, bends over her solicitously. She could not have been more than two or three months pregnant but was not considered well enough to accompany him. Already, there is a nurse. Dorothy Rodgers would have a tendency to miscarry, and perhaps the signs were already there, or perhaps being hovered over by a nurse was to be expected from a rich young husband who indulges the whims of a spoiled young wife. In any event, having Dorothy pregnant brought forth an even greater protectiveness in her husband, and it is surprising that he should have overruled her in one respect: her choice of doctor. He insisted that this be Morty. Her brother-in-law her obstetrician! Someone she had seen socially! It was mortifying, but the Rodgers family was obdurate. Not to engage Morty would seem like a vote of no confidence, they must have felt; and besides, Morty needed clients.

In *Kiss Hollywood Good-By,* Anita Loos wrote that it took five days on two crack trains to get to Hollywood; one took the Twentieth Century Limited as far as Chicago and then had to change trains and stations for the remainder of the journey on the Santa Fe Super Chief. "But what a de luxe five days! Compartments glittered with polished mahogany, shiny brass, and red brocade; the seats flaunted antimacassars of heavy lace." The service was impeccable, as was the food: "The maître d'hôtel would come to the compartment to announce he'd acquired some trout caught that morning in an icy mountain stream of Colorado or that the guinea hen had hung for just the proper time." Rodgers tended to take such luxury in his stride. Writing from the Super Chief, his energies were concentrated on reassuring his wife: "My disposition, my gut and my love for you still hold out, so don't worry. Give Kezebiah [his name for the baby] a reassuring pat for me and tell him that Dadda loves Mummy even though he's far away on a Choo-Choo, God damn the thing (the Choo-Choo)." He was looking for someone to talk to—there was usually somebody he knew, and sometimes a screen star like Gloria Swanson, with a retinue of husband, lover, manager, agent, hairdresser, and maid—but had found no one, which made him feel lonely. "It's hot enough" (for all of their deluxe accoutrements, the trains were not yet air conditioned) "but not really bad, and the scenery is at least worth looking at. My routine is simple: I read until my eyes get tired; I go out on the back platform till I get good and dirty; then I come in and wash till I'm clean; then I read till my eyes get tired." He would be in Los Angeles in twenty-four hours, and he was a bit anxious about it all; "what it's like—and how I'm going to get along with this strange business and these strange people."

Rodgers and Hart's first film was to have a screenplay by Herbert Fields and was a variant on the *Present Arms* formula, being about a young riveter who marries a rich heiress, with Ona Munson, who had made her name in the title role of *No, No, Nanette,* in the role of the heiress. Ben Lyon was to play the rough diamond. The next morning, after his arrival, Rodgers went to the studios in a valley behind Los Angeles, "the cleanest, pleasantest place to work in I've ever seen." They were given a good-sized anteroom and an office "the size of the big room in the apartment at the Lombardy," with banks of windows, fashionable furnishings, and a Chickering piano. His song "Ten Cents a Dance" was the talk of Los Angeles. Jerome Kern came to see him, he wrote a few days later, and said that it was "not only the best song we've ever done, but the best character sketch since *Camille!*"

They had lunch at the round table with all the "big shots" and went to see a film of Munson singing a song. At the end of the day they had "a song, verse and chorus, all finished and Larry is working on the lyric in the next room!" They had met the chief, Jack Warner, who was lunching late that day. They found him at the head of the table, drinking coffee "with the spoon *in the cup.* In the thickest Russian-Jewish accent I've ever heard he greeted me with, 'How do you do, Mr. Hart! Oh, no, you're the odder vun!' I was amazed as he was such a nice-looking man. After a few minutes of staggering conversation . . . he said, 'Now vat ve vant is some sonks wit guts, like "Yiddisher Mommer," Sophie Tucker's sonk.' My mouth was wide open by this time and I had visions of an early . . . return to New York. Suddenly he took a swallow of coffee, dropped the cup with a bang, and yelled, 'Dis vice-versa coffee is so God darnt hot it boined my mouse.' Everyone started to yell with laughter and I realized I'd been framed! I've never been taken over so completely in my life, and I loved it!" He was having a great time, and the one drawback was that she was not there with him. Still, she was coming as soon as she was well, and he hoped the journey would not be too hot and uncomfortable. A few days later, she had planned her trip. "I do hope your Dad will be all right," he wrote. "What rotten breaks the family have been having." He was perhaps referring to his father-in-law's stock market losses; even so, the Feiner family income would not be seriously affected. Rodgers's letter a day later reveals that Benjamin Feiner was ill, with no details.

They had only five numbers to write for the film and had finished all but the last. "It's only been the rush to get things finished in time that's made us work so fast." As for Hart, "Larry is less crazy than usual and has been working like the devil. It must be in the air." By the first of July Dorothy was on her way and they were about to film their first song, "Nobody Loves a Riveter." It was a complicated process. "In this song, for instance, we're making the sound of Ben Lyon singing and then later [filming] the picture. Then the two are put together. This is necessary because the song is sung while Ben rivets on the building and it's impossible to handle the orchestra in the actual scene. They say the process makes it impossible to tell that the singing isn't done at the time of the filming. I'm learning so much and there's still so much to learn that my head's swimming." In other words, he was in his element. This was not the case for Dorothy, after she arrived. Their lives were circumscribed, she wrote—it is interesting to see how quickly she calls his world "ours"—"by the studio, the hotel [the Beverly Wilshire] and the Brown Derby restaurant, which was just across Wilshire Boulevard." Her husband was much too busy to have a social life, and had no energy left anyway by the end of the day. They knew only two couples, Dick's agent and his lawyer and their wives, whom they saw occasionally. No one ever phoned. "We weren't even noticed; we weren't snubbed, just ignored. Coming on the heels of our marvelous reception in London, the contrast simply intensified my feeling of alienation . . ." Although in his life she was still outside it; she confessed that she often gave way to tears.

Her husband wanted to believe that his first venture into films, *The Hot Heiress,* was going to be a success. It was all so interesting, and everyone at the studio was so encouraging and optimistic (he would learn that this was a ritual, no matter how disappointing the film was becoming), but there were some danger signs. Ben Lyon, the leading man, had no voice, and Ona Munson's range was so limited that songs for her could hardly be adventurous. In the end only three of their songs were used, and the film received a disappointing reception a year later.

BY EARLY AUGUST they were back in New York, and two days after that, Rodgers was on the high seas, bound for London. Hart had gone on ahead.

Ben Lyon, Ona Munson, Tom Dugan, and Inez Courtney in *The Hot Heiress,* 1931

Morty had decreed that Dorothy must stay behind, so Dick, who detested traveling alone, had persuaded his parents to go with him (Dorothy's were already in Europe). Writing a kind of daily diary to her from the SS *Olympic,* he thought she had been "swell" about the business of letting them go, especially since he would be gone for two months. "I'm afraid that I, on the other hand, had a pretty bad time of it. We watched lower New York go by and I sank lower and lower by the minute." He went to his mother's room, and she asked him to move the basket of fruit Dorothy had sent as a farewell present. As he picked it up the handle broke and the fruit rolled everywhere. His mother laughed, "and so did I, but to my surprise, I wasn't laughing at all, I was crying." The weather was not worth mentioning, not much was happening on the boat, they had not met anyone, and the three of them spent one evening reading magazines.

He had dreamed about her all night. "All I remember is that we were at a large party and I chased you all over to compel you to join me in a certain act of pleasure. You refused at first and I had trouble convincing you. Finally you relented aboard the Century bound for Chicago. Things were fast reaching a pretty pass when I awoke to disappointment of the most acute order. Oh, well, dearest, perhaps tonight." He was lonesome and bored and deeply depressed, but two or three days later that feeling had diminished "into more or less of an ache which hurts most at night." One evening he and Pop had sat around drinking whiskey, and when Pop went to bed, he played sad songs to himself at the piano. In fact he was so bored he wrote a song for *Ever Green,* although he had promised himself a complete rest. It would save time later, and he had to confess that the aphrodisiacal quality of a sea voyage had to be countered somehow, particularly when he was feeling so healthy. But the time dragged by. He wrote, "If this trip gets any slower time will start going backwards, and the first thing you know it'll be last Thursday night [the evening before he sailed] and I'll be happy again."

He was making great progress with his score, which he wrote in his deck chair, because it was harder than sitting at a piano and therefore better practice. There was just one more song left to write. "I'm really awfully pleased with myself for being so diligent and clever." The days were boring and the nights intolerable, so it was a blessing that he could "drink a little," as it helped put him to sleep. "The disadvantage is that it makes me think too much, and you can imagine along what lines."

Then Thursday night came. "Angel," he wrote at one in the morning,

> if you were here I'd tell you that I was drunk and you'd laugh at me— as you do. I'm writing now for a reason . . . You see, it's this way: I'm absolutely livid with desire and I'd give my soul to have you in this room at this moment. Then I'd feel safe. As it is, I'm afraid! I'm not afraid of the work, or people . . . but (I'm writing now after four double brandies . . .) I'm afraid of something inside that's raising hell with me. I want to yell because I feel strong and I want terribly to feel that surge when you and I are close together. Baby, at the same time I know logically that I shouldn't be writing to you this way; that you'll worry. What can I do? I can't tell anybody here. You're the only person in the world that I could ever tell the whole truth to.
>
> Look, Angel, I *am* telling it to you now, and I don't care. I know at this moment that if I'd slept with someone on this boat that I'd tell you about it and you'd understand. I know that I'll tell you every single thing that happens between now and the time we kiss each other again. Will you please, please remember what I tried to say when we said our goodbyes? I've never loved anyone but you, and I swear it, I never will.

This incoherent confession of an almost overwhelming temptation was written one whole week after he left her. No wonder Dorothy Rodgers quoted forever afterwards the cautionary words of her father when she first brought up the subject of marriage to Dick. He told her, she said, "Look, I like him very much, but I think you must realize that he is going to be surrounded by the most attractive women and they'll be coming along new every year, younger and younger. And as you get older, they'll still be coming." So, Benjamin Feiner concluded, "if this is going to worry you, you shouldn't marry him."

Chapter Nine

"WHERE'S THAT RAINBOW?"

R ODGERS WAS SO CONFIDENT Dorothy would understand that he did not bother to reread his words the next day but simply mailed the "boat letter," as it came to be called, upon arrival in England. Larry had sent a wire saying that he could not find a flat in London and suggested Dick do what he was doing: i.e., take a suite at the Savoy with a parlor, bedroom, and bath. Rodgers found the rate very reasonable, in fact, half the price he had paid when they stayed at the Berkeley the previous spring. Thank goodness he had not moved in with Larry. He was "worse than ever, and if he doesn't go completely mad soon, I will!" He added, "However, I must admit he works hard and hasn't held me up a bit."

A day later, work was progressing. "As usual it took three times as long to put the opening number on paper as it did to write it, but we did a hot number called 'Harlemania,' which sounds very good indeed." He had not left the hotel by day since he arrived, but his nights had been free. The night before he had taken Joyce Barbour (who sang "You Took Advantage of Me" with Busby Berkeley in *Present Arms*) to the formal dress rehearsal of *Charlot's Revue*. They went to the Savoy Grill for a drink afterwards and bumped into Dorothy's parents and his. "Your Ma looked so surprised that I wondered what she thought," he wrote. But then, two days later, a cable came from Dorothy. She had received his boat letter, and, her cable added, I UNDER-STAND PERFECTLY BUT AM SLIGHTLY UNHAPPY MISS YOU HORRIBLY ALL MY LOVE. That worried him. He wrote, "I'm cabling you again now to ask you what you mean—if there was something in my letter that upset you. I know that I feel awful about you all the time, and if you were just speaking generally, it's all right. If you meant anything in particular, I'd like to know. Maybe I'm just stupid."

Three days after that, on September 9, he was writing again, after having telephoned her, a conversation that had "only made me feel worse. I had a miserable night. Really, Ange, you seem to suffer all out of proportion to what is actually happening . . . It's awful for me as it is, but if I'm to have added to my generally low spirits the worry that your attitude is morbid, I don't know what I'll do. You *must* buck up!"

Rehearsals had begun and there was the usual struggle to get things under way. He wrote, "I suppose you'll want to know what the girls are like? Fair, darling, only fair. At one time, I suppose, something or other might have looked good to me, but you've spoiled all that. Gawd, you've changed me! It's comforting to report that the monastical life is becoming a tiny bit less difficult, by the way . . . The only female I've been out alone with is Joyce and the night she took me to the Charlot thing, and she made me ill with her talk about her Dickie Bird [a reference to her husband, Richard Bird], I came back here with strength on my side." So work went on, and he "broke a record for speed in teaching the chorus the numbers. They learned everything in two days, and not full days, either. The stuff sounds great as they sing it and they seem to like it tremendously."

By September 10 his parents had left for Ireland and he was feeling bereft. He wrote, "You make me laugh when you say, 'This must never happen again.' Fat chance . . ." The baby, which he often referred to as a boy, was a constant subject of his letters. He wrote, "I dreamed of you all night, but I can only recall two fragments. The first was in the lobby of the Savoy. You came in, took off your hat, sat in a chair and didn't recognize me! It wasn't that you were angry, you actually didn't know me. Second, we were returning, you and I, on the *Leviathan* with our child. The baby was washed overboard and you begged me to save it. I tried to go after it, but a lot of men wouldn't let me go. I woke up in a cold sweat, and I guess I was yelling too." That did not mean that he was not completely delighted at the idea of becoming a father. "I had the grandest dream last night," he wrote from London a week later. "I was home with you and you were all smiles and terribly happy. Then you gave me the baby to hold and it put its arms around my neck and kissed me. Oh darling, that will happen, won't it?"

That same letter brought news that he had met a sweet young thing who, it turned out, was not only the mother of twins but had four other children as well. She had the figure of a sylph and the face of a young girl, very much like Dorothy's, and was visibly "untouched" by childbirth. "Obviously then, it isn't necessary to look awful, so be encouraged." This and similar soothing words revealed that he had correctly assessed his wife's fears about what the arrival of a baby would do to her attractiveness as well as her conviction that he would always have an incurably wandering eye where young women were concerned, the younger the better. At this stage he was honestly and truthfully trying to assure her that this was not the case. Writing one such letter after a phone call on September 14, he said, "You've no idea how it hurts and depresses me when you're unhappy . . . Tonight your voice sounded stronger and more vital, and thank God, you didn't cry so. Oh, I love you so much! Something had resolved itself in my mind now, and what we spoke about tonight—my boat letter—is no longer a problem. I can't explain it completely because I don't quite understand it myself. You know that moral precepts play small part in my life; my instincts certainly haven't changed; that I rely on you for complete understanding of that sort of thing. Nevertheless, here I am as you last saw me: your faithful loving husband."

He was going to so many places they had visited together and becoming very nostalgic. "Larry, Mother and Father and I had dinner at Kettner's, right next to the table we sat at for lunch . . . the day we looked at the house. Then we went to the Empire Theatre to see a picture, and the star was, of all people, Greta Garbo. I thought of the time we sat in the lounge and wondered if you really were going to have a baby . . ." It was wonderful to be able to talk to her but hard afterwards. "I always feel much worse, and last night especially you sounded so near. Oh, darling! If only your letters weren't always trying to beat me down and telling me how awful it is of me to be away. I'm sure you don't know what you've written—it's so cruel."

During his lengthy absence—he did not return home until the end of October—he prefaced another letter by telling her that when he got "an upset cable" from her he would go around looking worried and could not work for hours at a time. "Some day perhaps when this is all over and we have a purely academic discussion of the effect of wires on husbands, I will show you a few choice bits," he said, referring to hers. "Pop definitely shouldn't have told you and I do hope I didn't hurt your feelings, darling"; a tantalizingly cryptic comment. Occasionally, her constant need for reassurance would begin to grate. "Don't think I have been a good boy all this time. I have had no chance to tell whether or not I have any willpower. I haven't been able to look seriously at anyone that's all. That boat letter, you see, was written when I was alone and I was afraid. Now that I have had weeks of contact with people I know definitely where I am. I just don't care . . ." But when she was happy, he was covered with relief and gratitude. "I have got a strength that comes from loving and being loved and only you can take it away from me. Don't do it, Angel, and don't let me let you." They had been married for seven months.

WHILE FRETTING OVER what Dorothy might be thinking and feeling, Rodgers could not help being increasingly elated at the progress of *Ever Green*. Sonnie and Jessie sang their duets and solos for him one evening, and he was thrilled. "Dancing on the Ceiling" had been staged and looked marvelous. "It's being done as it should be, which is a rare experience for me these days." Rehearsals had a "joyous and successful air." Charles B. Cochran had actually paid them a visit to tell them how pleased he was with their work, as well as their attitude towards the show. "He was . . . terribly nice. I think that it was all caused by yesterday afternoon's rehearsal. We were to stage the opening of the show, a long, very complicated affair with about seventy-five people. Frank Collins and Buddy Bradley should have directed it, but they started to flounder about and asked me so many questions that before I knew it they were standing aside and I had done the whole thing myself—in two hours! C.B. was there, and evidently much impressed."

His social life was picking up. He always dreaded a Sunday in London because there was nothing to do. He and Larry had gone to the Mayfair to lunch with his parents, who had just returned from a trip to Ireland, and as they went into the restaurant, whom should they bump into but Gertie Lawrence. So she and her friend Helen Downes joined them. Then Jack Wilson, a theatrical producer and close friend of Noël Coward's, came along and was added to the party. He and Larry went back to the Savoy and worked all afternoon, and while he was in the shower Wilson reappeared with Joyce Barbour. They all went out to dinner and then on to see Jack Oakie in a very funny movie, *Let's Go Native*.

He continued, "Then the real fun began when we met Gladys Calthrop" (a theatrical designer and intimate of the Coward circle) "and Noël . . . brought the whole party up to my apartment." They sat around all evening while Noël listened to "all the new stuff and the picture songs. Really, I'd blush to tell you what he said. You've never heard such praise . . . He's written a play called *Private Lives,* in which he appears with Gertie under C.B.'s management, and it's a roaring success on the road, having paid its production costs in two weeks! . . . He wants to write a book for us as he says Larry and I could do the best romantic score of the past twenty years." Although they would only work together once, and not on this project, the two men struck up a lasting friendship. Perhaps Coward seemed to incarnate to Rodgers, as he did to the novelist Stella Gibbons, "the *myth* of the Twenties (gaiety, courage, pain concealed, amusing malice)." Ten days later Rodgers went to the opening of Noël's show and the party afterwards. *Private Lives* was wonderful. The surprise was Gertie, who under Noël's direction "turned out to be a superb comedienne—not the dull sort of sweet-thing she usually is . . . In the second act Noël sat down at the piano . . . and quite calmly delivered the first eight bars of 'Dancing on the Ceiling'!" At the party Gertie and Noël sang all his songs; he had to confess that he got quite "cockeyed." That was unusual for him nowadays. He was making an effort not to drink, because he felt much better "and a good deal less nervous."

Meanwhile *Ever Green* continued to blossom. He reviewed every one of the costumes, some of them truly lovely and all of them "startling." He enclosed a picture of the first-act finale so that Dorothy could see what it would be like—modeled on the finales at the Folies-Bergère. There was another big, important evening. They were rehearsing ten miles outside London at the Alexandra Palace, the only space big enough to accommodate a

Gertrude Lawrence and Noël Coward in *Private Lives*

Jessie Matthews and Sonnie Hale "Dancing on the Ceiling"
in a scene from *Ever Green,* 1930

succession of huge sets, among them a Parisian fair and cabaret. One night Gertie sent her car to collect them, "with a polite, but firm, request to appear at Major Butler's. It seems that Prince George (the Duke of Kent) had asked for us to be there. There were only the Prince, Gertie, Noël, Jack Wilson, Larry, the Butlers, and me, but the King of Greece was there for a while as well. We had supper and played and sang till quite late, which was a lot of fun. Larry only knocked over one glass." The same could not be said the night Tallulah Bankhead arrived at his rooms at the invitation of Bea Lillie in the company of three male ("?") "bright young things," he wrote. "Bankhead got badly boiled on champagne, which she demanded, patronized everyone, broke glassware, did imitations, looked awful and finally left at 3.45 a.m. Good old London!"

Soon they would be in Glasgow and he begged her to pray for a smooth opening. As Dorothy was urging, he had asked C.B. whether he could leave after the tryouts—he would stay long enough to make whatever changes might be needed, of course—in other words, miss the London opening. To do so must have cost Rodgers something, but his letters give no hint. He had been glad enough to get out of town when *Lido Lady* looked like a disaster, but every theatrical instinct told him they had a hit, and he had not had so many London successes that he could afford to be blasé about this one. It was Dorothy he was thinking of, with her floods of tears, her refusals to eat, her paralyzing insecurities, and her constant cables and phone calls wanting to know how soon he could come home. To his great surprise, C.B. had agreed to let him go.

After yet another phone call to her, Rodgers wrote, "I was so anxious to tell you that I thought there was a good chance of making the *Mauretania* on the twenty-fifth [of October], and when you said you thought that was *late* I could have bawled with disappointment! If you only knew how hard I've worked and how I've nursed every opportunity that might help us get away." To top it off he had just received a long letter from Dorothy's mother, back in New York, in which she told him "you weren't well for days after her arrival and that you cried all the time she and your Dad were with you. I felt great," he said, with a flash of sarcasm. "I don't think I can write any more just now. I'm more depressed than I have been at any time since I left you and I simply can't think of anything pleasant to say . . . I'll come to you as soon as it's humanly possible and I love you very much."

Ever Green opened in London at the new Adelphi Theatre early in December of 1930 and, as he and Larry had predicted, it was a huge success. James Agate, always a reliable guide, wrote in the *Sunday Times:* "To pretend that this lovely thing is a musical comedy is to evade truth, since Mr. Cochran's latest sophistication takes after its inept model about as little or as much as Man resembles his first progenitor . . . the whole show brilliantly captures the note and spirit of Paris . . . an entertainment so all-absorbing that I have no notion of what the new theatre looks like." Ivor Brown in the *London Observer* called it "the Ascot of musical shows." The reviewer in the *Tatler* said it was "a peep-show, a kaleidoscope, a merry-go-round, a miracle, all Hollywood and all Heaven . . ." The songs "Dear, Dear" and "Dancing on the Ceiling" were deemed particularly sprightly and original. (The set for the latter was designed in such a way that Jessie Matthews appeared to be actually dancing on a ceiling, twirling around an immense crystal chandelier.) Whatever private transgressions had been committed by Matthews and Hale were forgotten in the general admiration, and *Ever Green* ran for 254 performances. Rodgers must have been just a little bit chagrined as he sat in New York with his wife, now eight months pregnant, and imagined some of the parties with dear Bea, dear Gertie, dear Noël, and dear Prince George.

IN HOLLYWOOD, he and Larry had been given a suite of rooms and assistants to carry their papers but, on the other hand, one could not believe a word anyone said. *The Hot Heiress,* which would open in March of 1931, was sinking under lackluster advance reviews, not that any of them was really surprised, and Warner Bros., ultimate indignity, had bought their way out of the contract so they would not have to produce any more Rodgers and Hart films. Even before that happened, the triumvirate was dreaming of another show. As Rodgers said, "In the theatre we're lucky to find a quiet fire escape when we have to re-write something . . ." but it was a world they knew and understood. While Rodgers and Hart were in London, Herb Fields, in New York, was working on a libretto for a topical satire about Hollywood. It would tell the story (which had, with the advent of talking pictures, some actual counterparts) of a couple who arrive in Hollywood to make their fortunes: she becomes a silent-screen star while he flounders, but when the talkies arrive, he becomes the star and her career begins to fade. Herb's synopsis arrived early in October, while they were still rehearsing in the Alexandra Palace, and Dick and Larry sent a cable saying they did not like it. Now Rodgers was worried: "What trouble this opinion of ours will cause I can't say," he wrote Dorothy. "I am afraid Herb will be terribly hurt, but I'd rather have the whole proposition go to smack than do something in which we had so little faith . . ."

Whatever Herb did to revise the script was evidently enough to satisfy them, because they decided to go ahead, although there were new problems to surmount. Instead of their being besieged with offers from producers, as in the pre-Depression days, the situation was now reversed. Broadway was in a deep slump. Dillingham had been bankrupted. Theresa Helburn and Lawrence Langner did not care for their idea. Aarons and Freedley had a big success with *Girl Crazy* and did not want to risk another musical that year. Lew Fields, who had just had his last flop, was retiring as a producer. Billy Rose was an unknown quantity, and as for Ziegfeld, well . . .

Finally the team of Laurence Schwab and Frank Mandel agreed to take *America's Sweetheart.* Schwab was an old friend—he had been the one who took him to Max Dreyfus on that "miserable occasion when the publisher told me that my music had no value." They signed up Monty Woolley as director, and a new leading lady, round-faced and petite, named Harriette Lake, later to make a name for herself in Hollywood as Ann Sothern. There were tryouts to come in Pittsburgh, Washington, and Newark before they braved a Broadway opening at the Broadhurst in February 1931. But at least Dick was not in London or on the coast when his daughter Mary was born on January 11, 1931, at Lenox Hill Hospital, with Dr. Mortimer Rodgers in attendance.

Dorothy Rodgers recalled that as rehearsals began, Dick and Larry worked in their apartment and always in the daytime. Her husband was always ready, but Hart "had to be caught or trapped or tricked—practically locked up in a room with Dick before he would start. Even then Dick would have to write the tune first to get him going." Once a song was finished, she would be invited in to hear it. Dick would whistle and play, and if Larry was there, he sang the lyrics. When Dorothy really liked something, she would find herself teary-eyed. And when her husband was really pleased by something he had just finished, she wrote, "the hair on his forearms stands on end and his skin is covered with goose bumps."

They brought Mary back to the Lombardy, Dick's study serving as an impromptu nursery; but what with the pails and pots for boiling diapers, the weighing machine, the equipment for sterilizing bottles, all the bedding, and a perambulator, not to mention the addition of a nurse along with the maid and cook, they were clearly overcrowded. Meantime, her parents were considering a smaller apartment now that she and her brother had left home. It was agreed that her parents would assume their lease on the Lombardy Hotel's nineteenth floor and she and Dick would move into a nine-room apartment at 50 East Seventy-seventh Street, at an "unbelievably high rent," she wrote. Before that happened, Dick took some silent-movie films of Dorothy and himself, pushing the elegant perambulator around their spacious terrace, as well as some pictures of Edna Ferber cuddling the new arrival. Dick looks snappy, as his wife would have said, in faultlessly tailored clothes and a fedora. Dorothy, beaming her wide smile, is almost immobilized under a vast mink coat, her present from him for having produced their first child. She then had, for her, the exquisite pleasure of redecorating a large apartment, and took great pains with the nursery, designing her own baby furniture: chests with rounded edges and units that sat squarely on the floor (to avoid the problem of lost toys). Dorothy Rodgers was especially good at such minutiae, a fact her husband was quick to appreciate, and she soon became the family accountant—her daughters said she taught herself double-entry bookkeeping. Bennett Cerf, who dated her before her marriage, had also noticed what he called "her eye for exactitude." One evening when they went to a musical, from the first row in the balcony "she was able to detect that the third chorus girl on the left was wearing shoes slightly different from those worn by the other girls." Cerf called her "La Perfecta."

For Rodgers, that winter of 1931, the routine was depressingly familiar as he and Larry fought to get *America's Sweetheart* into the right shape. There were hopeful telegrams from him in Pittsburgh: FIRST ACT NEARLY PER-FECT. SECOND NEEDS PLENTY. STOP. A day later he wrote that it would be so nice to have a success, so that he could "not work and not worry." He had

Edna Ferber, circa 1930

a feeling it would be. "Then! We'll have fun, won't we?" Performances had begun, and Gus Shy, the comedian, "gave a terrible show and started the evening off so badly that it really never came back." But the Forman Sisters (Hilda, Louise, and Maxine) were a great success with their first trio, "Sweet Geraldine," and Harriette Lake, as Geraldine March, and Jack Whiting, playing Michael Perry, were splendid in their song "I've Got Five Dollars." The press was kind and advance sales were good. Then they went on to Broadway.

"Where do people get these ideas about the thrill of a theatre opening?" Hart asked an interviewer for *Cinema*. "A Broadway first night is agony. Everything goes wrong. The actors are so nervous their greasepaint melts . . . Nothing gets a laugh because everyone's waiting to see the reviews before they pass an opinion. The juvenile goes up in his lines and the leading lady has hysterics and weeps mascara on her costume.

"It's ghastly. Herb won't go into the theatre. When something goes wrong and he is badly needed I go crazy looking for him. He walks up and down in the alley outside or sits on a fire-escape smoking four packs of cigarettes, or hides in the men's room." Hart would sit in the audience for a while, then go out and smoke a cigar and look for a drink. Rodgers, who was becoming equally addicted to nicotine, was never without a cigarette in his hand. "Afterwards they gather," the *Cinema* writer reported, "broken old men, and wait in a speakeasy until morning for the notices to confirm their conviction that this is the end." More than the usual angst attended the opening of *America's Sweetheart,* so they must have sighed with relief when, despite mixed notices, the show went on to have a run of 135 performances. It would be the last musical they would write with Herb Fields and their last appearance on Broadway for four years.

With an expensive household to maintain and two musicals that would close in the summer (*America's Sweetheart* and *Ever Green*) there was no hope of not working and, especially, not worrying. Despite their best efforts and the pride they had taken in such shows as *A Connecticut Yankee, Peggy-Ann,* and *Chee-Chee,* at this point, Cecil Smith observed, they were hardly more than "bright and fluent workmen, able to turn out attractive and moderately successful work," without having moved strongly to develop their best talents. But now, given the state of the Broadway theatre, thoughts of artistic direction seemed almost beside the point. Just then they had a new offer from Hollywood, this time from Paramount. "Things had changed, they were assured. Musical comedies were no longer being transferred to the screen, but pictures with a musical background were being made. Would they return and work on a vehicle for Maurice Chevalier?" They certainly would.

RICHARD AND DOROTHY RODGERS and Larry Hart had made a quick trip to Hollywood in the late spring of 1931, with the real work on the new film, *Love Me Tonight,* to begin in the autumn. When they got back to New York Dorothy had only been away for a few weeks but was shocked at the change in her father. True, her mother had written to say he was depressed, but this did not seem alarming. Then she saw him. "His whole bearing and demeanor had changed. He was a big man—over six feet tall and on the heavy side—yet he had always moved quickly and easily. Now he seemed to have grown smaller, and his movements were slow and lethargic.

Jeanne Aubert in *America's Sweetheart,* 1931

He spoke only in answers to questions and then in a low monotone . . . his eyes looked out on his world with terrible despair and pain. Even his breath smelled stale. He had no interest in anything; he didn't want to see people or go out; he wasn't able to concentrate on reading, and no spark ever lit up his face."

Feiner, then fifty-five, had recently contracted diabetes and was being given insulin, but this did not seem an adequate explanation for the despair that enveloped him. Nor could she blame the financial crash entirely. She wrote, "his practice was a large one and his earning capacity was unaffected." There was no question of putting him in a sanatorium, and even the words "mental illness" were too terrible for anyone in the family to contemplate. "Nervous breakdowns, like cancer, sex and venereal disease, were never spoken of out loud." The solution was to consult a psychiatrist, then called an "alienist." The diagnosis was that the patient would improve with time. Nursing care around the clock and occupational therapy were prescribed—

jigsaw puzzles, for instance. So, day after day, her brilliant father sat at a table in the living room "with hundreds of little pieces—a little like the pieces of my father's life, I suppose—waiting to be interlocked." Every day she would arrive at the apartment on the nineteenth floor to give her mother some relief, and spend "several silent hours" visiting her father.

She wrote, "Those visits were difficult and occasionally quite disagreeable because sometimes my father would get a fixed idea about something or other and he'd keep on nagging about it." (She also said, "He was completely absorbed in fancied or real anxieties.") She continued, "On the afternoon of October 22 my mother had gone to a concert and I was spending the afternoon with Father. His worry that day was that Mary, then nine months old, was too fat and I must put her on a diet." (Films of Mary at that age show her as a pudgy baby.) Dorothy's first impulse was to defend her child, but she listened as patiently as she could. Finally, she lost her temper. "Daddy, if you go on that way, I'm going home!" Ben Feiner continued to complain and his daughter to protest with increasing vehemence. Mary was too fat: it must have sounded far too familiar. So she left.

That evening, she and Dick went to an opening of Jed Harris's production of *Wonder Boy* at the Alvin—the same producer whose negotiations with Rodgers and Hart she had been accused of disrupting in London the year before. "At the end of the performance, as we reached the outer lobby of the theatre, someone connected with the show asked Dick to step into the box office for a moment . . . A few minutes later, Dick reappeared, and I remember thinking he looked rather pale, but the lobby lights were over-bright and unflattering . . .

" 'Anything wrong, darling?' I asked.

" 'I'll tell you when we get in the car,' was his answer—and then I knew that something had to be very, very wrong." That evening Feiner and his nurse took a stroll around their terrace on the nineteenth floor. "They stopped to rest and were leaning against the rather low brick wall when, according to her account, without effort he simply fell to his death."

It was years before Dorothy could talk about it, years before she could face the idea that it might have been suicide, and the guilt she felt lingered for decades. "No matter how often I told myself that he always knew how much I loved him . . . that I had really been a good daughter, I still felt I had let him down." It finally dawned on her daughter, Linda Rodgers Emory, that whenever her mother got up and left the dinner table in tears the date would invariably turn out to be the day of her grandfather's death. "Nothing was ever talked about," Linda Rodgers Emory added. It was one of their family secrets.

Jeanette MacDonald and Maurice Chevalier in *Love Me Tonight,* 1932

LOVE ME TONIGHT would prove to be Rodgers and Hart's most success-ful film during their Hollywood years of 1931–34, in its way a landmark. Talk-ing films had solved the technical problems of how the hero sings a song on film, as in *The Hot Heiress,* but not the artistic ones, i.e., how to keep the audience's interest during the two or three minutes (interminable on-screen) that it takes to sing it, the kind of conundrum that would rivet Rodgers's attention and bring out his very best ideas. In this case, the three of them decided "there was no reason why a musical sequence could not be used like dialogue and be performed uninterrupted while the action took the story to whatever locations the director wanted." The technique is almost routine nowadays; then, it was revolutionary.

One of the film's most famous sequences was its opening, the start of an early morning in Paris. The director, Rouben Mamoulian, a thirty-four-year-old prodigy from the Theatre Guild, had already tried this successfully in a Catfish Row context for the 1927 play *Porgy* (the basis for Gershwin's *Porgy and Bess*). As the streets gradually awaken, the sounds of workmen digging, horns honking, hammers clanging, and a baby crying are picked up in an accelerating rhythmic pattern and woven into the film's opening number, "That's the Song of Paree." Mamoulian insisted Rodgers supply incidental music as well as the songs. Rodgers wrote: "It is more or less stop-watch composing, with the writer creating musical themes to fit precisely into a prescribed number of frames."

Chevalier plays a Parisian tailor who falls in love with an aristocrat, played by Jeanette MacDonald, and masquerades as a baron to win her affections. In one scene, he is fitting a portly bridegroom into his wedding finery while singing "Isn't It Romantic?" The customer picks up the tune and walks down the street humming it. A taxi driver begins to whistle the refrain. His passenger, a composer, whips out some music paper and writes down the notes. Pretty soon the composer is boarding a train, and that transfers the refrain to a group of French soldiers, who take to a country road, and then there is a Gypsy camp and, finally, a chateau, where the heroine waits wistfully on a balcony and has the final word (or in this case, note). Such a relentless set of coincidences ran the risk of looking contrived, but in the case of *Love Me Tonight* it not only solved a nearly intractable problem but gave the song such a handsome set of repetitions that its success was assured. Just as *Chee-Chee* had done, *Love Me Tonight* offered Rodgers an opportunity to put into practice his theories about artistic coherence, ones he had cherished ever since he and Hart began their collaboration in 1919. They had demonstrated that, not only could it be done, but it was by far the most satisfying solution and not even the most difficult. What was harder was to be denied the opportunity, and in Mamoulian they had the ideal collaborator.

Rodgers and Hart were lucky in another respect. They liked Chevalier despite his penurious ways. (He was the only man he ever met, Rodgers wrote, who when offered a cigarette tucked it away in a pocket for later.) Since Chevalier had sung celebrated songs to Louise and Valentine, they decided to write one in a similar vein, "Mimi," after the heroine of Puccini's *La Bohème* which, to their surprise, became a standard part of his repertoire. Another song that surprised them was "Lover," sung by Jeanette MacDonald as she is out for a drive in a horse-drawn cart and is constantly interrupted by the need to rein in a frisky horse. The song was written as a joke and not given a reprise, and they were unprepared to have it, too, become a favorite. In short, *Love Me Tonight* was just what Rodgers and Hart had needed to establish them in films, the way that *The Garrick Gaieties* had done in the theatre. The *Illustrated London News* summed up the general reaction by calling the film "wholly enchanting, gay, witty and exhilarating." Although they had been under contract for only one film, Paramount signed up Rodgers and Hart for a second, *The Phantom President,* to star George M. Cohan.

The young director Rouben Mamoulian with Maurice Chevalier
in *Love Me Tonight,* 1932

BARELY A MONTH after the trauma of her father's suicide, Dorothy, along with Dick, the ten-month-old Mary, Mary's nurse Sophie, and Louise, an Alsatian girl who worked for them in New York, made the trek out to the West Coast. May Feiner went with them. Her husband's death had left her so distraught that Dorothy and Dick decided they could not leave her alone. As soon as they arrived they went hunting for a furnished house and, after seeing some hopeless examples, were taken to 724 North Linden Drive in Beverly Hills, owned by Elsie Janis, a music-hall singer of World War I days. Dorothy Rodgers wrote, "The architecture was vaguely Spanish, with interiors complete with the rough plaster walls, over-wrought iron and Moorish arches. There was a swimming pool, and the house itself might almost have been designed for our needs. The main part was two storeys high, but attached to the large living room there was a one-storey wing with three rooms, bath and its own front door that would make an ideal suite for Larry . . ." (He would later move to much grander quarters elsewhere.) The departing tenants had been married in the house the day before, and huge bouquets of lilies and white flowers decorated every room. "What could be more romantic? We signed the lease that day . . ."

By the end of 1931 a huge theatre colony had settled on the West Coast. Just as the era of the talkies had destroyed some careers (John Gilbert's being a conspicuous example), it had also opened up undreamt-of opportunities for actors like John Gielgud, who knew how to speak, and Ronald Colman, who had also had classical training in England. There were all kinds of writers under contract without much to do, including William Faulkner. Dorothy said, "Each writer was given a cubicle and expected to punch a time clock. Well, they're not used to working like that. Dick spent most of his time at the Beverly Hills Tennis Club, where they could reach him any time, but there was no point in his staying and sitting in the office." Faulkner once famously asked whether he could work at home and was given permission. Dorothy Rodgers said, "So he went home to Mississippi. And that really upset them quite a lot when they found out about it."

In contrast to their first visit, their social life was booming and, to judge from the Rodgers home movies, Dorothy was a natural organizer. In addition to Ronald Colman, the producer Edwin Knopf and his wife, Mildred, Fredric March and his wife, Florence Eldridge, Rouben Mamoulian and Myrna Loy (who had appeared in *Love Me Tonight* in an unflattering role), they got to know Helen Hayes. She and her husband, the playwright Charles MacArthur, also had a small daughter named Mary. There on film are the daughter of John Lodge, actor and later ambassador to Spain, and the son of Norma Shearer and Irving Thalberg, eating ice cream and cake with a crowd of other "screen children" at Mary Rodgers's third birthday party, their nannies hovering in the background. Dorothy, in a white brocade jacket with black velvet collar and frog closings, directed the program.

Now Dorothy is in Mexico, drinking champagne, or coming to the table for a breakfast al fresco in the mountains of California, or a group of them are swimming, diving, and lounging beside the pool. Or Dick, his head bent, pretends to be asleep as his daughter tries to give him a flower, then raises it with a smile as he pulls her towards him. He looks so relaxed, so at ease and self-assured, in the white cashmere cardigan (an ascot tied round his neck) that sets off his bronzed good looks, the curve of his mouth, and the cleft in his chin. Dorothy is a prettier version of her mother, advancing shyly across the grass with her delighted smile, a ribbon of hair blowing across her eyes, as

Richard and Dorothy Rodgers with the two-year-old Mary at the El
Mirador Hotel in Palm Springs, 1933

slim and exquisite as any of the movie-star mothers. As Ernest Boyd wrote of
Zelda and Scott, "They can realize to the full all that the Jazz Age has to offer,
yet appear as fresh and innocent and unspoiled as characters in the idyllic
world of pure romance. The wicked uncle, Success, has tried to lead these
Babes in the Wood away and lose them, but they are always found peacefully
sleeping in each other's arms."

Elaborate birthday parties, with a whole carousel in the garden and someone to film the occasion, were just one aspect of a plethora of unfamiliar customs in Beverly Hills. Most of the gardeners were Japanese, and if told to
water on Tuesdays and Fridays that is what they did, even if it was pouring
with rain. The enormous and costly houses were built on minute plots of
land, "so that you could almost open your bathroom window and brush your
neighbor's teeth . . . There was no privacy at all." Sometimes it rained for
days, and the houses, being built without foundations, could be musty and
damp. "They had a wonderful heating system; you just pushed a button in
each room and the heat turned up right away; it was natural gas and
cheap . . . There were no sewers, which was terrible. They also didn't have

any air conditioning, because they never acknowledged that it was needed. Now of course it's all air-conditioned."

She was used to getting around in a car, and in Beverly Hills they of necessity became a two-car family. One birthday Dick gave her a twelve-cylinder navy-blue convertible coupe Cadillac with real leather upholstery, which had belonged to Adolphe Menjou. It had hardly any mileage and was almost new. She drove it around the block and came back in tears: "I can't drive with that big motor in front of me." But Dick told her she would get used to it, and she did.

Among the other quaint customs of Beverly Hills was the matter of "protection." Shortly after the Lindbergh kidnapping of 1932 a number of frightened movie stars with children, among them Marlene Dietrich (who lived on Sunset Boulevard), bought guard dogs and burglar alarms and put iron railings on their windows. One day a man came to see Dick and Dorothy Rodgers and offered to protect their house for fifteen dollars a month. It was not very much money, "but Beverly Hills had been, and I think still is, one of the best police departments in the country. If you take a walk, you are a suspicious character. So we said, 'Thank you but we feel we are sufficiently protected,'" she said. "A night or two later we drove the car into the garage. The

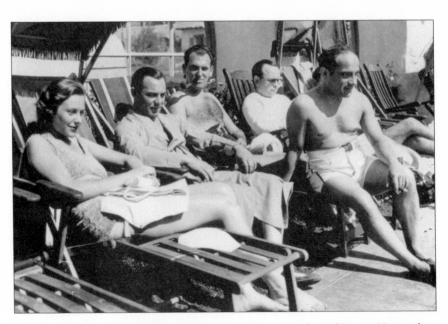

Dorothy Rodgers, Richard Rodgers, Moss Hart, Harry Brandt, and Lorenz Hart at the El Mirador Hotel, Palm Springs, in 1933

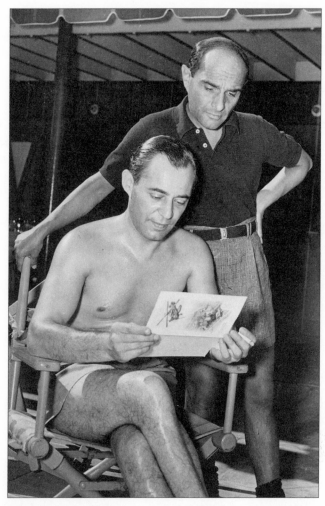

Richard Rodgers and Lorenz Hart in Hollywood in the early 1930s

garage had a window that opened into the house, and it was open. The next day we got a phone call saying, 'Did you notice your window was open? And would you like to reconsider fifteen dollars a month?'" They paid up.

It was a one-industry town, as she discovered; if they met a lawyer, all his clients were in the movies, and so were each doctor's patients. Dinner parties centered around films: what had been released and what was about to be released. In the home built by Bill Goetz and his wife, Judy Mayer (of Metro-Goldwyn-Mayer), "a wall of the living room swung out and up (with three beautiful Impressionist paintings staying in place), exposing a projection room with seats for the Goetz staff. After dinner everybody would go into the projection room and a film would be run. You never dared to express an opinion because you never knew who was sitting next to you." In a way already becoming archaic, after dinner the men huddled and talked about the financial side of pictures while the women huddled and talked about children and the servant problem.

Even though Larry had his own quarters, he remained something of a trial. He often had dinner with them but then took off afterwards to be with his cronies. "Where he went we seldom knew. Our friends, the writers and directors with whom Dick and Larry worked, held little interest for him socially. Most of his friends were chorus boys or women much older than he." Fortunately, he had never learned to drive, which Dorothy Rodgers was sure added years to his life. She recalled that early one morning she and Dick were awakened by loud voices and lights going on in the garden. Soon her mother was awake and Mary was crying. Dick went downstairs "just in time to stop Larry from putting Worcestershire Sauce into the martinis he was making." His guests, Jack Oakie and Joan Marsh, another film star, had no idea anyone else was living in the house. They quietly left and Larry disappeared for two days, but sent "a huge basket of orchids" by way of apology. The story is that Dorothy gave Dick an ultimatum after Larry decided to bring home the entire Count Basie band at two one morning. "It's Larry or me," Dorothy said, so Larry found a place of his own.

Her husband was making determined efforts to keep Larry from spending all his money, either by lavishing it on his cronies or by gambling it away, with scant success. On a trip to Mexico in October 1932 Dick wrote to Dorothy, "I watched Larry win two hundred bucks in nine straight passes. He's ahead three fifty on the trip and if I could only kidnap him all would be well. He'll probably lose it all and more tonight." In his role as Larry's savior and overseer, Rodgers was becoming increasingly discouraged. The following summer, June of 1933, he wrote that they had only one more item to write but Larry had to write the lyric first, and "I just can't get it from him." He did not know what to do. He and Herb Fields had had long talks about the problem, but there seemed to be no solution. There was something else as well; Hart seemed increasingly prey to paranoid fantasies, and he was "bitter about everything. He's back to his old conviction that [Howard] Dietz (a fellow lyricist and an executive and producer at M-G-M) is out to get him, when Howard has been nothing but a tremendous help and stabilizing influence . . ."

His letters to her were written during her periodic absences. She had become pregnant again and carried a baby almost to term but one night had

George M. Cohan and Claudette Colbert in *The Phantom President*, 1932

premature contractions. She was rushed to Cedars of Lebanon Hospital in Los Angeles. The baby, a girl, lived for only a few moments. This was in August 1932. He wrote in his autobiography, "I had never before realized how traumatic such an experience is. Dorothy was physically depleted and emotionally drained." She went back to New York to recover, taking Mary, then about eighteen months, and was away for a couple of months. A year later she became pregnant and again lost the baby. She went to New York in late May of 1933 for a minor operation and this time left Mary with Dick and his parents. Shortly after she left, he wrote, "Mary kept me company at breakfast. She looked wonderful and added to the joy of the occasion by asking for you all the time . . ."

They moved two or three times, always to rented houses, and Rodgers went on working in Hollywood until early in 1934. He felt he had little choice. Broadway musicals had shown no signs of reviving, and "a man with a family to support, particularly given the ephemeral nature of my profession, had to acknowledge the financial importance of a contract with a major studio . . ." He was intrigued by film technique and heartened by the success of *Love Me Tonight,* so at first everything pointed to the wisdom of his decision. Then the problems began. Rodgers and Hart's next project, *The Phantom President,* about political shenanigans during a presidential campaign, starred Jimmy Durante and Claudette Colbert, as well as George M. Cohan in the title role. But Cohan, who had exaggerated notions of his own songwriting abilities, resented their presence and everyone else's, as far as Rodgers could tell. The film was released in time for the Roosevelt-Hoover election campaign and made no impression. He wrote, "I think even Hoover was more popular than the film."

In pursuit of an unbroken transition from dialogue into song, Rodgers and Hart experimented with rhymed dialogue in *The Phantom President* and made even more extensive use of it in *Hallelujah, I'm a Bum,* about out-of-work and homeless men living in Central Park, with Al Jolson in the leading role. That consummate artist sang the movie's most ingratiating song, "You Are Too Beautiful," which has survived to become a repertory standard. It is a song that insinuates itself on the ear rather than immediately engages it, with a wit and sophistication worthy of Cole Porter. It has all the Rodgers hallmarks: his facility in step writing, his "adroit use of successive fourths, opulent but unintrusive harmonic progressions," and his striking originality. Yet, as Alec Wilder wrote, up to that point it would be hard to say what constituted a Rodgers song, when one looked at the enormous range of his work: from "Manhattan," "The Girl Friend," "Mountain Greenery," and "The Blue Room," to "Dancing on the Ceiling," "Ten Cents a Dance," "Lover," "Mimi," "Isn't It Romantic?" and all the others. His songs had captured the popular imagination, but he had yet to write a score that seemed, and sounded, characteristically his own. He was a one-song phenomenon or, put more diplomatically, a musical dramatist with the chameleonlike ability to disappear behind the work itself. And his position in Hollywood was by no means secure. Rodgers wrote of *Hallelujah,* "We tried to keep the score relatively light but we were defeated by the theme." Since there were real shantytowns in Central Park, "the subject of homelessness . . . didn't strike many people as something to laugh . . . about." The public's mood had been misjudged once more, and from that point on Rodgers and Hart found themselves cajoled into movie projects that were either abandoned or failed to make any impact. *I Married an Angel,* for instance, a pet project of Irving Thalberg's of M-G-M, sounded particularly promising. It was to be an adaptation of a Hungarian play about "a banker whose wish comes true when he marries an angel," and the unknown writer assigned to the project was Moss Hart, "an intense, almost Mephistophelian-looking fellow, fairly bursting with ideas." They finished the entire project within a month or so, and then Louis B. Mayer canceled it. That ended the matter for the time being. A few years later Rodgers and Hart made *I Married an Angel* into a musical, and a film followed: "Thus Larry and I ended up in the happy position of being paid for the same material three times."

There was to be one more disastrous year while they were under contract with M-G-M. With the success of *42nd Street,* starring Al Jolson's wife, Ruby Keeler, film musicals were all the rage, but everything Rodgers and Hart were asked to work on seemed to turn to dross, with the exception of one song, "Blue Moon." It began as a song for Jean Harlow in a film, *Hollywood Party,* in which she expresses her longing to become a movie star: "Oh Lord, if you're not busy up there / I ask for help with a prayer / So please don't give me the air . . ." The scene was never used, and since Rodgers "rather liked" the music, they invented new lyrics for a Harlem nightclub sequence in another film, *Manhattan Melodrama,* starring Clark Gable, Myrna Loy, and William Powell. It became "The Bad in Every Man" ("Oh Lord, what is the matter with me? / I'm just permitted to see / The bad in every man . . ."). That should have ended the matter, but Jack Robbins, head of the studio's music publishing company, persuaded Hart that if he would write a more commercial lyric, he would promote the song from coast to coast. Hart sat down and wrote, "Blue moon, you saw me standing alone / Without a dream in my heart, / Without a love of my own . . . ," and the song was made.

They were reduced to writing single songs for occasional films. Samuel Goldwyn wanted an appropriate ballad for Anna Sten to sing in her first Hollywood film, *Nana;* the result was "That's Love," for which they had high hopes, but nothing came of it. There were other desultory one-number obligations, hardly amounting to much of an intellectual challenge. Rodgers spent most of his time on the tennis courts. There were, very occasionally, busy days. One of them started out with "writing, manuscripts to be done, conferences about orchestrations, rehearsals and everything else," he wrote to Dorothy in October of 1932. He worked all day and did not get to bed until two a.m. Such days were rare. More often, when he wrote he described dinners in which he talked about pictures and then went to see a film, then went back to somebody's house to talk about more pictures. Or he would write music he liked and be disappointed. In the summer of 1933, "I turned out a tune that was pretty bad, and I didn't know it till I played it for the boys. They were awfully nice about it . . ."

He was still attempting to reassure Dorothy sexually: "I've been hideously faithful to you, my pet, and not through a sense of duty! I just don't seem to care. I have a deep need for the activity that you and I enjoy most and sometimes it makes me pretty uncomfortable but, outside of exchanging mild pleasantries with various members of your attractive sex, my efforts and results have been nil." He went to a party occasionally. One was given by Dorothy di Frasso, a noted Hollywood hostess, and "I was warned not to come without a costume so I got me a sailor suit." Other people were in wigs and uniforms and everyone was much too hot. That was the night he got extremely drunk and had to be taken home at six in the morning; he had just spent three hours straight playing the piano. "I wouldn't know whether it was a good party or not—I only know that I was trying frantically to consume as much whisky as possible." His letters show that he was either drinking too much or trying to cut it out entirely. "The glass of beer I had at Milly's tonight was my only drink in four days. How'm I doing?" Getting drunk seemed to be especially necessary whenever he was discouraged and/or angry. After she left their house on Angelo Drive in Beverly Hills in May of 1933 he wrote, "Now I know what you felt like when I left for Europe, except that you didn't have to go back to a big house all alone. However, I don't believe I'll fill my letter to you with all the gory details of my lonesomeness," he added with a flash of irritation. Then he found a note from her on the bed. "As for that, I can only tell you that I went directly into one of the best little solo drinking bouts you've ever seen. I don't know who won, but it couldn't have been me."

It was a gloomy time. He wrote, "It's bad enough to know you're wasting your time and not accomplishing anything; what really hurts is to realize that others are aware of it, too." A writer who had a syndicated column about Broadway in the *Los Angeles Examiner* posed a question one day: "Whatever happened to Rodgers and Hart?" Rodgers was so unnerved that his hands began to tremble. That was all he needed to read. He and Larry were going back to Broadway.

Chapter Ten

"LITTLE GIRL BLUE"

THAT NINE-ROOM APARTMENT on East Seventy-seventh Street which had been furnished with such care, and then had to be abandoned, was always in the back of their minds. Perhaps at Dorothy Rodgers's behest, they had never bought anything in Hollywood that could not be carried onto a train, and after three years of living with other people's possessions, they were anxious to get back to their own. Before leaving New York in 1931 they had taken out a loan of thirteen thousand dollars, presumably to help pay for the redecoration, and then, in a fit of extravagance, left the apartment empty for a year. The second year they rented it to a careful elderly couple. The third year they rented it again.

When they came back they found that their new tenants had bought a puppy (despite the "no dogs" clause in their contract), and the results were everywhere in ruined rugs and chewed chair legs. The butler had pressed clothes on the dining-room table. A chandelier was broken, along with three dozen of their best glasses. There were pieces of broken glass and liquor stains everywhere. The kitchen was unspeakably filthy. Dorothy Rodgers told the young lady of the house, who had just had a baby, "You know, if you had gone into that kitchen you wouldn't have eaten anything that came out of it." The girl replied, "I'm not surprised. I went in there once and it was just so awful I never went in again." By then Dorothy Rodgers was in the early stages of her pregnancy with their daughter Linda, and in despair. She said to Dick, "I just wish I could wave a magic wand and have it put back." He replied, "Why don't you start such a place?" That led to her first business venture, Repairs, Inc.

If there is a moment at which Dorothy Rodgers ceased to be just "Dick's wife" and struck out on her own, the day she surveyed the destruction of what had once been a beautiful apartment was such a moment. During the thirties she would build a successful business repairing furniture and objets, using top specialists, just one in a series of enterprises she would undertake over the years. Being Dick's wife was changing her, whether she knew it or not, from a charmingly insecure girl in his shadow to someone of consequence. Neither of them made a point of it, but no doubt Repairs, Inc., would have seemed like a useful idea, given the state of Rodgers's career at that moment. Their attitudes toward money were similar but not entirely identical. Both of them enjoyed sybaritic living and indulged in their discriminating tastes with zeal. But whereas Rodgers, so clever about getting advantageous contacts, was casual about disbursement and spent to the limit of his income, as keeper of the books Dorothy Rodgers was always aware of exactly how fast that income was disappearing. She was the one who wanted everything in place so that there would be no unpleasant surprises. No doubt her precision had its manic edge, but it also meant that, when things looked bad financially, she would rise to the occasion.

As Rodgers soon discovered, there was still no work on Broadway; it was the same disheartening situation he had left three years before. When Arthur Hornblow Jr., Goldwyn's production chief, who had become a producer at Paramount, offered Rodgers and Hart the chance to write the score for his first musical, *Mississippi*, they jumped at it. It was back to Hollywood for six weeks in the summer of 1934, writing songs for a bright young singer named Lanny Ross. They came up with three songs for which Rodgers had high hopes: "Down by the River," "Soon," and "Roll, Mississippi." The last-named disappeared into oblivion, but the first two were real successes, which was reassuring. Then Ross turned out to be hopeless as an actor and was replaced by another "singing sensation," a portly and youthful Bing Crosby. He needed one more song, which became another hit for Rodgers and Hart: "It's Easy to Remember." It was a consolation to have their songs heard on the screen since, in the year and a half following their return to New York, only one Rodgers and Hart song had been heard on Broadway. That was "You Are So Lovely and I'm So Lonely," in a play called *Something Gay*, starring Tallulah Bankhead and Walter Pidgeon. The play lasted for 72 performances and the song was never heard again.

While Dorothy, now heavily pregnant, was restoring the apartment and beginning to organize Repairs, Inc., Dick and Larry were developing a story idea that would be suitable for RKO's dancing team of Ginger Rogers and Fred Astaire. They had just had a great success with the film *The Gay Divorcee*, and Rodgers and Hart came up with the idea of a former song-and-dance man in vaudeville who moves into ballet and falls in love with a ballerina. It would be called *On Your Toes*. Astaire liked the idea, but rejected it because he thought his public would not accept him in anything less than white tie and tails. Then Harry Kaufman, producer of musicals for the Shubert brothers, who also liked the idea, thought of Ray Bolger, who had caused a sensation as Georgie in *Heads Up!* in 1929. That was an even more splendid idea, they agreed. Lee Shubert gave them a contract and an advance. It would be their first show on Broadway for four years, and their first ever as authors of their own book. Meantime, Dick and Dorothy celebrated their fifth wedding anniversary, March 5, 1935, by becoming parents of another baby: daughter Linda. Mary, in Brearley School kindergarten, and one of the actors in a school play, "proudly announced to one and all that her mother had just had a baby and couldn't possibly come to see the play because she was getting married." At that moment, Billy Rose reappeared in their lives.

After selling his Fifth Avenue Club, Rose had opened a theatre-restaurant called Billy Rose's Music Hall. Samuel Marx and Jan Clayton wrote, "Observing a law he claimed to have originated, 'Never use your own money,' he sought the backing of bootleggers for this venture. They seemed charming associates, putting their booze on the tables and their girls in the chorus." However, when that venture also failed, and the backers lost their money, "Rose fled to Europe to escape their uncouth methods of showing displeasure."

While wandering around Hungary, so the story goes, Rose came upon a company that was performing a play about feuding families, with a traveling circus as the setting. It was a variant of the Romeo and Juliet theme (in this version, all ended happily), and it gave Rose new impetus. Returning to New York, he got in touch with Ben Hecht and Charles MacArthur, who had recently co-authored *The Front Page* and *Twentieth Century*. Rose's imagination had leapt ahead, and what he envisioned was a full-sized circus musical, with animals, acrobats, tightrope performers, clowns, singers, and, of course, a leading lady: entertainment on a vast scale. As Ben Hecht remarked, Rose was "a song writer, café keeper and fame hunter who found invisibility painful." This would be the most spectacularly visible musical ever to arrive on Broadway, that is, if it ever got there. The Hippodrome was judged large enough to accommodate the enormous cast, but it had to be completely redesigned and refurbished to make room for a huge circus ring in the middle of the auditorium. *Jumbo,* as the show came to be called, was postponed five times, and by the time it did open, in the fall of 1935, it had cost about $340,000. Most of the money, Rodgers believed, was advanced by the mil-

The billboard for Billy Rose's *Jumbo* at the
Hippodrome, 1935

lionaire John Hay "Jock" Whitney. Rodgers concurred with the general verdict that Rose "never parted with a dime if he didn't have to."

That brought them back into the Billy Rose–Fanny Brice social circle,
and Dick and Dorothy spent a weekend visiting them on Fire Island. Bea
Lillie was there with her teenage son and eccentric mother, who was very
vague. "If you said something to her about her daughter, she'd say, 'Who?'"
Dorothy Rodgers said. Anyway, Jimmy Durante, who was playing the comedian in *Jumbo*, was there too, and she, Bea, and Fanny Brice went fishing for
flounder in a flat-bottomed boat. Bea caught her first fish and when it began
to flap around in the bottom of the boat she became very alarmed and tried

to run away. Dorothy said, "It's very hard to tip a flat-bottomed boat, but she almost made it. Then she announced to us that she didn't know how to swim." Moss Hart was spending the weekend with the Gershwins and came over to see them. He was introduced to Bea Lillie's mother as Mr. Hart. "Now, she had met Mr. Rodgers, and here was Mr. Hart, but somehow she got all mixed up, and she thought that Moss Hart was *Buddy* Rogers. So she said to him, 'Well, you're the man all the girls are so crazy about!' He simpered and seemed terribly pleased until she looked him up and down quite boldly and said, 'Whatever for?'"

Work on *Jumbo* was particularly welcome just then because it transpired that Lee Shubert really did not want to produce *On Your Toes* after all. Once his option had expired they thought they had another producer, Dwight Deere Wiman, but in the meantime they needed work. Even though Rose had not paid them for their last assignment, the money being invested—he was lavishly redecorating the shabby Hippodrome as well as redesigning it— and the originality of the idea were irresistible, and Rodgers and Hart came up with the best score they had written for years. "The Most Beautiful Girl in the World" was sung while the hero, played by Donald Novis, and the heroine, Gloria Grafton, rode around the ring on horseback. Then there was "Little Girl Blue," in which the heroine dreams she is a child again, being entertained by circus performers in dazzling costumes. The song ends the first act, and something about it deeply affected Dorothy Rodgers when she heard it:

> Sit there and count your fingers.
> What can you do?
> Old girl, you're through.
> Sit there and count your little fingers,
> Unlucky little girl blue.

There was "My Romance," also introduced by Grafton and Novis, and so many others that have drifted into obscurity, although one more memorable song was cut before the opening. Frederick Nolan wrote that Hart disliked the tune so much that he refused to write a lyric for it at first. This may be why, Nolan claimed, Hart wrote such irreverent dummy lyrics, i.e., lines jotted down on first hearing in order to fix the rhyming scheme:

> There's a girl next door
> She's an awful bore
> It really makes you sore

The grand finale of *Jumbo*

To see her.
She's got a forty waist,
But she's got no taste,
I know I sure would hate to be her.
By and by perhaps she'll die—
Perhaps she'll croak next summer;
Her old man's a plumber,
She's much dumber.

After being introduced in *On Your Toes,* "There's a Small Hotel" would go on to have a long life.

Rodgers and Hart were again in luck in Rose's choice of George Abbott, who by the time he joined the company as book director (John Murray Anderson, of *Dearest Enemy* fame, was overall director) had been on Broadway for over twenty years, first as an actor, then as writer, director, and producer. George Jean Nathan wrote, "His is the theatre of snappy curtain lines, wisecracking dialogue . . . periodic excursions to the lavatory . . . and various analogous condiments, all staged as if the author had used a pepper shaker in lieu of an inkwell." Rodgers remembered him as a "tall, sharp-featured ramrod of a man," who was indispensable in pulling together the myriad elements of their ambitious musical. Abbott would go on to make an invaluable contribution to *On Your Toes,* as co-author of the book and also uncredited director, and worked on four other musicals with Rodgers during the next two decades.

Reviews of *Jumbo* were wildly enthusiastic; the world's smallest showman had come up with the grandest show in town. John Mason Brown, in the *New York Post,* summed up the general reaction with the words "If you think the mastodon is extinct, you have only to travel to the Hippodrome to realize that at least so far as a theatrical endeavor is concerned, he still stalks the earth. His name is *Jumbo.*" The critics predicted a long run, so it was disappointing to have *Jumbo* close five months later. Despite its 233 performances the musical had been so expensive that it was still $160,000 in the red. Since Rodgers does not mention it, one gathers that this time they were paid.

The encomiums lavished on the score were enough to put Rodgers and Hart back on Broadway. Roosevelt had been elected, the country was beginning to recover from the worst of the Depression, and producers had started remembering who they were. As Cole Porter wrote in later years:

> It's smooth!
> It's smart!
> It's Rodgers!
> It's Hart!

DOROTHY RODGERS WAS BECOMING launched on her career as a hostess. During her pregnancy with Linda she was sent to bed by brother-in-law Morty for five months to guard against another miscarriage. Her memory of Christmas Eve 1934 is that George Gershwin came to dinner with a composer, Kay Swift, then married to James Warburg, and one of his close friends. The Rodgers apartment had a dropped living room, entered by means of a staircase one and a half storeys high. Mary, then aged four, was running around in her nightdress and wrapper, and Gershwin and Rodgers carried Dorothy down the stairs and put her on the sofa. Then Gershwin played what he had just finished of the score of *Porgy and Bess.* It was "quite a wonderful evening." George used to come and visit her. "He was so brilliant and a wonderful pianist. He could talk about himself in the third person [and] admire his work that way. When he started to paint he told me he'd never had a

Producer Billy Rose, with one of the principal backers for *Jumbo*,
the millionaire John Hay Whitney, at left

lesson." She would have liked to say he would have done even better if he had,
but was too polite. He said, "'If I had decided that I was going to be a painter
instead of a composer, I would have been just as good . . .' And somehow
when he said it, it didn't seem boastful." When Gershwin died of a brain
tumor in the summer of 1937, Rodgers, who was in Beverly Hills, wrote, "I'm
so upset at the moment I can hardly think enough to write."

They knew everyone in the theatre, writers, directors, and composers.
Cole Porter was "a darling man." Noël had great wit and charm and once
invited them to Goldenhurst, his house in Kent, for the weekend, but it was

Back on Broadway and loving it: Richard Rodgers with Charles MacArthur,
who wrote the book for *Jumbo* with Ben Hecht

November and "rather bleak and cold." They were somewhat too young to be
regulars at the Round Table but knew the dramatis personae and were
friendly with all of them. Robert Benchley, drama critic for the *Herald Tribune,* was, like the others, "marvellously witty" and very fast on his feet. Once
Benchley was successfully sued by an actor for having called him "the worst
in the world"; the next time the actor appeared onstage, Benchley wrote:
"Mr. So-and-So's performance was not up to its usual standard."

Dorothy Parker, another frequent dinner guest, had a much more acid
tongue. Dorothy Rodgers recalled that she was dining at their house one

George Gershwin, 1937

night in the company of Marian Thompson, who wrote a history of the Palace Theatre called *The Palace,* and Ilka Chase, the actress and writer. "And the subject of the discussion was Clare Luce, who was not a great favorite." Ilka Chase defended her: " 'Clare is my friend, and I'm very fond of her. She's very loyal to her friends, and she's very kind to her inferiors.' Dorothy Parker was eating and she never stopped; she was drinking soup, as I remember it. And without missing a beat, she said, 'And where does she find them?' "

Dorothy and Dick were often invited to visit the island in Vermont, called Bomoseen, that members of the Round Table had bought; "but Alexander Woollcott behaved as though he really owned it." Woollcott invited whomever he pleased and ran it to suit himself. She first met Wooll-cott when he took them to dinner on their honeymoon in Paris at a little restaurant called Chez Nini that he remembered from World War I. He was wearing a long black coat, and although he was only in his mid-forties, to her, at age twenty, he seemed impossibly old. As they went toward the restaurant they were obliged to walk in single file because the sidewalks were so narrow, and she found herself, in deference, stepping aside to let him pass.

Woollcott set great store by a portrait of himself that had been painted in his World War I uniform, with books under one arm. It hung over the man-telpiece in an apartment he shared with Harold Ross, editor of *The New Yorker,* and Ross's wife, Jane Grant. One time when Woollcott was away for several months, Ross and Grant took the portrait to an artist to be copied in every detail save one. In the original version, Woollcott looked straight ahead. They wanted the new version to show his head slightly turned, so that he would now be in three-quarter face. Ross and Grant then told all their friends, " 'Now when Woollcott comes back, he will undoubtedly notice the change and he will ask everybody about it . . . And we are all to say, "No, we don't notice any change." ' So, sure enough, Woollcott eventually came home, and they gave him a welcome-home party. He glanced up the mantel, and then he did a take. He . . . said to his friends, 'Does that look different to you?' They looked and said, 'No.' Everybody who came into the house was asked the same question, and no one admitted to seeing any difference. It was bothering him quite a lot. Then he went away for a weekend, and they took it out and it was back to the original. Poor Woollcott died without ever being told."

It was a time for elaborate practical jokes, some of them of the harmless "Let's fool a policeman" variety in which Bertie Wooster and his pals liked to indulge. Only, instead of swiping policemen's helmets, the Round Table gang's capers were somewhat more elaborate and costly. "They'd have a dupli-cate of a park bench made and they'd have a bill of sale for it and would carry [the bench] surreptitiously into the park and leave it there, and they went [back] and waited until a policeman was walking around, and then a couple of them would get up and carry this bench straight out of the park. And of course, the policeman would say, 'What are you doing with park prop-erty?' . . . And they would produce a bill." One of the best practical jokers was their friend Jules Glaenzer, who had a charming apartment and a huge living room graced with two pianos, where the likes of Noël and George or Cole or Harold Arlen would entertain and Gertie would be singing. Even though the food was dreadful, nothing but canned corned beef accompanied by gushing fountains of champagne, they were the best parties, the equal of

Dorothy Parker in the 1930s

those given by Elsa Maxwell, although her apartment was bigger. "The guests at the party were of two kinds: the talented people with famous names who loved being with each other and performing; and then there were the customers: they were all extremely wealthy . . . they loved meeting the people of the theatre. So everybody was happy." The vice-president of Cartier's was described as "a rich socialite" by *Life* in 1937, when he was host at a party given for the French actress Danielle Darrieux to show off her new, upswept coiffure: among the other guests were Dick and Dorothy Rodgers; Noël Coward; Doris Duke's then husband, James H. R. Cromwell; Dwight Fiske, the nightclub entertainer; and Mrs. Jock Whitney, who had just been screen-tested for the part of Scarlett O'Hara in *Gone With the Wind*.

Occasionally the joke would be on Glaenzer, and once, again, it involved a painting. His living room was graced with a canvas of an old lady wearing a frilly nightgown, with a cap tied under her chin, by the artist Bernard Lamotte. One day Glaenzer decided the time had come to clean the painting, so he took it back to the artist to have some smoke marks and other discolorations removed. Weeks passed, and finally Lamotte called to say it was ready. "The painter had taken out the face and done a . . . marvelously lifelike portrait of Jules, still wearing the nightcap . . . but with these piercing, lecherous eyes. It was like the wolf in 'Little Red Riding Hood.'" Glaenzer threw a big party to formally unveil the new version and enjoyed the joke as well as anyone.

Games were all the rage, and Dick and Dorothy loved playing them. Woollcott was always ready to teach people cribbage, "but he would play you for money while he was teaching you, which was rather unfair." They played bézique and backgammon and something called "the Game," an elaboration of old-fashioned charades, requiring two teams. Dick was especially fond of puzzles and liked such challenges as finding how many of a single letter there might be in a sentence, or trick questions about mathematics; if puns were involved, so much the better. One evening in Beverly Hills he played games at a dinner party, which made him homesick for New York. "You'd have been quite proud of me. We played Guggenheim, Pick-up-Sticks, and one that was new to me called 'Likes and Dislikes.' I won them all, believe it or not." By the time she came to write her book about decor and entertaining, *My Favorite Things* (1964), Dorothy Rodgers had become not only sophisticated and knowledgeable about games but definite in her tastes. Those she liked could not be too obscure, and they must never be mean: "Games that show up people as clumsy or badly informed end by making everyone uncomfortable." If Dashiell Hammett's Nora Charles had been organizing games for a dinner party at which she and Nick were the hosts, she, too, would have steered a diplomatic course between games that were too obvious, therefore banal, and those that were too demanding, and therefore even more boring.

As exemplars of the smart young things in the 1930s, Dorothy and Dick could hardly help resembling, in some superficial respects, that inimitable couple, as played by Myrna Loy and William Powell. Like Nora, Dorothy had the flawless features and the figure needed with which to display a dazzling wardrobe of designer outfits. For the most part, one imagines her, like Myrna Loy, greeting guests at the door in another amazing hostess gown, taking telephone messages with matter-of-fact aplomb, the receiver held slightly away from the ear, and passing out martinis with a practiced hand. She is wise enough to stay in the background (while keeping her husband under control with a few ever-so-slightly tart remarks), but she is always prepared to resolve a crisis by resolute action when necessary. As for Nick, the gentleman detective, as personified by William Powell, he too is debonaire, street smart, equal to any emergency and on easy terms with underworld characters, while knowing all the right people. He smokes (a man's man), drives a fast car, goes to prizefights, bets on horses, is recognized everywhere, and conveys an air of "tranquil assurance," as Anita Loos said of the playwright Wilson Mizner. No

Alexander Woollcott with Charles Chaplin, 1930s.

evening can begin until Nick has downed at least five martinis in a single gulp (without showing the least effect). Occasionally Nick is seen with their off-spring, a small boy dressed in a uniform; Nick behaves as if he has never seen the child before.

MARY RODGERS REMEMBERS being dressed up in a good bathrobe and taken downstairs when her parents were giving a party. She would be told not to ask for autographs and then be given plates of hors d'oeuvre to pass around. She has vivid memories of at least one of the houses in California in which they lived and could describe it when she went back years later. "I remember there was a chart at the head of my bed with gold, red, and blue stars, red for when I wet my bed, blue for when I had to be picked up at night and taken to the bathroom, and gold for when I was dry all night long."

She also remembers the day Linda was born. She was sitting in a patch of sunlight on a red rug in her nursery and her father came in to tell her she had a little sister. She knew her father was hurrying to go somewhere, and she asked what the baby's name was. Then she asked her last name, trying to keep him there. He asked her what she thought it was. Mary said perhaps she thought Linda had a middle name, and felt terribly embarrassed because he would not take the time (nor did most adults) to try to figure out why children did what they did. Most adults went through an invisible wall and could not remember having been children once they were on the other side. In those early California days she would ask her father every day where he was going, and every day he would be going to the studio. "And he'd pat his pockets full of Lucky Strikes and take off." He smoked three packs a day. He also had "this famous bottle we referred to as daddy's little black medicine, that turned out to be a tranquilizer for alcoholics. A very strong sedative that looked like very dark maple syrup. It may be that he needed it in order not to drink in front of people."

Mary was always fascinated by matches and, like most children, had been forbidden to play with them. So when she was seven she pocketed a book of matches from her father's study, got up very early next morning, lit a match, and set the organdy curtains in her room on fire. "I was instantly terrified, because they went up in a flash. I ran to the next room and got my nurse, who was sleeping with my sister, and my father yanked the curtains down and stamped out the fire." When questioned about it, Mary virtuously denied all knowledge. She had been asleep and suddenly smelled smoke, she said. Her father said the superintendent of the building was very good at deciding how fires started, so he would be consulted. Nothing more was said, and Mary went off to Brearley, where she was playing one of the cookie children in *Hansel and Gretel* and had to stand onstage with her eyes closed, "and all I could see were flames." She went home for lunch and then her father wanted to see her in his study. "I knew I was either going to be spanked, or lose my allowance, or be locked in my room forever . . . I went in and he closed the door, put out his hands, and said, 'Do you see these hands? These are the hands that hold yours at lunch. These are the hands that play the bass of 'Chopsticks' when you're playing the top. And these are the hands that put out the fire that you lit.'" All she could think about was that "nothing terrible was going to happen." But she did recall thinking that her father was trying to be a true father.

He was always indirect. She took a dime from him once. "He was very careless with money. He couldn't have cared less, and used to put it on his bureau, toss it there," and she thought her allowance was probably a dime a week, so she stole it. Some time later, feeling guilty about it, she asked him why he left his money out like that. "Couldn't somebody take it?" she asked. "I could take it." Her father replied, "If I thought either of my children would steal, I would be so unhappy, and depressed, and disappointed." Mary thought, "Oops. There it was again—trying to instruct by indirection."

Dorothy Rodgers was the disciplinarian; her father never wanted anything to do with that, and that included every area of his life. "He had the

meanest secretary in the whole world . . . a tiny little angry shrew, totally
devoted to Daddy, and everyone hated her . . . He had these special people
working for him so he could stand around being mild-mannered." Nevertheless, on occasion Rodgers could be biting and humiliating. His and his wife's
worries about Mary's figure dogged her throughout adolescence. Since her
father set such store by outward appearance, Mary thought she must have
been a source of disappointment and embarrassment to him. He once said to
her, "You are so fat that when you walk your arms swing out by your sides like
an ape." He was capable of that kind of remark. Both she and Linda were
musically gifted, but Linda showed outstanding talent as a pianist, and in retrospect, would have made that her career, but her parents had made the early
decision that she should not be groomed for the concert stage. Mary privately
decided to stop memorizing so she would not be asked to play and compared
with Linda. Her father's blunt response was that it was about time.

Her mother was "gracious and completely covered, though not for anyone who knew her, a surface-charm queen . . . She fitted his purposes wonderfully as a chatelaine. She kept a perfectly beautiful house and wore
wonderfully tasteful clothes and gave charming dinner parties and he was
dependent on that, and appreciative." At least when they were small, their
parents presented a united front, and she and Linda would be sternly repri-
manded if they tried to play one off against the other. She later believed her
father became sympathetic because her mother was so rigid, but he would
never rise to defend her. Her mother, on the other hand, was "a confronter,"
who wanted her own way. From about the age of three or four she felt she was
being controlled by her mother, "and I didn't like it much." At breakfast time
Mary would be summoned to her mother's bedroom, and find her with a
little pad of paper and a gold Cartier pencil with a ball at the end with her
initials on it, containing an eraser and extra lead. Her mother would begin,
"Did you . . . Have you . . . Why didn't you . . . When will you . . . ?" Mary
Rodgers said, "I hadn't even had orange juice before that started. I used to
have terrible fights with her about 'Why can't I keep it the way I like it? It's
my room.'" Mary called herself "terribly rebellious and determined, with
these two parents who had such strong personalities. I felt I had to fight for
my own identity."

Both of her parents were usually angry with her, he because any unpleasantness between his wife and his daughter disturbed the surface of his life. He
could come home and her mother would say, "Guess what Mary's done
now?" Mary knew her father would be frosty, but not much worse, "except
for once every six months when he would blast at me." Their way of punishing her was by withholding money, or the threat of it, and Dorothy made

that decision. Another way of punishing was with coldness. Both she and Linda were sensitive to nuance, because they had been brought up to believe that hitting was bad. "You fought with words and my mother would communicate her displeasure very accurately with her tone of voice." There was a further issue between them. Dorothy Rodgers felt her daughters did not love them enough, and this led to tears and accusations. Mary did not think their father would have noticed at all if his wife had not been "so busy" pointing it out. "I think she shouldn't have had any children, and under a truth serum would have confessed she did not want any."

After Stephen Sondheim and Mary Rodgers became apprentices at the Westport County Playhouse, they became friends, and "Mary used to complain about her parents all the time," Sondheim said. "They were as bad as parents can get. Selfish, and I don't know why, much worse to Mary than Linda. My guess is that they wanted a son and Mary was such a disappointment they made her pay for it all her life. And although Mary tended to exaggerate in those days, she told me of enough slights to convince me. She wouldn't have made up the things her mother said. Her mother, as you know, was homophobic. The dynamic of that relationship is that she hated homosexuals, and there was Larry Hart! Whenever Mary would bring a boy home her mother would say, 'Well, you know he's a homosexual.' Dorothy Rodgers is one of the real monsters of the world. And unlike my mother you can't tell funny stories about her. My mother was crazy. I don't think Dorothy was crazy. I think she was genuinely an awful person."

Daniel Melnick, the Hollywood film and television producer, who married Linda Rodgers, remembered how Dorothy "was constantly bitching about how she had to call her mother every morning, because if she didn't May would torture her with comments like, 'Too busy to call your mother, are you?' Coming from a working-class Jewish intellectual family I thought I had the only mother who said, 'Don't worry about me. Just take my head out of the oven when you come home.' And here these grand people were doing it to each other."

Linda said, "Mary was so much more angry on the surface that I got the message you didn't show what you were feeling because if you did you got clobbered." She thought her mother was obsessive, demanding, very insecure and hard to understand. She never felt really loved by her, in contrast to the warm relationship she and Mary had with their maternal grandmother. "She played with us, took us to movies, had Friday-night dinners in her apartment which was across the street from ours, and I always felt I could relax with her. I felt accepted . . . What I'm talking about is having felt love there, and not having had it at home." She remembers some humiliating spankings, the first when she was seven. "I said I needed more soap, new soap, and [my mother] came into the bathroom and saw I had put a healthy sliver of soap in the wastebasket; I didn't really *need* a new cake of soap. She sat on the toilet on the side of the tub and said, 'When you get out of the tub I'm going to spank you.' So . . . I stayed in the tub until my skin shriveled . . . To have to lie down over her lap while she spanked my bottom was probably more humiliating than it was painful."

As for her father, when he was in a good mood he was "very bright and funny. He could be extraordinarily warm. He would reach a hand out at lunch and you would put your hand in his. Next evening he could look at you with the coldest brown eyes in the world." She was so upset when he was rejecting and cold, and always assumed, as a child, that it must be her fault. Composing gave him "the breath of life. It was the only thing he really enjoyed. There was an exuberance about him when he played." Both she and Mary knew he would be pleased if they shared his love for music. That was easy, because they were both musically gifted. They both agreed that "one of the ways to please him was to make him laugh," Mary said. So they tried to do that as well. Mary continued, "Our only joy when we were little, when we could forget who was playing the piano better, was the giggle syndrome, which we really could get into quite heavily." Occasionally both parents would get to laughing and would throw back their heads. Mary said, "One of the unexpected things about our mother was that she was great at being teased. She was really funny about someone making fun of her."

Linda said of her parents, "I think it was a very strange relationship. They needed and supported each other and were the worst people in the world for each other . . . When he had problems she was always there to take charge. I am not sure he had much of a say. He was quite a passive partner. She controlled his life." Linda had so many memories of hearing her father's footsteps going past her door at night, and then the clink and chink of ice in a glass. "It never occurred to me that people didn't do that. I think he was under the impression that vodka was the 'breathless drunk,' and more and more as he got older." Increasingly often her father would be in bed with "the flu," and she would go into his room and see his hand shaking as he tried to get a glass to his mouth. "I feel great compassion for him now. He was never as happy as he wanted to be. When I think of all the happiness that should have been his . . ."

Mary Rodgers Guettel once found herself quite shocked as she watched the early family home movies of herself, then a fat little baby, on the grass with her father, who was playing with her. "When this thing came on the screen I felt my whole stomach turning over, with this incredibly attractive and loving young father, and I looked at him and thought: 'Aw, shit, why didn't I ever see that or ever feel it towards me?' I mean . . . obviously he was feeling that towards the baby, which was me, but I never saw that again. I only saw it on celluloid . . ." Her sister believed their father loved her "when he was able to, but that wasn't very often. As I got older I was better able to understand the gaps. He had all he could do to take care of himself, and there wasn't much left over."

ONE AREA of her husband's life to which the door was locked and bolted, at least at first, was his work. Early in their marriage Dorothy Rodgers had been hurt and disappointed to learn that she would not be allowed at rehearsals. "Dick . . . felt it would be awkward and embarrassing to have a wife—or anybody who wasn't actively connected with the show—present. I understood his point of view, but I resented it at the same time." What was most annoying of all was having him gone night after night; "the theatre was so fascinating that, like most people, I wanted to be a part of it." Besides, she disliked entertaining alone and going out without an escort, "as though I didn't have a husband." Linda Rodgers Emory said that her mother "knew something about music and scores. She also knew about costumes and things like that, although that was never an important part of any show." She would join him on the road on weekends and always went to out-of-town openings. Just the same, there were many periods when she stayed home while he was "having a rollicking good time working."

At some point in his marriage Richard Rodgers had begun to compartmentalize. His work was his private world; Dorothy was not to enter unless invited. He had already ceded almost everything to her: overseeing their income, the house, the servants, children, friends, social life, the joint façade they presented to the world. Nothing must be allowed to disturb that careful division, not only because of the furor any ripple seemed to cause in her, but also because Dorothy's management of so many areas of his life might have begun to feel like a kind of entrapment. Mary Rodgers Guettel said, "When he got over admiring how pretty she was and all her various talents, he must have found he had fallen in love with a straitjacket." People like her father could tolerate such a situation because, ultimately, the only thing that mattered for them was writing music. "As long as nothing gets in the way of that, they'll put up with a lot of other things." A certain distance might be necessary if he were to speak his mind. Once in Los Angeles he could write teasingly that "Repairs Shopping," the name she had tentatively chosen for her new company, "stinks." He added, "I also do not like not having you here screaming curses in my ear, being generally disagreeable and refusing me the solace of your blonde whiteness . . ." Later, on the same trip, he wrote to say he was in bed by midnight and up again early to work on a manuscript. "Don't you think I have been good? I have been leading a very active but well-behaved life and I want a nice little blue star for not wetting my bed." Speaking to her on the phone was the most fun he'd had until he spoke to her again. "How do you like having a young attractive man so nuts about you? I should think you'd be flattered to death." She had been hearing certain (unnamed) rumors about him. "Damn these rumors!" he wrote. "If you believe anything you hear about me, I will kick the bejeesus out of you . . ." But some rumors had a way of persisting. Back in Los Angeles three years later, in the spring of 1937, he wrote, "Baby darling, when I mentioned Ginger last night on the phone, you said, 'Please be good.' I beg you, darling, don't think of things like that. We've gone over seven years without hurting each other and I love you more now than I ever did before. Let's put things like that out of our minds and remember what we have."

Chapter Eleven

"THE NIGHT BOAT TO ALBANIA"

B ETWEEN 1936 AND 1940, the team of Rodgers and Hart produced eight shows, three of which they wrote or co-authored in addition to providing the songs, and only one was not a resounding success. Even their triumphant days of the twenties had not surpassed this record in quality, such a profusion of wit, melody, and fecundity of imagination. They were established in the AA class of songwriters with the American Society of Composers, Authors and Publishers (ASCAP), along with Kern, Porter, and Ira Gershwin, as "smart" songwriters, i.e., those who had managed to please the multitudes while also satisfying more discriminating tastes. Their annual incomes from ASCAP (royalties due from dance bands and others for the privilege of playing their music) were about $20,000 apiece. In addition, they received six cents on every copy of their sheet music sold (by 1938, "Blue Moon" had sold 175,000 copies), between $50,000 and $60,000 for each film, which was divided fifty-fifty, and a combined royalty of 6 percent of the gross box-office receipts whenever they wrote, or collaborated on, the book for a musical. (They received a joint 5 percent for words and music alone.) Six percent could translate into a handsome sum: for example, a musical that brought in $24,000 on a traditionally slow week, Easter week, gave them $720 each. Added together, the royalties on shows, sheet music, records, radio, and concerts, plus the sales of musicals to Hollywood and foreign countries, provided individual incomes hovering around $100,000 a year.

They were subjects of newspaper and magazine profiles in *The New Yorker* and elsewhere. *Time* magazine wrote a cover story in 1938, erroneously claiming that the pair had written something like a thousand songs. Hart was not the first to have written sophisticated lyrics, nor was Rodgers the first to have fashioned melodies with a powerful emotional effect; but they were unusual, nevertheless, for the degree to which their words so perfectly matched the underlying feelings of gaiety, pathos, or humor implicit in the melodies: a Rodgers and Hart song had "the power of a single musical expression." In this five-year burst of creativity Rodgers and Hart demonstrated not only the extent to which their talents had merged seamlessly and with considerable expressive power, but the wisdom of their joint resolve not to repeat themselves. *Jumbo* had been a circus musical; *On Your Toes* took on classical ballet; and *Babes in Arms* was about the adolescent children of vaudevillians who put on a show of their own. *I'd Rather Be Right* was played against politics during the Roosevelt administration, and *I Married an Angel* was a fantasy about a man who literally gets his wish, with unpredictable results. *The Boys from Syracuse* recast Shakespeare's *Comedy of Errors. Too Many Girls* was set on a college campus; *Higher and Higher* was a farce about a maid who marries a millionaire; and *Pal Joey,* for the first time, took an antihero as its central character, in this case a nightclub entertainer.

In his spare moments Rodgers wrote a ballet, *Ghost Town,* and he and his partner produced the music for a couple of films, *Dancing Pirate* and *Fools for Scandal.* Both movies disappeared with inglorious haste. That ended Rodgers's attempts to master that medium for a number of years afterwards, leaving him free to vent his frustrations. "I hate Hollywood," he told the director Joshua Logan in 1945. He also told an interviewer that going to Hollywood was one of the most foolish things he ever did. "It was the five-year plague of the locusts. Back in New York it took me two years and all the money I had to get a show going . . ." He would never make that mistake again.

At this stage they were referring to themselves as musical dramatists. In their view, the advent of the radio and phonograph had made deep inroads into what was once the highly profitable sale of sheet music. This limited, if it did not end, the careers of composers who could write single ballads but had not attempted the greater intellectual challenge of fitting words and music into a plausible sequence. Even composers like Harry Warren, eight years Rodgers's senior, who wrote wonderful and memorable songs in the thirties and forties ("We're in the Money," "Shuffle Off to Buffalo," "You're Getting to Be a Habit with Me," "I Only Have Eyes for You," "There Will Never Be Another You," among many others), remained impenetrably anonymous; but that could be for another reason, because he had stayed in Hollywood. Enter the musical dramatist, who confines himself to Broadway and centers each song around a situation in the plot. Time and again, Rodgers and Hart had started full of hope, only to be defeated by the sordid commercial realities: "Most authors of musical-comedy books and most producers had a theory that any sentence implying the presence of the moon, the month of June, or a feeling of frustration was a sufficient cue for a boy and a girl to walk into a spotlight and sing about love," Margaret Case Harriman wrote. But as the years went on they were edging ever closer to their belief that a musical could be as coherent and ultimately satisfying as a well-crafted play.

They were also becoming shrewder. When they were asked by Paramount to produce one more song for Bing Crosby to sing in *Mississippi,* they did not hesitate and wrote the song in a day. That was the easy part. The hard part, given what they knew about Hollywood, was how to present it:

> "If we send the manuscript," Hart said, "somebody out there will play it and sing it the way we don't want it." Rodgers said, "If we send a record, they'll play it in some executive's office with the doors banging and the telephones ringing and nobody paying any attention."
>
> For a moment the two were baffled by the hellish intricacies of Hollywood art, but at length they brightened and sauntered over to the Paramount Studios on Broadway. With Rodgers at the piano and a radio singer to give the number . . . sales quality . . . they made a sound film and rushed it, special-delivery air mail, to Hollywood.

They knew that the Paramount producers would be forced to watch it in a projection room, free from distraction, and concentrate on their song. Needless to say, their ruse was successful and "It's Easy to Remember" remained a popular success long after the film from which it came was forgotten.

THE ULTIMATE CHALLENGE, in pursuit of their goal of a fully integrated musical, would be to write a book themselves. Since they had already come up with a plot outline for *On Your Toes,* they set to work with a will on a first draft; but writing proved to be more demanding than they thought, and the draft was "so heavy in its timing and so complicated in its plot structure that they decided to enlist the help of George Abbott," David Ewen wrote. Abbott, who would be called in so often when all seemed lost that he himself made jokes about it, had, as it transpired, not attempted a musical until he assisted John Murray Anderson with *Jumbo.* That same year he had triumphed again with *Three Men on a Horse,* and was happy to oblige. That turned out to be a pretty good idea. Abbott had soon untangled the story line, simplified the plot, quickened its pacing, and honed its jokes. He also brought into sharper focus their main intention, i.e., to introduce classical ballet into the modern musical at a time when, Brooks Atkinson wrote, "ballet on Broadway was a coterie art-form." How could two such disparate art forms (and Rodgers and Hart would always think of the musical in such terms) be fused in a way that enhanced the strengths of each? The authors thought they had a way, but to give the idea proper justice they needed a choreographer of rare talent. For once Doc Bender, whose role in Hart's life was so seldom constructive, had a good idea. He suggested George Balanchine, who had arrived in the United States in 1933 after a career in Europe with Diaghilev's Ballets Russes de Monte Carlo and its various offshoots to co-found the School of American Ballet. Bender introduced Balanchine to Hart, who was impressed, and so was Rodgers. Mr. Balanchine did not speak much English, but he "talked an awful lot of ballet," Rodgers remarked succinctly. Bender spent most of his time during the subsequent rehearsals hanging around with the male dancers. One evening, as Bender was kicking up his heels at the back of a line of Nubian slaves waiting to make their entrances, Hart improvised a merciless commentary to the tune of "There's a Small Hotel":

> Looking through the curtain you
> Can see six slaves and Bender.
> Bender's on the end-a—
> Lucky Bend-a.

Balanchine's primary role was to choreograph two ballets, the first, a parody of exotic Russian ballets like *Scheherazade* called *La Princesse Zenobia,* and the second, a ballet set to a modern jazz theme, *Slaughter on Tenth Avenue.* Ray Bolger, in the leading role, would be principal dancer, Tamara Geva would be principal ballerina; and the jazz ballet's plot would, not altogether successfully, tie into the story and form the evening's climax. *Slaughter* was to be Rodgers's first sustained piece of musical writing, and he brought to it all his gifts for theatrical color and nuance. The ballet's abrupt shifts of mood, its nervous rhythms, its brassy, reiterated themes, its atmosphere of menace, its sudden shrill climaxes, painted a portrait of Winchell's Broadway as vivid as Gershwin's of another city in *An American in Paris.* When *On Your Toes* was revived almost twenty years later Richard Watts Jr. wrote, "A sizable number of jazz ballets have passed this way since it first appeared, but it still is something of a classic in its field, and the music Mr. Rodgers wrote for it continues to seem one of the major achievements of his career."

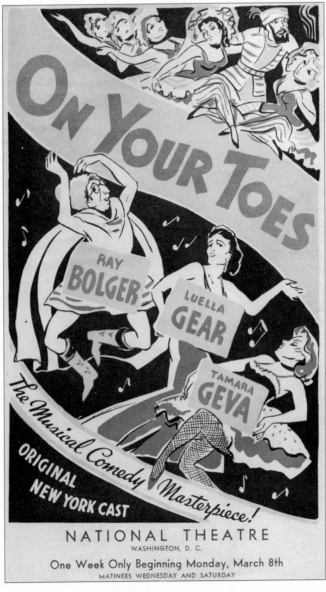

A billboard for *On Your Toes,* 1937

Although the songs did not completely fulfill Rodgers and Hart's ambitions for them, not being as wedded to the plot as they would have liked, the score was nevertheless fresh and enchanting, the second fine achievement in a matter of months. "There's a Small Hotel" was the most often played, but

Slaughter on Tenth Avenue, the balletic highlight of *On Your Toes,*
with Tamara Geva, George Church, and Ray Bolger

most of the tunes were popular, from the title song to the "sweetly forlorn"
"Glad to Be Unhappy" and Hart's satiric salute to upper-class folly, "Too
Good for the Average Man":

> Psychoanalysts are all the whirl.
> Rich men pay them all they can.
> Waking up to find that he's a girl
> Is too good for the average man.

Years later, after Lucius Beebe credited to Cole Porter the lines "Caviar for peasants is a joke / It's too good for the average man," Rodgers was moved to write a letter. "Both Cole and Larry Hart, who admired him greatly, would not have minded this error, nor do I who admire all three of you," he wrote, but the fact was that the lines had come from "Too Good for the Average Man." He ended with, "Kindest regards and caviar emptor."

On Your Toes opened at the Imperial Theatre in the spring of 1936 to huge acclaim, and ran until the following winter for a triumphant total of 315 performances. It went to London a year later; became a movie in 1939, starring Eddie Albert and Vera Zorina; and was frequently revived on Broadway. Along with *Jumbo's*, its success took Rodgers and Hart right back to their former positions of eminence, and with the exception of a single week, "there was no time between 1935 and 1938 when they did not have at least one smash success running on Broadway."

Encouraged by the success of their first book, Rodgers and Hart were determined to write another as soon as possible, this time without outside help. They got the idea for *Babes in Arms,* Rodgers said, when they were

Larry Hart, wearing hat, at far right, instructing the chorus
of a *Babes in Arms* rehearsal, 1937

George Balanchine with Lorenz Hart, 1936

strolling through Central Park and came upon a group of children who had invented their own games. That began a series of what-ifs. What if a group of adolescents, suddenly faced with the need to earn a living, were to put on a show of their own? It was a repetition of the genesis of *The Garrick Gaieties,* with even more youthful participants if possible. They took the idea to Dwight Deere Wiman, their producer, who liked its economical aspects: "I don't think the whole production cost him more than $55,000 and even with a top ticket price of $3.85, it turned a nice profit," Rodgers wrote.

The idea was to find the young talent, which turned out not to be difficult. Their principal actress, Mitzi Green, was only sixteen; and their principal actor, Ray Heatherton, then in his mid-twenties, was the oldest member of the cast. A number of others would become well known: Alfred Drake, the Nicholas brothers, Dan Dailey, and Robert Rounseville among them. Since the whole point of the show was spontaneity and improvisation, and elaborate scenery had been dispensed with, the funnier and cheaper, the better. In one of the musical's best-received numbers, "Johnny One Note," which unaccountably had an Egyptian setting, the cast appeared wearing towels, bath mats, and scrub mops. Such exuberant invention had an immediate appeal. The musical was gay and sprightly, youthful and captivating. So the critics wrote when *Babes in Arms* arrived at the Shubert Theatre in the spring of 1937. Furthermore, almost every song in it was a hit, including such melodies as "Where or When?," "The Lady Is a Tramp," "I Wish I Were in Love Again," and "My Funny Valentine." It was by far their best score to date, putting a triumphant flourish on their return to Broadway.

Alec Wilder devoted some space to the specific merits of the songs from *Babes in Arms*. There was "I Wish I Were in Love Again," which he thought a perfect marriage of words with melody, and music that was "strong enough to sustain itself as an instrumental piece." Then there was "The Lady Is a Tramp," a big favorite with jazz musicians: "And rightly so: for it swings," he wrote. As for "My Funny Valentine," he heard that nightclub singers loved the song so much "that the owner of a formerly famous East Side New York club inserted in all contracts with vocalists a clause which stated that they were forbidden to sing it." Its verse, "like an air for a shepherd's pipe," was published without piano accompaniment. "I've never seen this before, but it

Busby Berkeley directing Mickey Rooney and Judy Garland
in the film version of *Babes in Arms,* 1939

is exactly as it should be. Any accompaniment would vitiate the pastoral purity of the melody," Wilder wrote. He thought the song must have meant a great deal to both of them. "The lyrics show Hart's ability to keep his detachment and sympathy in perfect balance." The words, with their amused description of Valentine, one of the characters, who is nothing much to look at, remind one of the lyrics for "Bill," by P. G. Wodehouse and Oscar Hammerstein, which arrive at the same sort of conclusion. Ever so gradually, lovers in the mythical world of the musical were beginning to see their loved ones with some of the blinders removed (a trend that would reach its apogee with *Pal Joey*), lovers who expressed their feelings in original ways, as with "Where or When?," another ballad Wilder admired.

The musical ran for 289 performances, and there have been numerous revivals, including a revised version, written in the fifties, which placed the group in a summer theatre and updated the dialogue. But *Babes in Arms* would be best known for the film that followed it two years later (1939), starring Mickey Rooney and Judy Garland, although only "Where or When?" survived the usual Hollywood massacre. It also inspired an attempt by Harold Prince and Stephen Sondheim in 1981 to center a new musical around a youthful cast. They based their own showcase for young talent on a play by George S. Kaufman and Moss Hart, *Merrily We Roll Along*—disastrously, as it turned out. There is a further Sondheim parallel; Hart's lyrics for "I Wish I Were in Love Again," in which he celebrates the joys of being out of love, have an increasingly brittle and sarcastic edge. That tone of almost savage disillusion would find its echoes years later in Prince and Sondheim's lengthy examination of contemporary marriage in 1970, *Company.*

No sooner had *Babes in Arms* opened than they were already at work on a new musical, this one with a book by Kaufman and Hart. The co-authors, who between them had written three Gershwin shows and two Irving Berlin shows, thought "the time was ripe for them to collaborate on the most daring political satire of them all," Rodgers wrote, referring to such past social commentary as *Strike Up the Band,* an antiwar musical, and a presidential spoof, *Of Thee I Sing,* which won the Pulitzer Prize as best drama in 1932. "Their idea was nothing less than a musical-comedy lampoon about President Roosevelt himself," the first time a White House incumbent and his family had been so satirized. Kaufman and Hart asked Rodgers and Hart to write the music, and they were immediately enthusiastic. They were all, Rodgers continued, huge fans of FDR, but they thought they would poke some gentle fun at the spawning of agencies that had followed the New Deal, Roosevelt's blatant attempts to pack the Supreme Court, and other political derelictions.

George M. Cohan, impersonating Franklin D. Roosevelt
in *I'd Rather Be Right,* 1937

There was one small caveat: it meant working again with the detestable George M. Cohan, who had made their lives a misery during *The Phantom President.* How could they do it? Kaufman and Hart rushed in with soothing arguments. Cohan had been badly treated in Hollywood; well, that they could understand. He would be working with his closest friend and former partner, their producer, Sam H. Harris, who could be counted on to keep him in line. He had recently appeared in Eugene O'Neill's *Ah, Wilderness!* and been a perfect gentleman. They had to agree he was the only man for the part. So, on the theatrical principle credited to Lee Shubert, "Never have any-thing to do with that son of a bitch unless you need him," Rodgers and Hart allowed themselves to be overruled.

What everyone had chosen to overlook was that Cohan detested Roo-sevelt. Perhaps he thought the lampoon was going to be a rout, and he must have been deeply disappointed when the result was more benevolent than biting. He never did accept the uncomfortable fact that he was working with somebody else's songs: "His own school of melody was not theirs and he was inclined to think of them as upstarts in a game he had mastered when they were children . . ." In short, he carried long-term grudges, expressed in silences, shrugs, and acid asides. He made constant references to them as "Gilbert and Sullivan," which he did not mean to be flattering. When he brusquely asked for better work, his criticism hit a nerve. Moss Hart wrote, "Richard Rodgers can be talked out of any song—he is the most frightened composer of them all. One harsh look, and he completely believes his song is no good." This uncertainty may have had something to do with Kaufman, who had told Rodgers he was "deliberately setting out to prove that the book was more important than the songs," the effect of which was to make Rodgers believe, reasonably enough, that nothing he wrote for *I'd Rather Be Right* was going to be good enough. The result was a lukewarm score; his songs, "while filled with interesting, sophisticated phrases, never added up to memorable tunes." That would have been one more reason why Cohan dis-liked them.

One of the arguments centered around "Have You Met Miss Jones?," a song that, Moss Hart wrote, would have disappeared if he had not gone around singing it constantly. This was typical of Rodgers's understated style, having the sophistication and cachet of, for instance, Porter's "Miss Otis Regrets" of a few years earlier. This must have made it look peculiarly inap-propriate for the bombastic tone of *I'd Rather Be Right,* and Rodgers was as surprised as anyone when it stopped the show during a runthrough. He was led to utter one of his tart remarks about how their moment had come at last. "Now we can have an encore and maybe somebody will remember a couple of bars." The remark predictably infuriated Kaufman, who sent Moss Hart to remonstrate. Rodgers and Hart had a further grievance; it was customary for authors of a book to receive a larger percentage of the weekly gross than did the composer and lyricist (at 5 percent). But the 8 percent in this case was considerably above the usual 6 percent, and Rodgers filed that away in his unforgiving mental ledger. Then, to top it all off, Cohan decided to embellish one of the songs he sang at the Boston tryout, adding a few anti-Roosevelt

Producer Sam H. Harris, Lorenz Hart, Richard Rodgers, Moss Hart, George S.
Kaufman, and George M. Cohan, the creative team for *I'd Rather Be Right*

lyrics he had penned for the occasion. A full-scale battle was looming, and
only a last-minute retreat by Cohan saved the day.

Like others in the theatre world Rodgers was superstitious about the
chances for a new idea, and no doubt Hal Prince expressed his sentiments
when he observed that when a producer keeps encountering setbacks, "you
tell yourself you're running into bad luck, which translates as something is
wrong." Despite the tensions, *I'd Rather Be Right* was one of the exceptions to
this rule. This was partly due to the return of George M. Cohan in a Broadway musical; advance sales were excellent. And there was the further advantage that for the first month of its run, the show was competing against only
one other musical, *Babes in Arms.* It could hardly lose, and its opening night
has to go down in the annals of Rodgers's long career as one of the most
memorable. Of that evening at the Alvin Theatre on November 2, 1937,
Lucius Beebe wrote, "Probably no theatrical event has occasioned such civic
tumult since the Astor Place Riots . . . From the Battery to the Bronx . . .
New York seemed completely overwhelmed by the return of Mr. Cohan, and

popular rejoicing and Morris dancing in Longacre Square complemented the most insufferable crush, confusion and amiable uproar Fifty-second Street has ever known . . . All eyes and autograph books, the crowd, an hour before the announced curtain time, reached as far as Eighth Avenue on one side and overflowed in cascades of footless urchins into the bar of Ruby Foo's on the other." Everyone who was anyone in New York was there, wearing top hats, black ties, minks and tiaras. After the show there were just three places to go, the Stork, El Morocco, or the Kaufman-Rodgers party for the cast at the Carlyle; everyone who was anyone managed to appear at all three. Beebe concluded, "Everyone agreed that of all the Presidents since Harding, none had been so popular a chief executive as George M. Cohan and that no one since George Kessler had caused more wine to be uncorked in a single demented evening in Little Old New York." Despite less-than-ecstatic reviews, *I'd Rather Be Right* was well and truly launched and achieved 290 performances. Nevertheless, it convinced Rodgers never to try another political satire, and in later years he turned down one such idea by explaining that the music in these cases, he had found, was never more than an accompaniment for the book and lyrics.

LIKE MOST OF THE BOOKS for Rodgers and Hart musicals of the twenties and thirties, that of *I Married an Angel* is almost unreadable nowadays, and only some fairly terrestrial concerns can have persuaded them to revive it. One of the most compelling arguments must have been that they had already worked with Moss Hart on the film adaptation of the original play by János Vaszary. After M-G-M rejected it, Rodgers and Hart persuaded Wiman to acquire the musical-comedy rights. No doubt they felt it would be a shame to waste the work already done, and it would be a nice twist if they could sell it back to M-G-M which, as it turned out, they did. They cast the beautiful Vera Zorina to play the Angel, Dennis King as Count Willy Palaffi, whom she marries, Vivienne Segal in a cameo role as Countess Peggy Palaffi, Walter Slezak playing Harry Mischka Szigetti, sets by Jo Mielziner, choreography by Balanchine; and then Wiman engaged a talented young director named Joshua Logan. Clearly, Wiman thought the excellent work Rodgers and Hart had already done on the score would carry the plot, however featherweight. As for the composer and lyricist, they decided to go back to the original Hungarian play—the scene was set in Budapest—and write their own libretto. They were going to hand it to the audience: this fellow marries a real angel, take it or leave it. "The theme . . . was that it's possible for someone to be too good," Rodgers wrote. "Our angel nearly ruins her husband's life by

The wedding scene from *I Married an Angel:* Vera Zorina and Dennis King pledge
their troth with witnesses, from left, David Jones and Marie L. Quevli,
and Arthur Kent as Justice of the Peace.

her truthful but undiplomatic remarks. It is only when, under the expert
tutelage of Vivienne Segal, she becomes devilish instead of angelic that the
marriage is saved."

All went well for the writing of the first act at the Traymore in Atlantic
City. Then Rodgers had to return to New York, leaving Hart to write the second act. Almost Logan's first obligation as newly hired director was to go to
Atlantic City and get the second act out of Hart, dawdling as usual. Logan
described meeting Hart at the station and their developing friendship during
the week that followed. They spent hours looking for, and dining in, the best
restaurants. Hart was drinking heavily (a factor Logan was too diplomatic to
mention) and not in the least interested in writing. Instead they played interminable games of cards. One that Hart called "Cocksucker's Rummy" made
cheating acceptable, the more flamboyant the better, and Hart knew every
dirty trick. After one particularly diabolical maneuver Hart said, " 'Boy, if
only the principal could have seen that.'

" 'Who's the principal?'

" 'A certain five-foot-eight character back home with a sour-apple face.' It was the only reference he made to Richard Rodgers that week."

The days slipped by. Finally, the day they were to return to New York, Logan found Hart scribbling furiously on an oversized pad, "as fast as I've seen anyone write." The only problem was that what Hart finally thrust at him was incomprehensible. Logan said, "I spent my time just trying to keep [the papers] in some kind of order; it was difficult to tell what followed what, because . . . there wasn't one word on any one of them that could be read." While Rodgers stared at the pages, Hart stood beside him insisting that the material was wonderful; the show could be put on tomorrow. They began rehearsals without a second act, and after about a week, the three of them met in Hart's apartment to "thrash things out," Rodgers wrote. Logan was full of ideas, so between them they started a complete rewrite, with new dialogue and situations, even entirely new scenes. It took all night, but at the end of it "we finally had a script that worked."

That took care of the outlook for *I Married an Angel*, thanks to Joshua Logan, but the episode of the week in Atlantic City has some parallels with a similar story told by Budd Schulberg, whose mission as a young scriptwriter was to get F. Scott Fitzgerald working on a screenplay based on the Dartmouth Winter Carnival. After days and nights of alcoholic meanderings, Fitzgerald finally produced a script that was a parody of the work he had done at the height of his powers. At least Fitzgerald knew what he had lost. Hart honestly believed that the gibberish he had scribbled for pages and pages made sense.

BUDAPEST WAS THE RUNNING JOKE the afternoon Rodgers and Hart met Michel Mok of the *New York Post* at Dinty Moore's early in January 1938. They were there ostensibly to discuss their trip to Europe of a month or so before, but since *I Married an Angel* was to open for tryouts at the Shubert Theatre in New Haven in the spring the urge to slip in a reference must have been irresistible. So Hart kept trying to sell his Budapest joke and Rodgers kept interrupting. Mok faithfully recorded the resulting dialogue, which ran in part:

> HART: I didn't like Europe. They've got no women over there. When you look at the women in Europe, you realize what people mean when they talk about God's country. In Budapest—

RODGERS: This young Englishman asked me to explain our monetary system. I did. Then he asked me about the New York taxi drivers. "If you go a short distance," he said, "and your bill is fifty cents, do you give the chauffeur a ten per cent tip?"

HART: One night in Florence, it was raining like hell. Two o'clock in the morning. I dropped into a little night club called "Chez Moi," and who do you suppose was singing and dancing there?

RODGERS: Just a minute. I said to this ten-percenter: "Sure, if you want a broken arm." So, on New Year's Eve, whom should I meet—

HART: Jimmy Rogers!

REPORTER: Who's Jimmy Rogers?

HART: The guy who was singing and dancing in this bistro in Florence . . . He had three American women with him. One was a duchess, one a countess and one a baroness. They had ditched their noble Latin husbands and were dishing the dirt with Jimmy.

REPORTER: What did you do?

HART: What did we do? Got tight as hoot-owls, of course.

RODGERS: When you told that story to me there was some point to it. [To REPORTER:] Look here. He goes to Florence to revel in the beauties of the Renaissance. And where does he wind up? With Jimmy Rogers and three American hoopla ladies.

HART: The Renaissance closes at 3 o'clock.

The joke about Budapest was never told because, Rodgers explained, "what he says about Budapest can't be printed."

In short, they were still on joking terms. But the incident of the unwritten second act can hardly have escaped Rodgers's notice. Logan noted that when faced with Hart's hieroglyphics, Rodgers hardly flinched. Hart had always waited until the eleventh hour, but of late, midnight was striking and he still was not prepared. Gary Stevens recalled that there was a moment during *On Your Toes* when Hart assured Rodgers and Abbott that he had finished a song and only had to go and get the lyrics. Skipping out of the room, he ran downstairs to the men's room of the theatre, because he was stuck at the bridge of the song ("Looking through the window / You can see a distant steeple / Not a sign of people—") and, Stevens said, "he didn't know where he was going.

He didn't even rhyme it! He threw in, 'Who wants people?' A throwaway line just so he could run upstairs and say he was finished!"

Hart had always been a master at the act of disappearance; now he was actually leaving the city, going to Long Island and New Jersey, even Florida. The dancer Dania Krupska, who was married to the press agent Richard LaMarr, said that when Hart could not be found, one of her husband's jobs was to get on the train bound for New Haven and alight at intermediate stops where he knew there were Turkish baths, to see if Hart was in one of them, sleeping it off. Hart had always been in the habit of appearing after the theatre at Lindy's, Reuben's, and Dave's Blue Room, large delicatessen-restaurants that were packed and popular. Comedian Milton Berle recalled that Hart "came into Lindy's one night, wearing an overcoat but nothing underneath. 'He was drunk and had no recollection where he left his clothes,' Berle said." It was either no clothes—thinking himself at home one night, Hart took everything off and curled up on the floor of the men's room at Dave's Blue Room—or he would leave his overcoat somewhere and strike out in all weathers. Predictably, he was getting frequent colds, interspersed with bouts of pneumonia. He became so disheveled that friends started crossing the street to avoid him. His brother, Teddy, and sister-in-law, Dorothy Hart, persuaded him to check himself into Doctors' Hospital periodically, but, she said in *Thou Swell,* her book about Hart, too often he left prematurely and the drinking would begin again.

Photos of the time show Hart leaning over a table discussing the latest show with one of the cast, dark shadows under his eyes. Rodgers was well aware of his deterioration and worried about it. He still felt responsible for his increasingly irresponsible partner, as when Hart was the victim of a black-mail attempt, presumably for homosexuality. Rodgers tried "very hard" to persuade Hart to get psychiatric help. He told Dorothy Hart that Larry should be committed to a mental institution. She could never agree to that, but she did consult numerous psychiatrists and even arranged to have a ther-apist, acting anonymously, join them for dinner in the hope of getting an informal diagnosis. She also knew, as did Rodgers, that Hart was hopelessly prejudiced against the idea of getting help. Rodgers said, "He would be panic-stricken at the idea." Was Hart aware of the fact that he was, in a sense, destroying himself? an interviewer asked. "Yes I think he was, but this was compulsive," Rodgers replied. "He couldn't help it." During the tryouts for *Pal Joey* a year and a half later, Budd Schulberg, who was correcting proofs for his first book, *What Makes Sammy Run?,* was staying with John O'Hara, whose series of short stories formed the basis for the musical. "There were occasions when O'Hara and Schulberg had to take care of . . . Hart, who would disappear when he was drunk. Once they found Hart in an after-hours joint and took him back to the Warwick, but Hart refused to leave the cab and went into a fetal position. O'Hara and Schulberg picked up the diminutive lyricist by the arms and carried him into the hotel."

Joshua Logan caught Hart in a similar mood late one evening as they were going through the dress rehearsal for *I Married an Angel* in New Haven. They were about to rehearse "At the Roxy Music Hall" onstage when he heard a commotion at the back of the theatre. It was Hart staggering around, trying to light a cigar. He seemed otherwise quiet enough, so Audrey Christie began the song, with the words, "Now come with me, / And you won't believe a thing you see." Hart began shouting incoherently. Logan remembered:

" 'Hold the rehearsal. What is it, Larry?' [I said.]

"He kept screaming hoarsely, but I couldn't understand the words.

" 'Slow down, Larry. Say it a little slower.'

"Then he said very slowly and carefully, 'No now-singers in this show! No now-singers in this show! . . . Did you hear how she began my chorus? It's "Come with me" and she began "*Now* come with me"! *No now-singers!*' " The singer apologized and Hart, mollified, sat down onstage to keep an eye on the proceedings. In a few minutes he was fast asleep.

MICHEL MOK, the *New York Post* reporter, described Lorenz Hart as being "forty-two, very short, very broad-shouldered, black-haired, black-eyed and looks like nobody else." Richard Rodgers was "thirty-five, slim, of medium height, brown-haired and looks like anybody else." This was not the usual description. Most people found Rodgers, as Margaret Case Harriman did, "poised, immaculate and humorous." His hair was flawlessly parted; his hats were adjusted to the precisely right angle, and his suits were faultlessly tailored without being flamboyant; with Dorothy Rodgers in the background, he could be counted upon to be dressed for every occasion. But there was a certain enigmatic quality about him. Joshua Logan wrote that when his opinion was asked, Rodgers stepped into a private chamber in which "he commiserates with himself . . . After you ask him [a] question, his face is so wincing, so wrinkled, so acerbic, almost disapproving; he looks as if he has a bad case of indigestion. Then he says 'Great!' or 'Perfect!' or 'Go ahead!' But just before he makes that happy decision, he looks terrifying and unhappy . . . I don't think he means to show this. I don't think he even knows he does it but he does go through such a personal decision-making thing that it is actually painful." As the record executive Goddard Lieberson said, "He looks like he's at Rabbi Wise's funeral, even in his happiest moments."

That a look of stern disapproval might have been acquired in the upward fight to the rarefied heights of Broadway success occurred to a few of his friends who knew how arduous the battle had been. Alvin Cooperman, who began his career in the theatre by working for the Shuberts and met Rodgers and Hart when he was only sixteen, found Rodgers "very attractive as a man's man, with a lot of strength . . . He was a darling, sweet, wonderful person but, like the Shuberts, hard as nails, as that whole generation had to be." To some, Rodgers was intriguing; to others, "so cool, so calm, so deadly deadpan." The critic Eckert Goodman thought Rodgers showed another side of his personality to those who knew him well; "he holds in check, beneath an outward shell of debonair casualness and wisecracks, an inner sensitivity and emotionalism so strong that he hesitates to reveal them even to himself." Robert Russell Bennett echoed that sentiment: "He must be a man with a beautiful warmth somewhere deep down in his blood." That other side of himself was more likely to be revealed to a woman. His longtime assistant, Margot Hopkins, had seen his eyes fill with tears "when he hears a beautiful song beautifully sung," she said. Florence Henderson, whose first starring role was in a Rodgers and Hammerstein musical, said she understood why people might find him dour but that this was never her experience. "He was insecure at times. I remember when they were remaking the film *State Fair,* he was asked to write some new songs and he asked me to sing them. When I got to the studio his back was out of place and I think it was just nerves. He was so sweet and funny and very sensitive and his feelings were easily hurt."

For Ed Sherin, who worked with Rodgers in 1976 when he directed the musical *Rex,* Rodgers was "a very wily observer of rehearsals. He knew you didn't have to rectify everything that went wrong; that time was an ally, and that eventually . . . He had that kind of patience. He didn't give notes at the end of the day. He would give them to me any time he thought of something, which could be five times a day or once a week. How he thought a song should be sung. When the staging was not clear. The thing I liked about him was that he was a gentleman. He was always pleasant; he would smile when he came into rehearsal and sit there quietly. He was always focused on the work. You didn't have to fear his reaction; he didn't take up a lot of space, as some creative people do.

"I also think he was very seductive. He was so personable. And he had those eyes! Those eyes were slashing. They were inviting. They were seductive. And he had a smile that was seductive. That kind of went halfway across his face; you didn't quite know what he was thinking." Sherin added, "I can see in his younger days that he would have been quite a knockout. A lot of women fell down in front of him, I am sure . . . You see, I think it was the romantic in him that made his music. But that didn't come out of nothing. I think he perceived the romance in relationships."

ON THAT TRIP DOWN to Atlantic City to start writing *I Married an Angel,* Rodgers and Hart were more interested in talking about writing a new musical based on a Shakespeare play. The novelty appealed to them, but they also had in mind the fact that Hart's younger brother, Teddy, was making a name for himself as a comedian (having appeared in two of Abbott's farces, *Three Men on a Horse* and *Room Service*). The family likeness was strong, but Teddy Hart's resemblance to another gifted comedian, Jimmy Savo, was even more striking, so much so that he was continually being mistaken for him. Two funny men who could pass as twins was too good an opportunity to miss, and after some thought Rodgers and Hart agreed upon a musical that would take the greatest possible liberties with *The Comedy of Errors.* However, it would make use of Shakespeare's basic concept, i.e., having twin servants, Dromio of Ephesus and Dromio of Syracuse, who wait upon twin masters, Antipholus of Ephesus and Antipholus of Syracuse, giving endless possibilities for comic misidentifications. They proposed *The Boys from Syracuse* to Abbott, who was so enthusiastic that he immediately decided to produce as well as direct it. The agreement was that Abbott would help them write the script, but "he had it all finished before we could get started," Rodgers said. "The book was so sharp, witty, fast-moving and, in an odd way, so very much in keeping with the bawdy Shakespearean tradition that neither Larry nor I wanted to change a line." Abbott retained one line from the original play, spoken by the Abbess: "The venom clamors of a jealous woman poisons more deadly than a mad dog's tooth." To make sure no one missed the learned allusion, the line was followed by a sudden appearance from Jimmy Savo, bobbing out from the wings and proudly announcing, "Shakespeare!"

The tart wit and verve of the lyrics demonstrated that when sufficiently stimulated, Hart was still in command of his gifts. This, allied to the most delightful score Rodgers had written since *Babes in Arms,* made an irresistible combination: "Falling in Love with Love" and "This Can't Be Love" were songs that have remained popular, but there were others, like "What Can You Do With a Man?" and "Come with Me," that sound as fresh as the day they were written. There was also another clever little tune, "Sing for Your Supper," that went on to fame and glory:

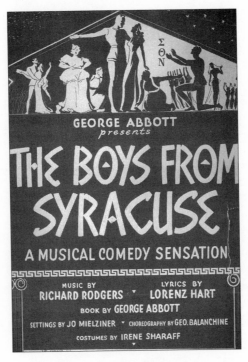

Window card for *The Boys from*
Syracuse, 1938

Sing for your supper,
And you'll get breakfast.
Songbirds always eat
If their song is sweet to hear.

Hugh Martin, a young composer and arranger, had cause to remember that song well. He said, "I wrote Mr. Rodgers a letter and probably sent it to ASCAP. I really believe in providence," because he happened to know a rehearsal pianist working in the musical, and his friend phoned and told him to come to the Alvin to meet Rodgers. Rodgers was willing to try him out. He was thinking of making the song into a trio for Marcy Westcott as Luciana, Muriel Angelus, playing Adriana, and Wynn Murray as Luce, and suggested Martin take it home and "fiddle around with it. He gave me the verse and two choruses with the piano part.

"I began to have ideas right away," Martin continued. "One girl had a deep chesty voice and two were really sopranos. Then it turned out that

Jimmy Savo as Dromio of Syracuse and Teddy Hart as
Dromio of Ephesus in *The Boys from Syracuse,* 1938

Wynn Murray couldn't read music, and when I showed her what I had done she burst into tears. 'I can't sing harmony,' she wailed. She threw herself on the sofa and I saw my golden opportunity going out of the window." He took her out for coffee with Westcott and Angelus and persuaded her she could do it. The resulting number was so successful in the show that Rodgers brought Martin back for their next show, *Too Many Girls,* to arrange "I'd Like to Recognize the Tune" as a quartet.

There was another song, "Dear Old Syracuse," introduced by Savo and Eddie Albert, playing Antipholus of Syracuse ("I wanna go back, go back / To dear old Syracuse"), that included the lines:

> And should a man philander
> The goose forgives the gander.
> When the search for love becomes a mania,
> You can take the night boat to Albania.

Marcy Westcott, Wynn Murray, and Muriel Angelus in "Sing for Your
Supper" from *The Boys from Syracuse*, 1938

Gary Stevens said: "There was a night boat to Albany that left Forty-second
Street at about eight in the evening and went up to Albany, 135 miles or so up
the Hudson, and returned next morning before eight a.m. It was a floating
motel. Lawyers, doctors, ad-agency men, Wall Street people had staterooms
on the boat and would take their models, girlfriends, mistresses, or whatever
you want to call them, on their one-night stands, and their wives thought
they were on a trip to Philadelphia. Larry Hart was the smartest of songwriters because he knew all about everything, and I was a miniature version of
that, knowing a little bit about everything. So when in the song 'Dear Old
Syracuse' he comes up with a 'mania' to 'take the night boat to Albania,'
everyone in the theatre laughed at the audacity of the rhyme but didn't get
the inner reference. But I knew what he was talking about."

Rumors about Rodgers's wandering eye began to circulate. John Jackson,
who later became a vice president at Radio City Music Hall, began as a
vaudevillian, and performed in the circus scene of *Jumbo*, cracking a whip
and taking a cigarette out of someone's mouth. Then Rodgers took a fancy to
a girl in *Jumbo* who also happened to be Jackson's girlfriend, and, another

friend said, was going out with her. "Rodgers never knew she was attached to this nothing, this sixty-dollars-a-week guy in the show, and they were sharing her. That's when she said, 'Look, I've got to be with Rodgers, because who knows? He may be able to help me.' " A similar story is told about the singer Earl Wrightson, whose girlfriend was in a Rodgers musical and being pursued by him. Wrightson knew about it, but Rodgers never did. The girl would call Wrightson from her hotel room and say, "He's just sent over some caviar and champagne. Come on up!" There were always pretty girls, very willing for obvious reasons to attract the attention of such a powerful figure; and as for that kind of philandering, Sherman Yellen, who wrote the book for *Rex,* joked, "if you are on the road it's not sex, it's recreational activity." Oscar Hammerstein's son, the late Jamie Hammerstein, was an assistant stage manager and began dating a girl "that I think [Rodgers] had his eye on." Jerry Whyte, Rodgers's longtime assistant and close friend, came to tell the stage manager, "You've got the boss's girl," and Hammerstein replied, "Tough on the boss." Hammerstein continued, "Infidelity is taken casually in a business like ours, where there are so many exceptionally interesting people of both sexes and you're working at a level where you know intimate things about people you are never going to see again after the six weeks are up."

Anna Crouse, wife of the playwright Russel Crouse, then Anna Erskine, met Rodgers when she was working for Joshua Logan, who directed *Higher and Higher* in 1940. She had "an outstanding memory" of how kindly she was treated by Rodgers from the beginning. "He was just charming, very attractive and attracted. For some reason we always got on well. Linda has her father's eyes, and when she starts to laugh, it begins in her eyes. That was Dick: this private amusement that you and he alone shared." She continued, "There was always one girl in the chorus. In *Higher and Higher* it was a dancer who had a small role. Dorothy Rodgers was reconciled, or tolerant, whatever it was, and very smartly included the girl in everything so that girl would have to be friends with both of them. He was certainly never going to leave Dorothy."

Rodgers dallied with chorus girls, but what he felt almost compelled to do was pursue leading ladies. In *The Boys from Syracuse* it was Marcy Westcott, a slim, pretty blonde, and he cast her in his next musical, *Too Many Girls.* This would be his special girl, for the duration of the run at least. Part of the pattern, which became habitual, might have to do, as Stevens suggested, with the struggle to make the show succeed. If he could win the girl, then his success became a hopeful omen: "Well, I did it again, didn't I?" Stevens explained: "To him it was like getting a great notice for a show." That was part of it, but much of it had to do with the role the girl played in bringing his fantasy to life. He had kept his wife at arm's length from his private world, the one she was so eager to enter. But he needed someone, some special girl who was bound up in its creation, someone in whom he could confide his fears, anxieties and fondest hopes. This pattern, familiar ad nauseam to most insiders, reminded Theodore Bikel, who knew Rodgers well, of a Broadway joke. It seems there was a director of musicals who was met at the gates of heaven by Saint Peter and told they had been waiting for him. His task in heaven was to put on a musical. He could have anyone he liked; Leonardo to paint the sets, Chaliapin to sing the leading role, Tchaikovsky or Verdi or Mozart to write the music . . . The director, quite overwhelmed, asked how soon he could start. "You can start at once," Saint Peter said. Then he added, "There is just one thing. God has this girlfriend . . ."

Chapter Twelve

"NOBODY'S HEART"

B Y 1 9 3 8, his sister-in-law Dorothy Hart wrote, whether Larry Hart was drinking any more than usual was hard to tell, but it was clear that it was having an effect on his health. He ate less and less and had frequent blackouts when he would forget whom he had just seen or what he was doing. Then, in the autumn of that year, during tryouts for *The Boys from Syracuse,* Hart took to his bed with pneumonia. Once he had recovered, he and his mother went to Florida, staying in his favorite hotel, the Roney Plaza in Miami, in an attempt to heal a persistent spot in one lung. As a result he missed the New York opening of the new musical and did not see it until a Saturday matinee some three weeks later.

His sister-in-law wondered whether he was losing interest in the theatre. During those rehearsals of *The Boys from Syracuse* that he did attend, he spent most of his time waiting for his chauffeur to bring him the racing results. She went with him to as many shows as before, but Hart was usually bored and left after the first act. His disappearances left more and more responsibility on his partner's shoulders, and Rodgers often found himself writing lyrics as well. In *Too Many Girls,* for instance, he had to make all the necessary changes and wrote the lyrics for the opening number, "Heroes in the Fall." The times when Hart was there and available were a godsend. Rodgers wrote that whenever a new line or a new verse was needed, it would take him no time to come up with one. "Once Abbott and I were deep in a conversation at a table and Larry was sitting with us. Our animated talk didn't bother him in the least; he just kept scribbling away and when he was finished he'd written the verse to 'Falling in Love with Love.'" Fortunately, *The Boys from Syra-*

cuse had not required any major changes once the company went up to New Haven. But, Rodgers wrote, "how much longer could our luck hold out?"

Their luck had certainly held for *The Boys from Syracuse.* The casting of Savo and Hart as twins was inspired; "Not only did the two diminutive comedians impart the same air of boyish innocence and pathos, but they looked so much alike they could almost have passed for twins," Bordman wrote of this "joyous romp," which ran for 235 performances. It closed in the summer of 1939, and by the autumn Rodgers and Hart had yet another hit running, produced by George Abbott: *Too Many Girls.* This relentlessly silly effort defied the laws of chance by having an even longer run (249 performances): Consuelo Casey (played by Marcy Westcott) is sent to Pottawatomie College in New Mexico by her millionaire father, who hires four bodyguards to watch over her, all former football players. Not knowing who they are, Consuelo falls in love with one of them (played by Richard Kollmar), causing the predictable complication before all ends happily. Van Johnson had a tiny song-and-dance role; Diosa Costello was another promising young talent and Eddie Bracken made his return, playing JoJo Jordan.

To the hackneyed theme of college and football Abbott added a Mexican twist, and hired Desi Arnaz, then beating the bongo drums in a club called La Conga in New York, to lead the dancing. According to Hart's biographer, Doc Bender was enamored of Arnaz—he became his agent—and so, Nolan wrote, was Hart. Whatever the truth of the claim, the musical interested Rodgers enough to write one memorable tune, "I Didn't Know What Time It Was," and several amusing, if unmemorable ones. One was "I Like to Recognize the Tune," in which Rodgers and Hart lamented the major distortions being perpetuated on songs by the swing bands of the period, or what Rodgers called "the musical equivalent of bad grammar." Another well-founded complaint had to do with the city of New York. "Manhattan" had celebrated its infinite charms; now Mary Jane Walsh, in the role of Eileen Ellers, was ready to "Give It Back to the Indians":

> Broadway's turning into Coney
> Champagne Charlie's drinking gin,
> Old New York is new and phoney—
> Give it back to the Indians.

In that connection Gary Stevens, then writing a column for a Broadway magazine and producing a radio show, happened to be acting as press agent for a group of Oklahoma Indians who were living in Greenwich Village. He thought up a stunt that brought sixty Indians, in full regalia, marching up the

Marcy Westcott, Richard Kollmar, Mary Jane Walsh, and Eddie Bracken singing
"I Like to Recognize the Tune" from *Too Many Girls,* 1939

Diosa Costello and Desi Arnaz in *Too Many Girls*

aisles between acts to present Manhattan to Mary Jane Walsh, along with numerous pieces of jewelry, drums, and similar trinkets. The audience roared and there were pictures in all the New York papers.

Too Many Girls was still running in the spring of 1940 when *Higher and Higher* opened for tryouts in New Haven and Boston. This improbable story about a maid from Iceland who is passed off as a debutante—a trained seal named Sharkey would play a prominent role in the proceedings—was written for the dancer Vera Zorina, but when she proved unavailable Rodgers and Hart cast the Hungarian singer Marta Eggert in the lead, a decision Rodgers would come to regret. Billie Worth Burr, who auditioned for the show, recalled singing a song by Jerome Kern called "In Other Words, Seventeen" wearing a silk blouse and patio trousers. "When I got through I heard Rodgers saying, 'Come back tomorrow and wear something short.' So I pulled up one of my trouser legs and said, 'The other one's just like it.'" She got the part. Marie Nash Walling, who had played a small role in *I'd Rather Be Right,* was hired as a ladies' maid for *Higher and Higher.* She was also given the role of Marta Eggert's understudy when the girl who had been picked was deemed to have "piano legs" and Rodgers and Hart said they would close the show unless she was fired.

The musical was hastily assembled and, given the circumstances, ran for a surprising number of performances—104—before collapsing in a quiet heap in August 1940. Perhaps because of its absurdist plot, Rodgers and Hart could never get the tone of the songs right. There was one called "Life, Liberty, and the Pursuit of You" that, Rodgers said during the Boston tryouts, was a failure. "Jack Haley [playing a bankrupt millionaire's servant] and Shirley Ross [a maid] shouldn't have sung it, it didn't tie up with the situation, and it never went well. The only excuse that I have to offer is that we had to write the show in a terrific hurry. So we did the song and it was unsatisfactory from the start. It's out of the show now and we have another one in that we hope is much better." His hopes for the show were already dim and collapsed completely after Eggert walked out in August. Marie Nash, who replaced her for the final weeks, said Eggert had done so because other members of the cast were constantly trying to upstage her. "She was a very big star on Broadway, a beautiful woman with an operatic voice. Those things happened in those days." She continued, "I can remember this seal coming up and putting his head on my lap, and I was supposed to be feeding him fish, and his breath was enough to knock you over." Rodgers concluded, "If a trained seal steals your show, you don't have a show." Despite the fact that the musical was deemed pedestrian and labored, in 1943 it was made into a film starring such

Vivienne Segal and the playwright John O'Hara discussing the
1951 revival of *Pal Joey*

unlikely figures as Michèle Morgan, Victor Borge, Mel Tormé, and Frank
Sinatra playing himself.

PAL JOEY, which opened at the end of 1940, took the team of Rodgers and
Hart to new heights. It was therefore ironic that the musical should almost be
their last great success (*By Jupiter* would run for over a year and 427 performances). Its genesis is curious enough; the novelist John O'Hara recalled that
he was trying to write a story but went on a drunken binge at the Pierre Hotel
instead. When he finally came to himself, full of remorse, the only person he
could think of who was more disreputable than he was was a nightclub master of ceremonies whom he knew. So he decided to tell the story of a fiction-
alized emcee, Joey, in terms of an ungrammatical letter to Joey's "Dear Pal
Ted," a bandleader. He sold the story of Joey's downward path to the *New
Yorker;* it was an immediate success and became the first of many. Finally,
O'Hara wrote to Rodgers and Hart, suggesting that his pal Joey series become
a musical. Rodgers said, "John and I had been more or less casual drinking

friends for a number of years but it never occurred to me that there was any point at which our professional careers might meet." The idea was a complete surprise, but within five minutes he and Hart were enthusiastically in favor.

As Gerald Bordman wrote, "Gigolos were not new to the musical stage. Until now they had been secondary figures, French comic characters, or coy mentionables in a Cole Porter lyric." To center a musical around a handsome, self-serving operator was perhaps the most daring of all ideas, and only a team with the stature of Rodgers and Hart could have attempted it. But Rodgers said he already knew he had the right kind of personable song-and-dance man in mind, whom he had seen as an aspiring entertainer in William Saroyan's play *The Time of Your Life*: Gene Kelly. As for the equally hard-boiled, rich married woman whom Joey seduces and who ends up opening a nightclub for him, there could only be one actress, Vivienne Segal. Hart remained perennially romantic about her and she had become a fixture in the ad hoc group of singers, dancers, and actors that surrounded them.

O'Hara, who wrote the libretto, used only two of his fourteen stories, "Bow Wow" and "A Bit of a Shock," serving to illustrate Joey's brisk exploitation of the married woman, Vera, which does not prevent him from romancing a young girl named Linda on the side. O'Hara's biographer Matthew J. Bruccoli wrote, "Comparison of an early script with the published script reveals that the plot toughened in revision. The working script hints at Joey's regeneration by Linda, suggesting that he may even end up driving a truck for her brother-in-law." In the final script, Vera has rejected him and Joey is in pursuit of a new "mouse."

What distinguishes the libretto from so many on which Rodgers and Hart had been willing to work was its literacy. From the opening lines O'Hara paints an unforgettable picture, spare and pointed, of a seedy world and a character so transparently boastful and naive one is almost ready to forgive him, except when he says unforgivable things:

VERA: I have a temper, Beauty, and I want to say a few things before I lose it.
JOEY: Lose it. It's all you got left to lose.

Vivienne Segal was ideally cast as the unsentimental Vera, and if anyone could reconcile the warring aspects of Joey's personality, that person was Kelly. The filmmaker Stanley Donen recalled, "I remember being impressed by Gene as soon as I saw him onstage. He had a cockiness, a confidence in himself, and a ruthlessness in the way he went about things that . . . I found

Gene Kelly, as Joey, in a dream ballet about the perfect nightclub, in *Pal Joey,* 1940

astonishing. I also found him to be egotistical and very rough." He added, "And, of course, wildly talented." Kelly's career as film actor, dancer, singer, and choreographer was about to begin in earnest, and most of the characters he would play were far sunnier and less complex. But Donen thought that Kelly never really lost the lingering aura of Joey; in contrast to Fred Astaire, Kelly would always seem "more common, venal, vulgar, selfish—in short, mortal."

Something about the mental toughness of the book itself, allied to the delightful raffishness of its setting, brought out the very best in Rodgers and Hart. "Here more than anywhere else in their career Rodgers and Hart's songs are a unique, curiously satisfying blend of Rodgers's warm lyricism and Hart's street urchin toughness," Bordman commented. The song in which Linda meets and falls in love with Joey, "I Could Write a Book," has a sweet wistfulness; and the song "Zip," which burlesques the famous stripper Gypsy Rose Lee, is an object lesson in amusing juxtapositions. Joey's triumphant little song, "What Do I Care For A Dame?," tells his listeners all they need to know about his ambition, and the song finally sung by Linda and Vera, "Take Him," has the authentic ring of revenge about it:

Gene Kelly and Vivienne Segal come to the parting of the ways in *Pal Joey,* 1940.

Take him, you don't have to pay for him.
Take him, he's free.
Take him, I won't make a play for him.
He's not for me.

But it was "Bewitched, Bothered, and Bewildered," sung by Vera as she realizes she is in love, that was destined to become famous, an almost perfect description of a sophisticated older woman who cannot believe she has fallen for such a worthless charmer. Geoffrey Block wrote, "Hart conveys the society matron's idée fixe by giving her thrice-repeated lyrics to conclude the first three lines of each A section . . . before delivering the 'hook' of the song's title, 'bewitched, bothered and bewildered,' to conclude each A section." Rodgers was still writing the music for the ballads first, but in the case of "situation numbers," as this one must have been called, Hart blocked out the lyrics first, and Rodgers came up with exactly the right melody to match. This, Block wrote, "presents an equally repetitive musical line, the note B ascending up a half-step to C." By turning the musical line upside-down in the B section, "Rodgers manages to maintain Vera's obsession, while providing [a] welcome musical contrast . . ." Disenchantment sets in, as it must, and when the song comes around again in the finale Hart has penned a succinct new set of words for Vera. Perhaps the ultimate commentary on "Bewitched, Bothered, and Bewildered" was written by William Bowers, a screenwriter who worked on the film version of *Higher and Higher:*

> I'm wild again, with child again,
> You might even say I'm defiled again,
> Betrayed, bothered and be-pregnant am I.

Hart's gift for finding just the right phrases for his well-educated heroine was matched by the language he crafted for the semiliterate Joey, who starts with a monotonous recital of the alphabet for his song "I Could Write a Book."

Rodgers and Hart were working with unusual concentration and finished the impossible task of writing fifteen songs in something like three weeks. That this could be done at this juncture spoke volumes about Hart's commitment to *Pal Joey,* a show that obviously stimulated him more than anything that he had worked on for years. He could be as wicked as he liked, and he would pen lyrics with double entendres and then call up Joshua Logan to read him the choicest bits, roaring with laughter, although some of the jokes were so obscure as to be impenetrable. For once, the tables had turned. Now they were ready for O'Hara, but was he ready for them? After weeks of silence, Rodgers sent him an imploring telegram: SPEAK TO ME JOHN SPEAK TO ME. O'Hara's refusal to act, the story goes, was the real inspiration for Hart's line "If they asked me, I could write a book." The author was not to be found once rehearsals began. O'Hara recalled that late one morning, Hart stormed into his apartment and dragged him out of bed to go to a rehearsal, no doubt full of righteous indignation.

George Abbott was producing, but his labyrinthine reasoning was always somewhat of a mystery to Rodgers, particularly during the making of *Pal Joey.* He began to throw up obscure objections. He was refusing to hire extra people, cutting money for sets, and suggesting that Rodgers and Hart reduce their usual percentages. For his part, Rodgers suggested that Abbott step down as producer, and that ended the matter. When he came to write his memoirs, Abbott made no mention of any possible misgivings he had about *Pal Joey.* Instead he talked about other people, namely the choreographer Robert Alton, who "thought the show was hopeless and wanted to quit."

Working on the score for *Pal Joey,* 1940: Lorenz Hart and
Richard Rodgers in characteristic poses, with Margot Hopkins
in the background

(Rodgers persuaded him to stay.) Far from skimping on sets, Abbott claimed, he authorized the designer, Jo Mielziner, to build an elaborate one for the end of act 1, in which Joey envisions the thrilling nightclub he will build from the money he intends to extract from his patroness. Abbott wrote, "It cost ten thousand dollars to build the set, a good deal of money in those days when a musical had a budget of one hundred thousand dollars, but I accepted the suggestion unhesitatingly."

Budd Schulberg and O'Hara soon teamed up with Larry Hart. "Let me buy you a stimulant," Larry would say every night, and off they would go on a round of bars. Gene Kelly soon made up a fourth. He knew all the bars, too, and had already met Hart in some of "the cheap saloons around Eighth Avenue and Forty-fifth Street." Kelly said that they got to know each other. "He'd come in and we'd be around the bar, and he'd tell stories, usually chomping on a cigar. He was a marvelous little fellow, and of course we all admired him . . ." Hart had found just the right audience in Kelly, not just a drinking companion who could turn up the next morning with a bright face—"I was a kid and I had all the energy in the world"—but who laughed at all his jokes and thought they should have been in *The New Yorker*. And everyone knew Kelly was the perfect Pal Joey; he looked the part, acted the part, sang the part, and "threw in a load of dancing for good measure," John Lardner wrote.

"Zip," which was introduced by Jean Casto, with its topical references to such men of the hour as Saroyan, Lippmann, and Salvador Dalí, brought down the house every time. Kelly rightly admired the way Casto sang it, and played some part in saving her life as well. One evening, as the actress was lighting a cigarette in her dressing room, the head of the match flew off and landed on her robe, which burst into flames. She began to scream and Kelly, along with another actor, hurtled through the door and landed on her full force, knocking her to the floor but snuffing out the flames. Although badly burned on her hands and an arm, Casto resumed her performance in time for opening night, December 25, 1940.

That evening, it transpired, was traumatic. As Rodgers explained it, "Approximately one half of the first-night audience applauded wildly while the other half sat there in . . . stunned silence." That night, nervously waiting for the reviews, John O'Hara threw up out of the window of a taxi. When the reviews did arrive, one of them, Brooks Atkinson's in the *Times*, asked, "Can you draw sweet water from a foul well?" Larry Hart, Kelly said, could not believe it. "I was standing right by him, he said, 'What, what?' He broke down, cried, sobbed, because he wanted Atkinson, for whatever reasons, to say this show was a milestone. He locked himself in his bedroom and wouldn't come out." Adding to Rodgers and Hart's misery was the fact that the songwriters' society, ASCAP, was involved in a fierce struggle with the radio networks and there was a blackout on Broadway music. Although *Pal Joey* would have a triumphant run of 374 performances, it was not until its even more successful revival of 1952 (542 performances), starring Harold Lang, that its music was widely heard and the musical recognized as a masterpiece. Even Atkinson changed his mind. In retrospect, *Pal Joey* "took the most nerve," Rodgers commented in 1963. "It was fool-hardy . . . Nothing but villains except the ingénue and she was stupid. I think it's the only one in show business to have had more success in revival."

ONE OF THE ESSENTIAL MEMBERS of the company of sixteen principals, twenty-five chorus girls and boys, the author, two songwriters, dance director and two assistants, scenic designer and assistant, orchestrator, orchestra leader, and producer was the stage manager, Jerome (Jerry) Whyte. A photograph of him, wearing dark glasses and a double-breasted suit, appeared in *PM's Weekly* in December 1940. Whyte, the caption said, had the reputation for being the best in the business, and his favorite exhortation was, "Shut up, girls, please!" He had worked for George Abbott and would become an indispensable member of the Rodgers inner circle for the rest of his life. He was, Rodgers's daughters thought, their father's closest friend. Linda Rodgers Emory said his name had originally been Jerry Jerkowitz and that he was "a rum runner from Canada" before turning to the theatre. Mary Rodgers Guettel said, "He was tall, blond, and a hunk. I don't mean good-looking. Big, husky, and all male. A gangster; a race tout." When he represented Rodgers and Hammerstein in London after World War II, he kept a very large suite at the Savoy, with people constantly coming and going; "the place had the smell of either horse shit or very fine leather, and I'm not sure there's a difference." She would arrive at his suite after rehearsals for her own musical *Once Upon a Mattress* "and he'd be playing poker with his cronies and the place was blue with cigar smoke and brandy. He was Daddy's procurer. He'd get him liquor; he'd get him girls; get him anything. He was wildly loyal to Daddy, and at one point I remember standing at the back of [the New York State Theatre at] Lincoln Center during one of the revivals when Daddy was producing and making some kind of sour crack about Daddy and he was terribly upset. He was wounded that I should say such a thing about this wonderful man. He worshiped him!"

Oscar Hammerstein's son Jamie remembered that while Whyte adored Rodgers, he was not above having a little fun at his expense once in a while. One time, during rehearsals for *Me and Juliet,* Rodgers kept asking for a certain lighting effect and Whyte finally "came down and said they had tried everything. What it would take was a certain light, he said, and he invented it, something like a 3,000-amp Kriegle, but that would have blown the theatre down. My father had to leave because he was laughing so hard, but Dick was nodding seriously and saying, 'Oh, okay.'"

Mary Rodgers Guettel went on to say that everything her parents did together was hierarchical and layered, to do with money and position, who had decorum, who knew the right way to do things, "and Jerry was down and dirty, so there was no class involved here at all. He was the only person for whom Daddy could emotionally take all his clothes off. And I'm sure he did. I can just imagine him saying of some actress, 'Well, she was a lousy fuck. Jerry, get me a better one next time.'"

Whyte had married a former showgirl whom he cared for tenderly, taking such complete charge of her life that he would not even let her write a check. This did not stop him from philandering. Duane Garrison Elliott, who was

Rodgers's secretary during the 1960s, said Whyte used to put his arm around her in the office and ask her what she was saving it for, the worms? Dania Krupska, who knew Whyte well, said he was the one who took the girls to Rodgers's room, using such a circuitous route in and out of hotels and through basement kitchens that it sometimes took an hour. They left the same way. All this was done because "it had to be a deep, dark secret." Sondheim called Whyte Rodgers's "minder"; and to Duane Elliott he was his bodyguard: "He carried a blackjack. He showed it to me once and I didn't know what it was." There were evident uses for this take-charge personality, this crass, unregenerate gambler and womanizer who was infinitely loyal and street smart. If Rodgers was ever bodily threatened or the victim of some sharp business practices, he never talked about it. But the sheer size of their success, the numbers of tickets being sold and the constant opportunities for box-office fraud must have been a cause of concern. Having someone like Whyte around would have been reassuring, if not essential. It seems providential that Whyte, who could have been a character straight out of O'Hara or Damon Runyon, should have arrived in Rodgers's life just at that moment.

IRONICALLY, RODGERS FOUND HIMSELF writing an article about his enduring relationship with Lorenz Hart—twenty-one years in 1940—at a moment when he knew he was going to have to leave it. In the summer of that year he wrote, "what has kept us together, and will probably continue to do so, is a mutual respect, a mutual responsibility and a mutual aim." There was no doubt about the mutual respect or the mutual aim; but as for the mutual sense of responsibility, that was a moot point. As far as Rodgers was concerned, his whole career was shackled to a man who had no such sense, either to others or to himself, and who seemed at his most self-destructive just as the partnership was at the pinnacle of its success. This Siamese-twin relationship, this indivisible team of Rodgersandhart, was going to have to be divided if Rodgers, who was still in his thirties, was to have a future. What he could not afford to do was let matters slide until Hart had ruined them both. *Pal Joey* was still running when George Abbott came to him with *Best Foot Forward,* again a musical with a college setting. This time Abbott, ever the realist, did not want Rodgersandhart writing the score. He wanted Rodgers as a co-producer and general overseer of the music and was ready to try his luck with the bright new composing team of Hugh Martin and Ralph Blane. Rodgers agreed, with one stipulation: since he was afraid that there would inevitably be gossip interpreting this as a rift, he insisted that his name not be used. That gave him something to do in 1941, the first year since 1935 that he and Larry had not had a new show on Broadway. Rodgers, at Hugh Martin's request, wrote the music for the song "The Guy Who Brought Me." Martin and Rodgers wrote the lyrics.

Rodgers was in Philadelphia for the pre-Broadway tryout of *Best Foot Forward* in the autumn of 1941 when he took Abbott into his confidence and asked him what he should do. Abbott was "even more pessimistic than I was." Rodgers was aware that Oscar Hammerstein was living nearby on a farm in Doylestown, Pennsylvania, so he invited himself to lunch. He wrote, "Dependable, realistic, sensitive Oscar Hammerstein was the right man, possibly the only man, who not only would be understanding about my problem but would make constructive suggestions." The truth was that Rodgers had been putting out feelers for a new collaborator for the past two years—he had approached Ira Gershwin, George's brother, in 1938 or 1939, without success—and had been talking to Hammerstein as early as late June of 1941, before the Abbott project. Edna Ferber was arranging a double contract for a Broadway musical and also a film of her colorful novel *Saratoga Trunk,* set in New Orleans and Saratoga in the 1880s, and sent a telegram to her old collaborator of *Show Boat* days to join Rodgers and Hart on the project. WE WOULD BE SO HAPPY IF YOU WERE WILLING TO DO THE BOOK. STOP. HOW DO YOU FEEL ABOUT IT? she wired. That same day, Rodgers wired him, LARRY AND I SIT WITH EVERYTHING CROSSED HOPING THAT YOU WILL DO SARATOGA TRUNK WITH US. It was the first step toward a collaboration with Hammerstein that could, if necessary, dispense with Hart, as perhaps Hammerstein was aware. However, he was trying at that moment to get a stage revival of *Show Boat* and not willing to take up the project. As early as a week later, on July 6, 1941, Rodgers was having second thoughts. He wrote to say that his old friend Edna had been "acting up," and, "I am trying to decide whether or not I can afford to let myself in for what appears to be endless aggravation." Shortly after that he, too, declined, and the project languished for some years before being made into a film and a musical, *Saratoga,* with music and lyrics by Harold Arlen and Johnny Mercer.

"Even if nothing comes of this difficult matter," Rodgers continued to Hammerstein, "it will at least have allowed us to approach each other professionally. Specifically, you feel that I should have a book with 'substance' to write to. Will you think seriously about doing such a book?" The answer was encouraging; and obviously relieved at the thought of Hammerstein in the background if the day came when Hart could not "function" (the word Rodgers used), Rodgers went ahead with yet another project with Hart. It

alcohol himself hardly counted. A real man could "hold his liquor"; getting drunk occasionally was being one of the boys, almost a proof of manhood, as long as it did not happen too often; such would have been his reasoning. Similarly, he would have shared the commonly accepted notion that homosexuality was also a moral failing, and he only had to look at Doc Bender and his disreputable coterie to have his beliefs confirmed. But the fact that he had weighed Hart and found him wanting would not have been lost on someone as sensitive to nuance as Hart, and the latter would have been inhuman not to take offense. All that being conceded, it is hard to imagine how any relationship could have continued, given Hart's severe addiction and emotional turmoil. Whatever satisfactions of friendship, common ideals, and the pursuit of a bright inner goal had bound them together for so long had vanished for Hart as well as for Rodgers. Each had reached the point where neither could stand the other. It would be the end of what Judith Crichton called "in their own curious way an extraordinary love affair." Years later Pat Suzuki, who played Linda Low in Rodgers and Hammerstein's *Flower Drum Song,* asked Rodgers what it had been like to work with Larry Hart. Rodgers replied, "There is a statute of limitations on gratitude."

THEN RODGERS AND HART were offered a new musical. Ever since the success of *The Garrick Gaieties* in 1925, someone from the Theatre Guild was always approaching them to do a musical, and Rodgers's response, paraphrased, was that the idea had to come first. "I never could think of anything." In the summer of 1940 the Westport Country Playhouse, which was owned by Lawrence Langner and his wife, and was not far from the summer home of Terry Helburn of the Theatre Guild, put on a revival of Lynn Riggs's play *Green Grow the Lilacs.* The Theatre Guild had produced the play ten years before (in the 1930–31 season), with a young Franchot Tone in the lead, when it had only a modest success. Riggs had made use of a chorus singing cowboy songs to bridge the scene changes, which suggested a more extended musical treatment. Elaine Anderson, later married to the novelist John Steinbeck, was working as a stage manager at the playhouse that summer. She said that Helburn came to see it "and was the first to say it would make a wonderful musical. So the two men who ran the summer theatre invited the Rodgerses over for a performance. I was present when Dick said, after the show that night, 'I think it would make a wonderful musical and I don't think it's Larry's cup of tea.'" According to her, Rodgers already had someone else in mind that night in 1940 but would not say who it was. Two or three

Ray Bolger showing his paces in *By Jupiter,* 1942

days later she asked whether anyone knew whom Rodgers meant, and the reply was, "Yes, Oscar."

That was the genesis of *Oklahoma!,* and the idea would have been in the back of Rodgers's mind when he visited Hammerstein in Doylestown a year later, that autumn of 1941. They might have discussed it then, although Rodgers does not mention it. What seems likely to have happened is that around the time that Hart went to stay in Doctors' Hospital early in 1942, and Rodgers managed to get him to write *By Jupiter,* Rodgers was sent the script of *Green Grow the Lilacs* and still found it enchanting. He said he "couldn't understand why it had not succeeded as a play. I gave it to my wife to read, and she loved it too." Rodgers also made the significant statement that Helburn and Langner "didn't know that I had stopped working with Larry," one whose pivotal importance has been missed in the usual explanations of the break between himself and Hart. He told his Columbia Oral History interviewer that by the time the script came to him he had already given Hart an ultimatum. After the success of the latest Doctors' Hospital stay, Rodgers had come to the obvious conclusion that the only way to get any work out of Hart would be to pin him down in a sanatorium. Without any alcohol on tap he could be counted upon to finish a score. Unless that happened, he did not intend to work with Hart. Not surprisingly, Hart did not jump at the idea. He was going to Mexico for a holiday instead. Rodgers said, "I knew that would be the end . . ." No doubt Hart did not like *Green Grow the Lilacs* much, either; but more important from Rodgers's point of view was Hart's refusal to act, as it would have seemed to him, in a responsible way. Rodgers often repeated that explanation, with variations. A few years after

The producer Dwight Deere Wiman and the writing team for
By Jupiter, 1942

the break he consistently said that he approached Hammerstein because Hart was "in no condition to work." *Oklahoma!* was on its way.

ONCE THE NEWS WAS OUT that Hart had separated from his longtime partner, there was no shortage of alternative offers. Paul Gallico came to Hart in late 1942 or early 1943 with a promising idea: to make a musical from *Miss Underground,* a novel about the Resistance movement in occupied France. Hart was intrigued. Doc Bender approached the Viennese composer Emmerich Kálmán, newly arrived from Europe, to write the music; Balanchine was to choreograph and Boris Aronson to do the sets. Hart and Kálmán worked rapidly and, it is believed, completed eighteen songs, although all but six have been lost: "Messieurs, Mesdames," "It Happened in the Dark," "Mother, Look, I'm an Acrobat," "The One Who Yells the Loudest Is the Captain," "Do I Love You?," and "You Crazy Little Things." They even discussed the cast, which was to include Vivienne Segal and Wilbur Evans. Kálmán was working in New York and, Dorothy Hart recalled, spent a lot of time wandering around Hart's large apartment "looking for a lyricist who did not want to be found."

Then, Dorothy Hart wrote, Alex Yokel, who had discovered *Three Men on a Horse,* came to Hart with a new musical idea, based on a book by Richard Shattuck, *The Snark Was a Boojum.* The title alone ought to have given him pause, but, nothing daunted, Hart went ahead with the project until, sensing a lessening of enthusiasm, he stopped work. Dorothy Hart wrote, "What followed was just like the scene in *Three Men* where the newly-wed Irwin is kidnapped by the three men who want him to continue picking the horses . . ." Yokel was trying remove Larry Hart bodily as he "lay on his bed in a helpless state." Brother Teddy intervened and there was "actually a tug of war," she wrote. "We realized then more than ever how dangerous it was to leave Larry in the hands of almost anyone who wanted to use him.'"

Hart had told his sister-in-law, "I don't want to work." She and others knew by then of the catastrophic effect of his mother's recent death upon him. Early one morning in April 1943, Frieda Hart, aged seventy-four, awakened in agonizing pain. While waiting for the ambulance to arrive, Larry Hart actually ran out of the apartment in a panic. An operation followed, but the outlook was hopeless. Hart, torn between tears and faked cheerfulness, sat chattering at her bedside. "It was frightening, because while he thought his laughter was reassuring, his sobbing was agonized, and Frieda wasn't fooled. 'Take care of my boys, Dorothy,' she whispered."

At his mother's funeral in April 1943, timed to begin at three in the afternoon, Hart could not be found. Friends went looking for him and he was finally discovered "in a deplorable condition," according to Mary Campbell, their cook and housekeeper for twenty years, in her deposition to Surrogate's Court. She said, "From what I saw of him . . . Lorenz Hart was not aware that he was attending his mother's funeral nor was he aware of what was going on about him. He was practically 'out.'" That evening Dorothy Hart tried to get him to bed without success and finally took him to the hospital in "an absolutely senseless condition." Those who knew him believed that with the death of his mother, Larry Hart relinquished his tenuous hold on life.

THE END OF HIS RELATIONSHIP with Hart was such a major event in Rodgers's life that it can hardly be overestimated, yet the clues to his state of mind are tantalizingly few. Even Dorothy Rodgers, who usually could be depended upon to offer insights into her husband's feelings, is silent on this question. His daughters, being seven and eleven at the time, were too young to have had any memories of their father's reactions. In retrospect they believed that he felt very little, if any, guilt and no sense of responsibility for Hart's subsequent collapse. Mary Rodgers Guettel said, "I don't believe he felt that at all. He was a one-track-minded person and all he cared about was writing music." Linda Rodgers Emory's view was: "I believe Hart was such an alcoholic it was clear that nobody was responsible, including my father."

Anna Crouse took a different view. She said, "Dick's loyalties were very strong. People who worked with him and for him were with him for years. He put up with Larry a lot longer than most people would have." Rodgers's comment that there had to be "a statute of limitations on gratitude" also points to a sense of loyalty and obligation, one further reinforced by the fact that he put up $100,000 of his own money to produce a revival of *A Connecticut Yankee* because he felt he owed it to Larry.

Hart had been so generous about the success of *Oklahoma!* On opening night he sat in a box roaring with laughter and shouting his approval. At the party afterwards in Sardi's, he came up as Rodgers walked through the door and said, "This is one of the greatest shows I've ever seen in my life, and it'll be playing twenty years from now." And Hart seemed so grateful and appreciative when he realized the lengths to which Rodgers had gone to get work for him, an effort that had been carefully tailored, by Rodgers and Herb Fields, to his present capacities. *A Connecticut Yankee* simply needed brushing off, updating, and the addition of perhaps half a dozen new songs. There was the additional incentive of writing new material for Vivienne Segal, who would play the formerly nonsinging role of Morgan Le Fay.

Dick and Dorothy had recently bought a house in Connecticut, and that summer of 1943 Larry was invited up there to work "regularly at reasonable hours," Rodgers wrote. "I don't think he took a drink the entire time. There was no question that he was making a genuine effort to rehabilitate himself and to prove that the team of Rodgers and Hart was still a going concern." Just how sober Hart was in that crucial period from May to October of 1943, and for how long, would become a matter of intense dispute later. But the fact was that during that period Hart did write new lyrics: "This Is My Night to Howl," "Here's Martin the Groom," "Ye Lunchtime Follies," "Can't You Do a Friend a Favor?," "You Always Love the Same Girl," and one of the wittiest songs he would ever write, "To Keep My Love Alive," for Vivienne Segal:

> I married many men,
> A ton of them,
> And yet I was untrue to none of them
> Because I bumped off ev'ry one of them
> To keep my love alive.

In that connection Hugh Martin recalled an amusing incident. "The song ends on a low note, and Vivienne complained jokingly, 'If I have to sing that low note eight nights a week, I'll develop balls.' Rodgers replied, 'If you do you'll be the only one in the show who has them." The new songs were sprightly, the topical references apt, the acting spirited, and "Vivienne Segal is a knockout in her streamlined sequin gowns and plumed headdresses. Her delivery of 'To Keep My Love Alive,' a song with the arsenic-and-old-lace style of . . . humor, had the audience arching its back and purring for more." Everything was going well, but as soon as his own work stopped, Hart began sliding away from them, and by late October, when the show opened in Philadelphia, Rodgers wrote, "Larry went on a drinking binge from which he never recovered." They were in Philadelphia for about three weeks, and, Rodgers said, he had to get Hart out of town twice. Once he sent for Hart's doctor and another time for his sister-in-law, Dorothy Hart, "because I was afraid he'd get killed. He'd step off a curve in front of a trolley car in those narrow streets, and it was a very cold, snowy fall month, and he'd leave his coat in restaurants and get soaked." The recklessness of his behavior at this period was frightening. The writer Max Wilk, an authority on the theatre, was working at a summer theatre in the period just after *Pal Joey*, and one afternoon Hart came to visit him, bringing the ever-present Doc Bender. The two of them had two bottles of Johnnie Walker Red and, without showing the least sign of being mentally affected, sat there and drank both bottles.

Vivienne Segal singing "To Keep My Love Alive" in the
1943 revival of *A Connecticut Yankee*

While Dorothy Hart was in Philadelphia with Hart, they happened to run into Oscar Hammerstein in a hotel lobby. Hammerstein, fresh from the triumph of *Oklahoma!*, was there for tryouts of his next show, *Carmen Jones*. Here was a man who until recently had had a decade of failure, striding through the hotel on top of the world; and there was Larry Hart, disheveled and shrunken, shuffling along beside her. The contrast was almost too much to bear.

THEN CAME OPENING NIGHT OF *A Connecticut Yankee* at the Martin Beck Theatre on November 17, 1943, an evening of high drama that was dealt with, after a fashion, in the M-G-M movie *Words and Music* (1948) purporting to describe the lives of Rodgers and Hart. The film began with their first meeting, skipped lightly past most of their early struggles, and arrived at the moment when Hart began to fade from the scene. As Bosley Crowther, in reviewing the film, described it, Hart, played by Mickey Rooney, went from "a bouncing, explosive little fellow who seems to drive everyone slightly nuts . . . into a grim, melancholic vein, for no other evident reason than he has been jilted by a girl . . . whose only objection seems to be that the gentleman is a runt." Rooney is given such lines as "Nothing seems to add up," and "Peggy [the girl who jilted him] isn't real anymore. She's a symbol of failure. I have done all right with my work but I have failed with everything else."

According to this version, as *A Connecticut Yankee* goes into rehearsal, Hart slips into a fatal decline. Since the nature of his ailment is never mentioned, the viewer is left to deduce that he must be dying of a broken heart. There is no reference to the break with Rodgers; and as for Hart's fondness for booze and boys, well . . . The voice-over narrative is given to Tom Drake playing a "solemn and soggily sentimental" Rodgers, as Crowther described him, who states mournfully that to do *A Connecticut Yankee* Hart had to "call on his last reserves." Hart is now hospitalized. It is the night of the New York opening. He is given a sleeping pill and is about to drop off, but then he remembers something. He must get up, but to do what? Ah, yes. It's opening night! He pulls a pair of pants over his striped pajama bottoms and struggles into a jacket. He is awake enough to dodge some nurses on his way out, but once he is down in the street the inner fog descends and he splashes, hatless and coatless, a small sodden figure, through the rainstorm. He arrives at the theatre and wanders in just as the curtain is rising. It's still light back there where he stands in the aisle, so that he can be seen weaving sadly as he listens to "My Heart Stood Still." Suddenly, he clutches his head. He is leaving the theatre, out into the rain. He is walking past the shoe store where, in happier days, he bought elevator heels in a naive, hopeful attempt to look tall enough for his only love. He suddenly falls flat on his face in front of the store. Death and curtain. This scene, Crowther wrote, was "among the most horribly inadequate and embarrassing things this reviewer has ever watched." Interspersed between some song-and-dance numbers "there oozes and gums the heavy treacle of a sluggish, maudlin plot." Or, as Richard Rodgers commented later, "They had a story written that at times impinged on the truth, but not very often."

On the night of November 17, 1943, far from being at death's door in a hospital room, Hart was alive and kicking and throwing back his usual dose of preperformance medicine. Accounts vary over exactly what happened that night, even where it happened—Dorothy Hart wrote that the musical opened not at the Martin Beck but at the Alvin, which was a CBS playhouse

Mickey Rooney as Lorenz Hart and Tom Drake as
Richard Rodgers in the 1948 film *Words and Music*

at the time. It seemed generally agreed that Hart, already far from sober, had
called at his brother's apartment that afternoon and handed out a dozen theatre tickets to be passed around to friends. Helen Ford said she and a young
couple had drinks with Hart at Delmonico's; "he was absolutely falling-down
drunk, and there was no food." They finally got him into a taxi. When they
got to the theatre, "there were no tickets for him at the box office. Imagine
the embarrassment! He was one of the writers, and he couldn't get in!

"I saw Dorothy Hart, and as I was talking to her about it, Larry disappeared. We went backstage to see if we could find him. He wasn't there, but
Dick was, and when we asked if he had seen him, he said, 'Is Larry *here?* Oh,
my God!' He had left orders for him not to be allowed in the theatre."

It seems strange that Hart would have a dozen tickets and that these had
not included a pair for himself. Or perhaps a pair was included, and in his
muddled state he had given them away, and by the time he reached the box
office they were sold out. Dorothy Hart's deposition in Surrogate Court sup-
ports Helen Ford's account that Larry Hart was not to be admitted. She said,
"It was Richard Rodgers who gave instructions to the door man not to let

Larry Hart into the theatre . . ." In fact she and her husband had stationed themselves outside the theatre to intercept Hart as he arrived and spare him an embarrassing scene. Billy Friedberg, a theatre publicist and cousin of Teddy's, was stationed in the middle of the block, Dorothy Hart was standing under the marquee, and yet another friend, Harry Irving, a writer, was in the crowd. All of them had missed him. Meanwhile, since she could not get a ticket, Helen Ford went home.

The audience began to arrive, along with several more friends of Larry's, asking Dorothy Hart for tickets which she did not have. A "grim-faced" Richard Rodgers was already inside. Suddenly Dorothy Hart saw Larry heading back toward the theatre, according to her, alone. He was intercepted by Friedberg and coaxed into a nearby bar. So far, so good, but then he returned. "He wasn't sober! I could tell by his walk." He checked his hat and coat—it was a chilly, rainy night—and noisily urged her to join him inside the theatre, but she made some excuse to stay in the lobby. "A moment later Dick was also in the foyer . . . He had seen Larry going in. Dick paced, and I stood rigid, staring straight ahead, apprehensive . . ." All went well for the first act. At the end of it Hart appeared and, shrugging off attempts to get him to put on a hat and coat, went back to the bar down the street. When he returned, the second act had already started. For a while he stood quietly at the back of the theatre. Then he began to pace up and down and started singing loudly. "There were annoyed murmurings of *shhhhh* from his immediate audience." The theatre manager moved in and asked Hart to leave, and when he refused, he was hustled out into the lobby. The manager helped Dorothy Hart get him into a taxi and she put him to bed on her couch. "When I looked in on him several times during this night, he was perspiring and breathing heavily, but by morning he had left the apartment without telling anyone."

The next day Hart had disappeared again. A cousin of Teddy Hart's, probably Friedberg, called the composer Fritz Loewe, Alan Jay Lerner's collaborator, to ask for help. Lerner wrote, "It was about three in the morning and raining heavily. Fritz went out looking for him. He found him sitting in the gutter outside a bar on Eighth Avenue, drunk and drenched to the skin. He put him in a cab and took him to the Hotel Delmonico's where Larry was staying at the time." On Friday afternoon, November 19, Hart was taken to Doctors' Hospital with a severe case of pneumonia. He was placed in an oxygen tent and sulfa drugs were administered as well as a blood transfusion. Dorothy Hart wrote, "I knew that Larry had had a bad reaction to sulfa the year before, but it wasn't until later, when I read the hospital records and the complete nurses' chart, that I learned that Larry's heart had stopped twice . . ." An appeal was made to Eleanor Roosevelt to release penicillin,

A late photograph of Lorenz Hart with his sister-in-law, Dorothy Hart

then in experimental use by the U.S. Army but not widely available, and the First Lady arranged to have it delivered to the hospital. But it was too late. By the evening of November 22 Hart was in a coma. Dick and Dorothy Rodgers sat silently in a corridor, along with his friends, waiting for news.

Suddenly there was a practice air-raid alert and all the hospital lights went out except for the emergency lights in Hart's room, where he lay inside an oxygen tent. Just as the all-clear siren sounded and the lights came back on, a doctor emerged from Hart's room. He was dead. Gary Stevens later spoke to the doctors who had treated Hart and was told there is a crisis at some point in the progression of pneumonia and that most people can fight it off. This did not happen in Hart's case because "he wanted to die." Mary Rodgers Guettel said that there was a great sadness around their house because Hart's death was such a waste and "everyone loved him. If only he'd loved himself as much."

Hart's funeral was attended by more than three hundred friends and associates, including the entire cast of *A Connecticut Yankee;* Teddy and Dorothy Hart; Richard and Dorothy Rodgers; William H. Kron, Hart's business manager; Dr. Mortimer Rodgers; Dr. William Rodgers; and Dr. Milton Bender. A burial took place in Mount Zion Cemetery, Maspeth, Queens, and the story, perhaps apocryphal, is that, as the mourners slowly left the burial plot, Dr. William Rodgers, standing beside Nanette Guilford, pointed to Bender and said, "There goes the murderer." Lorenz Hart was forty-eight years old.

RODGERS WAS RIGHT IN THINKING that M-G-M's motive in filming the life stories of Rodgers and Hart had more to do with getting access to their songs and dances than any interest in them personally. Rodgers went on to say he had no control over the script for *Words and Music* and never read it, but the claim seems disingenuous given that his brother-in-law Benjamin Feiner Jr., who had pursued a show-business career, is credited as having written an adaptation of the story. So how much of its bowdlerization could be explained by a lack of interest on M-G-M's part and how much to censorship from Rodgers and his wife is impossible to know at this stage. The fact that the musical glossed over the real story of Hart's life could be attributed to the censorship code, but what is harder to understand is why the writers deliberately ignored the ready-made drama of the breakup of the partnership. What is also puzzling is that the fact that Hart was thrown out of the theatre is not dramatized and that in his subsequent accounts of that night Rodgers never mentioned it, either. This could have been from a desire to spare the feelings of Hart's family, or out of a belief that he, Rodgers, was somehow responsible for Hart's death. In a sense, Hart was a suicide, as Dorothy's father had been. Now the same tragedy was eerily repeating itself.

Gary Stevens said he wanted to write a book about Hart and spoke to people involved in the night of November 17, 1943. "I had interviewed the doorman at the theatre and he corroborated what had been told to me: that Hart had been noisy, drunk and everything, and it was a rainy night, and Rodgers was adamant about getting him out of the theatre. The tone was, 'Get this drunken SOB out of here.'" Rumors were circulating on Broadway, Dania Krupska said, and "everybody felt [Rodgers] had been very cruel to Larry Hart," which she thought was unfair, given the circumstances. Stevens did about six months' research on the book and then took the idea to an agent. "I was told that Dick Rodgers would never allow me to do this book if I was going off on the premise . . . that Rodgers had Hart thrown out of the theatre. The word was, 'You'd better get yourself a passport or a visa to get out of the country.' So I gave up."

Chapter Thirteen

"MANY A NEW DAY"

D OROTHY HART had been seeing her doctor for a suspected ulcer and had a series of X-rays. This was all happening at the end of Lorenz Hart's life; she was surprised and delighted to discover that instead of an ulcer, she was pregnant. She found out the day her brother-in-law died. The new arrival was named for his uncle. With a baby on the way, Teddy and Dorothy Hart were therefore astonished and upset when they read the terms of the will Larry Hart had written that summer of 1943.

The Lorenz Hart legacy was complicated and paradoxical. There was no more devoted family man than he had been. Not only did he adore his mother, but he was fiercely protective of his brother, who, given his actor's unreliable income, was always in a precarious financial position. On the other hand, Lorenz Hart could not help being as recklessly generous to the world at large as he was to his impecunious family. Knowing this about himself, he had taken out a handsome life insurance policy, with his mother and brother as the main beneficiaries. After his death they jointly stood to inherit $100,000, a vast sum in those days. It was the life insurance, rather than a will, that Hart talked about constantly, and it was the life insurance that Dorothy and Teddy Hart confidently expected would provide them with a comfortable income once they became his heirs in November of 1943.

After Frieda Hart died that spring Hart had rewritten his will. He had previously revised the terms of his life insurance policy so that it would become payable in full to his brother once the latter reached the age of fifty, on September 25, 1947. That this was Hart's intent is clear enough from a letter written on his behalf to the New York Life Insurance Company in the winter of 1932. However, once the Harts presented the policy for payment they learned to their dismay that during the policy's revision, a clerical error had been made that had never been discovered. Instead of 1947, the policy contained a clause stating that it would be void if Teddy Hart was living on September 25, 1937. His brother had effectively been cut out of the insurance policy years before, and it was now going to the Lorenz Hart estate.

The issue was further complicated by the fact that Theodore Hart and his family were not the only ones to benefit from his brother's will. Hart had a money manager, William Kron, who had been recommended to him by Rodgers some eight years before to help him keep track of his income. Rodgers's version of events was that Kron had hit upon a novel way of protecting Larry from himself by opening checking accounts all over the city which his client did not know about, and then investing the income in bonds which went into a safe-deposit box in Hart's name. Kron seems to have become a good friend and, according to Rodgers, spent hours in Hart's company playing cards to keep him out of the bars. But if Hart had died a wealthy man, no trace of bonds in safety-deposit boxes could be found after his death. When he died, Hart left $4,000 in a checking account and debts of $15,000. He did have sources of income coming in; but technically, at his death he was bankrupt. His executors actually sold off his possessions, his family silver and first editions of rare books, to help pay his debts. Hart's nephew, Larry, said that after his mother's death, he found, among her effects, a cup that had belonged to his uncle with the auction ticket still on it.

Under the terms of the new will, written in the summer of 1943, Kron and his heirs would benefit from 30 percent of the residuary estate in perpetuity. So by having the life insurance policy absorbed into the estate, Teddy and Dorothy Hart not only lost control of a large investment, but 30 percent of that money went into a trust for someone else. They themselves benefited from the remaining 70 percent of Hart's estate, but not their unborn son. After their deaths the trust ended, and the income was to go to the Federation for the Support of Jewish Philanthropic Societies, a charity that, according to Hart's nephew, was not a particular favorite of his uncle's but was a great favorite of Kron's.

Not only were Dorothy and Teddy Hart the victims of an egregious error, but it seemed to them outrageous that this relative newcomer in their brother's life and his heirs should inherit in perpetuity, whereas Hart's only nephew should not. They promptly challenged not only the terms of the New York Life Insurance policy but the will itself. Teddy Hart filed an affidavit in Surrogate's Court at the end of 1943 claiming that his brother had been an alcoholic during the last three years of his life and therefore "did not know what he was doing and did not understand the nature of his acts."

Since insiders knew that Hart had been addicted for years, the argument was plausible, but not to Rodgers. Rodgers was co-executor of the will with Kron and had been given broad powers over their joint works, which in effect made him the dominant voice in the disposition of Hart's artistic legacy. Naturally enough, Rodgers was not anxious to see the will challenged. Far from being of unsound mind, Rodgers said, Hart's condition from May to October 1943, when he was working on a revised version of *A Connecticut Yankee,* was the best it had been for years. Rodgers testified "that during that period of six months Larry was not only competent but a little sharper than I'd ever seen him, that he knew exactly what he was doing . . ."

Exactly what Larry Hart's state of mind had been during the months from May to October of 1943 became the battleground for the challenge to the will that followed. If, as Rodgers said, Hart was exceptionally clear-minded during that period, there was nothing more to be said. If, however, as the Harts claimed, he was slightly worse, then their argument would have merit. Testimony from them, the faithful housekeeper Mary Campbell, Harry Irving, Milton Bender, and even the assistant maid and doorman all argued that Hart was in a hopeless drunken state for much of that time.

Mary Campbell said that he hardly knew what he was saying and next day could not remember what had happened. "During the entire month of May he was hopelessly drunk . . . morning, noon and night and with little sleep in between." That summer was a difficult one for Irving, usually ensconced at the Lambs Club, because he would either find Hart asleep in a nearby doorway, or curled up on his own bed, or across the road drunk in a bar. The only solution seemed to be another trip to Doctors' Hospital. Records show that between April and October, Hart was in Doctors' Hospital six times for acute alcoholism. In addition, he saw his doctor, Jacques R. Fischl of 870 Park Avenue, almost daily at some periods. According to Dorothy Hart and also Milton Bender, much of the lyrics for *A Connecticut Yankee* were written during Hart's periodic hospital stays. Bender said, "He was taken there while in a paralyzed condition . . . and after he sobered up he was induced to . . . work. Mrs. Theodore Hart was with him almost all of the time . . . Immediately after he did this work . . . he went back to drinking."

The battle over Hart's legacy continued until 1947. Teddy and Dorothy Hart succeeded in having the probate of his brother's will postponed for four years while they attempted to overturn the erroneous insurance clause. They lost their case in a lower court, and after taking it to the Court of Appeals, they lost there as well. They could have contested the will, but by then it was 1947 and they were tired. They accepted a settlement that awarded them $5,000 cash, $9,000 insurance, and the life income from the residuary estate.

A studio portrait of Oscar Hammerstein in the 1940s,
autographed to Mary Martin and her
husband, Richard Halliday

By then, thanks to the life insurance policy and royalties that had accrued since Hart's death, the estate was valued at $197,000.

Larry Hart said, "One problem for my father was having to say that his own brother was a drunk, which was a terrible thing to say in those days. And of course, copyright royalties were not that large. Originally they were about $12,000 to the beneficiaries but that sum has gone up monumentally since because Rodgers and Hart have grown so popular as the years went by." The present value of the trust, he said, is $8 million. As a result of Rodgers's decision to testify against the Harts there was considerable ill will between the two camps, Hart's nephew said, that took a long time to dissipate, although by the time of his mother's death in April 2000 the parties involved were back on good terms. Robert Kimball, a musical-theatre historian, believed that Rodgers's attitude towards Hart mellowed over the years. Kimball recalled that he had a teaching fellowship in American history at Yale when Rodgers came through town during tryouts of *No Strings* in 1962 and later when *Do I*

Hear a Waltz? was playing at the Shubert Theatre in New Haven in 1965. On both occasions Rodgers's references to Hart were dismissive, a typical response being, "Well I had first to find out which bar he was in." But when Rodgers's musical *Two by Two* came to New Haven in 1970, and he was invited to speak on campus, he happened to notice a poster advertising a revue of Rodgers and Hart songs. Rodgers was amazed that college students would want to hear those songs and, Kimball thought, nostalgic. Kimball said, "I could see he was surveying his career and beginning to look back. He seemed like someone who felt maybe he had been too harsh and too tough in his earlier years and was trying to do things a little differently."

Larry Hart recalled a curious incident which took place in 1955 or 1956, a year of crisis in Rodgers's life in which he had cancer followed by a breakdown. Hart and his mother happened to go into Sardi's just before or after the theatre. They ran into Rodgers unexpectedly. Seeing Dorothy Hart, Rodgers suddenly broke down in tears and collapsed in her arms. Hart did not remember what was said, but the gist of the meeting was how sorry Rodgers felt for all that had happened. To see someone so outwardly in control give way to his feelings was almost shocking. He said, "I'll never forget it as long as I live."

WHEN HE BEGAN HIS FAMOUS collaboration with Richard Rodgers, Oscar Hammerstein was at a low point in his career. An aristocrat of the theatre, he was born into a family of impresarios. He was named for his grandfather, whose Manhattan Opera House was briefly as important as the Metropolitan Opera. His uncle Arthur was a noted Broadway producer, and his father, "Willie" Hammerstein, managed a theatre, the Victoria. As has been noted, he attended Columbia and almost immediately began to make a name for himself as a librettist and lyricist; while Rodgers and Hart were still struggling, his uncle Arthur had produced what Oscar Hammerstein chose to call "a musical play," even in those early days. *Wildflower,* with music by Vincent Youmans, was his first successful collaboration with Otto Harbach, who became his mentor; it ran for 477 performances and went on to London. Hammerstein and Harbach followed that with an even more successful musical play, *Rose-Marie,* with music by Herbert Stothart and Rudolf Friml, which ran for 557 performances. *Rose-Marie* went to London, was twice made into a film, and has been repeatedly revived. All this was taking place before *The Garrick Gaieties* established Rodgers and Hart as a bright new team; when that show opened in 1925, Hammerstein was just twenty-nine years old. *The Desert Song* of 1926 was yet another success from the Hammerstein-

Oscar and Dorothy Hammerstein, shortly after a second marriage
for them both in 1929

Harbach team, with music by Sigmund Romberg and 471 performances; it
was made into a film as late as 1953. Towering over them all was the magnificent *Show Boat* of 1927, from the novel by Edna Ferber, with music by Jerome
Kern and lyrics by Hammerstein, which ran for 572 performances (1927–29),
has been made into films and revived down through the decades, one of the
great musicals of all time.

Hammerstein had a new success with *The New Moon* in 1928, for which
he co-authored the libretto and wrote the lyrics, with music by Sigmund
Romberg; it ran for 509 performances. From then on, his luck began to fail
him. *Sweet Adeline,* for which he wrote book and lyrics to the music of
Jerome Kern, had a respectable 234 performances in the 1929–30 season. The
team collaborated again for *Music in the Air* in 1932, that did even better with
342 performances. But *Rainbow* (1928) closed after 29 performances; *The
Gang's All Here* (1931) had 23 performances; *Free for All* had only 15; *East Wind*
had 23; *Three Sisters* (1934) had 45; *Very Warm for May* (1939) had 59 performances; and *Gentlemen Unafraid* (1938) did not even make it to Broadway.

There was a string of films, most of them forgettable. The year of his greatest success, *Oklahoma!*, 1943, Hammerstein paid for an announcement in the annual issue of *Variety*, in which most members of show business congratulate themselves on their successes. Instead Hammerstein listed five of his abject failures, with the comment, "I've done it before—and I can do it again!"

That was typical of Hammerstein. Stephen Sondheim wrote, "His own humor was dry and restrained, distanced. I suspect he preferred to chuckle because it was a moderate action, and I think of him as a moderate man." He is always described as a liberal and was known for musicals that had socially daring themes, e.g., *Show Boat*, which was about miscegenation. He was a true humanist in an age when communism and fascism were on the ascendant, and an early opponent of Nazism. Hammerstein was always concerned and committed but not always benign, something he himself acknowledged. Writing to Joshua Logan, Hammerstein said, "Magazine articles call me that 'nice, modest, unenvious Oscar Hammerstein.' When will they discover the scowl behind that benign mask?" The playwright Arthur Laurents said he was "as tough as nails," and others perceived the ruthlessness behind the charm. Mary Rodgers Guettel said, "He talked a good game but he didn't want intimacy." His children were occasionally subjected to his idea of a joke, which might be, she continued, to trip them up with a branch just as they were learning to ice-skate. His son Jamie was often subjected to what Sondheim called an irony that "lurched into sarcasm." Sondheim conceded that "Ockie" did not have much in the way of parenting skills. "He and my father shared something, I think, which is that they were not good parents until you were at a rational age, and the trouble with that is, by the time you are at a rational age a number of wounds have been inflicted and scars have formed."

By the time he and Rodgers began to collaborate, Hammerstein and his second wife, Dorothy, were living in Bucks County in a house surrounded by acres of undulating Pennsylvania countryside that they always called "the Farm." This became home to Sondheim and others like him whose lives had been broken up, either by divorce or war. They joined the large extended family of his children by his previous marriage, hers by her previous marriage, and their own son, Jamie. Their large-hearted acceptance of waifs, mostly adolescents, must have had something to do with a curious family history among the Hammersteins, of children bereaved at a young age. Hammerstein's father, Willie, had lost his mother when he was four. Oscar would lose his mother when he was fifteen and his father at the age of nineteen. Although he claimed not to have been scarred by the experience, some buried sense of unfairness must have made him a champion of children similarly afflicted.

Dorothy, his warmhearted, impulsive, artistically gifted Australian wife, had been a showgirl in the Coward–Bea Lillie circle, and turned to interior decorating to supplement the family income. Jamie Hammerstein said of Dorothy Rodgers, whose decorative talents became well known, "She was all taste and no flair whatsoever. I mean, it was just perfect. You didn't want to touch a thing. And my mother—you came in and went, Wow! Yellow! Red! There were splotches all over. It was gorgeous. And the taste was just the same, probably for half the money." Sondheim wrote, "I remember being overwhelmed by the extraordinary serenity of their house in Pennsylvania. The huge living room was dark and cool and chic, the atmosphere . . . unhurried . . ." Theirs was a vital, intimate, close-knit world, one that kept the frenzied uncertainties of Broadway at a comfortable remove. They were famous for disliking large social gatherings. "Ever heard of the Hammerstein shuffle?" Jamie Hammerstein asked. "My father would be going home as the last guests were arriving. But he'd go out backwards so that it would look as if he was coming in. That's the joke. This is not Dick and Dorothy." In his youth, Hammerstein had been ruggedly handsome rather than striking and always slightly at odds with the age; he never acquired that slick, clean-cut twenties look that Rodgers was born to exemplify. As he got older, he always looked like "a rumpled paper bag," Mary Rodgers Guettel said.

What Hammerstein did have was immense experience as a man of the theatre: as director, stage manager, producer, librettist, and lyricist. Jamie Hammerstein said, "I think my father was much easier to get along with than Rodgers. He was an artist too and he had an ego, too. My God! But he could control his ego easily, very much better than Dick. And he had a thicker skin in that way." He continued, "My father hated rules, but he said if there was one rule he had to follow it was that the first act had to be twice as long as the second, and the second had to have twice as much in it." For all of his experience and knowledge there remained something hesitant about him. Stevens said, "I met him once in Sardi's. He was a very fine man; he was almost like a human tree . . . The first thing he said to me was, 'Do you realize how difficult it was for me to follow behind Larry Hart? I was such a great admirer of Larry's that I never thought I could do it.'"

AS MARK STEYN OBSERVED IN *Broadway Babies Say Goodnight*, the Oklahoma envisioned by two New York sophisticates was an idealized, romanticized version of reality. "Let's be frank," he wrote, "the place is a nondescript urban sprawl in the middle of a dreary plain." Since their concept of life in the Oklahoma Territory just after the land rush of 1889 was no more realistic, say, than Rodgers and Hart's idea of the Venetian Lido (*Lido Lady*), or Budapest (*I Married an Angel*), or Peking in the days of the Son of Heaven (*Chee-Chee*), that should not have mattered much. But *Oklahoma!* held a promise, even in its embryonic stage, so foreign to Hart that he was right to distrust it; on the other hand, it was one in which Hammerstein saw the glimmerings of an American folk opera. In 1943 Oklahoma as a state was only thirty-six years old (it joined the Union in 1907), and so when people thought of it they thought of immigrants struggling to put down roots in a brand-new world, a struggle that, far from being in the distant past, was very much alive in people's memories.

Something about the very ordinariness of this love affair between Curly, a cowboy, and Laurey, a farm woman's niece, appealed to that side of Hammerstein that yearned to make an affirmative statement. And what better moment to make such a statement, a little more than a year after Pearl Harbor, when young Americans were being shipped abroad to fight the second world war of a generation? Musicals that succeed in as spectacular a way as did *Oklahoma!* are more than artistic successes alone. They speak to a human need which becomes insistent at such moments, i.e., the need to believe in a brighter future. One could argue that *Oklahoma!* was as perfect an expression

The "Kansas City" number for *Oklahoma!*

The poster for *Oklahoma!*, 1943

of its time, place, and mood as any piece of theatre yet invented. Hammerstein, that consummate man of the theatre, had sensed such a longing, and so had Rodgers.

The great period of Rodgers and Hammerstein brought with it a new wave of success for Rodgers personally. Even his best shows had contained songs that slipped into obscurity. *Pal Joey*, for instance, has several songs few remember, such as "Chicago," "The Flower Garden of My Heart," and "Plant You Now, Dig You Later." From *Oklahoma!* on, practically every song in the hit Rodgers and Hammerstein shows would become not just familiar but universally beloved, played over and over again until the words and melodies had become meshed, it seemed, with one's very existence. To have one's complete score memorized by a whole population would, it would seem for a composer, to have been given all that life has to offer. For Cecil Smith, this was easily explained: "The sunny homeliness of Hammerstein's book and lyrics . . . inspired in Rodgers an upwelling of friendly melodies whose inflections often suggested a folk feeling, even though they were not literally based upon folk idioms. Without quite knowing what had happened to him, perhaps, Rodgers took a long step away from Broadway toward a more universal and less insular type of light music," Smith wrote. In other words, Hammerstein and Rodgers were perfectly suited, in a way that Hart, with his astringent style, and Rodgers, with his lyricism, had not been.

Alec Wilder dissented: "Though he wrote great songs with Oscar Hammerstein II, it is my belief that his greatest melodic invention and pellucid freshness occurred during his years of collaboration with Lorenz Hart. The inventiveness has never ceased. Yet something bordering on musical complacency evidenced itself in his later career . . ." Something about Hart's high-wire act and the challenge he presented to Rodgers had imbued the music with an impish sparkle, a sophistication and nuance that faded from his work. Sondheim was not referring to the sweet-and-sour combination Sullivan and Gilbert exemplified, but he might have been, when he explained (speaking of his own collaboration with Leonard Bernstein on *West Side Story*) that music that wears its heart on its sleeve almost demands ironic understatement from its lyricist. The special quality, unique to Hart, that gave their songs such complex and rich shadings, such density and weight, was replaced by uncomplicated optimism that occasionally trembled on the edge of bathos.

In the volumes of commentary written about *Oklahoma!* much is made of the startling nature of the metamorphosis that Rodgers's music underwent. Ethan Mordden wrote, "Gone are the syncopation and altered chords he used with Hart . . . Now he sounds squared off, with a heavy-footed base and a lot of strings . . . Granted that *Oklahoma!*'s ethnicity begged of Rodgers a style he had not had to wield in his slick city shows with Hart, still the turnabout is astonishing." What seems common to the temperament of any great musical dramatist is a suffused sense of empathy. He or she is able to appreciate not just what a certain character is feeling but, at least temporarily, to become that character. To switch from the worldly-wise tone of *Pal Joey* to the celebration of Americana required for *Oklahoma!* took no great effort on Rodgers's part. That volatile strain, that high, nervous impressionability run-

Celeste Holm, singing "I Cain't Say No," in *Oklahoma!*

ning beneath the placid surface, might make for a very uncomfortable inner life, but it would provide him with a creative bonanza. And something about *Oklahoma!*'s qualities appealed to the idealist in Rodgers. He, like Hammerstein, was taken out of himself and into this sparkling, sunlit landscape of wish fulfillment.

SINCE HAMMERSTEIN not only wrote the book but wrote the lyrics first—a dramatic departure from the method Rodgers and Hart had followed—his influence on the play's evolution in musical terms was critical. Rodgers wrote that

> up in Connecticut, where I live with my paranoiac wife and my two schizophrenic little girls, I once sat under an oak tree with Oscar Hammerstein 2d. (He has to use the "2d" because he, too, is a split personality.) We spent the better part of a week end trying to devise an

"Laurey Makes Up Her Mind": the dream ballet from act 1 of *Oklahoma!*

opening curtain for *Oklahoma!* that would not do violence to Lynn
Riggs' *Green Grow the Lilacs* but which would instead express to the
audience the personality of the play.

I should like to itemize for you some of the decisions involved in
the discussion of this one song: not to have a chorus on-stage (phony);
utilize three-quarter time in short sixteen-bar verses and repeated
refrain (indigenous); have Aunt Eller on-stage churning butter to
emphasize rhythm (self-evident); let Curly enter singing but unac-
companied (intimate); better not seat audience during song (impressive).

So how would they open the show? "Well . . . we got out Lynn Riggs's
script . . . and in the stage direction . . . you will find many of the words and
certainly the entire theory of 'Oh, What a Beautiful Mornin'.' . . . A very
good example of not seeing something because it's too close to you. And it
turned out to be kind of explosive, because it was so simple and pure."

Oscar Hammerstein has been quoted as saying that if the opening num-

Richards Rodgers conducting the two thousandth performance
of *Oklahoma!* on Broadway

ber is right you can read an audience the telephone book for the next twenty
minutes and they will still love the show. He knew that this particular opening was crucial. Two years later, he said, "Why, I could kill *Oklahoma!* right
now by giving it a different beginning. Let's see . . . I'd have an opening chorus sung by a row of cowgirls in high boots, short skirts, bare knees and ten-
gallon hats. Aunt Eller would be a musical-comedy heavy woman making
wisecracks, and Ado Annie's comedy would be broader and noisier. No matter how much the audience laughed, I'd have killed *Oklahoma!* because the
rest of the story wouldn't go with that beginning . . . I'm generally fussy and
slow with the words of a song, but that one came to me in a hurry almost as
if I'd known it beforehand. And I wrote it inside of an hour at my farm in
Doylestown, looking at the corn in the fields."

Hammerstein always made careful notes about the local history, flora and
fauna, and would assemble an ad-hoc collection of colloquialisms, writing his
lyrics in the vernacular. He also wanted to follow the play's original outlines
as closely as possible and used sections of the same dialogue. He tied up some

loose ends and enlarged the comic subplot. *The New Yorker* subsequently commented, "the building up of such secondary characters as the Levantine peddler, firmly not the marrying kind, and Ado Annie Carnes, a sort of Topsie of the prairies, has been done so skillfully that it is hard to imagine how *Green Grow the Lilacs* got along with only offhand sketches of these lovely people." Just as Riggs had done, Hammerstein made studied use of the kinds of repetitions found in speech, although, Bordman observed, it would become an increasing trait and was not always appropriate. In this case, however, his lyrics had an "affecting simplicity." He had made a successful effort to match Hart's wit, particularly in such numbers as "Kansas City" and "I Cain't Say No," and the musical's general sprightliness went a long way toward mitigating Hammerstein's occasional descent into operetta prettiness, as in "Out of My Dreams." His description of the terrifyingly available Ado Annie is priceless:

> I'm jist a fool when lights are low.
> I cain't be prissy and quaint—
> I ain't the type thet c'n faint—
> How c'n I be whut I ain't?
> I cain't say no!

That Rodgers was writing the melody after the lyrics had the natural result of allowing him to tailor his effects much more precisely than had been possible before, and Hammerstein's lyrics had as electric an effect on him as his work had had on Hart. The soaring waltz for "Oh, What a Beautiful Mornin'" came in a flash; one would have to be made of cement not to respond to such a sentiment, he commented. As for the eternal problem of boy falling for girl, Curly and Laurey had only just met before the play began and could hardly launch into a love song. So Rodgers and Hammerstein hit on the idea of having them tell each other not to be attentive: "Don't throw bouquets at me," because otherwise "people will say we're in love." Rodgers wrote, "This follows an obvious technique of indirection, but the audience is responsive to it for apparently they have all been shy in their lovemaking at one time or another."

The melodies were all new, with the single exception of "The Surrey with the Fringe on Top," Hammerstein said. "He had the beginning of it, but not the middle. So I started with words for that much, and the rest of what I wrote made him think of the rest of the music." Rodgers's work had lost none of its lyricism and dramatic appropriateness, but his musical palette had changed. "When we began to prepare *Oklahoma!* I thought long and hard about the orchestra problem," Rodgers wrote. "In my past few shows I had yielded to the demands of fast, furious 'hoofing' on the stage and had filled the pit with saxophones and brass. Against this metallic battery were opposed four frustrated fiddles." He decided on the "outrageous" expedient of returning to the old-fashioned orchestra, cutting out the saxophones, reducing the brass to a minimum, enlarging the strings, removing the piano, and adding a harp. The average theatregoer would not know what happened, he wrote, but would know that something was different and would ask, "What is that lovely sound the orchestra makes?" Bordman wrote, "The melody of 'The Surrey with the Fringe on Top' unerringly captures the clippety-clop of a horse pulling the vehicle. Rodgers's long-sustained opening note of his title song coupled with the driving melody that follows was one of the freshest inventions of the sort since 'Who?' And the impeccable mating of words and music in 'People Will Say We're in Love' justifiably made it the most popular song of the year."

One idea Langner and Helburn had for the leading roles was to try to get Groucho Marx to play the peddler. Rodgers said, "And Oscar and I rose up, you know, and screamed. We thought this would ruin the show and it damn well would have. We . . . wanted fresh people, young people, people who hadn't been seen before." Alfred Drake had appeared in Babes in Arms as an adolescent; he became their Curly. Joan McCracken, a brilliant young dancer, played Sylvie, and Bambi Linn, another phenomenal dancer, was cast as Aggie. Howard Da Silva played Jud, the ranch hand by whom Laurey is both attracted and repelled. Dania Krupska, who took over the role of Ellen a couple of years after Oklahoma! opened, was even younger than they, being only sixteen when she auditioned for the first national company. "I had been a soloist at Radio City Music Hall, so I came in wearing a tutu and toe shoes. Agnes de Mille asked, 'Are you any good at pantomime?' so I did a scene from Johnny Belinda because I had played the leading role on the road. Agnes said, 'Very good; wait a minute.' All of a sudden this man came running down the aisle, and I didn't know who he was. It was Richard Rodgers." Rodgers offered her the part, so she borrowed a very grown-up hat from a Polish friend and went to negotiate her contract at Sardi's. She told Langner she would not accept anything less than $250 a week, which she thought sounded right for a soloist's pay. She said, "At that time there was a great divide between ballet and Broadway. Everyone looked down on it. You might only be paid $35 a week to dance with Balanchine, but it was so much more prestigious." She did not quite say she thought she was too good for Broadway. She got the money.

Joan Roberts was somewhat more diplomatic when Hammerstein, who knew her work—she had appeared in one of his ill-fated shows, *Sunny River*—asked her to audition for the role of Laurey Williams. Although she seemed everyone's choice, she kept being called back for auditions. Every time she went, there was a different actor playing Jud. Then there was a series of auditions for backers at Steinway Hall on West Fifty-seventh Street, with Rodgers and Margot Hopkins playing two pianos. Joan Roberts sang all the female vocals and Hammerstein sang "Pore Jud Is Daid" in a foghorn kind of voice. She desperately wanted the part but, being a devout Catholic, would not use the swear words she was shocked to find in Lynn Riggs's text. Rodgers tried to persuade her it was all in a day's work. Hammerstein said, "You don't have to worry about that, Joan." She said, "He was such a perfect gentleman. A living doll. If he had to make a criticism, he did it so gently. He made you feel good." Although she was not given a contract until the tryouts in Boston (she thought they held off on that to save money), she knew she was their choice. Every morning before rehearsals she went to mass to pray for the show's success. One day she was half an hour late. "They were all lined up, looking at me with fiery eyes. The director, Rouben Mamoulian, said, 'How dare you come in so late! Where were you?' and I said, 'I was at mass, praying for the success of the show.' Richard Rodgers said, 'Let her pray!'"

Elaine Anderson knew she had the perfect Ado Annie: Celeste Holm, an experienced young actress who was a friend of hers. However, no one knew whether she could sing. Holm's description of tripping as she walked onstage for her audition, falling flat, and breaking her belt is famous, as is the response from a voice in the auditorium: "That's pretty funny. Could you do it again?" It was, of course, Richard Rodgers. After trying, and failing, to impress them with a well-bred version of "Who Is Sylvia?" Holm was asked if she could sound like a farm girl, and obliged with a hog call that rolled through the St. James Theatre and up to the balcony. She was hired. Agnes De Mille said of her, "She was a comedienne in the French sense, playing a stupid girl with a knowing air about her, and she could suggest all sorts of wicked things without saying or doing anything off-color. She was the essence of provocation and fun."

The critics agreed that one of the outstanding aspects of *Oklahoma!* was its sophisticated use of ballet, an innovation Rodgers and Hart had pioneered with Balanchine in *On Your Toes*. De Mille had just created *Rodeo* for the Ballets Russes de Monte Carlo and had heard about the new musical. She got the job through "persistence," she said. "I caught Oscar Hammerstein in a drug store on Fifty-Seventh street one day and said, 'Let me do the show,' and he said, 'I'd like to but Dick Rodgers doesn't think you can do a musical, which is very different from a ballet . . . We are not sure you can work under that kind of pressure.' That was their theory, but they finally agreed to take me on. I got $1,500 for the entire job, no residuals." Not being paid what she was worth would be a constant complaint from De Mille, who eventually did get a raise and received one half of one percent. De Mille's main grudge was against Langner and Helburn of the Theatre Guild. "For my first year's Christmas present they sent me a bottle of bath salts."

The first three days of rehearsal were agonizing. "Dick Rodgers sat beside me right by the piano watching every move. The girls were so nervous they were almost sick and I explained to them that he was not watching them, he was watching me. At the end of the third day we had done the postcard section [in which a battery of naughty postcards in Jud's smokehouse come to life] when Dick Rodgers put his arms around me and said, 'Where have you been all my life, Aggie?' "

He was, she wrote, "moderately short and squarish, with a strong compact torso, the developed hands and forearms of a pianist, a strong short neck on which sets and turns a head almost archaic in its concentrated power. When considering . . . his piercing black eyes grow as opaque as an Aztec's, his face expressionless. The rest of us wait and hold heartbeat because the decision will be Star Chamber and final." They crossed swords almost at once over the issue of dancers. De Mille naturally wanted them classically trained and was particularly happy about the work of Joan McCracken and Bambi Linn. The latter soared effortlessly into space, thanks to phenomenal calf muscles that gave her speed and grace, but not beauty. Rodgers wanted girls with legs, and if they could dance as well, so much the better. De Mille had to threaten to leave in order to keep her two favorite dancers, who, of course, became stars. She took "two girls because Dick wanted them. They were pretty little starlets, chorus girls who didn't have a brain in their heads and couldn't dance. They used to sit clinging to each other . . ."

Next she tangled with Hammerstein over his concept of the dream ballet, the great scene that ends the first act. He had envisioned a circus with Laurey's aunt Eller riding around in a surrey with diamond wheels, Curly as ringmaster, and Laurey on a flying trapeze; "they were literally going through hoops." She objected that this had nothing to do with the first act, which was, she insisted to a startled author, "all about sex. Laurey wants Curly and Curly wants her, but she's scared to death Jud will kill him. She's been down in the smokehouse and seen his postcards and they have a lurid appeal for her." Having won the day on that issue, she set to work.

Joan Roberts thought that rehearsals were wonderful, "because everyone knew what they were doing. If there were any criticisms, I think it's that there were too many directors. I would have been very happy just to have had Mamoulian, Rodgers, and Hammerstein. But then I had Jay Blackton, who was the music director, Langner, and Helburn—six people saying do it this way or that. You couldn't ignore their direction. I do remember Mr. Mamoulian standing up and saying, 'There can only be one captain of this ship and I am the director,' and it stopped." She thought Mamoulian brought out the best in her, but such was not the case for De Mille. She and he were almost instantly at war. As De Mille saw it, "He was nervous about me and jealous of my work. When he saw it was new and fresh and had a good deal of vigor he was just frantic and did everything to block it." She was rehearsing in a separate room, and in the middle of a very technical passage she would be stopped by Mamoulian because he wanted the dancers onstage. A thwarted De Mille was likely to become hysterical, and on at least one occasion Marc Platt, the leading male dancer, had to drag her off screaming and hold her head under a cold-water faucet until she stopped. Calming De Mille was a role Hammerstein also assumed. He lent his large, comfortable chest and she would weep damp patches on his shirt. And she said later, "Rodgers saved me in that show. He rode herd on rehearsals and when Mamoulian just wouldn't leave me alone, he put a stop to it." She got to like Mamoulian later, "after we didn't have a show to wrangle over."

Another source of irritation for De Mille was the need to interrupt rehearsals because backers were coming. The Theatre Guild was banking on this musical to avert bankruptcy and looking for the fairly modest sum of $83,000; all it could provide was some seed money. The Guild had managed to interest M-G-M in the project, which took out an option (Rodgers and Hammerstein later bought them out). It paid $200 on signing to Rodgers and Hammerstein and agreed to a generous 8 percent of the weekly gross. Backers were almost nonexistent. Rodgers explained this was partly because of the war, partly because the team was unknown and no one knew whether Hammerstein could break his record of steady failure; and also because the subject matter seemed to strike everyone but them as a dismal idea. Their most famous audition took place at the home of Natalie Spencer, a friend of Helburn's, who owned a penthouse apartment just off Fifth Avenue large enough to contain a ballroom and had a great many rich friends. Rodgers wrote, "It was a lovely evening . . . the whole thing was full of entertainment and charm, and came the pitch, trying to get money for it—which was not done that evening, of course. Everybody was much too subtle to do that.

They were all approached later, and not one single penny came out of the evening . . ."

Howard Cullman, another experienced Broadway investor, turned them down and later hung Theresa Helburn's letter over his desk to remind himself of what he had missed. Helburn approached the playwright S. N. Behrman, many of whose works had been produced by the Theatre Guild and said, "Sam, you've got to take twenty thousand dollars of this because the Guild has done so much for you." Behrman thought he was being blackmailed, and Helburn admitted as much. She got her money, and he was eventually richer by $660,000. Max Gordon, head of Columbia Pictures, tried to get his board to provide the remaining financing without success, so he put up fifteen thousand dollars of his own money. Slowly, the necessary funds came together.

Finally the musical, then called *Away We Go!* was deemed ready for its New Haven tryout on March 11, 1943. That period was like "being in a cement mixer," De Mille said. "Opening night went on far too long and everyone went home in the middle." Mike Todd's famously wrong verdict was "No gals, no gags, no chance." Joan Roberts said, "Everyone thinks the show was not a success in New Haven, but that is not true. Because we had the Yale boys in the audience loving the show, and you know how difficult they can be. As a matter of fact, Howard Da Silva, who played Jud, got on the stage and they were hissing at him! It upset him very much. We had a wonderful notice in their magazine and raves everywhere. I remember when we did 'Many a New Day,' with Joan McCracken, and even in New Haven that stopped the show, because she was so adorable and feminine."

After the authors began cutting, the song "Boys and Girls Like You and Me" was cut, along with a three-minute dance sequence. What bothered the leading lady was Mamoulian's somewhat arbitrary decision not to let the dancers and singers acknowledge the applause, and the hardest part of the evening was the freeze they had to maintain while the clapping went on and on. This idea was finally abandoned. So was Mamoulian's ambitious notion to have a real cow onstage—it mooed all the way through "Oh, What a Beautiful Mornin' "—and real pigeons flying about. "We got a little man with pigeons and asked him whether the birds would come back if he released them. Of course he said they would. The first time they tried it, fortunately at a dress rehearsal, the pigeons flew up into the flies, and I don't think they ever did come down."

The show's lame title, *Away We Go!,* was obviously unsatisfactory, but no one could think of an alternative until Helburn casually remarked to Hammerstein that there should have been a song about the land itself. Hammerstein brooded on this thought and came up with the title song. Either he or Lawrence Langner added the exclamation point, and the musical was finally the way everyone wanted it to be. The tryout in Boston was so satisfying that Rodgers would invariably remark in future that he would not open a can of tomatoes without taking it to Boston.

Opening night at the St. James Theatre on March 31, 1943, was far from sold out. De Mille said, "I had had several Broadway shows, but I'd always been fired, so this was my first opening night." She bought six or eight tickets but could hardly give them away. As the first song, "Oh, What a Beautiful Mornin'," came to an end, "it produced a sigh from the entire house that I don't think I ever heard in the theatre. Just 'Aaaaaah!' Like people seeing their homeland. The Dream Ballet was a sensation, but after 'The Farmer and the Cowman' in act 2 the audience was screaming and yelling and I was making love to Dick Rodgers and somebody rapped me on the back and said, 'Look what's happening to the theatre!' And they were just whooping and hollering." As for Joan Roberts, she recalled that in act 2 she had to take a bow for the reprise of "People Will Say We're in Love," and then hurry offstage and get into her wedding dress for the final scene. "I left the stage and was half undressed but the applause wouldn't stop. So they made me get back into my costume, and as I ran back onstage I was holding my dress together at the back because I hadn't had time to do up the zipper."

Hammerstein, who faced the possibility of yet another failure, took a walk with his wife near their farm in Pennsylvania a few hours before they left for New York. He told her, "I don't know what to do if they don't like this, because this is the only kind of show I can write." Almost as soon as the musical began, he knew they had a success. "Not only could I see it and hear it, I could feel it. The glow was like the light from a thousand lanterns."

DESPITE THE CLAIMS made for it, *Oklahoma!*'s uniqueness did not altogether lie in the willingness of its creators to tackle serious themes; *Show Boat* had done so sixteen years before, and so had Gershwin's *Porgy and Bess*. Nor was the claim, so often made, that this was the first integrated musical particularly valid. Gilbert and Sullivan had led the way; the Princess Theatre shows had emphasized a logical meshing of song and story; and Hammerstein had made it his lifelong ambition and demonstrated his growing mastery of that goal with *Rose-Marie*. Similarly, the single-mindedness with which Rodgers and Hart had pursued a flawless blending of song and story had been demonstrated, with varying degrees of success, from *Peggy-Ann* and *Chee-Chee* to *Pal Joey. Oklahoma!*'s uniqueness stemmed from the extent to which song, dance, story, costumes, scenery, and lighting had coalesced into the kind of total theatre so often extolled in theory and so difficult to achieve in fact. As Mark Steyn wrote, "Rodgers and Hammerstein . . . fused the naturalism of the straight play, the musicality of operetta, the colour and imagery of musical comedy lyrics and the emotional sweep of dance. Not bad for one revolution."

This quintessentially American invention was, nevertheless, eminently exportable. Gemze de Lappe, a dancer who was hired for the first national touring company and then opened with the show in London in the spring of 1947, dancing the part of Laurey in the Dream Ballet, recalled her surprise at the extent of the musical's success there. (Until it was overtaken by *My Fair Lady* in 1962, *Oklahoma!*, at 1,380 performances, was the longest-running production in the Drury Lane's three-hundred-year history.) She said, "There was a trial run in Manchester for a week. We were in digs and you took a bath in cold water, there was food rationing, and they gave you a hot brick to put in your bed every night.

"Drury Lane still had a hole in the roof, there was no heat and the audience came with blankets and hot-water bottles. On stormy nights there was so much wind inside the auditorium that they needed four or six men just to hold down the big gold curtains." There was also fog. Elliott Martin, who played Fred, remembered there were times when the pea-soupers were so heavy that "we couldn't see the orchestra conductor, old Reggie Burston, down in the pit of the Drury Lane." Nothing dampened the audience's enthusiasm. Martin said, "London was incredibly exciting, because obviously the war had been such a strain on everyone that the British public just opened their arms and hearts to this fresh and exhilarating Rodgers and Hammerstein musical." Princesses Elizabeth and Margaret often came, the latter, it was said, twenty-seven times. Dania Krupska toured with the national company and found the same response. Her stay of a year and a half in Chicago was one of the most dazzling experiences of her life. "We were invited everywhere and sent flowers, taken to dinners, given parties, because we were with *Oklahoma!* We were treated like fairy princesses." And everyone knew the songs by heart. Celeste Holm recalled that Sam Goldwyn was one of them, as he earnestly told Richard Rodgers, "every word, every song, right from the moment when Curly sings, 'Oh, how I hate to get up in the morning.'"

For years after it closed, *Oklahoma!* held the record for the longest-running Broadway musical, at 2,248 performances. Three plays had longer runs: *Life with Father* (3,224), *Tobacco Road* (3,182), and *Abie's Irish Rose* (2,327). It saved the Theatre Guild from bankruptcy, earned a profit of

$4,245,500, and made Rodgers and Hammerstein rich. It won a special Pulitzer Prize citation in 1943, and its national company toured for a decade. It was the most spectacular collaboration that could be imagined, but it came with a sting. Rodgers recalled meeting Goldwyn after he had seen *Oklahoma!* for the first time. Goldwyn said to him, "This is great! You know what you ought to do next?" "What is that?" Rodgers asked, and Goldwyn replied, "Shoot yourself!"

IF RODGERS AND HAMMERSTEIN had achieved a new vitality in their work, a new unanimity of tone, the reason for that could be discerned in the discoveries each was making about the other. Jamie Hammerstein thought that in those early days, they excited and energized each other. "Here were two mature, successful artists, and what did they write? A young show. The only show I can think of which had close to that feeling was *Hair.* For its day, it was the *Hair.* The same ebullience onstage. Neither of them was young, but they were young together." Rodgers was not a visitor to Jamie's father's farm more than two or three times altogether; and Hammerstein may have visited Dick and Dorothy in Connecticut once or twice, that was all. "Dad would come to the farm for long weekends, and if he was writing, stay all week. Before that happened he and Dick would meet constantly. Then Dad would write an outline and Dick would be preparing things in his head for certain characters he was beginning to see, which is why he was a dramatist. The music wasn't just a pretty song." They had to work that way because "if you don't, the temptation is to write a wonderful song that is perfect for what you are doing, but what you are doing can change tomorrow, and by then you love the song so much that you can't bear to part with it, so you find some way to put the perfect song in imperfectly. It's a very confusing business, doing a musical." That underlined the wisdom of Sondheim's remark "Make sure you are all writing the same show." As the early experiences with *Oklahoma!* had shown, Rodgers and Hammerstein's minds worked together toward the same goal.

The advantages of working with Hammerstein were immediately evident. He was a disciplined, creative writer who made appointments and almost shocked Rodgers by keeping them. A man who talked thoughtfully about what he intended to do and then went away and did it. Instincts honed from a lifetime of working in the theatre meshed perfectly with those of his partner. For Rodgers, knowing whether a show would succeed or fail came down to a physical sensation at the back of the neck. Hammerstein, by contrast, proceeded with a methodical investigation of minute signals. While a show was being put together, Hammerstein would sit with his back to the audience, listening for those stirrings in the auditorium such as a shifting of feet, coughing, and a fluttering of programs that were the telltale signs of waning interest.

For Rodgers, the disadvantage of working with this meticulous personality was that, as his pupil Sondheim also did, Hammerstein tended to agonize. He was always sure there was a slightly better way, and Rodgers, who was used to Hart's ability to churn out a thousand alternatives at a minute's notice, was still waiting, as weeks went by, for that one perfect lyric. Dorothy Rodgers said, "During that time, Dick would be unable to do anything, but he couldn't stop thinking about it. And he had all of this going on in his head about who was going to sing it, the range of the voice, and what the mood of the music should be. He said really he was thinking about it, consciously or not, while he was shaving, while he was taking a shower or a walk, it would be there. People accused him of writing very quickly, and Oscar even said, 'I hand him a lyric and then get out of the way.' It wasn't quite true."

Although they enjoyed writing together, Jamie Hammerstein said they did not always enjoy putting on a show together. "I think Dad had an exercise in patience, in a way. Dick tended to express himself in absolute terms . . . Dad would come by sometimes and say, 'You've got to have a thick skin in this business,' and just walk on by. I felt about a quarter of the time it related to Dick. At the same time they could make each other laugh. Dick had a quick sense of humor, and would resort to terrible puns; that was his weakness. I know Rodgers revered Kern, and who was Kern's best collaborator but my father? The fact that they had known each other since college was another factor, as well as the kind of operetta and musical plays that came up. Rodgers realized he wanted to go in that direction. I think he was a genius to think of my father. It shows how smart Rodgers was, and artistically adventurous. He was a musical comedy writer, after all; he was *not* Sigmund Romberg! But he liked to break the form. I think this was something people do not give him credit for."

Oscar Hammerstein was delighted to discover that Rodgers actually liked going to an office, "because [Dad] never went into the office at all," Jamie continued. "I think they must have had a receptionist who would not recognize him when he walked in the door." Jamie Hammerstein recalled an incident that demonstrated Rodgers's theatrical acuity. Some Las Vegas producers had asked to do *South Pacific* in an abbreviated version, and he went to Rodgers to tell him what they were offering. "I said I thought I could cut it down to an hour and thirty-five minutes but I doubted whether I could get it down to an hour and thirty. I thought it would be well cast. I did not think it would be true to every value we know. I asked him what he thought. And all Rodgers did was make expressions, wincing, nodding his head one way and the other. Then he said, 'Okay.' In those moments of just watching, I thought, That's the theatre. That's when you say, this is my instinct here, this is my instinct there, and weigh them up. A businessman would be calling his accountant." Rodgers also kept a close eye on box-office receipts, from bitter experience. Besides, his wife said, he liked going to the theatre. "Dorothy and Oscar . . . would usually leave right after a show opened and take a long holiday. Whereas Dick never wanted to leave the show. He wanted to . . . look in on it a couple of times a week, at different times, to see if the timing was right and how it was going. Because the pace can speed up or slow down, and actors can be hammy, and stage managers can be careless about watching. Death scenes have been known to take an extra ten minutes or so without a word having been added."

For all of their complementary characteristics and common interests, there was a gulf between the two men that was never bridged. William Hammerstein, Oscar's firstborn, who also had a lifelong career in the theatre, recalled having lunch with Rodgers several times after he returned from the navy at the end of World War II. "I was never comfortable with him, and I mentioned this to Dad one day and he said, 'Nobody is. It's not you; it's Dick.' And he was right. He had great difficulty relating to people in a casual way. And was very easily offended by nothing at all. Both he and Dorothy were very sensitive about themselves and very insensitive about other people. I worked with Dick and we got along extremely well but we were never close friends. Nobody knew Dick, because he was a very difficult man to reach.

"Everybody admired him, certainly for his work, which was superb. And for his personality, oddly enough. He was a mean son of a bitch, but he was very kind. And amusing to be with. But he was not warm. He was not the kind of person you'd want to call up that evening and go out with. Yet I knew a fellow, Stanley . . . who was very close to both of them and used to see them all the time. He told me one night he and his wife were to meet them at the Four Seasons and got there on time, and Dick and Dorothy didn't show up. Finally Dick arrived alone and Stanley said, 'Where is Dorothy?' And Dick said, 'She's a pain in the ass, that's where she is.'"

Chapter Fourteen

"ALLEGRO"

Dick, Dorothy, and the children had moved out of New York. Soon after war in Europe began, and when it looked as if Britain would be invaded, the socialite Myrtle Farquharson, laird of a large Scottish estate bordering that of the Queen Mother, wrote to ask whether the Rodgers family would take in her daughter. They had all become close friends as a result of the Rodgerses' trips to London, and Dick and Dorothy warmly agreed to take care of Zoë d'Erlanger, then aged ten, and Zoë's nurse. But the addition of two more people meant they must either take a larger apartment or move into the country, since they could not afford both, and the latter course was decided upon for the time being. After the success of *Oklahoma!*, and once their financial future was secure, they kept the house for weekends and moved back to Manhattan during the week.

For the moment they were in Fairfield, Connecticut, where Dorothy found a white frame house on Black Rock Turnpike with a pillared front, twelve rooms, five baths, and a separate guest cottage that was big enough for everyone. There Linda, Mary, and Zoë went to the local schools, often dressed alike. After Myrtle Farquharson was killed in the London Blitz, Zoë's stay was indefinitely prolonged, and Mary Rodgers Guettel took to calling her "my English sister." There was a two-hundred-year-old oak tree in front; there were apple trees down by the gardener's cottage and a brook in the back garden. It was the ideal family house. A photograph taken shortly after Zoë arrived showed Dick and Dorothy on a garden settee with Linda between them, Zoë peering around from behind Dick, and Mary, also in the back, with her chin on her mother's shoulder: a close-knit family group.

Richard Rodgers and Dorothy Rodgers at Radio City
Music Hall for a stage tribute to Rodgers and Hart in 1941

Dorothy Rodgers had become not only an accomplished housekeeper but something of a businesswoman with a flair for invention. Repairs, Inc., which she closed down after they went to Fairfield, had been a success. Then she got the idea of a disposable mop for cleaning toilets, on which she took out a patent; she eventually sold it to Johnson & Johnson as the Jonny-Mop. There was a universal dress pattern that could be altered to fit and used again and again; she sold that to McCall's Patterns. She had an idea for a wristband refrigerant for keeping cool and another idea for a simple mechanical device that would allow refrigerator doors and freezers to be opened from the inside when pushed, after learning how many children died trapped inside them. It would have cost only an extra dollar per appliance, but she could not find a manufacturer willing to buy the patent. She thought of combining soap with detergent to eliminate the ring around the bathtub, but made the mistake of suggesting it to someone in the business, who appropriated it. Then she got the idea of a book-toy designed to teach children to read. She was always coming up with inventions, some of them quite ingenious, of the practical household variety, and sometimes they sold.

Mary, Dorothy, Linda, and Richard Rodgers with Zoë d'Erlanger
in the grounds of the house on Black Rock Turnpike

She was, of course, helping with war work. She took courses in first aid
and map reading, worked as a member of the Writers' War Board (heading a
committee to collect dramatic material for men in the armed forces), and
became involved in the Red Cross Blood Program. (She later worked with a
private group to help improve conditions in public schools.) Deciding that
she did not know enough about cooking, she went to the Culinary School of
New York, and then the Cordon Bleu Cooking School, headed by Dione
Lucas, and became an expert at "quite elaborate dishes and all kinds of
sauces," she wrote. Mary Rodgers Guettel said, "They never could keep any
maids in the country. They had this wonderful dog called Patience who was a
big poodle and had been trained elsewhere. She adored my mother but didn't
like maids because some maid had dropped a tray on her. So a new chamber-
maid would appear every Thursday and be frightened by the dog on Friday
and leave on Monday. That's how my mother learned to become a brilliant
gourmet cook, because she got tired of eating her own tuna fish casserole."
Her niece Judy Crichton remarked, "There was a point at which Dorothy,
like many women who find themselves in similar situations, in which they

Linda and Mary Rodgers, with Zoë d'Erlanger

are basically battling for their souls, for their own personae, began to make an independent life for herself."

The war brought other changes. Dick's father and mother liked the Traymore Hotel in Atlantic City and would stay there for lengthy periods of time. They had been there for about a month in September 1940 when Rodgers got a phone call from his father to say that his mother was very sick. When Rodgers told him that he and Dorothy would take the next train to Atlantic City, his father told him not to hurry. In short, his mother was already dead, from a stroke. Although Mamie Rodgers had had breast cancer, she had survived it, and her death came unexpectedly. Whatever her shortcomings, the world's tiniest mother had been a constant source of emotional support and comfort, and her loss was a real blow. His father's delayed grieving—after appearing unaffected, he burst into tears in a taxi a month later—seemed curiously like his son Richard's pattern. Dick and Dorothy were with him when it happened and knew what he must be feeling, but neither of them said a word.

Rodgers tried to get a commission in the air force and passed the physical, but, he explained, "because of a sudden crackdown on civilian commissions,

I was never able to get one." He believed himself to be disappointed and filled with guilt, and perhaps he was. Writing to Joshua Logan in 1945, he said he had been congratulated by a friend for failing to serve, leaving him free to write *Oklahoma!* instead. "All of this has been gratifying and I would be a blind fool not to recognize it. It's also fatuous to suppose that a piece of shrapnel in the back of the neck is the only answer to the question, 'What did you do in World War II?' " And, since most of the profits from *Oklahoma!* had been eaten up by taxes, he did not feel embarrassed on that score. Just the same, it was hard to "sit comfortably on one's plush behind while other men are wallowing in mud." His daughter Linda Rodgers Emory commented, "My knee-jerk reaction at the thought of him in the air force is to giggle, since he was terrified of flying. In 1953 he took the train all the way to California from New York because he wouldn't fly." So, whether he knew it or not, Rodgers must have been secretly relieved at some level not to have been in the air force.

He had equally mixed feelings about the success of *Oklahoma!* As his wife remarked insightfully, *Oklahoma!* had set a terrible precedent. "So people would say to Dick things like, 'You'll never write anything as good as that.' Well, that was a terror he had deep inside. I mean, every writer thinks he'll never be able to do anything as good as his best work." However he tried to hide it, that was the probable cause of much more inner angst than his failure to serve in the war had been.

After *Oklahoma!* and *A Connecticut Yankee* had been launched, Dick and Oscar filled in the time writing songs for a musical remake of a 1933 film, *State Fair,* starring Charles Winninger, Dana Andrews, Jeanne Crain, Dick Haymes, and Vivian Blaine. True to form, they refused to go to Hollywood and wrote the songs in Fairfield and Doylestown, respectively. As a screenplay *State Fair* was barely acceptable, but it had another superb group of songs, every one of which became popular: "Our State Fair," "It Might as Well Be Spring," "That's for Me," "It's a Grand Night for Singing," "Isn't It Kinda Fun?" and "All I Owe Ioway."

Kitty Carlisle, the actress and singer who married Moss Hart, agreed that the pressures of success were as intolerable, in their way, as those of failure, "because it was not only their reputation but their livelihoods that were at stake." In her husband's case she thinks those pressures "ate him up inside" and contributed to his early death. She never thought Rodgers showed these pressures, at least socially. "He was always imperturbable, charming and full of goodwill." They went to parties where Dick was invariably at the piano and people drank elaborate cocktails and smoked incessantly. Conversation

Dana Andrews and Jeanne Crain in *State Fair,* 1945

was an art. "People sharpened their epigrams ahead of time, and I can remember Mossy talking to himself in the mirror before a party, orchestrating the conversation for the dinner." After Moss Hart did *I'd Rather Be Right* with Rodgers and Hart, he and Dick began to see a great deal of each other. One time, much later, Dorothy came to stay with the Harts in Bucks County because Dick was on the road. "The first morning she came down to breakfast she said, 'Darling, I have to tell you, there's a kind of pillow they have at Hammacher Schlemmer or someplace, it is the best pillow in the world. You must get it for your guest room.' Then she took a taste of the food and said, 'Darling, it's very good. But you just have to know . . .' I was a nervous wreck!" Nevertheless, they became good friends. "I loved her. I thought that she was interesting, intelligent, and fun. And she was absolutely ravishingly beautiful. She looked like a movie star. She had that classical profile and she wore her hair pulled back in a bun. An extraordinarily good body. And she always wore clothes well. She was very chic. And her houses were beautiful and comfortable. We went to stay with them often.

"As for Dick, he was so gifted, one admired him so. Very good-looking. I thought he was sexy. You see, he had such vitality, such energy, ideas and enthusiasm, and for me that is sexy."

They were all fanatical croquet players, a game that had long been popular in society and show-business circles, its enthusiasts including Averell Harriman, Vincent Astor, and Alexander Woollcott as well as Moss Hart and Dick and Dorothy Rodgers. Kitty Carlisle Hart said, "Dorothy was the only woman allowed to play croquet with the men, she and Mrs. Vincent Astor. They only used me if they couldn't find a fourth. It was a grown-up game with an English mallet and the very, very, narrow iron wicket. You could get right up in front of it and be sure you were going to get through it, and you still couldn't. The games were fierce and taken very seriously; in California people built lawns just for croquet. I stayed with the Zanucks and she was a passionate player. One day they got so mixed up on the score they practically hit each other over the head with their mallets. They were going to kill each other." Mary Rodgers Guettel said, "It was the real English game involving two and a half hours of strategy, and they trained me to play. When I was my father's partner, if I missed a shot, he'd say, 'Oh, shit.' And if I missed a shot with my mother, even though she was behind me and I couldn't see her, I knew just what she was doing. She was clapping her hand over her mouth with dismay and then saying, 'That's all right.' But I knew it wasn't." Her mother's passion for precision made her excel at everything she did, whether she was sending flowers, writing notes of appreciation, remembering birthdays, or throwing herself into philanthropic activities. "She was a woman of great principle, but she did not want unacceptable emotions."

One evening when they were dining with Dick and Dorothy, Kitty Carlisle Hart said, Dick excused himself early because he was going back to the theatre to check on the show. Afterwards she reproached her husband. "Why don't you do that?" she asked him, and he replied, "Do you want me to go for the same reason?" Mary Rodgers Guettel said that despite her mother's professed pride in not being jealous of other women in her father's life, "I think her jealousy showed up in the fact that she was constantly sick from the age of about forty on, but even before that. She became addicted to a drug. When she got pregnant with Linda and was threatening to miscarry her doctor at Lenox Hill Hospital kept her in bed, and for whatever reason she was on Demerol. She knew, she told me later; she was really quite frightened even then of being addicted to it; it was a very strong narcotic. I think that from that point on, in some convoluted fashion, her brain managed to persuade her body at quite frequent intervals, and more and more as she got older and the chorus girls got younger, to have all sorts of illnesses, some more threat-

Playing the eternal game of croquet

ening than others, that would require Demerol. It started with intestinal obstructions that went on for the rest of her life. She was addicted to laxatives as well, as that generation was, and she had very bad headaches, especially after her father died. She was something of a hypochondriac, but she actually had these things." Asked whether she thought her parents had an intimate relationship, she replied, "It's hard for me to imagine that they did, but children never think their parents do. All I know is she was incredibly fastidious . . . I remember her saying once, 'Women are constructed dirty. With men, everything's on the outside, but with women you have to be terribly careful, and you have to use douches and things,' and she was very reliant upon them. She managed to make us both feel sex was a tricky proposition."

Tricky, perhaps, and also fraught with tangled emotions. This most fastidious of women had had two difficult pregnancies, at least one miscarriage, and a child born dead. At the end of the day she still had not provided her husband with the son he wanted. To be somewhat afraid of intercourse was almost routine in an age when contraception was unreliable and abortion illegal. Whatever dramas were played out in the privacy of their bedroom, she would not be the first woman to take refuge in chronic ill health, and he not the last man to maintain his wife and his affairs in separate compartments. If, in the company of his closest friend, Rodgers surveyed the latest crop and cynically made arrangements for his next rendezvous, his daily penance was to assure his wife that he loved her. Meantime, Dorothy Rodgers "never, ever, acknowledged that Dick 'fooled around,' " Judy Crichton said. She told her children that everything about lovemaking was wonderful, had storms of tears when she declared she was not loved enough, and had frequent stomachaches and headaches. If either of them knew what they really felt, they hid it. Both tried to feel what they ought to feel, telling the other what each wanted to hear, reinforcing the fragile edifice of their marriage. In 1945, during the Boston tryouts for *Carousel*, she must have written to complain that she was "shut out of things," because he earnestly assured her that whatever fame he had garnered was at least half hers. "If the things a man writes are an expression of his personality (and they can't be anything else) then what greater influence can his personality and his writing have than a woman with whom he has lived for fifteen years? It's terribly important for you to understand and remember that. It's *your* name on the program or in the newspaper . . . When an audience applauds something I've done, you are certainly entitled to a gracious nod of the head . . ." He ended with, "I'm crazy about you."

Oscar Hammerstein had a secret long-term affair with a beautiful showgirl, and "Dick was very protective of that," Judy Crichton remarked. "As for his own affairs, he is said to have had an apartment above Sardi's for that purpose. There is no doubt he adored beautiful women, and if you looked nice he was very quick to tell you. I know any number of women who flirted with him, not all of whom wanted something from him. And I know some reasonably well who went to bed with him, friends of Dorothy's, and who remained so. They just thought of it as an amusement, a not-that-important sport. It was part of the world and the times."

There was some gossip, never substantiated, that he and Margot Hopkins, his rehearsal pianist, had had a "fling," but if so it seems to have been brief. Celeste Holm, tall, blond, slim, and outgoing, was very much his type, and he apparently saw something of her, but if she had any romantic thoughts about him, a couple of incidents she witnessed disturbed her greatly. One concerned an actress whose work he did not like; she quotes him as saying, "What can you do with a woman over forty who can't sing or dance?" The other happened one night when she went with him to the Lotos Club on East Sixty-sixth Street. There they ran into a beautiful older woman—she might have been in her early forties. Rodgers barely acknowledged her and turned away. Celeste Holm did not say so, but the inference was that this was a former girlfriend who was now "too old." "He had no eyes for her. I was all, as far as he was concerned." It made her conclude, "Don't hold your breath." As he saw himself aging, youth was the prize. The girl he married was no longer "the child," "the baby," and "a damned sweet kid," with himself as "Daddy." Many of the girls he chose were very young, blond, admiring, and delighted to be hangers-on in the life of a famous man. They were always pretty and occasionally bright-minded as well. Elaine Anderson said, "The first time Dick and Oscar came on stage with the Theatre Guild people to rehearse *Oklahoma!* I went up to Dick and asked if I could take his hat and coat. He said, 'Why should a pretty girl like you take my hat and coat?' But he gave it to me. A few days later he came to read and I came up and he just handed his coat and hat to me. The third time he came to read I wasn't around and he said, 'Where's that nice girl who takes my hat and coat?' " It was not hard to become friendly with Dick and Oscar, she said. They were warm, some of the most wonderful people she ever met in the theatre.

"Dick was very witty and very attractive. Women always found him so. Oh, yes. Was he smoking a lot? Oh, sure. We all were. In the theatre during rehearsal; everywhere. I got to know Dick very well and our friendship blossomed greatly after we went on the road. We would go out after the theatre every night and sometimes to dinner beforehand. The company never said anything; everybody was going out with everybody else." At the time Anderson was married to the actor Zachary Scott, who was in Hollywood, and they had a small daughter. She never thought of her relationship with Rodgers as serious, but lightly, affectionately. On opening night he gave her a medallion on a chain with an inscription that expressed it perfectly: "To Elaine, Allegro con amore. From Dick." Before the show opened, some rewrites had been made, and Rodgers asked her to bring them over to the Volney Hotel, where he and Dorothy then had a suite. It was a Sunday, and Dorothy was there. "I had a new gray gabardine suit and I got all done up and went over to the hotel. Dorothy, who hated making a mistake more than any human being I've ever known, was very gracious. She stood up to make a drink, and said, 'I always shake my martinis,' or whatever it was. 'This happens to be my way of doing it,' and just as she said that the top flew off the shaker and she hurled her martini mixture all over my brand-new suit. I burst into laughter, Dick started laughing, and she burst into tears."

Rodgers with Jeanne Trybom, chorus girl, during rehearsals
for *Pal Joey* in 1940

AS HAD BEEN THEIR PRACTICE, neither Rodgers or Hammerstein
was willing to tackle another down-home subject or anything like it, and the
jolting success of *Oklahoma!* had only made them more cautious. The Theatre Guild was just as determined to engage them for another project and
badgered them for nine months. The play in question was *Liliom,* by Ferenc
Molnár, which Lorenz Hart had translated in the days when he was doing
such work for a living. The sometime actor and producer who commissioned
Hart then sold the play to the Theatre Guild, which produced it during its
third season to great acclaim in the spring of 1921. Eva Le Gallienne played
Julie, a simple servant girl, who meets Liliom, a worthless barker at a circus
(played by Joseph Schildkraut), marries him, and has a daughter. Liliom

The *Carousel* window card, 1945

turns out to be a wife beater and also a thief and dies attempting a robbery. As the story continues, Liliom has been sentenced to sixteen years in purgatory, at the end of which he is allowed to make an effort at restitution by returning to earth for one day. The drama critic Richard Watts Jr. wrote, "Sixteen years in purgatory do not quite destroy the stubbornness of his spirit, so that even then he cannot resist slapping his daughter in desperation as he sees his chance for that one good deed being taken from him." The play was revived on Broadway in 1940, starring Ingrid Bergman and Burgess Meredith, and

Jan Clayton and John Raitt in *Carousel*

at the Westport Country Playhouse a year later, with Tyrone Power and Annabella.

The character of Liliom, critics said, was one of the great creations of modern theatre. "It is strange how touching the story of this violent young scapegrace and his loyal wife can be, and it is a great tribute to Molnár, who has combined fantasy with realism amid so much romantic effectiveness," Watts concluded. John Mason Brown wrote that the theatre had often dealt with the hope for a second chance, for instance, in *Our Town,* in which a young girl who has died is allowed to look in on her family at a past birthday of her own choosing. "But no dramatic statement of our dream of the second chance seems to me to have been more moving than was that final scene in *Liliom* in which a Budapest barker returned to earth to strike his daughter even as, when living, he had struck her mother. In fact, few plays to have come out of the modern theatre have equalled Molnár's fantasy in imagination or pathos, in charm or universality, in tenderness or timelessness." One last chance, if only "to lessen the horror of death's finality"—thoughts of this kind were bound to be particularly insistent during a war, which was perhaps part of Helburn and Langner's reasoning. There was no doubt of the play's dramatic values, but, Rodgers wrote, they spent months "talking about the 'tunnel' in the story through which we could see no light at the end." In *Oklahoma!* they had gambled by including a violent death, but at least it was the death of a villain, and all ended happily. In *Liliom,* the hero fails his last chance for restitution. They could soften the ending so that the hero was redeemed instead of destroyed, but he still had to die. How would audiences react? It was a serious concern.

Robert Wright, the lyricist, who wrote musicals and films with his partner George Forrest in the thirties and forties, had rewritten one or two of Hammerstein's lyrics while at M-G-M, and, in fact, they had contributed new material for Rodgers and Hart's *I Married an Angel* in its 1942 film version. They were most embarrassed about having to desecrate what they felt to be superior work and sure Rodgers would hold it against them, but he had been extremely generous and forgiving, Wright recalled. In the summer of 1944 Wright and Forrest had a new hit, *Song of Norway,* an operetta about Grieg's life using his music set to their lyrics. The ending was sad, and one night Wright ran into Rodgers outside the Imperial Theatre, where the musical was playing. It transpired that Rodgers and Hammerstein had been coming to the show regularly at the very end, ten minutes past eleven, to gauge the audience reaction. "They said they wanted to see whether something so daring could succeed. Night after night they saw these hard-bitten audiences wiping their eyes, and this was when Hammerstein decided to go ahead and make a musical of *Liliom.*" This was not quite the case, because Rodgers said they had decided to write the musical early in 1944, before *Song of Norway* opened, and talks were going on with the Theatre Guild even earlier. But *Song of Norway*'s success would have confirmed their belief that such an ending could be made acceptable to Broadway audiences, the right kind of ending. When they first broached their desire to make changes to Molnár, he refused permission. Hammerstein persisted and Molnár eventually yielded. Hammerstein said later that if the point had not been conceded, "we could never have written *Carousel.*" The ending was, nevertheless, so affecting, Langner said, "I doubt whether anyone will pay $6 for tickets to have their hearts completely broken."

Shirley Jones and Gordon MacRae in the film version of *Carousel,* 1956

Liliom, moved to a New England setting and retitled, used the *Oklahoma!* team of Mamoulian and De Mille (who presumably continued to bicker), the youthful talents of Jan Clayton as Julie Jordan, now a textile worker, and a young singing discovery, John Raitt, as Billy Bigelow the carousel barker. Instead of the usual comic subplot, Hammerstein brought in Carrie Pipperidge, who dreams of an ordinary marriage to Mr. Snow. Mark Steyn commented of their duet, "The song has become so familiar we forget how unusual it is to make memorable singing material out of contentment, tranquility, routine . . .":

> When the children are asleep
> We'll sit and dream
> The things that every other
> Dad and mother dream . . .

The lyrics may seem ordinary, but the music is far from that. "Rodgers tugs and tweaks here, squeezes and extends," Steyn observed, adding

When the children are asleep
And lights are low
If I still love you
The way
I love you
Today
You'll pardon my saying—
I told you so!

"The phrase begins as its predecessor does," Steyn continued, "and then goes into the briefest of sub-phrases, with rests after the two 'love you's and a gorgeous octave leap on 'saying.' You don't notice the musical structure, because Hammerstein's lyric glides smoothly over it. This is mundane reflective domesticity but the music makes it magical and exciting. And Rodgers is artful enough to construct his tune so that its welling emotional force can be resolved only as a duet. Subliminally, he has told us that the sentiments are true, that the love between Carrie and Mister Snow is real and will endure." The love affair is in placid counterpoint to the doomed romance between Julie Jordan and Billie Bigelow. It was show writing of a very high order, "but you don't think of it in *musical* terms, because it suits the drama so well," Steyn wrote.

Just as Jerome Robbins in *West Side Story* tweaked and tugged at the material until it became a vehicle for his choreography, Rodgers designed *Carousel,* and particularly act 1, as an almost continuous stream of music. Asked if he had ever considered writing an opera, Rodgers said he and Hammerstein were sorely tempted a couple of times, and he imagined *Carousel* in those terms, from the five-and-a-half-minute overture which introduces the meeting of Julie Jordan and Billy Bigelow, "The Carousel Waltz," to the famous seven-and-a-half-minute "Soliloquy," in which Billy Bigelow voices his thoughts about becoming a father. Rodgers added, "We came very close to opera in the Majestic Theatre [where the musical opened]. I had a brass section in there the size of the brass section at the Met. Only I didn't let them play as loud. I had forty men in the pit. That's the size of an opera orchestra in France, outside of Paris, of course. There's much that is operatic in the music . . . But I have found more flexibility in the theatre and I like this freedom."

Having directed *Love Me Tonight*, Mamoulian was the ideal choice for this particular musical, the gossamer-like texture of which would have to be delicately handled if it were not to disintegrate. Mamoulian said, "Take that song, 'You're a Queer One, Julie Jordan,' in the first scene of the first act. If it were done just as a song—sung to the audience, presentational style—the play would stop. It must be given a feeling of dialogue to music. And the . . . nearer [speech] comes to a song, the more rhythmic it becomes . . . What you finally have is a balance, or a blend of rhythms, but all so sustained that it seems perfectly natural." Max Reinhardt, he continued, called it "psychological realism through stylization."

Perhaps the most difficult aspect of the musical, calling for the greatest tact and understatement, had to do with its ending, which introduces a deity presiding over an afterlife, and a daughter and mother who have to take what comfort they can from continuing their journey alone, the famous pseudo-hymn, "You'll Never Walk Alone." Hammerstein's original scene put heaven in a bare New England parlor, with a straight-backed Yankee playing the harmonium (He) while She listened respectfully: Mr. and Mrs. God. For reasons unexplained, Rodgers objected strongly to this scene during the Boston try-outs and Hammerstein obligingly transported his deity heavenwards, to a ladder, polishing stars in the sky. It was a definite misstep, one that would be criticized as having created "a Rotarian atmosphere congenial to audiences who seek not reality but escape from reality, not truth but escape from truth," the *New Republic* commented years later. It was, perhaps, the only faltering of tone in an otherwise flawless work. Brooks Atkinson wrote, "Hammerstein's compassionate lyrics drew more deeply on Rodgers's reservoir of melodies than anything he had written before, and every song is either delightful, or moving, or both . . . ," a reference to "June Is Bustin' Out All Over," "If I Loved You," and "What's the Use of Wond'rin'," among others. Rodgers's phenomenal gift for creating exactly the right song had triumphed once again.

The musical was fortunate in the choice of Jan Clayton, an engagingly intelligent young actress and singer, who brought just the right straight-backed naïveté to "You're a Queer One, Julie Jordan." And John Raitt, who was spotted by Lawrence Langner's wife on the West Coast singing in women's clubs and churches, was another inspired piece of casting. Billy Bigelow would become his favorite and most famous role, although perfecting his vocal delivery in the face of Rodgers's demands was not an easy matter. Rodgers took to calling Raitt "Junior," and the two were slow to arrive at a joking truce. "He had a wry sense of humor," Raitt recalled, "but I found him a very strange man. He didn't relate to people well." He recalled the famous day when Billy's "Soliloquy" was handed to him on what seemed like a five-foot scroll and all the problems they faced in staging such an audaciously extended song, problems he felt were never quite solved. Raitt sang the song eight times a week for two years without a break and was startled, one time, to look down into the orchestra pit and find that the double bass player was holding an umbrella: it seemed Raitt was spitting out his words too energetically and the bass player was bald. He said, "I should have paid for that umbrella."

With a world at war in 1945, finding adequate dancers, particularly male, was harder than casting the leads. John Fearnley, Rodgers's casting director, recalled a conversation he had had with Rodgers. The composer said, "You know our policy with dancing boys?" He replied, "No sir, what's that?" Rodgers said, "We hold a mirror in front of their face and if it clouds up, they're in."

LILIOM as retold by Hammerstein may have been frayed around the edges, Molnár's subtleties blunted and his poetic tone diminished by Hammerstein's sunny homilies, but just the same, the play was successfully addressing an almost universal fantasy of what might have been. What counted was whether *Carousel* succeeded on its own terms, and there could be no real doubt about that. It opened at the Majestic on April 19, 1945, and closed two years later after 890 performances, having made a profit of $1,250,000. As with *Oklahoma!*, its songs swept the country. Rodgers and Hammerstein had achieved, with these two brilliant musicals, an almost iconic status. Brooks Atkinson wrote, "*Carousel* was the Rodgers and Hammerstein masterpiece: it best illustrated their dedication to the musical stage as a legitimate art form." It was Rodgers's favorite of all his musicals. He wrote, "It affects me deeply every time I see it . . ."

AFTER THE IMMENSE SUCCESS of their score, the sheet-music sales, the recordings and radio performances, Rodgers and Hammerstein could afford to establish their own publishing identity as Rodgers and Hart had done for their own work early in the thirties; they called it Williamson Music. From the start of their association, it would seem, Rodgers and Hammerstein had discussed producing plays, an idea that would have seemed perfectly natural to the latter as the son and grandson of theatrical managers. Almost immediately they took a liking to *Mama's Bank Account* by Kathryn Forbes, a novel Mary Rodgers had liked and recommended to her mother, who passed it on to her husband. They commissioned John Van Druten to turn it into a play and produced it at the Music Box in the autumn of 1944, with Mady Christians, Oscar Homolka and the young Marlon Brando in the cast; Rodgers called him "a bit of a brat." *I Remember Mama* cost $75,000 to produce and ran for 714 performances, with a combined profit from Broadway and the road of $500,000. Then Rodgers and Hammerstein took on a comedy by Anita Loos, *Happy Birthday*, with a starring role for Helen Hayes; it was produced in 1946–47 and scored another success, with a profit of $75,000 after 564 performances. Joshua Logan directed the play, and he in turn invited Rodgers and Hammerstein to join him in producing *John Loves Mary*, a featherweight but extremely funny postwar comedy by Norman Krasna. It starred Nina Foch, Loring Smith, and Tom Ewell.

Logan recalled that while the show was doing extremely well during its New Haven and Boston tryouts in the early spring of 1947, they were having trouble ending the second act. There were all sorts of suggestions: "the boy goes out, the boy comes back, the father and . . . mother get furious, they don't get furious . . . And our tempers rose as we found no answer," he wrote, recalling the late-night sessions with Krasna, Rodgers, and Hammerstein. "Then I had a flash of an idea. 'I know what should happen! . . . the boy comes back in the room, kisses the girl and takes her off into the bedroom.' " Hammerstein's face reddened. He stood up. "Anyone who would make a suggestion like *that* is a *cad!*" After he had left, Krasna turned to Logan and said, "Everybody used to tell me that Oscar Hammerstein was cool as a cucumber. Well, he's the most belligerent cucumber I ever met." Another ending was finally found, and the play settled in for a run of 423 performances and a profit of about $225,000.

But perhaps Rodgers and Hammerstein's biggest success as producers in the immediate postwar years was a musical they themselves did not write: *Annie Get Your Gun*. It started as an idea in the minds of Herbert and Dorothy Fields. They came to the office one morning and said, " 'How would you like to see Ethel Merman play Annie Oakley?' And that was it," Rodgers said. "We said, 'Go home and write it and we'll produce it.' " There was never any question about writing the music and lyric themselves. This would be a big, old-fashioned musical and they wanted to concentrate on musical drama. They immediately contacted Jerome Kern, who wanted to do it, "and it was when he came East to talk about writing the score that he was picked up in front of the Bible Society and taken to Welfare Island Hospital, and then died a week later," Rodgers said. Their next choice, Irving Berlin, took some persuading, but he finally agreed and came up with an ideal score. Berlin, who had a reputation for being difficult, behaved charmingly and came to all the backers' auditions. After Berlin had done this for a few times Rodgers realized that one song he particularly liked had been dropped. He asked Berlin why, and Berlin replied that "when we came to that song I looked at your face, and you weren't enjoying yourself." He had observed the

Richard Rodgers, Irving Berlin, and Oscar Hammerstein during auditions
for Berlin's new musical *Annie Get Your Gun* in 1946

usual facial contortions and drawn, as usual, the wrong conclusions. Rodgers
reassured him, so Berlin put the song back in the show. It was "There's No
Business Like Show Business." The musical opened at the Imperial Theatre
in the summer of 1946 and ran for 1,147 performances. Mary Martin took
over Merman's role for the tour, and Rodgers thought of her when the time
came to cast for *South Pacific.*

In his chosen field Rodgers was spinning fast and ever more furiously.
Oklahoma! and *Carousel* were sending out road companies; *Mama* closed at
the end of June 1946, a month after *Annie* opened. *Happy Birthday* was about
to open in October, and *John Loves Mary* was set for the following February.
In 1944, once they began producing *I Remember Mama,* they set up an office,
and by 1953 it had become a tastefully furnished, ten-room suite on Madison
Avenue, with ten or twelve employees overseeing the affairs of Williamson
music and as many as thirteen play companies, either touring or on Broadway. By 1950 their annual payroll was $1,750,000. Rodgers was duly elected to
act as chairman of the board and supervised every business detail down to,

and including, signing the weekly paychecks. In 1953 unofficial estimates put the partnership's annual gross at $15–$20 million and the annual incomes of Rodgers and Hammerstein at $500,000, not counting something like $30,000 annually that each received from ASCAP. Part of their success was their willingness to seek out new actors and, if necessary, keep them working in touring companies until the moment came for a leading role in a new musical. Jonathan Bush, now a stockbroker, the brother of one president and the uncle of another, was "a song-and-dance man on Broadway" for five years. He played Will Parker, who sings "Kansas City," and he could have gone on playing the same role forever, but he got tired of it. He said that if an actor was wanted by a music fair to play a part, he or she would be sent to Rodgers and Hammerstein for their approval before being assured of the role: "They exerted complete control over casting. However, once you were accepted, that gave you a kind of passport, and the next time you auditioned for one of their shows you only had to compete against five or six people instead of a hundred." (The Rodgers and Hammerstein Organization still has the power to approve actors, directors, conductors, and orchestrators for first-class productions of their shows.)

SUCH A DEMANDING producing schedule was bound to engage most of their time and energy, and so perhaps it was not a surprise that *Allegro,* Rodgers and Hammerstein's third musical, the last to be produced by the Theatre Guild, did not make its appearance until 1947. It was about the son of a small-town doctor who follows his father into medicine, goes to the big city, and ends up "giving vitamin injections to rich people and laying corner-stones of hospitals," Stephen Sondheim said. The book was by Hammerstein, who had based it on discussions with his own doctor, a good friend. Hammerstein had wanted, in the manner of Thornton Wilder, to tell a universal story about the life of a man from birth to death, but was pressured to redeem his hero in midlife, because to have another leading man die onstage was more than he dared to attempt. But in reaching for universality, Hammerstein's usually confident tone faltered, and what came through was "a vast and woolly morality play."

So, despite its innovative staging—a Greek chorus was used, and an inge-nious set design allowed for almost instantaneous scene changes—*Allegro* was a disappointment. Rodgers and Hammerstein made a further miscalculation in allowing De Mille, who had choreographed two shows, to act as director. Perhaps they thought there was enough emphasis on movement in *Allegro* to justify the decision, but a De Mille who was unsure of herself became bel-

Looking over the chorus line for *Allegro,* 1947

ligerent and abusive. Gemze de Lappe said, "Agnes was her own worst enemy. She'd lay down the law, but she was never mean the way Jerry Whyte could be. He had a terrible reputation for caustic, mean remarks. He'd look at you with great disgust if you were a soloist, call in your understudy, and tell her she had better learn this." This was demoralizing, because, on the other hand, he was the most charming of men, "and if he looked at you with disgust it really hurt, because you wanted him to like you." As a substitute director, he could be unbending. Barbara Cook, who, to her eternal regret, never originated a role in a Rodgers and Hammerstein musical, was frequently cast for national tours and revivals. She recalls one revival of *Oklahoma!* in which she was playing Ado Annie. "I was having trouble because I felt I was not being allowed to find my way to doing it. Whyte wanted me to play the role exactly as Celeste Holm had done. 'When you sing this, you put your hand here; when you say that, you cross on this syllable.' I can understand Rodgers and Hammerstein wanting their shows not to get too far from what they knew worked, but this was rote learning. Just before we opened, I rebelled. I went onstage and did it my way. Whyte was furious. He was livid. He said, 'You put that back exactly the way I have told you, or you'll never work in show business again.' Nowadays I would have appealed to Rodgers, but I was just a little girl scared to death."

The rebellion of a single cast member could be dealt with, but in the case of *Allegro* the whole cast was up in arms, and this could not be dismissed so easily. Although De Mille continued to receive the official credit, unofficially Hammerstein took over as director. He in turn sought the advice of Logan, who, as an exchange of letters reveals, made some interesting proposals. Instead of the ending Hammerstein had devised, in which the hero turns down the opportunity to become physician-in-chief of a big hospital to return to his hometown and help his father run a small hospital, Logan suggested an alternative. The hero should toy with the idea of going home, but then decide to take over the large hospital and change its focus from catering to rich, spoiled clients to the needs of the poor and truly ill. "Believe me, Oscar, this is not idle playmaking on my part. Whether this is the solution or not, I feel you are in more trouble than evidently most other people feel." He wrote that Oscar should be ruthless in making the necessary repairs. But as the show made its way to a New York opening on October 10, 1947, Hammerstein retained his original ending, and the show received a barrage of reviews making more or less Logan's point. "No one can deny there is virtue in villages," John Mason Brown wrote. "It does seem fair, if unnecessary, however, to remind Mr. Hammerstein that villages have no monopoly upon it . . ."

Stephen Sondheim, who became Hammerstein's protégé and was working on the set as a glorified office boy, said, "It was a seminal influence on my life, because it showed me a lot of smart people doing something wrong . . . Oscar meant it as a metaphor for what had happened to him. He had become so successful with the results of *Oklahoma!* and *Carousel* that he was suddenly in demand all over the place. What he was talking about was the trappings, not so much of success, but of losing sight of what your goal is . . . To the end of his days Oscar said, 'I want to rewrite the second act of *Allegro* so people will understand what I was talking about,' because all the critics pounced on it as being a corny story, the doctor who gets corrupted by money. That's not what he meant . . . It wasn't about money; it was about losing sight of your goal . . ."

Even before the reviews appeared, Rodgers had understood that something was basically wrong. Gary Stevens said that he was producing a radio show called *Luncheon at Sardi's*, which was broadcast daily from that restaurant for about seven years. One day Rodgers was one of the guests. As producer, Stevens provided the show's host with material and had given him a press release to the effect that *Allegro* had a large advance sale. "Which meant in the parlance of things that he had another smash hit that would run for years." After the radio show was over, Rodgers invited him to a late lunch, "and he delivered a semi-monologue, instructive diatribe, on the fact that an advance sale means nothing. How after the notices everything falls apart . . . This was not a short conversation. It was a monologue that went on for at least twenty minutes, and I saw a side of him that I had not seen before, authoritative and dictatorial. He lectured me. Unfortunately, everything he said came true. The show got very poor notices, business dropped off, and it was obvious four weeks later that *Allegro* was not going to be there for too long." *Allegro* ran for a respectable 315 performances, but since it had cost $400,000 to produce it needed a year to break even and ended with a loss of about $50,000. It was an omen for the future. Rodgers said, "You now have to have a smash or you have nothing."

AGNES DE MILLE, who was not an entirely unbiased witness, said, "By the time I did *Carousel* Rodgers had become quite a different man from the one I had done *Oklahoma!* with. He was nervous. He was tense. He began to be power-driven and very jealous of his rights. You couldn't gainsay him about anything at all. You could at first in *Oklahoma!* And by the time we got to *Allegro* they were both manic."

It was true, though, that Rodgers had changed. Mary Rodgers Guettel said, "I get a very peculiar feeling that gradually over the years he changed from somebody who had a wonderful time to somebody who had a terrible time." In those family home movies taken just before the war Dick and Dorothy and the girls are seen in a carefree mood behind immense rented summer houses on Long Island with pillared fronts, palatial awnings, and fountains. The girls, wearing matching polka dot romper suits, dance hornpipes and do forward and backward somersaults with their mother, or are seen falling all over their delighted grandmother. In a home movie from 1944, they have moved to the house on Black Rock Turnpike, and Dorothy's hair, which had been loose around her face, is tied back into a chignon. She is tending the vegetables and displaying their well-kept Rhode Island reds. Then Mary, a teenager, and Linda, aged nine, suddenly appear on either side of their father, walking toward the camera. Rodgers, then aged forty-two, seems much shorter. His hair is thinner and his waistline has thickened. His face looks puffy and he manages a tired smile. Sondheim, who first met

Rodgers at about this time, remarked on the difference between the prewar Rodgers, "when he was kidding around with Hart and seems kind of fresh and pulled together," and the marked change in him just a few years later.

He said, "From the minute I got to know him he was always sour, and that's also what made him quite funny: sour-funny, which is a taste I share. I never saw Dick in what I would call a happy or generous mood. Something always seemed to be bothering him." Sondheim's very first memory of him was when he and Hammerstein were writing *Carousel*. They were upstairs in Hammerstein's study in the farm and came down to ask him a question about treasure hunts. They knew that, even at the age of fourteen, he was an expert on the subject and were thinking of using a hunt to begin the second act. Sondheim was flattered. "I don't remember anything about Rodgers then except that he was there with Oscar. The first time I actually remember talking to Dick was after Oscar got me to join Williamson, and I just remember having an interview with Dick in his office. Then I asked him about the release of 'People Will Say We're in Love.' We were chatting and I was then very aware of structural things and I've always been so impressed at the ingenuity of the release of that song, because of the inversion of the main theme [which begins with "Don't start collecting things"]. And he blinked at me. I realized he had no idea he had done it. He then quoted a line from *Pal Joey* to the effect that, when Vera asks Joey for the secret of his charm, Joey says he never looks into it because if he does it will disappear. Dick quoted that. I know that feeling because I've had it myself."

He continued, "To me the change in Dick had something to do with the joining-up with Oscar. Oscar was a generous, big-hearted man who devoted himself to good works such as the United World Federalists and all those things. He was more than just a book or lyric writer. He was a man of the theatre. I suspect Dick began to believe Oscar was seen this way and he was the mean little man in the office." Rodgers was no longer the white knight riding to the rescue of his partner, but cast into the role of . . . Sondheim: "Absolutely. The drunk. He became a whole other person. It was like Wilde's *The Picture of Dorian Gray* come to life."

Even before he married Dorothy, Richard Rodgers was aware that he tended to get sick under the stress and uncertainty of mounting a new show; and the more anxiety he felt, the worse his nervous stomach, or cold, was likely to be. He could be running a temperature and flat on his back, as he was for the ill-fated *She's My Baby*. And there were accidents as well. The gallon of peaches that fell on his head during the tryouts for *Dearest Enemy* was a genuine blow of fate, but the accident just before the opening of *Carousel* was self-inflicted. Outwardly, the cause seemed simple enough. Arriving at the Bridgeport railroad station, where Dorothy and Mary were waiting to take him to Fairfield, he had to carry his two heavy suitcases to the car. "I suffered no ill effects that night, but the next morning when I got up I coughed. With that I felt a pain in my back that was so excruciating that I simply collapsed on the floor. I had wrenched one of my lumbar vertebrae." It was just after the Boston tryouts and shortly before opening night at the Majestic. There was no porter, and perhaps he was tired and careless, carrying two bags when he should have been lifting them one at a time. Perhaps some part of him found the tension unbearable. It is true that he began to suffer from back problems, and there was often a connection between the arrival of pain and a moment of stress in his life. He saw the show on opening night from a stretcher concealed behind a curtain. He was so drugged with morphine he did not hear the laughter and applause, and the truth did not dawn upon him until afterwards. Given the circumstances, it was probably the most painless opening night he ever had.

Around this period, his phobias began to manifest themselves. Judy Crichton, who had married the novelist Robert Crichton, author of *The Secret of Santa Vittoria,* recalled that they were living at Thirtieth Street and Lexington Avenue when Dick and Dorothy came for dinner one night. "We had an extremely good time and they were both very funny and stirred each other up. They left to go to Connecticut, and about ten or fifteen minutes later Bob got a call from Dick. He could not get onto the West Side Highway. He didn't explain it; he just couldn't. Bob left in a taxi, met them somewhere on the West Side, drove the car up onto the highway for Dick, then got out of the car, got a cab, and came home. Yes, Dorothy did drive, and I'll be damned if I know . . . This is as much as I can remember. Dick had panicked in some mysterious fashion, and we never understood why."

Judy Crichton never saw Rodgers overtly drunk in her life, and she saw him constantly at parties and dinners. She was never, ever, aware of its being a problem. Everybody drank in those days, just as everyone smoked. It was "all very confusing, because there were small symptoms of breakdown." Rodgers would occasionally go to the hospital, "and no one would explain to us just why." Mary Rodgers Guettel said it took her years before she realized that her father had a drinking problem. He fooled everyone, and Dorothy Rodgers was very good at finding new and ingenious excuses; she put up a protective wall so that no one would suspect the truth. Judy Crichton explained, "If you grow up being thought of as a princess, La Perfecta, in a family that has jumped out of one class and into another very fast, you surely are not about to let the world see your warts."

The first time Mary Rodgers Guettel suspected her father might be abusing alcohol was once when she came home from Wellesley with very good grades. She knocked on her father's study door to show him this excellent report card. "When he opened the door and I looked at him, something went flashing through my head and right out again, because I obviously didn't want to look at it: drunk! I just completely rejected it." She learned that at one point her father was consuming a bottle of vodka a day, a secret he kept hidden successfully from almost everyone, since he never appeared to be drunk. Then the period came, after the war, when her father was having nervous breakdowns that were not identified as such. "I think he was probably having the D.T.'s, just a complete physical breakdown. He was probably an alcoholic all his life."

In those years just after the war, Dorothy Rodgers got pregnant for the last time. Mary Rodgers Guettel said, "I graduated from high school in 1948 and mother was pregnant and lost a baby because my uncle didn't have the guts to tell her she had a fibroid tumor and never would have carried a child full-term. I was thrilled. It was the first time I felt close to my mother. It was the best time. We'd get out the books and say, 'How big is it now?' I was as crushed as she was when she lost the baby, her fourth girl. And my father cried all over me. I realized how much he'd always wanted a son. It was upsetting to see how vulnerable he was. Frightening."

Chapter Fifteen

"SO FAR"

A S THEY ACHIEVED EMINENCE as masters of the Broadway musical, Rodgers and Hammerstein continued to expound their goal, paraphrasing Frank Lloyd Wright, that they would not do today what they did yesterday, or tomorrow what they were doing today. That dictum, Hammerstein said confidently, did not include worrying about what the public wanted. "We decide on what we want to do and then we hope the public will want it." The comment was somewhat refuted by his further observation that they had removed *Carousel* from its Central European setting as a precaution, because "there was no way of knowing how the public would be thinking." It seems obvious that part of their uncanny success in the decades of the 1940s and 1950s was exactly this ability to sense what the public wanted. Of their five most successful musicals: *Oklahoma!, Carousel, South Pacific, The King and I,* and *The Sound of Music,* four are concerned in one way or another with World War II.

Given the mood of the times, they could hardly avoid dealing with subjects that a world at war had brought to the surface, e.g., the fragility of life itself, the courage of ordinary people in extraordinary situations, and the longing for a belief in life after death. To this Hammerstein added his particular set of homilies: hatred could be unlearned, there was light at the end of the tunnel, and "you'll never walk alone." Perhaps it was true that the lyricist could hardly underestimate the popular desire for a fairy-tale ending, but if so, the assessment was made without a trace of irony. Part of his and Rodgers's success in those days was an ability to redeem such statements from cliché and get audiences to respond viscerally by the strength of their own personal commitments. Once their faith in the message weakened, their power to do so began to falter. But in those days there was a vigor and conviction to their work that swept all before it. And with the first of their musicals to tackle an actual war setting, they were dealing with real people in real situations.

The musical *South Pacific* evolved from a book by the novelist James Michener, who found himself as a navy lieutenant stranded on a small Pacific island in 1945 with nothing to do and so decided to write a group of short stories based on his actual wartime experiences. *Tales of the South Pacific* won a Pulitzer Prize when it was published in 1947. The book was seen by a story editor at M-G-M, who passed it around, and it fell into the hands of Jo Mielziner, the scene designer, and Josh Logan, then rehearsing the play *Mister Roberts.* Logan saw its possibilities and made an arrangement with the producer Leland Hayward and the author to develop the stories into a play. In due course Logan suggested the idea to Rodgers; and once Rodgers and Hammerstein had read the book, they wanted it as a musical.

Interest centered around "Fo' Dolla," a story about the love affair between a young American naval officer and a native girl, which was going to be the main theme. There was also interest in another story, "Our Heroine," dealing with a middle-aged French planter, Emile De Becque, and his affair with a young American nurse from Arkansas. The perfect candidate for De Becque soon presented himself in the form of Ezio Pinza, a celebrated Metropolitan Opera basso, who was interested in making a highly unorthodox transition from opera into popular musical theatre and film. Rodgers said, "Pinza came East in June to do a radio show, and we arranged to meet him at lunch at the Plaza. In walked this great, big, attractive-looking fellow. We went to his broadcast and heard him sing in front of an audience." Hammerstein said that the moment they saw the audience reaction their minds were made up. They would rewrite the script to make De Becque the hero. As for the heroine, they had the perfect candidate for Nellie Forbush from Little Rock in Mary Martin, who was then playing the lead in the touring company of *Annie Get Your Gun* on the West Coast. But when she learned she would be appearing with an operatic bass, Rodgers said, "she was scared to death. She didn't want to get out there and be made a fool of by a Metropolitan Opera star. She has no illusions about her singing—she knows what it's good for, but she doesn't think it's vocal." Rodgers knew there was a simple solution, one that he in fact would use for them, of never having them both sing at the same time. In the meantime, they had two high-powered actors lined up and no script.

As envisioned by its authors, *South Pacific,* however muted the theme, was to be about racial prejudice. Nellie Forbush is almost ready to marry

Joshua Logan showing how it's done for *South Pacific*

De Becque until she learns that he has children by a Polynesian woman; her struggle to come to terms with this forms the basis of their story. Lieutenant Cable, the young American naval officer with a Philadelphia-and-Princeton background, has an affair with Liat, a native girl, and also has to grapple with his prejudice. Threads of other stories were incorporated into the plot. One was about a coast watcher hiding in the hills who reports radio movements of the Japanese fleet, and there was some comic relief about the handling of laundry by the GIs. All this should have galvanized Hammerstein, but, as Logan discovered, after months had gone by he had only finished the first scene and written a few lyrics. He had serious writer's block and Logan, who was now director as well as co-producer, went to the farm for the weekend to see whether he could help. He ended up staying for ten days, but at the end of that time they had a script. In *Josh,* his autobiography, Logan described his efforts to gain credit as co-author (finally given) as well as receive a percentage of the profits (denied). (He must have been privately reassured, however, because when the film of *South Pacific* was finally made in 1958, he, as director, received a substantial percentage of its profits.) As Logan described it, Hammerstein would have been ready to do the right thing, but Rodgers absolutely refused.

Mary Martin, who liked to tell stories against herself, said that the first time she heard "A Wonderful Guy" was when she met Rodgers and Hammerstein in Joshua and Nedda Logan's New York apartment. They said they had a present for her; it turned out to be a new song. While Rodgers played the song, Hammerstein croaked out the lyrics. She decided she had to sing it at once, so she sat down on the piano bench, getting more and more excited and making ever wider gestures. When she reached the final words, "I'm in love with a wonderful guy," she flung back her arms and threw herself off the bench. Rodgers peered down at her and said solemnly, "Never sing it any other way."

An even more famous fall came about during rehearsals for the same song. Mary Martin had executed cartwheels all her life and felt so sure of herself that she suggested she intersperse them while singing the repetitions of "I'm in love, I'm in love . . ." at the end of the song. The director agreed, and when they got to New Haven, all went well until she came up from one of her cartwheels and was so blinded by a spotlight that she could not see where she was going. But the momentum took her forward. She went flying into the air and down into the orchestra pit. She knocked out Trude Rittman, the musical and vocal arranger, who was at the piano, and struck a glancing blow at the conductor, Salvatore Dell'Isola, before collapsing in a heap. Rittman thought her neck was broken. Although a mass of bruises, Mary Martin was not seriously hurt and went on like the trouper she was. Fortunately, Rittman and Dell'Isola were not seriously hurt, either. Mary Martin sent them both football helmets filled with flowers.

Don Fellows, who played Lieutenant Buzz Adams, recalled Mary Martin's generosity when he and his wife had their first child. She had made special arrangements to have the hospital room full of flowers the moment his wife returned from the delivery room. There were other aspects to her personality, he discovered. He stuttered as a young actor and had a bad case of stage fright, so one night he asked her how she dealt with it. Mary Martin said, "Don, it's very simple. I come to the theatre half an hour before the half-hour call, and get made up, and get into my costume. When they call the half hour I go into the john and I stay there until Gladys [the maid] comes and says,

'You're on, Miss Martin.' Then I lean down, pull up my panties, and go out onstage. Well, that's the way you deal with stage fright."

She had absolutely no illusions about herself. She had given Hammerstein a photograph of herself as a gawky and bedraggled teenager at summer camp and he had put the picture beside his shaving mirror with the words, "This proves there is hope for everyone." Despite the teasing tone of the caption, Hammerstein somehow knew she would become the quintessential Rodgers and Hammerstein heroine. Even before they had developed a script for *Oklahoma!* they had offered her the leading role, but she had turned it down in favor of another Broadway musical, *Dancing in the Streets,* which came to an ignominious end in Boston. But now she had played in *Annie* and become one of the leading lights in that loosely knit, heterogeneous group of actors, directors, and scene designers who formed an ad hoc Rodgers and Hammerstein repertory company. Never conventionally pretty, Mary Martin was always pert-looking in a fresh, guileless way, spunky and tomboyish. Then in her mid-thirties, she *was* Knucklehead Nellie, the cockeyed optimist who was "stuck like a dope with a thing called hope," every man's ideal girl next door. But there was something more to that special equation that made this actress so incomparable onstage, a quality aptly identified by the English theatre critic Kenneth Tynan after he saw *South Pacific* at the Drury Lane Theatre in 1951. He wrote that he had been transported by delight, and for this he held Mary Martin responsible. "Skipping and roaming round the stage on diminutive flat feet she had poured her voice directly into that funnel into the heart which is sealed off from all but the rarest performers, and which was last broached, I believe, by Yvonne Printemps." Something about her lack of affectation, her natural gift for burlesque, her enthralling ability to put across a song and her generous spirit melted not only her audiences and Oscar Hammerstein, but whatever gulf lay between her and Rodgers. There is a faded black-and-white television film showing her after the opening of *South Pacific,* again seated on a piano bench while the composer played, but this time she is singing the same song to him. As she does so, his serious expression relaxes into the small, secretive, and enormously attractive half-smile that was one of his special gifts to the people he liked. When the song ends, she throws her arms around an obviously delighted Rodgers. She had the knack.

She was also sexy. One of the open secrets about *South Pacific* concerned Ezio Pinza's efforts to have an affair with Mary Martin. The columnists were busy, Hammerstein told Logan, "with the most fantastic rumors that ever surrounded a show. It is said that Pinza . . . and Mary are carrying on a hot backstage romance and those who hear this take it up from there and invent their own details." This was in spite of the fact that Pinza was happily married with two young children, and Mary Martin was married to Richard Halliday, who managed her business affairs and guarded her with ferocious solicitude. He took her to the theatre, picked her up, took her home every night, allowed her a single drink, and then she would sit and do needlepoint. Leland Hayward complained they lived such a dull life that when they got to London, Martin and Halliday went nowhere and saw no one. Mary Rodgers Guettel, who knew them both, said Halliday was by far the more difficult person of the pair and often drank too much. He could have "a really mean tongue and a really mean temper when he got frustrated and angry." But his wife loved him and depended upon him completely, and only a few people knew she had formed a discreet attachment to the film star Janet Gaynor.

Pinza's long and enthusiastic onstage kisses had convinced their public that he and Mary Martin were madly in love, which was good for business but anathema to his co-star. Don Fellows said, "Pinza knew her entrances and he'd go to her dressing room door and take her by the hand and lead her on stage. I'd hear her in the wings saying, 'Ezio, when you kiss, kiss me nicely,' and he'd be saying, 'When I kees, I kees!' She'd be singing on stage and he'd be whispering, 'Mary, I love you!' into her ear." But Pinza was like that with all the girls. As Rodgers reported to Logan with evident amusement, "Pinza is in fine shape and keeps the girls in a pleasant state of anxiety. They just never know what end to protect." The playwright Russel Crouse said of him, according to Fellows, " 'Pinza has three balls and when he sings they all light up.' I'd be standing in the wings of the Majestic and when he started singing you'd feel it in your feet. He used to get love letters and he'd put them on the call board. Some of them were crazy, women offering to leave their husbands for him. There was a gorgeous young girl in the company, Patricia Northrop, just beautiful" (she played Ensign Sue Yaeger), "and they'd both be waiting to go on stage together, and he would kiss her. One night she said, 'If he kisses me one more night I'm going to bite his tongue. I'm tired of this.' So he did, and she did, and Pinza cried out in pain; and then he said, 'Wonderful!' "

ALTHOUGH, as Emile De Becque, Pinza had a starring role in the drama, he was curiously underemployed vocally. He had only two solo songs, "This Nearly Was Mine" and "Some Enchanted Evening." Granted, the latter, which became one of the most famous romantic ballads of all time and was reprised several times during the performance, has made him a Broadway legend. Still, Mary Martin's numerous songs, "A Cockeyed Optimist," "Honey

Mary Martin and Enzio Pinza: an enchanted evening,
and enchanting moment

Bun," "A Wonderful Guy" and "I'm Gonna Wash That Man Right Out-a My Hair," placed the emphasis where it belonged. Musicals had been about heroines almost since the dawn of time; at least since 1919, when *Irene* took Broadway by storm, leading Rodgers and Hart to write songs for a string of impoverished heroines with hearts of gold.

Nellie Forbush, with her coltish high spirits, flashing smile, and polka-dot allure, cheerful and uncomplicated, was the perfect musical-comedy heroine, a role Rodgers and Hammerstein were never quite able to duplicate again in its almost universal appeal. The hardworking nurse from a hick town who sees what is really important in life was the kind of person every woman could identify with and every man find disarming. Questions about the long-term survival of a marriage between a sophisticate who read Proust at bedtime and a girl who liked Dinah Shore and did not read anything were raised by Nellie Forbush only to be brushed aside. As for the interracial complexities of raising two Polynesian children, all such issues were subsumed in the general euphoria of true love. As the song said, "And somehow you know, / You know even then," the moment a stranger entered a crowded room. Good-hearted, corny American optimism would build a braver, truer

Martin and Pinza falling in love in *South Pacific*

world. It was left to filmmakers with a more complex view of life to explore the paradoxes and contradictions implicit in such a belief, as William Wyler did in *The Best Years of Our Lives,* which actually predates *South Pacific* by two years.

South Pacific marks a great dividing line in the Rodgers and Hammerstein oeuvre between heroes and heroines who are more or less evenly matched in age and stories about powerful older men and the younger women who are attracted to them. The pattern is arresting: a young Englishwoman goes into a Siamese court *(The King and I),* and a young girl goes to take care of a rich widower's children *(The Sound of Music),* and, once Rodgers was on his own, a young black model falls for a famous writer *(No Strings).* Such a departure from the usual was praised at the time; it even seemed courageous. *South Pacific* had "made a romantic figure of a man in his late fifties and has, undoubtedly, brought home to many a man of such an age, and even older, that late-in-life romance is by no means unachievable," wrote Ward More-house in 1951. Yet the pattern of the older man marrying the younger woman was already a truism of American culture, reflected at every turn in its films, novels, advertisements, newspapers, and magazines. A woman's asset was her youth and a man's, his social and economic status. Her value faded with the color of her hair, but his wrinkles just made him seem more interesting. What might have made the story look especially attractive to the musical's creators was the undeniable fact that they themselves were getting older. When *South Pacific* opened, Hammerstein was fifty-four and Rodgers, at forty-seven, too close to fifty for comfort.

As the years passed, a note of envy and longing begins to enter Rodgers's correspondence. His telegram of birthday congratulations to an old friend said, FROM THIS ANCIENT PINNACLE WE ENVY AND CONGRATULATE YOU ON YOUR YOUTH, ENERGY AND BEAUTY. That was evidently meant to flatter but the inference is clear, and other comments are even more straightforward, as in the telegram, WISH I COULD BE THERE AND WISH I WERE YOUR AGE." It was as if he saw his very essence dwindling, leaving him, in his overly critical view of himself, an aging juvenile; as he wrote in answer to a complimentary letter, "I'm only a small boy trying to get along . . ."

Meanwhile, his discreet liaisons (as he fondly believed them to be) continued. Joshua Logan remarked that Rodgers always wanted to double-date with him, because "that made it all right." Logan was never quite sure how far matters went, but Rodgers did have a key to his hotel room. One day a chorus girl said to Logan, "You're a manic depressive, too!" It seemed she knew what kind of medicine he was taking and Logan concluded the only way she could have known was to have seen the inside of his medicine cabinet.

Logan thought Rodgers was a great success with women, so sure of his looks and charm that he could be crude; he could walk up to a girl and say "Do you want to fuck?" and get away with it. Theodore Bikel, who would play Captain Georg von Trapp in the original production of *The Sound of Music,* liked Rodgers and used to joke with him constantly. He recalled that one time, one of the ladies of the chorus complained she had gained too much weight during the out-of-town tryouts. Patting her right buttock, she said she had gained that in New Haven, and patting her left, that this one came from Boston. Quick as a flash Rodgers said, "I prefer Providence myself." He could, however, be bested on occasion. The composer David Raksin recalled that his first wife, Pamela Randell, a beautiful singer and dancer, was appearing in one of Rodgers's shows. Raksin would come to New York as often as he could to visit her. One night she received a message that Mr. Rodgers was expecting her that evening. She coolly told his emissary, "Go back and ask Mr. Rodgers how he would like to see this in the *New York Times.*"

. . .

SOUTH PACIFIC opened at the Majestic Theatre on April 7, 1949, and ran for 1,925 performances, finally closing in January 1954. When Mary Martin left the production, in June 1951, Martha Wright took over the role of Nellie Forbush for two and a half years. She liked Rodgers but was on her guard against him. "Oh, he was very nice to me and very gentle, but I knew that underneath there was a tough guy, believe me!" People thought, mistakenly, that they were having an affair, because he would take her to Dinty Moore's for supper. "I must admit it made me nervous, but I went. One night we were sitting there and we had a drink and I said, 'Do you mind if we eat?' and he was very surprised." She was married but separated, which was a small protection for "whatever stresses might be coming my way." She got on well with him for the most part. "He'd tell a joke and it would be fine, but he always had this edge. You were a little apprehensive with him. You never knew why."

When Salvatore Dell'Isola left the show, a conductor was hired who was deaf and would rush the accompanying background music for a pivotal scene, throwing the actors off balance. One day Wright plucked up her courage and went to tell Rodgers about the problem. She asked, "Wouldn't it be wonderful if we could get Sal back again?" and he said, "Wouldn't it be wonderful if we could get Mary Martin back again?" Wright said, "That was typical of Dick Rodgers. He could do that. Instead of saying, 'Well, we just can't do that,' he jumped all over me." Billie Worth, who joined the company in May 1950, had a similar story to tell. "One evening Mary Martin and I started talking about the things that were wrong with the company, and Dick was furious. He said, 'Both of you have spoiled my whole evening.' He didn't take criticism well and he was always getting his feelings hurt."

Joshua Logan was aware that a change had taken place. Rodgers was no longer a crony, one of the guys, with whom he could take out a couple of girls in the cast and have a "warm, relaxed time of it," but had become, with his amazing worldwide success, "a monument." Logan wrote, "He was so sought after that he had to closet himself in an office and dictate letters daily in order to handle his business affairs and to fend off the many people who wanted to sap his talent. To me, his fun seemed gone—the fun he and I used to have." Something about success had brought to the fore a professional ruthlessness and increased his didactic tendency. Where he might once have ignored criticism or deflected it with a joke, he no longer troubled to mask his resentment. Perhaps it was only a coincidence that he had stopped smoking after twenty-five years. It was well known along the street that Damon Runyon, a chain smoker, had developed cancer of the larynx and died after two painful years, in 1946, an event that deeply shocked his friend Walter Winchell. Rodgers appears to have stopped in the autumn of 1948, the year that his father, Dr. William Abraham Rodgers, died in New York at the age of seventy-eight. Rodgers wrote that when his father told him he had intestinal cancer, he, Rodgers, was "terrified." He added, "Eight months later he died quietly and with remarkably little pain." In 1955 one of his friends commented in an article that Rodgers had "suddenly" given up smoking six and a half years before and liked to quip that "after the first five years I never missed 'em at all!"

That smoking was an addiction was probably known at the time, but that withdrawal symptoms included dizziness, fatigue, lack of concentration, and irritability might not have been known. Recent studies also indicate that smokers, and former smokers, are "more than twice as likely to have suffered from major depression at some point in their lives than those who [have] never smoked." Rodgers had had periods of depression going back to the twenties, if his letters are any guide, and his withdrawal from nicotine could have triggered another. His daughters believe that he consulted five psychiatrists over the years, but since one of them was in Chicago, they did not know how often their father actually saw him, or how much he was helped by any of them. To add to his unease, Dorothy, the capable one, was ill. *South Pacific* had barely opened in the spring of 1949 when she had a hysterectomy, perhaps related to her miscarriage of the year before. Rodgers wrote to Logan two weeks later to thank him on her behalf for the tulips and carnations because "she simply isn't up to writing for herself as yet." Early in May she was "organically and surgically quite recovered and perfect, but she's weak and unable to do much for herself. Today, nearly four weeks after the operation, she put on a dress for the first time, and her steps are still very slow and uncertain." Two years after that, by an interesting coincidence twenty years after her father's suicide, she had the first of several operations to correct an intestinal blockage. Rodgers wrote to their friend Bay Harley, "Dorothy . . . awoke one morning . . . in violent pain and then [after] a couple of days of careful watching the diagnosis was made of an intestinal obstruction. It took them 2½ hours in the operating room to find the thing, which they discovered had been brought about by an old adhesion. They found no growth of any kind and simply relieved the constriction which the adhesion had caused. The difficulty since then has been in getting her system to function normally. It has been slow, tedious and painful . . ."

Crohn's disease, an acute inflammation of the digestive tract, tends to run in families, and at least one of her relatives had it; but her daughters believed her problems were caused by her gynecological difficulties and dependence on laxatives. The Demerol she always took for pain exacerbated the symptoms. Mary Rodgers Guettel said, "When she was in Lenox Hill Hospital a few years before she died, they sent in this guy who was going to straighten out all her problems. The first thing he said was, 'We'll have to take you off all painkillers,' meaning Demerol, and nobody ever saw that doctor again." The reason was not hard to find. One day, while her mother was still hospitalized, Linda went to see her. "She was there for a long time and they weren't supposed to let me in, but they did not catch me in time and I went into her room," she said. "They had taken her off Demerol and she was frightening: crying and twisting on the bed and in absolute torture." She added, "It was a drug-infested family, as doctors' families often are."

Dorothy Rodgers was back in the hospital a year later for yet another unexplained operation, and recovering in the spring of 1952. Hammerstein told Richard Halliday that the four of them were planning to go "somewhere where there is sun." It would do their wives good to get away, "and possibly Dick and I can meet each other and get to know each other and perhaps get some work done . . . Here in New York it is just hell. I have had to swear off making any more speeches or doing any more good. Last week I spoke on the theatre at the P.E.N. Club, and up at New Haven at the Yale Drama Department, and two weeks before that I played Swarthmore. Goodbye to all that . . ."

OF ALL THE THINGS Rodgers chose to be testy about, how his music was performed was at the top of the list. If he was ready to write a song, rewrite it, and throw it away at a moment's notice, once the score had been fixed an understandable reaction set in and he would countenance no arguments. The very thought that someone might change a chord, let alone a phrase, without his approval would lead to an explosion of rage, as one young composer quickly discovered. David Raksin, then at the start of his career, was hired to orchestrate some songs for *On Your Toes* in 1936, for which Hans Spialek was the main orchestrator. "Rodgers was very persnickety about the composer's rights, exceptionally so," Raksin said. He already knew this because one of his friends, on the board of ASCAP, produced a radio program and got a call from Rodgers afterwards, "in a rage about what they had done to his stuff," when in fact, "they were all but worshipful." There had not been any changes to his melodies, but there might have been some changes in the harmony, "and Rodgers had every right to be persnickety about that because his harmonies were often rather odd and even perverse." They were, nevertheless, "very good," he said with emphasis. "He was one of the great songwriters, and one of America's two premier writers of waltz, the other being Jerome Kern."

Raksin was given some work on *On Your Toes,* finished it with dispatch, and was invited to go on the road with the company. One night he was given a tune, and "I'm supposed to have it ready next morning for the rehearsal," so he went back to his hotel room to do the instrumentation for a thirty-five-man orchestra, prepared, as orchestrators had to be, to work all night. Raksin then discovered that two chords appeared to be in the wrong order. "Sometimes Rodgers would do that, but it was his way of doing things and of course you deferred to it, but in this case it looked wrong." He went to see Spialek, who agreed that it was an obvious error in this case. Nevertheless, just to be cautious, Raksin reversed the chords in such a way that Rodgers's original order could easily be restored if it transpired that this was what he wanted. Next morning the orchestra was reading through what Raksin had written when "Mr. Rodgers came charging up the aisle. I tried to tell him I had written it so it could easily be reversed, but he didn't want to hear any of that and so I finally lost my temper. Rodgers said, 'What have you done to my music?' so I replied coolly, 'What music?' " That was the end of the friendship.

Singers who were auditioning knew better than to perform one of his songs for fear of offending him inadvertently. Martha Wright said, "He knew exactly how he wanted his music sung, and you had to adhere strictly to that, including Rodgers and Hart songs. There is a line in 'It Never Entered My Mind,' that he wanted sung as "Now—I—even—have to—scratch—my—back—myself," she said, singing the phrase with long pauses between the words. "Peggy Lee would never sing it this way." In fact it was the mangling of song and dialogue that led to the downfall of Roger Rico, a handsome Frenchman who replaced Pinza in the role of De Becque. Rico had seemed like the perfect choice, but his command of English was shaky. After he continually mispronounced and reversed the order of words, Martha Wright again complained to Rodgers, this time with results. "I got him fired and I never regretted it." After that there were a series of replacements for Pinza, who was "almost irreplaceable." Another singer who played De Becque, Ray Middleton, was frowned upon by Rodgers. "Poor Ray, he was singing flat," she said. "He was a quarter of a tone flat, and I mean it was steady. He went into a show after that and didn't have any trouble at all." Something about Rodgers's displeasure had so unnerved him that he could not keep his pitch.

Rodgers's intolerance for less than an absolutely literal interpretation was well known by the *South Pacific* cast, who decided to tweak him about it one evening. Don Fellows said, "It was around Christmas 1949, and Peggy Lee had come out with a recording of 'Lover,' and we'd heard he was a little unhappy about it. So one night he came in the stage door and Bill Dwyer [who played Seaman Tom O'Brien] asked him if he had heard it. Rodgers turned around, took a step or two back, and said, 'Yes, I've heard it.' So Bill Dwyer asked, 'What do you think?' Rodgers thought for a second and said, 'I don't know why Peggy picked on me when she could have fucked up 'Silent Night.'"

Rodgers's deadpan humor was particularly well suited to such subjects. Fellows remembered him talking about Cole Porter once and saying, "The son of a bitch has made a career out of five chords." Rodgers also told a story about auditioning girl singers in London at which one of them sang "Let's Call the Whole Thing Off." The point about the song is that a disagreement about pronunciation, English versus American, threatens to break up a romance, but there is no indication of this in the printed score and the girl took it literally. When she came to the end of the song, Rodgers said, "Thank you very much, Miss Leveen," and she answered, "Oh, please, Mr. Rodgers, it's pronounced Le*vine*."

Rodgers always wanted his music played too loud, which was a perennial complaint from Larry Hart, to which Rodgers would reply, "Do you want the audience to go out whistling the music or the words?" And his tempi tended to be slow, causing much grumbling among singers who would lose their breath. In that regard the story is told that Iva Withers, who replaced Jan Clayton as Julie in *Carousel* and went on to perform in a revival of that musical at the Dallas State Fair, was having a heated disagreement about tempo with her conductor, Franz Allers. Her arguments were going nowhere until she finally said to Allers, "All right, did you sleep with Richard Rodgers, or did I?" She won.

RODGERS AND HAMMERSTEIN were working to the absolute limit of their energies. As producers they launched *The Happy Time,* a comedy by Samuel Taylor, which ran for 614 performances at the Plymouth Theatre in 1950–51, and then Graham Greene's *The Heart of the Matter,* which closed in Boston in 1950. They had high hopes for *Burning Bright,* a play by John Steinbeck, which Stephen Sondheim saw in New Haven. "It's about Barbara Bel Geddes, who played the heroine, and Kent Smith, who played the husband, and Howard Da Silva, who played friend Ed. The point is, the husband is impotent so she gets pregnant by the friend. At the intermission some guy was saying the first act was rather slow. Dick said, 'Listen. It gets better in the fecund act.'" That play closed in 1950 after thirteen performances, which seems to have convinced Rodgers and Hammerstein, particularly after *South*

Pacific won the Pulitzer Prize, to stick to musicals. But in the meantime they had built a producing organization for the copyright licensing, publication, and performance of their works which is still flourishing, more than fifty years later.

Rodgers was in demand. He was being awarded honorary degrees, his advice was being solicited, and concerts were being organized in his honor. He and Dorothy were making handsome contributions to charitable causes, medicine and the arts being high on the list, and becoming politically active. When a committee of prominent people in the arts and sciences was organized to help re-elect President Roosevelt in 1944, Rodgers was one of the signatories. Then, three years later, when the House Committee on Un-American Activities began its probe of supposed Communist infiltration into Hollywood, Rodgers joined another prominent group of playwrights, composers, authors, and actors protesting the investigation. This activism aroused the suspicions of the Federal Bureau of Investigation, which opened a file on him but could find nothing really nefarious about him except that the Roosevelt re-election committee might or might not have become a Communist front organization and that he had risen in defense of free speech and civil liberties.

Conducting his own music was one of his favorite activities. After "Rodgers and Hammerstein Night," an annual event on the closing night of the summer concert series at New York's Lewisohn Stadium, was inaugurated in 1948, he often appeared as guest conductor. Receptions were being held and awards were showered upon him and Hammerstein. They were becoming the equivalent of national treasures and the subject of numerous radio and television specials. There was an evening of Richard Rodgers on NBC-TV March 4, 1951, to celebrate his twenty-five years in the theatre, followed by two one-hour programs on the Ed Sullivan show devoted to his career on CBS-TV in 1952. A year later, in 1953, when four Rodgers and Hammerstein musicals *(Oklahoma!, South Pacific, The King and I,* and *Me and Juliet)* were running in New York simultaneously, the Mayor of New York declared a Rodgers and Hammerstein week. In 1954, a one-and-a-half-hour program featuring the works of Rodgers and Hammerstein was carried on all four networks: NBC-TV, CBS-TV, ABC-TV and DuMont-TV. Nearly everyone who had starred in their shows appeared, as well as some who had not, performing their works and singing their praises. But, to Rodgers, the crowning moment came in 1954 when he conducted the St. Louis Symphony Orchestra in a program of his own music. It was the fulfillment of a lifetime's ambition.

That Rodgers wanted to be recognized as a composer of serious works had become apparent in his speeches and newspaper and magazine articles. When

Richard Rodgers, with Mary Martin on his right, and Gertrude Lawrence, his new
leading lady, on his left, celebrating the second anniversary of *South Pacific* in
April 1951 and the successful opening of *The King and I*

he was awarded an honorary degree at Drury College in Springfield, Missouri, in 1949, he chose the moment to criticize what he called the arbitrary division between the high and low arts, on the ground that this was hindering the development of a distinctive American music, which would always draw its main strength from folk traditions. His solution was, not surprisingly, the genre of musical theatre, so perfectly suited to reconcile either end of the spectrum, from the crassly commercial to the most esoteric. He would become increasingly impatient with the argument that because his and Hammerstein's work was so popular, it must therefore be inconsequential, pointing (with some justification) to the success of Hammerstein's *Carmen Jones* as an example of what could happen to an opera once it was imaginatively translated and made accessible to English-speaking audiences.

Rodgers also chafed under the criticism that he was a composer of limited range, confined to show tunes. This was hardly fair, since he had written two ballets, *Slaughter on Tenth Avenue* and *Ghost Town,* demonstrating his ability to compose on a larger scale, and his seven-and-a-half-minute "Soliloquy" for Billy Bigelow in *Carousel* was rightly seen as a landmark example of what could be done with an extended form, one that would influence Leonard Bernstein and Stephen Sondheim, among others. But Rodgers was still dissatisfied. He wanted his name associated with a huge work, something everyone (even the music critics) would have to concede was important. His opportunity would come with *Victory at Sea*.

As was customary in his world, Rodgers had made use of arrangers and copyists since the early days. As he frankly acknowledged, orchestration was a special skill he had not learned, but even those composers fully capable of orchestrating their own work, Leonard Bernstein among them, left the work to others, primarily because of time pressures. As Professor George Ferencz, who edited the memoirs of Robert Russell Bennett, explained, "In an opera you are writing for the cast and the role but in the theatre the music is being written for a particular actor/singer." That meant so much last-minute work on the road that there literally was not enough time to put together a completed score. In the twenties Rodgers had tended to use Roy Webb, who was also his music director, and in the thirties, Hans Spialek or Don Walker. Bennett had worked with Rodgers and Hart on *One Dam Thing After Another* and *Heads Up!* but was primarily Jerome Kern's arranger, known for his brilliant work on *Show Boat*. When Hammerstein joined Rodgers, Bennett came with him, and with the exceptions of *Carousel* and *Me and Juliet*, which were orchestrated by Walker, Bennett was the one who gave the distinctive sound to the Rodgers and Hammerstein scores. Rodgers was always ambivalent about the role of the arranger-orchestrator. While acknowledging the contribution of men like Bennett, he resisted the claim, put forward by such other masters of the genre as Irwin Kostal, that arranging someone else's work was just as creative as writing melodies. Kostal decried the custom of awarding the melodist and ignoring the work of the man who constructed the orchestral framework around the tunes. To counter that, Rodgers liked to tell an apocryphal story: "An arranger claimed that the composer was nothing without the arranger's work. The composer took from his pocket a sheet of music paper that was totally blank. He tossed it across the table to the arranger and said, 'Arrange me a hit.'"

Alec Wilder, who thought some of Rodgers and Hart's music was as close to perfection as anyone could get, was not as enthusiastic about the work he did with Hammerstein. He wrote, "While Rodgers continued to write great songs, and even to top himself, generally speaking I find missing that spark and daring flair which existed in the songs he wrote with Hart." Speaking of *South Pacific,* he did not like "Some Enchanted Evening," finding it "pale and pompous and bland. Where, oh where, are all those lovely surprises, those leaps in the dark, those chances? I'm in church and it's the wrong hymnal!" Wilder was voicing a common complaint, that Rodgers's uncanny ability to reflect the personality of his lyricist had led him to write with an earnestness and solemnity that was absent in his earlier work. His melodies were as irresistible as ever; but the whimsicality, surprise, and sheer inventiveness, those aspects of his own nature that Hart had stimulated, had been replaced by something more didactic and sentimental. Be that as it may, no one doubts that the lushness and polish of the Rodgers and Hammerstein scores were due in large measure to the work of the self-effacing Bennett. Bruce Pomahac, music director for the Rodgers & Hammerstein Organization, said that Bennett "instinctively understood Rodgers's style. His arrangements were very simple and unadorned. He didn't add a lot of flashy ornamentation at the end of phrases, what musicians call 'a mayonnaise arrangement.' It was always tasteful and understated. Once in a while he would add a countermelody. Rodgers didn't do very much of this, and Bennett believed that counterpoint was one of the building blocks of good orchestration. As in a fugue, he gave each instrument its own voice, which is what gives the result its richness and depth." Stephen Douglas Burton, a composer who has written a book on orchestration, said, "Like Mozart's orchestrations, you hear everything. Nothing is covered up. It is a minor miracle to be able to do that with twenty-six musicians on Broadway." Brooks Atkinson proposed a word of thanks to Bennett after the opening performance of *The King and I* at the St. James Theatre in the spring of 1951, praising his "colorful orchestrations that make a fresh use of individual instruments and that always sound not only interesting but civilized."

Rodgers and Hammerstein had been offered a very large compliment by the Metropolitan Opera: they were invited to write an opera based on *Moby Dick*. It was hugely flattering but obviously completely wrong for them, as Rodgers was quick to appreciate. Then NBC-TV asked Rodgers to write the background music for twenty-six half-hour television films documenting U.S. naval operations during World War II. After seeing a run-through of the films, he agreed to provide the music if Henry Salomon, the historian who had assembled the series, would be willing to make adjustments in the films, if necessary, for the sake of the music.

That Rodgers, said to have written the entire score of *Oklahoma!* in six working days, should have agreed to tackle thirteen hours of music was evidence, to his admirers, of his phenomenal abilities. In *Some Enchanted Evenings,* the composer and critic Deems Taylor was so impressed that he italicized the number of hours of music Rodgers would write. He added, "While

Dick has never claimed to be the peer of Richard Wagner he can, if he chooses, point out that the score of *Victory at Sea* equals in running time the combined scores of *Tristan und Isolde, Die Meistersinger,* and *Parsifal*—and it took Wagner a total of twelve years to write them!" Eckert Goodman wrote in a similar vein, "The score for *Victory at Sea* . . . a work that considered in the aggregate is undoubtedly the longest sustained musical composition in history, took Rodgers relatively quite a while: he labored over it for nearly six weeks." What Taylor and Goodman did not know, or chose to ignore, was that of those thirteen hours of music, Rodgers wrote about an hour. The chief themes were his, plus some of the subsidiary material, with suggestions about tonal color. Robert Russell Bennett wrote the other twelve. As an illustration of what that meant, David Raksin referred to "No Other Love," the slow tango that Rodgers originally wrote for an episode called "Beneath the Southern Cross," which was picked up and set to words by Hammerstein for *Me and Juliet.* Raksin said, "Russ had to turn that song into something that was appropriate for battleships." Bennett did all the technical work involved in timing and cutting the music to fit the twenty-six episodes and acted as music director for the series, which was highly praised. He also conducted the orchestra for the best-selling RCA record album, and was doubtless very well paid.

LIKE MANY OTHER Broadway producers, Rodgers and Hammerstein had an unvarying rule. No matter what the notices, they would sit down within a few days to talk about a new show. At their particular stage no single failure was likely to bankrupt them professionally or financially; their futures had been secure ever since *Carousel.* But there was nevertheless a necessary dimension to their determination to keep going, something like the dictum that requires a man thrown from a horse to get back on it as soon as his bones have healed. This was truer of Rodgers than of Hammerstein once the latter passed the magic age of sixty and began to think of himself as someone who had earned the right to stop and watch the shadows cross the grass. For Rodgers, this was more than the work of a lifetime; it was a lifeline. As he said to Don Fellows, when the subject of success or failure arose, "if you lose your momentum you're dead."

Since they shared the same ruthless self-interest in matters of business, it was not difficult for them to present a united front during contract negotiations. Consultations were confined to whispered exchanges in the far corners of a theatre, or outside on a fire escape if necessary, in pursuit of the golden rule that governs theatrical collaborations in all but exceptional circum-

stances. But since Rodgers and Hammerstein had had so many careful discussions about a show beforehand, these differences were minimal, and others have remarked on how seldom there would be a last-minute crisis on the
road. They even agreed on delicate matters of theatre etiquette. When it
looked as if Constance Carpenter, who had jumped into the leading role in
The King and I when Gertrude Lawrence died, would take her vacation so
that she could attend opening night at the Drury Lane Theatre to watch
Valerie Hobson in the same part, Hammerstein, who was already in London,
sent a strongly worded letter to Rodgers to the effect that he did not want her
there. He did not want the publicity to focus on Carpenter, or to have Hobson, who had made her reputation in films, to be any more unnerved than
she was already. Rodgers replied by return mail that he had "completely
stepped on the idea."

Their back-and-forth correspondence is full of such letters as this from
Hammerstein: "Did you get one of these letters? If so, what have you done
about it? If not, what do you think *I* should do about it?" Neither of them
was shy about putting his foot down when necessary. Responding to a letter
from the Museum of Modern Art asking for the rejected footage from their
films, Rodgers wrote, "My feeling coincides precisely with yours—that it's
completely ridiculous to preserve for posterity materials which we are not
even willing to preserve for present use . . ." They also agreed that any new
idea that one of them did not like was automatically dismissed. Hammerstein
told Rodgers, "The very conception of 'Tragedy of Man' makes me tired
when I think of it. I want to go straight to bed and sleep . . . If I feel this way
I am sure you feel even more so in the same direction . . ." Or Rodgers would
write to him, "I have no idea what should be done about the enclosed," referring to a letter from a record company enclosing a postcard with a scene from
South Pacific on one side and a recording on the other. "I do know it makes
me feel creepy and I imagine we don't want anything to do with it." On occasion each felt emboldened to speak for the other without prior consultation.
When Hammerstein received a letter from John Van Druten, who directed
The King and I, saying that his theatrical friends in London were astonished
at the choice of Valerie Hobson, Hammerstein replied, "We are aware of
some of the English public and press believing that they should cast *The King
and I* but we still believe we should cast it, and I think it will all die down if
she is as good in the part as we think she will be, and if she isn't there is nothing that we can do about it." He was sure English producers would make predictable, and wrong, choices, naming some leading ladies who had been in
their prime two decades before. Speaking of the actress he was sure would
have played Lady Thiang, he wrote, "I mean the lady who played all of Ivor

[Novello]'s plays and sings out of the side of her mouth. This is why we do not leave the job to English producers any more. Dennis Hoey would have automatically been cast as the Kralahome and Tuptim would be Doris Day. This is giving me a nightmare, so I will stop." No doubt Rodgers completely approved.

Even though they took great care not to let anyone else drive a wedge between them, they irritated each other often enough. It was clear to everyone that Rodgers was the dominant partner in the relationship and expected everything to go through him first. He would get extremely upset if he was not the first to know, however minor the information. When Rodgers had to find out from a stage manager that the Hammersteins would not be attending the opening of *Annie Get Your Gun,* he took it personally. Bruce Pomahac said, "Joshua Logan was once asked about the importance of cooperation in the theatre and said, 'It's not cooperation, it's confrontation.' He thought the same dynamic had to be operating with Rodgers and Hammerstein, but they were so good at concealing this that you could never see it happening."

This was true, because Rodgers did not so much confront—as has been noted, he left that to others—as refuse to comment. He was particularly annoyed at Hammerstein's dilatory attitude, as it seemed to him, when it came to writing lyrics. Waiting for lyrics made him feel helpless, and that was too uncomfortable a reminder of what he had gone through all those years with Hart. A suspicion formed in the back of his mind that Oscar, too, did not like to work, one to which he unkindly gave voice in later years. So his way of dealing with the situation would be to punish his partner with silence when the long-awaited lyrics finally arrived. One of the most difficult songs Hammerstein ever wrote was "Hello, Young Lovers," a poignant musing about a past love that is one of the high points of *The King and I.* It took him five weeks of struggle to master the form and the sentiment, but he eventually had something he felt proud of. He sent the lyrics by special messenger to Rodgers, instructing the man to wait for an answer, but no answer came. There was no word that day from Rodgers, or the next, or the one after that. In fact, Hammerstein did not hear from him for four days. Finally Rodgers called on another matter and, at the very end, said that, by the way, the lyrics were fine. Then he hung up. They were four of the most painful days of Hammerstein's life.

GERTRUDE LAWRENCE, whom Rodgers and Hammerstein had known ever since she appeared with Bea Lillie in *Charlot's Revue,* had not been in a musical for ten years, since she starred in *Lady in the Dark* in 1941. Music by

Gertrude Lawrence as Anna Leonowens in *The King and I,* 1951

Kurt Weill, lyrics by Ira Gershwin, and a book by Moss Hart had made this
an imaginative, intelligent concoction about an editor of a fashion magazine
who has never been able to find true love. In particular, the song "My Ship"
seemed exquisitely tailored to the special qualities, both fragile and authoritative, that Lawrence conveyed. Despite a small singing voice that was often
gratingly off-key, she had a quality that Rodgers and Hammerstein rightly
valued, that of seeming to be the only person worth watching on a stage. She
was looking for a new vehicle and in 1950 thought she had found one in *Anna
and the King of Siam* by Margaret Landon, which was based on an account of
a young British widow, Anna H. Leonowens, who went to Siam in the 1860s

Yul Brynner as the King of Siam with Gertrude Lawrence

to become tutor to King Mongkut's children. In the play "Mrs. Anna," as she would be called, is in her twenties and the king she serves is middle-aged. In actual fact Lawrence was fifty-two that year and Yul Brynner, the actor who would play the King and make it so completely his own that no one has ever surpassed him, was in his thirties. But Rodgers and Hammerstein knew that actresses can get away with playing younger women on a stage far longer than they can on a screen. When they came to make the film of *South Pacific* in 1958, Mary Martin had reached her mid-forties and, they thought, was no longer persuasive as a young nurse, so they cast Mitzi Gaynor. This led to a distinct cooling between Martin and her husband and Rodgers and Hammerstein, if only temporarily. (Martin would play the role of the young novice Maria onstage in *The Sound of Music* two years later.)

Gertrude Lawrence was no prettier in the conventional sense than Mary Martin; like her, she had the wide eyes and somewhat blunted, larger-than-life features that seem almost a caricature at close quarters but which serve so well when seen from a distance. She had made her reputation playing sophisticates, albeit ones with a sense of humor, and it was by no means clear that she could convey the youthful uncertainty of an English girl catapulted into an alien world. But she had the poise and authority Anna needed to assert her worth in the face of absolute royal power, and she was determined to play the part.

There remained the small problem of her voice, which had become thinner and more reedy as she aged, and less certain in pitch. That was a very sore point with her, and Rodgers did not endear himself by having Doretta Morrow, the young, beautiful, highly trained singer who had been cast as Tuptim and was rumored to be his "girl," introduce Lawrence's numbers to her before rehearsals began early in 1951. Although offended, Lawrence knew she had to at least appear to cooperate with her composer, and she agreed to study with his vocal coach. For his part, Rodgers would tailor his songs to her vocal limitations: no high notes, or low ones, either. By then Rodgers and Hammerstein were convinced that even though they were writing for a star, which was not the way they liked to write, the story was so engaging, with its exotic setting, its conflict of cultures, and its hint of a love interest between Anna and the King, that audiences would not be able to resist it. "There was the most perfect stillness," a purser on an American sloop-of-war wrote when he went to visit King Mongkut in 1857. It was broken only by "the sound of our footsteps on the marble, and, except ourselves, not a creature was moving. Here and there . . . with faces on the stone, in motionless and obsequious reverence . . . grovelled the subjects of the mighty sovereign into whose presence we were approaching." The King stood beneath a gold umbrella of state, "dressed in a grass-cloth jacket, loosely buttoned with diamonds, a heavy silk panung, jewelled babouches, and a cap that blazed with gems of great size and beauty."

Such a baroque display would tax the gifts of even someone as accomplished as set designer Jo Mielziner or his colleague Irene Sharaff, Broadway's leading costume designer. In addition, Rodgers and Hammerstein had engaged the talents of the brilliant young choreographer Jerome Robbins, whose challenge would be to adapt the highly stylized movements that had evolved from centuries of Siamese culture into dances that looked exotic but not too foreign. Similarly, Rodgers had to suggest the musical coloration of the setting without imitating it. He wrote, "Western audiences are not attuned to the sounds of tinkling bells, high nasal strings and percussive gongs . . ." It had to sound like Siam, "but Siam as seen through the eyes of an American artist." Interestingly enough, *The King and I* would serve as a model for the Harold Prince–Stephen Sondheim–John Weidman musical, *Pacific Overtures,* a quarter of a century later, but in reverse. What if, Prince proposed, they showed the arrival of Commodore Perry's historic visit to

Japan in 1853 from the perspective of the Japanese? They had set themselves an almost insuperable task. That of Rodgers and Hammerstein was at least theoretically achievable, and for Rodgers at least, not unfamiliar, since he had experimented with the same kind of setting twenty years before, with *Chee-Chee.*

Work on the new musical play began early in 1951, a $300,000 production which they were producing themselves. No longer dependent on anyone else to find money for them, they were in the novel position of actually turning backers away, albeit with profuse apologies. But controlling all the profits also meant shouldering all the risks, and they were still not sure how well their star would respond to the demands of the part. They were soon to be reassured. There is a scene in which Anna sings and talks to herself, giving vent to her frustrations and privately summing up what she thinks of the King. James Poling, a writer for Collier's who sat in on the rehearsals, wrote, "She took the center of the barren stage wearing, for practice, a dirty muslin hoop over her slacks, with an old jacket thrown over her shoulders for warmth. She began rather quietly on the note, 'Your servant! Your servant! Indeed I'm not your servant!' Then she gradually built the scene, slowly but powerfully, until, in a great crescendo, she ended prone on the floor, pounding in fury and screaming, 'Toads! Toads! Toads! All of your people are toads!' When she finished, the handful of professionals in the theatre burst into admiring applause."

Gemze de Lappe, who played one of the Royal Dancers, said, "I had two big revelations during *The King and I.* I used to listen to Gertrude Lawrence on the public address system every night in our dressing rooms and she'd get onto a note and sag down off it. The night after I left the show to go into *Paint Your Wagon,* Yul Brynner gave me house seats and I saw her from the front, and I was so taken by her. She had such a star quality, you didn't care whether she sang off-key. She more than dominated the stage. Boy, was that a lesson to me."

Her second revelation came during rehearsals for *The Small House of Uncle Thomas,* the famous ballet devised by Jerome Robbins as a Siamese version of Harriet Beecher Stowe's novel, in which de Lappe danced King Simon of Legree. "One day everybody was sitting around the periphery, and Jerry called me out into the middle of the floor and started showing me the movements, and I did fine. Then he said, 'I want you to growl like a lion.' Well, in those days you were trained to make no noise at all. The whole illusion of ballet is that it's effortless, and you can't let anyone hear your footsteps; you can barely even breathe. And here was Robbins demanding that I roar. I was so self-conscious at that moment, because everything had stopped and all eyes were glued on me. But when Jerry Robbins tells you to do something, you do it! So I started growling, and realized how useful it was, because if you have the right image and the right sound, you will get the right movement," she said. This was something Robbins knew instinctively.

She continued, "They took out a wonderful scene. Mrs. Anna's first entrance into the palace comes with a song in which she sings, 'Over half a year I have been waiting, waiting, waiting, waiting, waiting, waiting outside your door.' At the end she points her umbrella at him, or something like that, and the King says, 'Off with her head,' or words to that effect, and the eunuchs pick her up and carry her off. The King says, 'Who, who, who?' with great satisfaction, and finds out he has just thrown out the English schoolteacher. So he says, 'Bring her back!' and she is ushered in." The scene was removed because it was considered too undignified an entrance for a star, but "we all loved it." (The songs "Waiting," "Who Would Refuse?" and "Now You Leave" were cut before the New York opening.)

In the person of King Mongkut Hammerstein draws a subtle, compelling portrait of a man at the crossroads: the inheritor of a feudal tradition who takes his godlike status for granted, yet cannot help being thrown into doubt by the challenge to his set of values that his European schoolmistress represents. Hammerstein dramatized this inner confusion in "A Puzzlement," a monologue in which the King gives vivid expression to this dawning realization. "There are times I almost think / I am not sure of what I absolutely know," he sings. Speaking of his heir, the Prince Chululongkorn, he asks himself,

> What, for instance, shall I say to him of women?
> Shall I educate him on the ancient lines?
> Shall I tell the boy, as far as he is able,
> To respect his wives and love his concubines?
> Shall I tell him every one is like the other,
> And the better one of two is really neither?
> If I tell him this I think he won't believe it—
> And I nearly think I don't believe it either!

Once again Hammerstein had demonstrated his gift for drawing, in the radically simplified manner demanded by the form, nuanced portraits that when heightened by all that a master composer can achieve, become fully believable human beings.

He and Rodgers also showed again their mastery of casting, perhaps the least understood and most important aspect of a theatrical undertaking. They had been waylaid briefly by the idea of Rex Harrison, who had played the role of the King in a recent film, but, fortunately for them, he was not available. When Mary Martin, who had played with him in *Lute Song*, recommended Yul Brynner, they had only to see him onstage to realize they had found an actor who had an uncanny understanding of the part. Richard Watts Jr. wrote, "Never does Mr. Brynner fall into the facile way of being a dashing leading man putting on a superficial Oriental masquerade. To an amazing extent he gets the depth, honesty and complete credibility into an authentic characterization of a man whose awakening mind and emotion are at work." Brooks Atkinson called him "vehement, restless and keen-minded . . . a terse and vivid characterization." And at least in this production of *The King and I*—the revival in 1995 starring Donna Murphy and Lou Diamond Phillips made the attraction explicit and therefore far less convincing—there was only a hint of something between the King and Anna. That was deliberate. As Hammerstein explained, "I think that Anna and the King are really in love with each other . . . but I don't believe that either one of them knows it . . . what I really mean to say is that they felt this attraction but were inhibited, not only from expressing it to each other, but each to himself."

That he would underplay a romance and eschew a conventionally happy ending was further evidence of Hammerstein's adherence to believable plots and consistent characterizations. This aspect of *The King and I* was immediately recognized and appreciated. Atkinson said, "Like *South Pacific*, *The King and I* is a skillfully written musical drama with a well-designed libretto, a rich score, a memorable performance and a magnificent production . . . Being genuine artists . . . Mr. Rodgers and Mr. Hammerstein have got way beyond the mechanical formulae on which musical shows are founded and are saying something fundamental about human beings. Again like *South Pacific*, *The King and I* is literature; and since the literature is expressed largely in music, it is tremendously moving." When the musical opened on March 29, 1951, there were only occasional, and polite, demurrals. John Lardner wrote, "Even those of us who find [the Rodgers and Hammerstein shows] a little too unremittingly wholesome are bound to take pleasure in the high spirits and technical skill that their authors, and producers, have put into them." As the musical began its three-year run and 1,246 performances, not to mention another lengthy run of 926 performances in the Theatre Royal, Drury Lane, and a film (1956) that would be considered the most successful of all those made of their work, the money was rolling in. John Steele Gordon, author and historian, wrote, "In 1951, when *The King and I* was on the road trying out, someone (Bea Lillie, perhaps?) had a luncheon party at an apartment on East End Avenue, overlooking the East River. During lunch a huge barge pushed by a tug chugged down the river. In it was a vast mound of something, covered by a tarp. 'What do you suppose is in it?' someone asked. Moss Hart looked out of the window and said, 'It's Rodgers and Hammerstein sending their money down from Boston.'"

There were two setbacks during *The King and I,* the first involving the death of Gertrude Lawrence. It must have been evident during rehearsals that her health was fragile. She missed the final week of rehearsal in the winter of 1951 because of pneumonia. She had repeatedly complained about the weight of the costumes around her waist, and the metal crinoline hoops were replaced by bamboo ones in an attempt to lighten her load—something like thirty-five pounds of metal and fabric—but still she complained. She played the role for a year and a half and then left for a vacation in the summer of 1952, replaced by Celeste Holm. She returned in August seemingly restored to health but left again almost immediately. She was diagnosed as suffering from hepatitis but in fact had a rapidly advancing stomach cancer and died on September 6, 1952.

It was a severe blow to the production. Although there have been many competent and spirited renderings of the role since, by such actresses as Constance Carpenter, Annamary Dickey, Patricia Morison, Barbara Cook, and Florence Henderson, there was something about Gertrude Lawrence's performance that was unforgettable. But before that happened, Rodgers had suffered a blow that was even more unexpected: lukewarm reviews. To a man, the critics seemed convinced that the score had not measured up to the standard set by Rodgers and Hammerstein in their previous musicals.

The verdict seems incomprehensible nowadays. As later critics have pointed out, Rodgers's soaringly beautiful melodies, with their overtones of operetta, give the evening its particular glow. "For his fine singers he was able to write as much arioso music as the market would tolerate, while for Miss Lawrence he wrote gay, simple, appealingly sentimental melodies," Bordman wrote. He was no doubt thinking of "Hello, Young Lovers" and "Getting to Know You," a melody that was originally intended for *South Pacific* and then replaced by "Younger Than Springtime." For the illicit and doomed romance between Tuptim and Lun Tha, Rodgers provided "We Kiss in a Shadow" and one of his loveliest ballads, "I Have Dreamed," which sets a mood of poignant longing. *The King and I* is really a celebration of love in all its guises, from the love of Anna for her dead husband; the love of the King's official wife, Lady Thiang, for a man she knows is flawed and also unfaithful; the desperation of forbidden love; and a love that is barely recognized and can never be acted upon. Finally, there was "Shall We Dance?," in which Anna gives the King his first lessons in the polka, "a whirling invitation to romance," as Cecil Smith wrote. Given the irresistible nature of the score, the critical reaction was as inexplicable as it was painful. These were the first bad reviews Rodgers had received since he began his partnership with Hammerstein. In his autobiography, written a quarter of a century later, he made light of the comments and pointed to the enduring success of the score. But at the time his confidence in himself and his partner had been severely shaken. He had grown used to paeans of praise and anything less felt like a rejection. He did not know whether he wanted to work with Hammerstein ever again.

Chapter Sixteen

"THE MAN I USED TO BE"

T HE NEXT RODGERS AND HAMMERSTEIN musical, *Me and Juliet,* was Richard Rodgers's idea. It would be a story about life in the wings, and the action would be confined to the theatre itself, its dressing rooms, offices, orchestra pit, an alley, even the electrician's bridge which controls the lights high above the stage. A play would be running and the story would be about the cast and crew and their daily relationships. Something of the sort may have suggested itself to him during *On Your Toes,* after Balanchine made use of the ballet *Slaughter on Tenth Avenue* to further the plot and bring it to a climax. There could be no clearer statement of the central role the theatre had come to play in Rodgers's life. In creating such a story he was not just holding a mirror up to nature but putting life itself inside an imaginary proscenium. Perhaps the idea of multiple reflections was meant, as in a play by Luigi Pirandello, that master of illusion, to obscure or obliterate the line separating fact from fiction. Perhaps, at this stage of his life, life itself had become the ultimate illusion, in which one acted a part to someone else's script, and the world of make-believe was the single reality. He wrote without irony, "I had thought it would be fun to do a piece about the musical theatre itself and do it as truthfully as possible." Behind that thought was an implicit threat.

Sondheim said, "Oscar was able to keep the partnership together by taking Dick's suggestion, which he did not want to take." After all, *Allegro* had been Hammerstein's pet project, and now Rodgers wanted them to do the story he wanted. That was fair enough, and even though Hammerstein accepted the idea with a good grace, he had to struggle to hide the fact that he was basically not interested. That there was such a struggle is clear enough in

Bill Hayes and Isabel Bigley in *Me and Juliet,* 1953

Margot Hopkins, Rodgers's longtime rehearsal pianist,
seated beside the composer, with, from left, George Abbott,
director of *Me and Juliet,* and Oscar Hammerstein.
Isabel Bigley is at far left and the other person
is not identified.

retrospect. The melodramatic plot, about a stage manager's love affair with a singer, and an electrician who tries to kill them in a drunken rage, sounds more like a one-act opera by Mascagni than what they said they intended to write. The musical would not have a message, even a subliminal one, but would simply be a lighthearted story about life in the theatre. There would be some gay little tunes—it was back to saxophones, which Rodgers had not used since *By Jupiter*—as well as trumpets and trombones. There would be plenty of dancing and a cast of bright young things. A few trenchant asides might be made about unglamorous realities, but for the most part it would be a return to the kind of old-fashioned musical he and Hart had written so many times over. So from the outset there seems to have been a dichotomy between what Rodgers said he wanted and what Hammerstein thought he wanted, as he vainly tried to clothe his cardboard characters with recognizable human feelings. It did not help that George Abbott, their director, found the plot trite and sentimental and was concerned about the play within the play. This had certainly been tried before, most successfully, in 1948, with Cole Porter's *Kiss Me, Kate,* in which the story of a divorced couple, now playing the leading roles in a theatre company, is given momentum and resonance by the play they are performing, Shakespeare's *Taming of the Shrew.* As with *Oklahoma!* Hammerstein could not, or would not, provide a plot-enhancing dance sequence, and choreographer Robert Alton was at a loss. "No one had thought it out," Abbott complained, and the dancing merely got in the way. Perhaps the only person who could have helped was Pirandello.

The singer Bill Hayes, who at the age of twenty-seven was already established as an actor and television performer, was hired to play the role of Larry, the stage manager, and Isabel Bigley was the chorus singer he falls in love with. Mark Dawson was playing Bob, the jealous electrician, and Ray Walston and Joan McCracken had leading roles in a secondary plot. It was to be a company of over sixty singers, dancers, and actors, many of them unknown. Hayes was thrilled to have been chosen and could not believe he would be working with these legendary figures. Abbott, he found, wanted him to parrot lines exactly, but "Hammerstein would wait for a quiet moment to whisper, 'Think of it this way' . . . and then he would explain succinctly and precisely how the character was feeling." Rodgers was everywhere at once, giving copious notes on the music. "He would tell the rehearsal pianist how to voice accompanying chords . . . try different endings to make the most of a singer's vocal abilities, endlessly try different keys to get the most out of the lyrics . . ." And he wanted his songs sung exactly. One of Hayes's numbers was "No Other Love," and "to this day, if I sing it, or even just hear it playing

Isabel Bigley and Joan McCracken in *Me and Juliet*

in the background of some restaurant I hear Dick Rodgers saying, 'No, Bill. It's written eighth-quarter-eighth-quarter-eighth, with the whole note preceded by an exact eighth-note syncopation . . . Don't linger on the word "love" and then come in on the downbeat. Do it the way I wrote it, thank you.' " It was, Hayes concluded, a very difficult song to sing.

They blocked and rehearsed in New York for four weeks early in 1953 and then went to the Alvin Theatre for a run-through, one Hayes found genuinely stirring. "And I've often found that to be true in subsequent shows. There's something magical about the first run-through, when the actors really become emotionally involved for the first time." Afterwards Abbott gave some notes, but they were minor. They were then taking the train to Cleveland for twelve days of tryouts at the Hanna Theatre and then the Shubert in Boston before a Broadway opening at the Majestic at the end of May. "We clambered on board that train, threw our suitcases on our tiny bunks, and gathered to laugh in the men's room lounge. No one could sleep." Things became more and more stimulating until the opening night in Cleveland. The audience was responsive and the applause was warm, but, as Rodgers explained, "when a show is in good shape you don't have to wait for the newspapers to tell you; you can feel it in the air. In the same sensory way, you also know when a show is not in good shape." Isabel Bigley sensed it. She had just come from performing Sister Sarah Brown in *Guys and Dolls,* and "there wasn't the same energy." Even "No Other Love," the melody from *Victory at Sea,* seemed to have been interjected arbitrarily. There was a hint of tension between Rodgers and Hammerstein as well. Jamie Hammerstein, who was second assistant stage manager for *Me and Juliet,* remembered Rodgers as difficult and demanding. "We had a scratchy relationship. He would come backstage and say to me, 'Shouldn't you be on the other side?' meaning the off-prompt side, and I would say, 'No. I've got everything under control from here.' I think he thought it was his show and his bailiwick. Why should a Hammerstein be back there?"

Jamie Hammerstein continued, "He liked pretty girls, in a very conventional way. I had a very embarrassing time with that show because there was a fabulous, aquiline-nosed ballet dancer in the lead and Dick hated her looks. She had that Russian look, you know, and his idea of a beautiful girl was Shirley Jones. I thought she was terrific and I remember asking her for a date. And I was to go out with her for the first time when Dick walked up to me and said, 'I want you to fire her.' So I had to go—I said to her, 'Are you ready?' She said, 'Yes.' I said, 'Well, you're fired. Can we still go out?' "

Suddenly what had seemed to be a show needing minor adjustments became a musical in serious trouble. Hayes wrote, "It was difficult unlearning five weeks of memorizing to insert new words and staging and scenes. Sometimes it became confusing to play Version A at night and be rehearsing Version B in the daytime . . . to be followed by Versions C, D, E, F, and G." One of the first changes to be made had to do with the way the show opened. As originally designed there was no overture; the curtain went up on a bare stage and actors and crew drifted in and began work. Hayes wrote, "The audience never bought it. They talked continuously, all through the opening dialog . . . the opening songs and the dancers' warm-up dances, until finally when it came time for the overture they would . . . settle down." Rodgers and Hammerstein fought against the inevitable but finally had to admit defeat and begin with an overture, which solved the problem.

After they closed in Cleveland they boarded the train for Boston. "This time no laughs in the men's room lounge. Everyone was pooped, from rehearsing all day and playing all night and changing the memorized material. No drinking parties, no poker, no giggling between the upper and lower berths, just get on the train, find your place, get into bed and try to catch a few winks on that old rocking roadbed . . ." As for Hammerstein, despite determined optimism—"*Me and Juliet* looks like a great big hit," he told John Van Druten—a certain defensive tone crept into his letters. "It is a change of pace for us and in some quarters we may be criticized because it is not as high-falutin' as our more recent efforts. It is in fact an out and out musical comedy. If this be treason, make the most of it." There were more changes in Boston, more polite reviews, and interminable extra rehearsals until the Broadway opening on May 28, 1953. In predictable reflection of the story they were telling, some backstage dramas were developing, ones with a ring of authenticity. Joan McCracken, married to the choreographer Bob Fosse, became pregnant during the run of *Me and Juliet* and lost her baby "about the same time she was losing her husband to Gwen Verdon," Hayes wrote. McCracken had originally been given a song called "Meat and Potatoes," which she sang to Bob Fortier, who played the principal dancer, Don Juan in the play-within-a-play. After hearing the song as delivered by McCracken in her "low-down, gutsy way," and the audience's reaction—they thought it was full of double entendres—Rodgers and Hammerstein hastily removed it and gave her another one, "We Deserve Each Other." The song was followed by a dance just before one of Hayes's entrances. Her Irene Sharaff costume was extremely skimpy, and after some energetic contortions she would be lifted up by Fortier and almost out of her costume, arriving at Hayes's feet night after night in a state of magnificent undress. He wrote, "You might say that from Joan McCracken I learned my wonderfully intense ability to concentrate."

After so much exhaustive effort they had all become good friends. Hayes would discuss folk songs and Burl Ives with Joan McCracken, have dinner at Sardi's with pals, and play recorder quartets with company members. The one person he could not figure out was his leading lady, Isabel Bigley. "I played opposite her for fifteen months, played her lover-then-fiancé-then-husband, and I don't remember ever having a conversation with her." He concluded, "I doubt that the audience ever believed we were deeply in love."

When he came to sum up his experience with *Me and Juliet*, Abbott wrote that the score was not the best. "They were too talented to write a bad score but it was not top-drawer Rodgers and Hammerstein." Thanks to a handsome advance sale the play ran nearly for a year (358 performances) and transferred to Chicago for two more months of capacity business, but the reviews were disappointing. Abbott thought that their string of successes had made Rodgers and Hammerstein too sure of themselves. That could well be true, but there was the further factor of Hammerstein's attitude toward this particular musical. John Steele Gordon, whose mother, Mary Steele, was Hammerstein's secretary, said he remembered her telling him about one incident.

"Oscar was in the habit of dropping into matinees of his shows to make sure that they were not beginning to run long and that the actors weren't getting up to their usual tricks . . . In the summer of 1953, after *Me and Juliet* had opened to decidedly mixed reviews, Oscar went to see it and when he returned home, he stuck his head in my mother's office to see if there were any messages or whatever. My mother asked him how the show was. He looked at her for a second or two, said, 'I *hate* that show,' and turned and entered the house."

As a kind of coda to *Me and Juliet*, Abbott convinced Rodgers to let him do a revival of *On Your Toes* and presented it, with the original choreography by Balanchine, at the Forty-sixth Street Theatre in the autumn of 1954. Vera Zorina again took the lead, Elaine Stritch played Peggy Porterfield, and the musical was polished to Abbott's usual professional standard. But almost two decades later, what had seemed a mildly amusing plot was exposed for the hopeless sham that it was. The production closed after a humiliating sixty-four performances. Rodgers wrote to a friend, "I'd be an awful liar if I said that I was not disappointed in the reception of *On Your Toes* but I feel very much the way Adlai Stevenson did, 'It hurts too much to laugh and I'm too old to cry.' " (Rodgers's faith in *On Your Toes* was finally vindicated in a 1983 revival, when the musical ran on Broadway for 505 performances.)

ISABEL BIGLEY RECALLED that when the wives of Rodgers and Hammerstein turned up at a dress rehearsal for *Me and Juliet*, Irene Sharaff said under her breath, "Here comes the wrecking crew." Isabel Bigley said, "They hated to see the wives because they would get all that criticism." This may not have been entirely true, but it is likely that, given the professional interests of both women, the dress designer would have come in for special scrutiny. John Steele Gordon recalled of that period that Dorothy Hammerstein was still an extraordinary beauty, "an absolute knock-out and as elegant as could be. She had blue eyes that could see across a room." Dorothy Rodgers was equally soigné in a Duchess-of-Windsor kind of way and always charming, but she had "a complete dead-fish handshake." As time went on, Dorothy Rodgers, once very much in the background where her husband's work was concerned, continued to make inroads. He always played his songs to her first and soon knew whether she was politely enthusiastic or genuinely moved. One of the songs that always reduced her to tears was "Hello, Young Lovers" from *The King and I.* How Dorothy reacted had become important to him, and he always wanted her there for an opening, at which she always wore a gray dress, on the theory that buying something new and dazzling was

Richard Rodgers getting some stiff criticism from his wife in the 1950s

just asking for trouble. She and Dick always sat in the very last row so that at intermission, and just before the final curtain, they could "make a break for it." Like him, she was very cautious about planning a large party for something that might turn out to be a flop, preferring to wait out the reviews at Sardi's and celebrate afterwards, or quietly disappear. *South Pacific* was a rare exception. They felt sure enough of its reception to plan an opening-night party at the St. Regis. The orchestra played, the champagne flowed, and all the tablecloths were pink.

Since the end of the war they had lived in a spacious cooperative apartment duplex at 70 East Seventy-first Street, with ample space for the girls, guests, and a staff of three. On the main floor was a large living room big enough to accommodate two grand pianos, with olive-green carpeting, walls, shantung curtains and woodwork, Louis XV occasional chairs, and Regency-period furniture. Dorothy was very fond of accent pieces such as antique Korean chests and cabinets with painted peasant motifs. The library was decorated in shades of beige. Since they also liked warm yellows, the dining room was in tones of yellow and green—the room had been enlarged from two smaller rooms to give it a separate seating area. Upstairs were the bed-rooms; his was in gold and forest green, hers in blue chintz with rose accents. Weekends, and much of the summers, were spent at Rockmeadow, a house in Southport they bought soon after *South Pacific* opened, an imposing six-bedroom center-hall colonial on forty bucolic acres, to which they added a pond. They had thought they wanted to move to Long Island but were entranced by this estate, not far from their first house on Black Rock Turn-pike. They immediately set about adding a sizable cottage, and Dorothy Rodgers spent many happy months immersed in decorating decisions.

As in New York, the living room's walls and carpets were the same color, a clear yellow, with a paler yellow sofa, green cushions, and pink, yellow and green flowered curtains for the nine-foot bay window. The dining room was in green and white, olive green was the prevailing color of Rodgers's study and there were walls of bookshelves in the paneled library with its angled fire-place. This was where their main entertaining was done. Dick and Dorothy embarked on a series of weekend visits to friends, making notes about the guest rooms they encountered, Deems Taylor wrote. Then they went home and planned their own. As a result, absolutely everything had been thought of, right down to the postage stamps already applied to the envelopes in the writing desks. What guests might be expected to need formed a whole chap-ter of Dorothy's book *My Favorite Things,* published in 1964. It made for a very long list.

Winthrop Sargeant, who interviewed them for the *New Yorker* in 1961, remarked on the lavish use of floral arrangements in their New York apart-ment, beginning with potted plants en masse in the vestibule outside. It turned out that the numerous bouquets were replenished every few days from the Connecticut garden and winter hothouse, presided over by a full-time gardener. They had begun to assemble an extraordinary collection of art, not just theatrical scene designs by Jo Mielziner, which decorated Rodgers's study, but sculpture and paintings by French Impressionists, Post-Impressionists, and Abstract Expressionists, and American and Italian works of the same periods. This solved their birthday and Christmas presents to each other; they just bought paintings. Among those Sargeant saw hanging on their walls was a Toulouse-Lautrec of a woman in a box at the theatre and a rare Vlaminck still-life. It would be characteristic of Dorothy Rodgers to place a bouquet of violet and red anemones beneath a painting of the same flowers in the same colors. Although she insisted that she aimed for a casual look, since her husband disliked a room that did not look lived in, the results were always exquisitely tasteful and somehow inhibiting.

Like her mother, Mary had left college before graduating to get married, in December 1951, to Julian B. Beaty Jr., always called Jerry, a lawyer more than ten years her senior. She had gone through her plump adolescent years and slimmed down considerably. When she was still in school, her father had written to her mother, "Mary is bursting with energy and good spirits, possibly because she is not bursting with fat," one more telling example of his intolerance for less than perfection in his children. She was a music major and wrote some two-piano pieces after they acquired their second piano; and after serving as an apprentice at the Westport Playhouse in 1950, she knew she wanted to be involved in the theatre somehow. While at Wellesley she was also writing songs, and she published her first book of children's songs in 1952. She did this "because it seemed like a step removed and something kind of modest and uncomplicated and nobody could accuse me of being stupid enough to try to do what my father was doing." Linda was still the pianist in the family. The two girls were rebelling in large and small ways. In March of 1951 Mary announced her conversion to Catholicism, and her alarmed father wrote a letter to Walter Winchell begging him not to use the item in his column. He complied. Then she was in love with Stephen Sondheim, got engaged to another man briefly and broke it off after she met Jerry Beaty.

It was an interfaith marriage and, Beaty said, his future mother-in-law asked him what they were going to do about that. She told him, "We are not religious but we are social Jews. Dick is well known and everyone knows he is Jewish. I think it would be embarrassing if we don't have something to say. Maybe we would like a Rabbi." Beaty said, "It's whatever Mary wants." But he added, "Mary was not being consulted at all. She would have been married by a judge." They finally settled on a wedding at her parents' apartment presided over by a minister and a younger rabbi from Temple Emanu-El.

He said, "Dorothy managed these things. She presented herself as the spokesman. She would say, 'Dick and I think . . .' He didn't want to be troubled. He dressed in Brooks Brothers clothes which she chose. She was the one with the culture, Capital C. She added the polish to the marriage."

Like her mother, Mary became pregnant immediately, and their first child, a boy, was born nine months later. He was named Jeffrey Tod Beaty, but out of deference to his grandfather, who had always wanted a boy, the name on the birth certificate became Richard Rodgers Beaty. Still, he was always called Tod. This obviously disappointed his grandfather, who showed his displeasure in a typically oblique way. He would say to his son-in-law, "I don't understand why you kids don't use the names you call your children." He would make jokes about the fact that Jerry was not using his own name; "I understand you have just had a julian-miad from some terrible people . . ." Or he would joke that their house had been julian-built and call jerry cans

Richard Rodgers with his first grandchild, Tod Beaty

julian cans. Beaty said, "It was a running joke that could be stretched only so far and he and I could think of nothing to say to each other." He was advised to get Rodgers talking about himself, and this was a help. "But if you asked a dumb question he would cut you off with 'Oh, we're past that,' or 'You should know that.' He was not really interested in other people's doings.

"Dorothy was much easier to talk to. She could have been a good lawyer. She managed their business affairs and I used to hear endless stories at the dinner table about decoration and which came first, the words or the music, and we would roll our eyes. I've seen Dick many, many evenings when his eyes would wander and he would look blank. One evening we were sitting in the lovely dining room at Rockmeadow. It was a warm evening and the French doors were slightly ajar. Dorothy was at one end trying to make conversation and suddenly the wind blew the doors open and the curtains flew up into the air. I said, 'Oh my, it's getting windy.' Dick banged the table, 'Oh my God, don't say we are so desperate now that we are discussing the weather.' I didn't confront him. I could have said, 'What are *you* doing to help?' But I didn't, so the remark just hung there." He thought Rodgers was often very cutting to his wife. "He'd be silent and she'd think of something to say and he'd snap her head off. You could see he was restive under her control. He was feeling he was in a cage and longing to escape."

PIPE DREAM, Rodgers and Hammerstein's next musical, had a complicated history. It began as an idea in the minds of the producing team of Cy Feuer and Ernest Martin, who had produced the masterful musical *Guys and Dolls* in 1950, based on the stories and characters of Damon Runyon, with songs by Frank Loesser. They were looking to repeat their success and thought they had found their next vehicle in *Cannery Row*, John Steinbeck's series of stories about an equally raffish bunch of characters living in Monterey that included a marine biologist with a beard. "In those days guys never wore beards," Feuer said. They went to Steinbeck to see if he would write a book for their musical. He declined, but went on to write a novel based on the characters, which he called *Sweet Thursday*. By then Loesser, who Feuer and Martin were sure would want to write the songs, had turned them down, so they thought of Rodgers and Hammerstein. Feuer said to them, "Look, you've been in the sweetness and light business. You're always writing shows with little girls running around the stage with bows on their asses. We're in a gritty business. Why don't you come down to our level? Get into this. It has John's literary stamp on it." Feuer and Martin owned all the rights but accepted an agreement with Rodgers and Hammerstein by which they were paid half the profits. In return, the producing credit would go to Rodgers and Hammerstein.

Feuer and Martin had envisioned Henry Fonda as the marine biologist and had spent a year trying to teach him to sing without success. Rodgers would have nothing to do with that idea. Feuer said, "They were very excited about the musical but the minute they started casting I started to worry. They had settled on [Metropolitan Opera diva] Helen Traubel to play the madam of the brothel, this tough dame with the heart of gold, and we knew they were in trouble. Dick claimed they were not uncomfortable dealing with prostitution, but they did pretty it up. Our more muscular name for the musical was the *Bear Flag Café*, which was the name of the brothel. *Pipe Dream* became full of doilies, and both of them were responsible, not just Oscar."

When he was interviewed for his oral history by Columbia University Rodgers did not remember that Feuer and Martin had played any role in the genesis of *Pipe Dream* and thought it had come through Steinbeck, who had married his friend Elaine Anderson and whose play, *Burning Bright*, he and

Helen Traubel and William Johnson in *Pipe Dream*, 1955

Hammerstein had produced. But, he said, "we were seduced by the writing, and didn't recognize . . . that the characters were not right for Oscar and me. We shouldn't have been dealing with prostitutes and tramps." It was pointed out to him that *Pal Joey*'s characters were disreputable; that, he said, was Rodgers and Hart, not Rodgers and Hammerstein. He conceded they made a bad decision by casting Traubel as the madam. They had seen her perform at a nightclub in Las Vegas and were impressed, but had not realized how much her voice had deteriorated. Furthermore, she could not act. They hired her without an audition: "a mistake I haven't made since," he said. In other words, they had begun badly and "these things are epidemic within a show . . . everything seems to become infected."

It was a curiously appropriate metaphor. For some years he had been get-ting yearly physical examinations and would consult specialists at the least sign of a symptom. He might have been guilty of hypochondria were it not for the fact that many of his suspicions turned out to have been justified. He had been prone all his life to benign growths—he had had a tumor removed from the back of his neck and a growth removed from his foot that was the size of a golf ball when he was still in his twenties—and seemed vulnerable to every flu germ that came around, as well as periodic stomach upsets, backache, and headaches. Always at the back of his mind was a terrible, irrational fear of cancer amounting to a phobia. He wrote that when he was twenty and studying music at what would become the Juilliard his father told him, "Son, your mother has a strange lump inside her that's got to come out. After it does we won't know for some time if it's malignant." Rodgers wrote, "When he saw the consternation on my face he said quickly, 'But she'll be all right. I know she'll be all right.' Would she? My mother! She was only forty-nine—and facing death! I was frightened sick." His mother survived breast cancer and lived for another twenty years. When he learned his father had cancer, "I was as terrified as when he told me about my mother," he continued. "Their experiences should have given me some immunity against the fear of cancer. They didn't."

During the summer of 1955 Rodgers began to feel pain in his left jaw. His dentist assured him there was no cause for concern, but suggested he come back again. Six or so weeks later the pain was still there and this time the dentist was alarmed. Some X-rays were taken and Dr. Milton Rosenbluth, Rodgers's physician, diagnosed cancer of the gum posterior of the last tooth. He and Dorothy returned home, deeply depressed. "She put two lunch trays before us, then cried and apologized for crying and for not being able to eat . . ." But then, he told the interviewer Arnold Michaelis two years later, "a curious thing happened to me. I got a little angry and mostly I got determined. Dorothy was terribly upset; much more than I was." Michaelis said, "Well, she loves you more than you do." Rodgers agreed, after a pause. Then he said, curiously, "She doesn't know me as well." He continued, "I remember exactly what I said to her: 'I am going to lick this.' " He knew he had no control, "except that too many doctors had told me determination has a great deal to do with recovery. The fellow who goes into the operating room licked usually is. And I wouldn't have any part of it. The fright is so much worse than the actuality. Plus there is a very curious thing . . . in a time of crisis we behave well." Was it a life-threatening illness? he was asked. He answered, "Oh, sure. I wouldn't have it. I didn't want to die."

He was told the bad news on a Friday and was to enter the hospital the following Tuesday, the very day *Pipe Dream* was going into rehearsal, and he still had three manuscripts to copy and a song to write. On the Tuesday morning he went to the rehearsal and played the score for the company, then went out to lunch with Dorothy and into the hospital. Shortly after noon the next day an operation was performed and the malignant growth, numerous lymph glands, and part of his jaw were removed. He also lost all of his teeth on that side. Mary Rodgers Guettel said, "One of the most horrifying memories I have is of him in the hospital right after he'd had the jaw cancer . . . And my mother said, 'He's going to be very self-conscious about the bandages and the tracheotomy here. Don't wear your glasses and he'll feel better. Then he will feel that you can't see.' Well, it may have been better for him, but it was appalling for me, because being nearsighted anyway, my sense of hearing is twice as acute in some compensatory fashion, I suppose, and when I was led to the door of his room after this horrendous operation, the sounds of a tracheotomy are just ghastly—they're the sounds of somebody trying to breathe . . . and here I was: I couldn't see that he was perfectly safe, because I can't see a damn thing across the room . . . And so to stand in the door of a hospital room and see . . . lots of white bandages and hear this ghastly rattling sound! I remember feeling all the blood leaving my face. It was just terror."

Jerry Beaty said, "The only thing I remember in general was when he had this jaw operated on he went into seclusion. He wanted to see how he was going to look. They had replaced the bone with titanium and the only thing one noted was just a tiny drop at the side of his mouth and a tiny slurring of speech. Dorothy saw to it that publicity was minimal."

Daniel Melnick, who had a warm relationship with his father-in-law, thought the operation was a critical turning point. "Before that happened he was still very outgoing, and in years to come he started to retreat. For someone of that period, cancer was the plague, a death sentence. So when it hit him it had a disproportionately devastating effect. However, I think it would be a simplification to ascribe his depression and withdrawal to that experience alone; it had been going on earlier. There were manifestations in disguise. He was even able to hide from himself! I didn't realize until much later that he had been in therapy for years. In the end, we were all terribly worried about him."

TRUE TO HIS LIFELONG PATTERN, Rodgers tried valiantly to brush off the operation's effects. He insisted on walking around and later published an article about the fact that it was possible to recover from cancer, and protesting the illogic of a social climate in which the word was never mentioned. Here he was, well and working again. Well, not quite. It was true he was back at rehearsals ten days later, but in a wheelchair, losing so much saliva that he had to keep a handkerchief over his mouth, barely able to speak or eat. His friends and colleagues were horrified and tried to shield him as much as they could, jolly him along. While Rodgers was still in Memorial Hospital,

John Steinbeck wrote to tell him how well they were coping. "You will be glad to know that Elaine is doing a really adequate job in your place in *Piece Pipe*. She has changed some of the songs around and rewritten a few lyrics and I am sure you will approve. She had to fire three actors but she replaced them with her friends—good, ambitious kids who could learn probably." Steinbeck was in a teasing mood, but the fact was they were all deeply worried. Elaine Steinbeck said, "When we opened in Boston we were having terrible problems with the show and Dick couldn't help, and Oscar and John were rewriting. My John suddenly realized they were the wrong ones to be doing it, and wrote Oscar the following letter, 'You have changed my whore into a visiting nurse.' And Oscar laughed so hard, but it was true." Had this been a Hollywood movie, Rodgers wrote, at the end the composer, now a hero, would have been well enough to attend a fabulous opening night and would, with a tearful smile, take a bow to tremendous applause. "Well, if there were any tears in my eyes, it was because *Pipe Dream* was universally accepted as the weakest musical Oscar and I had ever done together."

Rodgers refused to make any allowances for himself, physical or emotional, but it was a bleak period in his life. He told Michaelis, "You ask too much of people who have been successful and they're human too. I'm tremendously worried right now about the next show. This isn't because *Pipe Dream* only ran one year instead of five [it actually ran for seven months], it's a natural wariness at the nature of the business. It's very easy to fail and I've always known that. *Oklahoma!* didn't make me think for one second that we weren't vulnerable. My point is that if you are reasonably rational and you have any kind of objectivity you know that after you have had *Oklahoma!*, *Carousel*, and *State Fair* in a row that it's a very good time to be cautious. This is when it's liable to sneak up from behind and hit you on the back of the head." Mary Rodgers Guettel said, "He dealt very gracefully and graciously and attractively with success and was generous about other people . . . He knew how good he was, and that was terrific. What was hard was that he didn't know how to deal with failure."

OUTWARDLY NOTHING HAD CHANGED. Williamson Music Limited at 14 St. George Street in London had found a large and loyal audience despite British reviews for Rodgers and Hammerstein musicals, which invariably found them "treacly," and was acting as a production office headed by Jerry Whyte, not just for its own works but other American transplants, along with plays of promise. Letters flew back and forth between Rodgers and Hammerstein and Whyte, who gave frequent detailed reports about casting, contract negotiations, touring companies, the status of a run, and the weekly box office. In the autumn of 1954 Whyte was in charge of six productions: *Oklahoma!, South Pacific, The King and I, Teahouse of the August Moon, Can-Can,* and *Guys and Dolls,* although *Oklahoma!,* a road tour, was about to close. Rodgers depended on him more and more. When Whyte had a slight coronary that year and was hospitalized in the London Clinic, Rodgers sent flowers and telegrams inquiring about his daily progress. He cabled at the end of August, DELIGHTED WITH THIS MORNING'S WONDERFUL NEWS THAT ALL IS WELL. PLEASE KEEP IT THAT WAY. THIS IS AN ORDER. LOVE FROM DOROTHY AND ME.

The telegram came from Culver City, where they were shooting *Oklahoma!* He and Hammerstein had retrieved the rights from the Theatre Guild for the vast sum of $850,000 and formed their own movie company, Rodgers and Hammerstein Pictures, Inc., in adherence to their unvarying rule of cutting out the middleman wherever possible. This, Rodgers conceded later, had been a mistake. *Oklahoma!* was considered disappointing when it was released in 1955, a verdict he thought was fair. But at the time he was immersed in all the decisions that went along with it, such as casting and locations. He wrote to Jerry Whyte in the summer of 1954 that he had just come back from Arizona, where much of the film was eventually shot, and found it beautiful and invigorating. That verdict was to be amended later. He told Florence Eldridge, Fredric March's wife, "Someone terribly bright at M-G-M told us that clouds in Arizona would photograph beautifully. There were clouds all right, but with them came sudden and . . . terrifyingly violent thunderstorms. What with the accompanying floods and the loss of light it took twice as long as the studio told us it would. We also found a coral snake in the swimming pool at our motel, so southern Arizona is yours for the asking."

They had found their new Curly in a handsome young singer, Gordon MacRae. Fred Zinnemann, who directed the film, had not been in favor of MacRae, considering him a wooden actor, and had tested James Dean for the part. Moreover, MacRae had a drinking problem and, the story went, had to have his lyrics taped to his horse's neck so that he would not forget them. Everyone agreed that he did have an ideal singing voice. Rodgers had settled on Shirley Jones, a young unknown, as Laurey after she was discovered in one of their Thursday-morning open auditions. He put her straight into the chorus of *South Pacific* and then gave her an understudy role in *Me and Juliet,* grooming her to take the starring roles in the films of *Oklahoma!* and *Carousel.* He liked her voice and everything else about her. She recalled that before they went on location for *Oklahoma!* she was invited to Rodgers's big office at M-G-M. He came around the desk and kissed her. She thought she

Oscar Hammerstein and director Fred Zinnemann on the film set of *Oklahoma!* in 1954

saw him slip over and lock the door. Then he came to sit beside her and patted her arm. He asked, "Do you have a boyfriend? Are you engaged?" She said, "He had a reputation with his leading ladies. The first thing he did was try to take them to bed. Young and naive as I was, this was something I already knew. He was getting a little too close, and I got the picture." So she fibbed and told him she was going to be married. As he moved even closer, she looked him in the eye and said, "You're just like a father to me."

The summer that Rodgers had his jaw operation they were at work planning a film of *South Pacific,* and since Rodgers was too ill to travel, Hammerstein was scouting for locations and sending back reports. Early in 1956, Hammerstein was on vacation in Montego Bay, Jamaica, where he and his wife habitually stayed. Rodgers wrote to say that *Pipe Dream* was looking better and better. Life was rather dull. Dorothy Rodgers was still having some pain, which he did not describe. He himself felt fine. Mary Martin and Dick Halliday were en route to Brazil and were urging him to find a new idea for her. He wrote, "So far I haven't got a thought." That month he saw excerpts from the films of *Carousel* and *The King and I,* which Rodgers and Hammerstein had turned over to Twentieth Century–Fox. The last-named "had me half out of my seat with pleasure"; Yul Brynner and Deborah Kerr could not be improved upon. "My feeling is that we have two very big hits coming up, especially the latter." He was right about *The King and I,* by far the best of the Rodgers and Hammerstein film musicals.

They had already met another up-and-coming young star, Julie Andrews. The set designer Tony Walton said that when his former wife was playing in Sandy Wilson's *The Boy Friend,* which arrived from London in the autumn of 1954, her clear, crystal voice, precise diction, and trim face and figure attracted the immediate attention of Rodgers and Hammerstein. She auditioned for *Pipe Dream* and Rodgers told her the part was hers. However, he happened to know that Alan Jay Lerner and Fritz Loewe were looking for an Eliza for *My Fair Lady,* their musical adaptation of Shaw's *Pygmalion,* a project that Rodgers and Hammerstein had also considered but had turned down because they could not figure out how to do it. Far from wanting to monopolize this enchanting young actress, Rodgers kindly told her about the Lerner and Loewe search. He said she was ideal as Eliza, which indeed she was, and hoped one day they would do something together. That opportunity came a couple of years later when her agent called to ask if they were interested in writing a televised production of *Cinderella* with Andrews in the leading role. To attempt their first television musical was a stimulating challenge—in those days, television programs were in black-and-white and most performed live—and an animated correspondence between Rodgers and Hammerstein, then in Australia, attests to the painstaking lengths they took to fashion a book and score. It was a great success when it aired in 1957, went to London as a Christmas pantomime the following year, and was revived twice. In 1965, Lesley Ann Warren played Cinderella, Ginger Rogers was the Queen, and the Fairy Godmother was played by Celeste Holm. Rodgers was gratified and everything was fine. And yet . . .

He was below par emotionally and physically. He had barely recovered from the severe psychic insult of the disfiguring operation when, he wrote to Hammerstein in November 1956, he was prevented from working on *Cinderella* by "a most peculiar illness. Apparently I picked up a bug or got some bad food and in some mysterious manner my central nervous system was affected . . . I couldn't retain my balance, I walked unsteadily and kept bumping into things. I couldn't even sign my name properly. Milton [Rosenbluth, his doctor] wanted to send me to a neurologist, but I was so fed up with going into my history with doctors that I begged him to wait a few days and see if I didn't improve spontaneously. That was exactly what I did do . . ."

Julie Andrews, as Cinderella, with Oscar Hammerstein and Richard Rodgers
before the live telecast of the fairy tale in 1957

But once *Cinderella* was behind them in 1957, there was nothing else on
the horizon. Something had happened to their unvarying rule of beginning
work on a new musical the minute they had opened the last; a year and a half
had gone by and there was no new project or prospect of one. Mary Martin
had been appearing with Giorgio Tozzi in a revival of *South Pacific* with the
Los Angeles Civic Light Opera that summer, and Dick Halliday had sent him
a glowing report. Rodgers agreed it seemed scarcely credible that they had
been unable to come up with another project for her. He had written to
Hammerstein about it, but Hammerstein had no ideas for that or anything
else, it seemed. After two musical flops Rodgers must have begun worrying
that his lyricist no longer wanted to work with *him*. He told Halliday that
Dorothy Rodgers had fallen downstairs and hurt her back but that otherwise
"we've had an uneventful but very pleasant late spring and early summer."

This was a polite social lie. As usual, whenever he was angry, resentful, or
discouraged, Rodgers had retreated to the bottle, and the winter and spring

months of 1957 were no exception. Kitty Carlisle Hart recalled that some time early that year she and her husband were invited there for dinner. Dorothy went to bed afterwards and they stayed up with him to hear a radio program of an all-Rodgers musical evening. While they were listening, Moss Hart began to take silent note of the number of Scotch-and-sodas Rodgers consumed and counted sixteen. This was when they realized he had a serious drinking problem.

That Rodgers was capable of abusing alcohol in this way was surprisingly little known. Jamie Hammerstein had no idea this was so. On the other hand, the writer William Goldman said, "Everyone knew he was a drunk." Dorothy Rodgers's reaction to her husband's problem was complex. On the one hand, Linda Rodgers Emory said, she was "a classic enabler," making excuses for him, protecting him from the outside world, and keeping his periodic falls from grace a secret even from his family. On the other hand, Mary Rodgers Guettel recalled that while she was having marital problems— she and Jerry Beaty were divorced in 1958—she found herself starting to drink at lunch and "whenever Jerry was around." When she told her mother about this, "I think she was shocked and some months later decided to tell me there was a history of this and I should be careful." Nevertheless, Dorothy Rodgers remained on her guard against even the idea that her husband had been an alcoholic. When the subject arose with Linda years later, in 1985, she wrote, "The only purpose that would be served in allowing this inaccurate rumor to become public would be to mar the image of a very private man in the eyes of his public—and to cause me excruciating pain."

The fact was, as Judy Crichton said, behind the façade Dorothy Rodgers's attitude was censorious. Judy Crichton's husband, Robert, had become a heavy drinker, and "[Dorothy] felt powerfully that he had gotten into trouble because he was an alcoholic, and she wouldn't forgive him, and was extremely ungenerous in every way." She had not viewed drunkenness as a symptom of a severe emotional problem; to her it was simply a lack of willpower. "That is what makes the story interesting, because clearly she had to have been caught in her own psychic jail. She was much too smart for the arbitrary lines she drew." What it must have cost her to watch this downward slide in her husband cannot be known. How often had he raged against Larry Hart's failing, which seemed to him the clearest possible abdication of responsibility for himself and others, a moral flaw? Now he, too, was spinning out of control.

He had always punished those around him with bouts of silence, but the silences became longer and deeper. Linda Rodgers Emory said, "He wasn't a falling-down drunk. When he was drinking he would just retreat. He'd get quieter and sleepier and fall asleep in a chair. I remember the Fourth of July weekend in 1957. My first husband [Daniel Melnick] and I were living in a little apartment in New York and my parents invited us to the country for the weekend. He was barely able to function. They had put him on tranquilizers, which was normal in those days. They didn't recognize then that its effects on the brain are similar to those of alcohol and the synergistic effects could be lethal. He had ground to an absolute halt. Essentially he was not there anymore." Rodgers referred to the episode obliquely in his memoir. "I began sleeping late, ducking appointments and withdrawing into long periods of silence." He claimed he "*began* to drink," a bland understatement, adding, "I simply didn't give a damn about . . . anything . . ." In common with the Arabist Freya Stark, Rodgers had taken refuge from an unstable emotional upbringing with flights of imagination that had sustained him and around which he had built his life. He had constructed "a kind of dream safety," as Stark's biographer, Jane Fletcher Geniesse, wrote. Stark had wrapped herself in romantic adventure stories in which she always played a leading role; Rodgers, too, had taken a leading role in his own never-never land and clung to it with single-minded purpose through decades of success and failure, sure of himself as long as it was there. When that world threatened to collapse, he, like Stark, ignored what was happening for as long as he could, staving it off with retreats into alcoholic oblivion. But that, as even he realized, was doomed to fail. To everyone's surprise, when it was suggested on that July 4 weekend that he enter Payne Whitney Psychiatric Clinic, he agreed. He was there for almost four months.

Payne Whitney, a division of the New York Hospital–Cornell Medical Center, has treated many famous clients, including Robert Lowell, Marilyn Monroe, Mary McCarthy, and the novelist Jean Stafford, who called it "a high class booby hatch." For those patients only moderately in need, the atmosphere was plush and permissive; there were regular visiting hours, a variety of activities, and private rooms. Linda said that on her father's first weekend there she went "scampering" to buy him pajamas without strings, because he was being put on the suicide floor and "couldn't have anything he could hang himself with," an indication of how seriously his doctors took his state of mind. While at Payne Whitney, and for some time afterwards, Rodgers was under a psychiatrist's care; Linda, her sister, and her mother were also interviewed. Linda called the psychiatrist, now deceased, "a cold son of a bitch," someone incapable of making real contact. She did not see any sign that he had been helpful, although that did not necessarily mean, she added carefully, that no help had been given.

Linda Rodgers Emory continued: "I think the most touching thing about my father is the alcoholism. As for the bouts with cancer—I think he had great courage with television. When photographs were taken, he tried not to show the side of his face that had surgery, but he was remarkably good about talking. I don't think he tried to keep the cancer a secret. It just wasn't much fun to talk about. But the alcoholism was devastating, along with the other psychological problems he had and didn't apparently get much relief from. And he had a life that, for me, was more fearful than anything else. He was scared of traveling, scared of leaving home, scared of dying . . . There were so many things that frightened him."

Her mother, she said, never had any problems with alcohol. She did smoke, about a pack of cigarettes a day, and continued to smoke even when she learned she had emphysema. She would never have consulted a therapist, because she had such trouble taking criticism, or what she would have construed as such. "But it's all kind of Catch-22, you couldn't get through to someone who was that rigid, wasn't ready to listen and didn't want to change. She was quite happy with the way she was and didn't understand there was a better way to live. I don't think she had any idea of how miserable . . . she was."

Edna Ferber wrote to Dorothy Rodgers in August 1957 that since learning of "Dicky's" hospitalization she had thought of them countless times. She wrote, "In these past two years Dick has had to face up to some difficult things. Most people (myself included) screech and tear their hair and carry on something feverish and boring when things pile up in life's usually orderly routine. Dick, so far as I know, not only doesn't actively rebel against them. He behaves, to us, his friends, at least, as though they (the unpleasantness) didn't exist. That course is easy on us, but hard on Dick."

Similarly, Rodgers dismissed his emotional crisis with the airy assertion, in his autobiography, that he recovered fast. He wrote, "untroubled by problems and pressures, I felt fine. My spirits soon picked up . . ." Once free of the depressant effects of alcohol, his natural resilience began to assert itself, but it is not true to say that he was relieved of problems and pressures. He was about to be visited by a host of new ones and he could not have been happier about it.

Barely a month after his arrival at Payne Whitney there was a new musical on the horizon. Joe Fields, Lew's eldest son, a man he had known all his life but with whom he had never worked, had come up with an idea. He had read *The Flower Drum Song,* a best-selling novel of that year by C. Y. Lee about the clash of generations between members of a Chinese family living in San Francisco. Fields had obtained the musical and film rights and approached Rodgers and Hammerstein. Rodgers must have been thrilled to find Hammerstein as enthusiastic about the idea as he was, and in short order the latter had taken over the negotiations. Writing to Rodgers from Beverly Hills in August of that year, Hammerstein said that Joe Fields seemed content to have

Oscar Hammerstein at work on a lyric for *Flower Drum Song* in 1958

Hammerstein collaborate on a book with him and would allow the musical to be presented by Rodgers and Hammerstein. Fields had come to an informal agreement with Twentieth Century–Fox, which Hammerstein did not like, but Oscar thought these issues could be resolved. (The film was produced in 1961 by Universal-International.) Oscar was en route to Hawaii when he wrote but would write again. They were back at the old stand. Even the fact that Dorothy had gone into the hospital "for a rest" in July, after her fall, and had to return a few months after that for another operation, had not dampened Rodgers's spirits when he wrote to Jerry Whyte in October of that year. He said, "Oscar tells me he'll have some material for me in a week or two, and, as usual, the people here [Payne Whitney] seem to be anxious to have me active . . . as much as possible. That, of course, is okay with me. I am in excellent spirits and have never felt better . . . in my life."

Chapter Seventeen

"THE SKY FALLS DOWN"

F*LOWER DRUM SONG* is about Sammy Fong, who lives in San Francisco's Chinatown with his straightlaced parents. Fong loves a nightclub hostess but is obligated to make an arranged marriage with a girl his parents have brought over from China, and the plot concerns his energetic efforts to free himself from his romantic entanglements. Rodgers and Hammerstein's first choice to direct this newest Oriental enterprise was Yul Brynner, already an experienced director, and telegrams flew back and forth between New York and Vienna in the spring of 1958. But then Brynner could not be released from his contract with Twentieth Century–Fox for *The Sound and the Fury,* and had to drop out. In the meantime, Rodgers and Hammerstein had approached Gene Kelly. Hammerstein was staying at Claridge's in London and Kelly flew in to discuss the show. "I was very favorably impressed," Hammerstein cabled to Rodgers on April 21, 1958, and Kelly was hired. The dancer, singer, and choreographer had spent seventeen years in films and the idea of directing his first full-scale Broadway musical was enthralling. Kelly told his biographer, "It wasn't one of Rodgers and Hammerstein's best shows but it had a warmth about it and a sweet sentimentality . . . I knew that as long as I crammed the show brim-full of every joke and gimmick in the book, I could get it to work." The comment was made after the reviews were in, and these had been mixed. As usual, it illustrated that tenet expounded by William Goldman in his seminal work *The Season,* that in a group endeavor it's always *Rashomon.* What Goldman did not add was that the blame tends to be selectively apportioned, depending on the person consulted. From the producers' point of view the problem was Kelly. Jamie Hammerstein, who acted as the musical's production stage manager, realized that Kelly was tentative and uncertain, a lack of conviction that had soon communicated itself to the cast. Brynner would have been better, but now it was too late.

From the point of view of Eddie Blum, who was Rodgers's casting director, the biggest headache *Flower Drum Song* presented was finding actors. He said, "The problem is that Asians are generally very poor actors because they are too shy. The Japanese are slightly better. I remember when Miyoshi Umeki, who played Mei Li, came to us. She was also very shy, but fortunately she had a wonderful sense of humor. We sent her to a vocal coach. As for Sammy Fong, we had to cast him with an American, because there are no Oriental comedians! It took a long time and was a tough job.

"We started off with Larry Storch, who was my idea, but by the time we got to New Haven or Boston, it wasn't happening. If you are in a musical and even if it's an evil character, there has to be something nice about him. This is what Rodgers says, and he is right." It was agreed, as Jamie Hammerstein observed, that "Larry S. got completely tangled up and was just not funny nor charming and seemed to get worse the harder he tried." Then Jamie Hammerstein thought of Larry Blyden, an old college friend, who took the precaution of preparing an Oriental makeup before he was auditioned. Fields, Rodgers, and Hammerstein were convinced and he replaced Larry Storch. "Is there a nice way to fire someone?" Blum asked. "If you are Richard Rodgers you don't do it yourself. You send Morris Jacobs," a reference to a member of the Rodgers and Hammerstein staff, someone Blum did not particularly like. "You send one of your lieutenants, and I guess it was all right. No one's good at it."

Rehearsals began in September 1958 for a December opening. Their co-author Joe Fields was in attendance, but Oscar Hammerstein's appearance was sporadic; he was convalescing from major surgery. He had entered Doctors' Hospital in the summer and was there for a month. He had gall-bladder surgery, and then his prostate was also removed. He had been too ill to work for a crucial month and a half, and there was still plenty to be done in the form of new material as well as rewrites. Fields, too, was in poor health. He would suffer a heart attack during the Boston tryouts at the end of October. Dick Rodgers was there every day, but he was beginning to drowse at rehearsals. Jamie Hammerstein said, "We all had to keep an eye on Dick, and whenever he fell asleep we'd turn the house lights off, if we were rehearsing in the theatre, so nobody could see him." If he was aware of this strange new habit of his, Rodgers made no mention of it when he wrote to Dorothy, who had left for Europe in mid-September. He told her he was still waiting for material. "Oscar has slowed up again, Joe is doing nothing, Gene is paying too much attention to details in directing, and I'm the only one who's

Richard Rodgers, Pat Suzuki, and Jerry Whyte discussing a point
during a rehearsal for *Flower Drum Song*

faultless. Aren't you proud?" Still, the first big advertisements announcing the
December opening at the St. James had brought in over two thousand mail
orders for an average of $20 each, which was "All Right!" he wrote. "The cast
still is doing very well, but I wish I had more score to teach them." A day later
he wrote that "Oscar had a session with the urologist that gave him a great
deal of pain . . . and he spent the rest of the day in bed. I'm terribly sorry for
him, not only because of the discomfort, but because he must be as worried
about the show as I am."

Two days later, Kelly and Fields were having a "fracas" and Kelly made an urgent request to see Rodgers and Hammerstein between rehearsals that evening. "Gene had nothing new to say and could have said it today. Neurotic? Again I remember how stable everyone was at Payne-Whitney . . ." Meantime Oscar was feeling better but he still had no lyrics. "Well this can't go on for much longer for the simple reason that we open in a few weeks and we'll have a score or we won't." A few days after that, he reported, "The show is horribly rough . . . but the cast, badly unrehearsed, is full of charm and potential talent. Even the intrinsic book doesn't appear to be too bad for this stage." The advance bookings now amounted to well over $1 million, and all would be well were it not for Kelly's indecisiveness. "If he seemed more sure of basic technicalities I'd be happier, but he flounders so," Rodgers wrote. He was going to that day's World Series game with Jerry Whyte, and when he recalled his state of mind a year ago he could barely believe "the enormity of the change" in his life. For that he had to thank Dorothy for her patience and "unbelievable understanding." He continued, "I've said in every letter that I loved you. I've got reasons. I love you."

Most of the major drama critics did not dislike the show, but they did not particularly like it, either. Brooks Atkinson, in the *New York Times,* while admiring the set and the winning cast, thought the musical lacked the crucial element of vitality that had been so apparent in *South Pacific* and *The King and I.* Walter Kerr in the *New York Herald Tribune* found it "modest and engaging." Richard Watts Jr., in the *New York Post,* thought that for all its color and liveliness it was "astonishingly" lacking in distinction. The implication was that a good effort was not good enough for Rodgers and Hammerstein. If they had not topped themselves, they had failed; it was back to Rodgers's fear that he would be unable to meet the accelerating expectations that each new musical brought with it. There were rumblings of the kind of criticism that would become more evident a year later. Harold Clurman, in *The Nation,* was clearly becoming impatient with Rodgers and Hammerstein's "Dutch-uncle" confidence and thought the musical just missed being cloying. Kenneth Tynan, who had just been appointed chief critic for *The New Yorker,* was less gentle. The spectacle of Rodgers and Hammerstein fluttering brightly past matters of any weight or consequence was made to order for his devastating, take-no-prisoners reviews, and he went to his task with gusto. The music was peopled with Orientals of "a primitive, childlike sweetness," who conversed with more than "a smidgen of pidgin," he wrote. He was reminded of Joshua Logan's production of *The World of Suzie Wong* and decided that Rodgers and Hammerstein had created "a world of woozy song."

It was perhaps the sharpest attack yet made on a Rodgers and Hammerstein musical, and the phrase "world of woozy song" was irresistible, even if not particularly apt; whatever the score could be called, woozy it was not. But the phrase stuck, and the miracle is that *Flower Drum Song* not only survived but prevailed. It ran for 600 performances, toured for a year and a half, had a successful London run, and was made into a film. The secret of its indestructibility, as would be the case with the last show they would write together, was advance sales. By now the name of Rodgers and Hammerstein alone was enough to sell tickets sight unseen, and whatever the critics said mattered as little as it could ever matter on Broadway. The customers voted with their pocketbooks despite the notices, a paradox that would give Rodgers grim satisfaction and a constant feeling of having been vindicated. Meanwhile, Tynan had declared himself as perhaps the most formidable opponent Rodgers ever encountered.

BACK IN THAT FATEFUL SUMMER of 1957, when Rodgers wrote to tell Dick Halliday and Mary Martin that neither he nor Hammerstein had the ghost of an idea what they should all do next, she already had an idea in mind, but one she could not talk about. A German film had been made in 1956 about the life of the Austrian baroness Maria von Trapp, who had started out in life intending to become a nun, but married a widower, Baron Georg von Trapp, after becoming governess to his seven children. After Hitler invaded Austria, they escaped to America and won renown as the singing Trapps; the German film was called *The Trapp Family Singers*.

Paramount Pictures took an option on the film and asked a young Hollywood director, Vincent J. Donehue, to direct it. After seeing the German film Donehue decided that it would make a perfect musical play and wanted Mary Martin, then too old to be passed off as a teenager in any film, as Maria. She was delighted and thrilled, but there were numerous obstacles. First, they had to wait for the Paramount option to run out. Then all kinds of permissions had to be negotiated, not just from the German film company, but from the Trapp family as well. Richard Halliday, who was to be the producer for the proposed musical play, was joined by Leland Hayward, and they engaged the playwriting team of Howard Lindsay and Russel Crouse. That left only the music to be settled, and their course was obvious: they would use the repertoire the Trapps had made famous. They needed one more song, and turned to Rodgers and Hammerstein.

Negotiations dragged on for months, and it seems clear that Rodgers and Hammerstein were not approached about writing extra material until the summer of 1958, during Hammerstein's hospital stay, because Halliday and Hayward brought the idea to Rodgers then. After watching the German film, Rodgers said he thought that doing a musical play was a mistake. They should either dispense with songs altogether or change their idea and make it a musical. That such an opinion might be self-serving made no difference. The general reaction was euphoric: the great Rodgers and Hammerstein liked their idea. Rodgers added the caveat that *Flower Drum Song* would have to come first, which altered nobody's mind. He said, "It was very flattering— they said they would wait."

That the character of Maria in *The Sound of Music* was romanticized and idealized was to be expected, given the nature of popular theatre; but this particular portrait had less resemblance to the real flesh-and-blood figure than most. What Lindsay, Crouse, and Hammerstein described was a beautiful, virginal blonde with a guitar whom the Mother Abbess farms out to be a governess because she is ungovernable: she wears curlers under her wimple, sings all day, continually cracks jokes, and wanders around in the mountains at night, a girl with so little attention span that she forgets everything she is told. The Mother Abbess laments, "How do you hold a moonbeam in your hand?" Even Maria von Trapp, who was in the audience and stood up to take a bow when *The Sound of Music* reached Broadway, must have squirmed over that one. She was a rather plain-looking, stockily built woman with a blunt manner. She had had a loveless childhood as the ward of a socialist judge who was a vehement atheist and who, she wrote in her autobiography, beat her. After finishing high school and experiencing a religious conversion, she joined the Benedictine abbey of Nonnberg.

Far from being a beam of light while there, she was so constricted by the order's regimen that her health was affected: this was why she was sent to be a governess. She grew up to be immensely resourceful and authoritarian, to judge from her children and stepchildren. It is said that some years after *The Sound of Music,* a visitor came to their Vermont lodge and told her he had been in love with her for years. Maria von Trapp turned to a friend and asked, "Do I know this man?" The friend replied that she did not. She turned on her heel and walked away.

Maria von Trapp was not sent to be governess of all Georg von Trapp's children but as tutor to his second daughter, Maria, who was bedridden. Since Trapp encouraged his children to sing and accompanied them on the guitar, mandolin, and violin, he was hardly opposed to having music in the house, as *The Sound of Music*'s authors had it. Instead of being a martinet he was, according to his family, a loving father whom they saw constantly. As for their escape over the mountains, in reality they made a prosaic departure on a

Mary Martin, as the new governess, arriving at the
home of the Von Trapps in *The Sound of Music,* 1959

Theodore Bikel, as Captain Georg von Trapp, demonstrating the
talents that helped him capture the role in *The Sound of Music.* He is
being heard by Marion Marlowe and Kurt Kasznar.

Mary Martin and Richard Rodgers listen to a playback during a recording
session for *The Sound of Music*

train to Italy, arriving in the United States by way of England. It was all rather
reminiscent of the day, recalled Theodore Bikel, who played Von Trapp,
when Zsa Zsa Gabor brought her daughter Francesca to see the show. After
the matinee she was in his dressing room backstage, crying, with mascara
running down her cheeks. "This is my life!" she said. "Escaping over the
mountains from Hungary . . . Magda, Eva, Mama . . ." He replied, "What
are you talking about? You were fifteen years old and some Turkish diplomat
married you and took you out of Hungary on the Orient Express." She said,
"It doesn't matter. It's my story. Over the mountains; over the mountains . . ."

Mary Martin's determination to play the part of Maria was equaled only
by her dedication. Eddie Blum, who cast the show for Rodgers, said, "She
was a consummate professional. If there was a nine o'clock rehearsal she'd be
there at eight-thirty. If someone said, 'You are going to have to play a guitar,'
she would take lessons. The big problem was finding someone to play opposite her. They tried to get a man with a Mitteleuropean background, even if
she didn't have one herself. We had to have just the right captain because we
had all seen the German film, but it was very hard to come to a consensus.

Martha Wright as Maria in *The Sound of Music*

Someone would get on the phone with an idea and come up with Bobby Darin! It was nutty.

"We had Lindsay and Crouse, Leland Hayward, Richard Halliday, Rodgers and Hammerstein, and the director, Donehue, who was a friend of the Hallidays' but, to my knowledge, had never done a musical. That was the group we had to please. Naturally we went the operatic route first, looking for another Pinza. No luck. We tried a great German actor but he couldn't sing. Then we called in Leif Erickson. We heard he could sing and they loved him. But not enough. Then I thought of this Israeli whom I had seen perform: Theodore Bikel. He played a guitar onstage and that was it. That was the other thing about Rodgers and Hammerstein; they were very good about using an actor's strengths." "Edelweiss," the last song Hammerstein ever wrote, was a heartfelt little melody written for Von Trapp to sing onstage as he realizes he is leaving his homeland forever. Bikel wrote, "This beautiful little tune sounded so authentic that one autograph-seeking fan at the stage door some months later said to me, 'I love that "Edelweiss" '—and then added with total confidence—'of course, I have known it for a long time, but only in German.' "

Eddie Blum continued, "Casting the children was also difficult, because we wanted children who were not obviously child actors. The stage mothers were dreadful. Some tried to proposition the stage managers to be sure their daughters got other appointments." Casting the nuns presented difficulties no one was prepared for. "The minute Mary Martin put on her habit she became one of God's children. The same was true of Patricia Neway, who played the Mother Superior. Rodgers would tell the story about going to upper New York State to visit a real Mother Superior, and she sat with her feet up on her desk. They just couldn't get the stage nuns to believe that yes, they were married to God, but they were also human beings."

Since Hammerstein was ill much of the time, Rodgers was the man in the foreground. Bikel said, "He would use humor whenever he thought a fight was looming, a humor that was sometimes raunchy and often impish," and he enjoyed poking fun at himself. They went to a Chinese restaurant one time, an unprepossessing kind of place with plastic place mats and Muzak in the background. "Whenever the Muzak played a Richard Rodgers tune— which seemed to be . . . about every forty-five seconds—Dick got up, turned toward the rest of the diners, and took a bow." His and Hammerstein's relations with Lindsay and Crouse could not have been more cordial. Anna Crouse said, "The thing that impressed me about that collaboration was, here were four writers who knew their business and I don't think there was a dissenting voice. They talked things out, made suggestions and changed each other's work. I remember particularly one of the first scenes Howard and Russel wrote was between the nuns and Maria, and the nuns were talking about curlers under her wimple. Oscar called up and asked, 'Would you hate me if I used that in a lyric?' And they said never, because if you can tell the story in a song in a musical, it's so much better. So he took the phrase right out of that scene. It was that kind of collaboration."

The person Rodgers did not "get on" with was Richard Halliday. "Richard Rodgers knew more about the theatre than he did, but Halliday was always out there protecting Mary," Anna Crouse said. "Mary was very smart. She'd let her husband bite the paddle and, when asked, she 'didn't know anything about it.' I saw Dick lose his temper with Halliday and speak his mind. Dick was not one to hide his opinions, anyway. While you are making a musical it gets very tense, particularly when you are just about to open, and things that really aren't important have to be dispensed with. So on a couple of occasions, Dick just took off after Mr. Halliday." She continued, "Mary

and Dick didn't speak for quite a while after that. One night the wonderful
man who owned the Ritz-Carlton in Boston gave a party for the company in
the dining room after the show. Mary and Dick were sitting on opposite sides
of the room and nobody was speaking!"

Audiences on the road had been giving them standing ovations, and the
advance sale of tickets was so heavy that performances were sold out for
months. So everyone's confidence was high the night of the famous opening
at the Lunt-Fontanne Theatre on November 16, 1959. Anna Crouse said,
"The shock of *The Sound of Music* was that no one expected such terrible
notices. When *South Pacific* opened, Dick and Oscar gave a huge opening-
night party on the roof of the St. Regis and they had the *Times* and *Tribune*
stacked high as you came in. They were raves. They were feeling so totally
secure that they gave an opening-night party for *The Sound of Music* in the
same place and they had the notices in the same place. As soon as they had
read them" (the *Times* thought it was disappointing to see Rodgers and Hammerstein succumbing to the clichés of operetta, and the *Tribune* wrote that
the musical became "not only too sweet for words but almost too sweet for
music") "they got rid of the notices. By then we all knew how terrible they
were but we had to be good sports. It was devastating.

"I remember going to the second night. We were all standing in the back
and being hit over the head by the show. Oscar said at the intermission,
'Make no mistake, this is a smash hit.' We all chorused, 'Do you think so?' "

Hammerstein, of course, was right. The musical would have 1,443 performances, and the film, which followed in 1965, starring Julie Andrews, would
become one of the biggest box-office hits of all time. That critics were so
pointed in their displeasure—Kenneth Tynan called it Rodgers and Hammerstein's "Great Leap Backwards"—said as much about changing tastes as
about the work itself. Asperity was the new order of the day. The writer Alan
Brien saw the musical as "a smudged carbon of what was once original and
progressive in their recipe . . . Here once more we have the rich, successful,
middle-aged, foreign hero with a brood of exotic children being saved from
himself by the sweet, shrewd, innocent young heroine from another world.
This time he is an Austrian baron who defies the Nazis as once he was a
French planter who fought the Japs, or a Siamese king who wrestled with
modern civilisation." None of this would matter, Brien wrote, if the lyrics
"showed the old Hammerstein command of simple emotions freshly
expressed." Instead, there were such bromides as larks learning to pray, hearts
beating with the wings of birds, and brooks laughing as they tripped over
stones.

Of recent years the fickle wheel of fashion has turned again, and audiences are rediscovering the virtues of earlier Rodgers and Hammerstein musicals, following the highly successful revivals in New York and London of *Oklahoma!, Carousel,* and *The King and I.* Even *The Sound of Music* has outlived its reputation for stickiness and entered the realms inhabited by fond High Camp, as audiences enthusiastically belt out its well-loved songs in movie-theatre sing-alongs. It may be trite, it may be "hopelessly square," but the stubborn endurance of *The Sound of Music* has made it, at the very least, "unignorable." As the ultimate compliment, Anthony Lane wrote from London, sing-along fans arrive appropriately attired as nuns (with underwear doing double duty as wimples), or in bright yellow body costumes (as Ray, a Drop of Golden Sun), or even as Brown Paper Packages Tied Up with Strings. No one, that writer noted, had so far had the temerity to ride the Underground attired as Schnitzel with Noodles.

OSCAR HAMMERSTEIN WAS TIRED. Two major operations in the summer of 1958, at the age of sixty-three, had left him physically exhausted, and that he received a long enough period of convalescence seems unlikely, given that he immediately launched himself into *Flower Drum Song,* with *The Sound of Music* waiting in the wings. True, he only had lyrics to write this time, but to a man running out of emotional energy such a task was daunting enough. His family knew, although Rodgers did not yet know it, that this would be his last musical. He wanted to write his autobiography, and since he was, as his letters demonstrate, a tart and fluid writer with a gift for self-revelation, it would have made a remarkable book. William Hammerstein said that when he was living in California working for Paramount Pictures he suggested that his father make a start by writing his autobiography in the form of letters. "He wrote eight or ten letters, and then something went into rehearsal and he stopped. Then I came East and never could get him to do it again. When he knew he was dying I found him in his study one day and he was at his desk writing a letter to me. What he wrote was how sorry he was that he had ever stopped these letters, and he wrote a little bit more. They were wonderful letters and a great start for an autobiography, but he never got beyond the age of six!"

If Hammerstein's gift was for writing about "simple emotions freshly expressed," that gift began to fail him in the final year of his life, but a refusal to accept adversity or even admit it was a marked aspect of his character at every age. His son continued: "He always looked at the positive even when there was nothing but negative. One of the stories about Dad concerned a play he tried out in New Haven when he was only twenty-three. After looking at it with an audience he realized it was a disaster so he took a walk through the Yale campus and decided to write a new play. Which he did. He once told me that if he was walking down the street and saw a blind person on the curb he would cross the street to avoid him, rather than getting involved. It was just part of a general decision to blot out unpleasantness. With his children he never remembered anything unpleasant about our lives. He never knew when we were sick, or had had an accident. He just put it out of his mind, and it worked!"

This selective myopia led to the decision his wife and children made in his final year. William Hammerstein recalled that the company was in rehearsal for *The Sound of Music* in September of 1959, when he remembers inviting himself to dinner at his father's house on Sixty-third Street. They waited for his father, who was late in returning from a doctor's appointment. When he came back he said the doctor told him he had an ulcer. The show went to New Haven for a tryout and Oscar had an operation. The whole family gathered at the hospital for a conference with the doctors and were told the bad news: three-quarters of Hammerstein's stomach had been removed, but they had not been able to get all of the cancerous cells, and he had six months to a year to live. William Hammerstein said, "Because of the kind of person he was and the super-positive attitude he had towards life, we decided not to tell him. Because it wouldn't have done him any good." Many months later his father told him that had been the right decision. "It gave him some time to come to the conclusion himself, which he eventually did." Hammerstein lived to see his sixty-fifth birthday—he died in August 1960—and learned the truth about two months before he died. He went to the Boston opening on October 13 and "cried as he watched the performance from an aisle seat next to Dorothy," Hugh Fordin wrote. Then he went to talk to the company, and now it was his wife's turn to cry, because she knew how little time he had left.

When they learned he was dying, the family took Rodgers into their confidence. This was perhaps necessary but put him in the excruciating position of being falsely optimistic about their joint future. This was happening just as *The Sound of Music* was coming into its final weeks of rehearsal, and he had to worry about whether Hammerstein could write whatever new lyrics might be needed. His daughter Mary was just about to open her first musical, *Once Upon a Mattress*, for which she wrote the music. She recalled that one day her father called her into his study to ask whether, if necessary, she would take over for Oscar, which was as close as she ever came to actually working with her father. As it happened, her help was not needed.

Julie Andrews, as Maria, entertaining the Trapp children on idyllic location
for the film *The Sound of Music*

The same phenomenon of robust advance sales that had saved *Flower Drum Song* despite a lack of critical enthusiasm was operating in the case of *The Sound of Music,* but this could only account in part for the musical's success. The fact that the film was, for a time, the most successful movie ever—its box-office receipts surpassed those of *Gone With the Wind*—had to mean that something about it had hit a nerve. *The Sound of Music* had transcended the limitations of its book and lyrics and perhaps even the appeal of its epoch, with its still-vivid memories of displacement and loss. Although critics were polite without being enthusiastic about Rodgers's score, it was inevitable that the film's enormous popularity should take his songs along with it, from the title song to "My Favorite Things," "Do-Re-Mi," "Climb Ev'ry Mountain," "Sixteen Going on Seventeen," and "Edelweiss," turning them into classics. The musical was, in its way, a backhanded compliment to operetta and just those shopworn formulae Rodgers and Hammerstein had earlier rejected. They knew better, even as they capitulated, but they also demonstrated the enduring strength of a hackneyed genre. Finally, after several failures, they could be forgiven for wanting to play it safe. They were human, after all, and neither, as has been shown, was at peak form, physically or mentally. Coming as it did at the end of a triumphant seventeen-year collaboration, *The Sound of Music* can be seen as more than a coda, if less than a culmination. Just the same, the era of the Rodgers and Hammerstein musical was coming to an end. Two years before, in 1957, *West Side Story* had ushered in another kind of musical theatre, with its dark meditations on formerly taboo themes that would lead, in due course, to Sondheim's chilling *Sweeney Todd*. It was the appearance of "boulevard nihilism," as John Lahr quipped, full of cynicism, ambivalent emotions, and bitter endings.

Hammerstein appeared to recover quickly from the stomach operation, and he and Dorothy left after *The Sound of Music*'s New York opening for a month at Round Hill, their vacation home in Jamaica. He was seemingly back to normal, but when he tried to play tennis again he almost collapsed. As the months passed he began to weaken and, losing his appetite, to shrink visibly. On August 15, 1960, the week before he died, Rodgers wrote to Jerry Whyte, "The latest news is even worse. He is now in no condition to see anybody . . . I understand this perfectly well. He's lost weight terrifically and doesn't want anyone to see him in this condition or to be sympathized with. Frankly I have no desire to see him myself. There is nothing I can do and I am not constituted so that I wish to deliver myself a beating if it can be avoided . . ."

In those last months when Oscar Hammerstein began to suspect that the truth was being withheld from him, he went to his doctor and demanded to know just how serious his condition was. He and Rodgers met for lunch afterwards and Hammerstein outlined his options in a ruminative way, as if he had all the time in the world. There were some last-minute measures to be tried, but none offered much hope. He thought he would just go back to his farm and wait to die. Then he began to talk about Rodgers's future and offer advice. As they were deep in discussion, a man seated nearby came over to introduce himself and asked for their autographs. He could not help observing that here were two men at the top of their professions who should not have a care in the world. "I was just wondering what could possibly make you both look so sad."

The news of Oscar's death early on August 23 was nevertheless horrifying. The *World Telegram and Sun* reported, "A spokesman for Mr. Rodgers, who was the first to be told of the death of his friend, said the composer was near collapse from grief. 'The guy is falling apart,' the spokesman said." That feeling was followed, Rodgers said later, by "this terrific drive to survive. Something takes hold of you—a determination not to get killed." Those around him knew that, unlike his wife, Rodgers was an atheist. At the age of twelve Mary Rodgers Guettel asked her father whether he believed in God and he answered that he believed in people. "If somebody is really sick, I don't pray to God, I look for the best doctor in town." At the same time his children and grandchildren came to believe he was very much afraid of dying, "and fought it every inch of the way," Kim Beaty said. His disinclination to visit a very sick Oscar Hammerstein became an invariable rule, amounting to a phobia, and he would decline to attend funerals with the explanation that his doctor advised against it as too emotionally taxing. With enough concentration and hard work death could be kept at bay, and his secretary, Lillian Leff, noticed that after Hammerstein's death Rodgers's dedication to his work became even more pronounced.

On the other hand, Oscar Hammerstein was, if not conventionally religious, curious and open-minded and had hewn a humanitarian philosophy that obviously sustained him. Explaining the guardedly hopeful ending of *Carousel,* his darkest musical, Hammerstein said, "I see plays and read books that emphasize the seamy side of life, and the frenetic side, and the tragic side. I don't deny the existence of the tragic and the frenetic. But I say that somebody has to keep saying that isn't all there is to life . . . We're very likely to get thrown off our balance if we have such a preponderance of artists expressing the 'waste land' philosophy." "Take me beyond the pearly gates," Billy Bigelow sings in *Carousel,* a lyric that is not included in the collected lyrics of Oscar Hammerstein II. "Take me before the highest throne / And let me be judged by the highest Judge of all!" Hammerstein was well aware of his partner's opinions on the matter. It must have been unsettling for Rodgers to have Hammerstein write that "in his heart, Dick is far more of a mystic than he knows . . ." Asked for a comment about that in a television interview after Hammerstein's death, Rodgers stumbled to find something adequate to say. He did not know what you called it, whether it was God, or mysticism, or something else. "It happens. And that's enough. Somebody makes . . . a fellow . . . paint a better painting, and somebody else . . . loves somebody more than anybody else." The whole subject made him acutely uncomfortable. "Leave it alone. Just do it."

SHORTLY AFTER Oscar Hammerstein's death Rodgers received a letter from Mildred Hunter Creen, always known as "Miggy." She and her husband Judson, called "Juddy," had known Dick and Dorothy since the thirties, when they gave lavish parties in their apartment in the Hotel Russell, just south of Grand Central Station, for people like Freddy March, Oscar and Dorothy, and Russel and Anna Crouse. She was in a reminiscent mood that day, remembering the night when the curtain first went up on *Oklahoma!* and the time when Rodgers was prostrate on a litter behind a curtain listening to his music for *Carousel.* Then there was the dress rehearsal of *South Pacific* in New Haven, with Mary Martin and Ezio Pinza "coming down to the footlights with out-stretched hands as the orchestra played the overture . . . The opening there, and the never-to-be forgotten first night in New York—the whole town ringing bells! A plane up to Boston with Linda (her first flight) for a week-end while Oscar sweated out the lyrics for 'Getting to Know You,' and you at the upright piano on the empty stage, playing 'No Other Love,' and Gertie rehearsing with the children . . ." If only, she wrote, she had the "right and shining words to tell you what my stumbling speech and choked emotion forbids." The letter had so moved Rodgers at breakfast one day that he cried. How could he forget those days, no matter how complicated his life had become, even frightening? How could he stop now? He was only fifty-eight and not ready to be "turned out to pasture. It's very easy for an upset man to retire. As you get older you get more scared. But what would I do if I retired? I'm not a golfer. What would I do after a cruise around the world—live on my memories?"

The question, in fact, was moot. Even while Oscar was still alive, in the spring of 1960, Rodgers had been exploring the idea of a new collaborator through intermediaries. He approached Alan Jay Lerner, then forty-three and fresh from his triumph in *Camelot,* a year later. Lerner had just broken up with his partner, Fritz Loewe, and was eager to work with Rodgers, but would not be available for a year. Since Rodgers had written lyrics before, and had just completed further songs and lyrics for a remake of *State Fair,* he decided to take the plunge and become his own lyricist. He made the decision with many inner qualms. At about this time he said revealingly, "My recollection is, I've been scared all my life," and now he was "just-plain-lousy-scared. With each new show, you croak. You fall apart. It's just torture.

People who tell you they aren't worried are one of two things: either they're extremely insensitive—or they're just not telling the truth."

He was looking for a new idea, and at such moments a man goes to his friends. He and Oscar had produced *The Happy Time*, a play by Samuel Taylor, which had been very successful, and the three men had remained close. Taylor said, "When Oscar Hammerstein died, Dick called me personally. He didn't sound at all like the cool, calm Richard Rodgers we knew. He was very emotional about it." Then about six months later Rodgers called again and suggested they do a show together. Taylor continued, "I was not particularly interested in musicals before, but I said yes. So we got together and talked about it." Rodgers already had a leading lady in mind, the young black singer Diahann Carroll, whom he had first seen in Truman Capote and Harold Arlen's *House of Flowers* in 1954 and had spotted as a future star. In fact, he and Oscar had wanted her for *Flower Drum Song*, but "we could not make her look sufficiently Oriental." Still, the idea had stayed in his mind. "All he knew was he wanted to do a show for Diahann Carroll and somehow involve Benny Goodman," Taylor said. The whole idea of their proposed cooperation was that "if we couldn't make up a good idea, we wouldn't do it."

Taylor said, "It was my idea to set the show in Paris. I suggested we do a very light comedy for Diahann, but he shied away from that. I finally came up with the story we used. I said I would like to write a story about a black girl with no problems with the world and a man burdened with them, and only in Paris could that be true. We never did find a character for Benny Goodman, but we did start the show with a clarinetist."

Taylor's plot put Carroll in Paris, where she is working as a successful model. There she meets an American writer, "a kind of Hemingway on the rocks," as John Simon described him, who has won a Pulitzer and come to Europe to write the Great American Novel, but finds himself with a monumental case of writer's block, from which he is too easily distracted. Eventually he decides that he must go home to Maine, where he will be able to write again; in a racially prejudiced America, she will be ostracized if she follows him there. What Taylor and Rodgers had in mind was a poignant, bittersweet kind of ending, but even in the sixties such a plot device seemed hardly convincing—there were, after all, places like New York, and broad-minded circles did exist—and what should have been a moving climax struck most critics as pretentious and false.

A more persuasive plot was put forward by the playwright Arthur Laurents after he was hired to write the screenplay for a projected film of *No Strings*. In Laurents's version, Lena Horne would play a French editor of *Vogue* who has left the U.S. because of its prejudice and says she will never

Diahann Carroll and Richard Kiley in *No Strings*, 1962

live there again. Rock Hudson would play a Southern senator, which would have made their marriage actually illegal. Laurents said that the film was ready to start when Hudson backed out. It seems his black cook had said, "Don't you do that, Mr. Rock." Laurents said, "It was before the civil rights movement. So he didn't," and that was the end of the idea.

Photographs taken during rehearsals show that Rodgers is always in close proximity to his leading lady. He is holding her hand, or giving her a neck rub, or his hands are on her shoulders or around her waist. Samuel Taylor energetically denied the idea that there was anything between them. "I know he had girls at one time, but there were never any signs in the nine weeks we were developing the show. Dick and I drank together almost every night after the performance. He was not too well by then and much more sedate," he said. Besides, Taylor thought, he had an understanding wife, "a very good solid marriage." He added, "We never talked about things like that." On the other hand, Jerry Whyte, who worked on the show, had confided in Dania Krupska that Rodgers was deeply in love and that Carroll was the great love of his life. "Jerry told me that Dick would stand there and beg her to go out with him with tears in his eyes. Whatever it was, she possessed him. I can't remember all the details, but there was something pathetic and sad about his behavior; he would go and stand outside her door. Jerry Whyte couldn't believe this was Dick Rodgers." At about this time Dorothy Rodgers was hospitalized for a series of X-rays. Rodgers told Whyte that they showed "absolutely no difficulty of any kind beyond the adhesions she's been so proud of for the last ten years."

For her part, Diahann Carroll had her own emotional entanglements. While married to Monte Kay, whom she met when he was casting director for *House of Flowers,* and mother of a baby daughter, she was desperately in love with Sidney Poitier, who was also married and had children. Although apparently charmed and flattered by Rodgers's attentions, she kept him at arm's length. Something he had said at an early stage had shocked her. He remarked of Lorenz Hart, "You just can't imagine how wonderful it feels to have written this score and not have to search all over the globe for that drunken little fag." She wrote that from that time onwards, she never quite trusted Rodgers. Nevertheless, to be in the company of this ravishing creature seemed almost enough for Rodgers. He had found a new protégée, young, insecure, and grateful, who needed him and had the wit to tell him so, in contrast to Dorothy, who had become so competent and was such exacting

Richard Rodgers and Diahann Carroll, at right, with cast
members of *No Strings*

company. As he once told Florence Henderson, another of his leading ladies, "The thing about Dorothy is she not only demands perfection but she gives it." Henderson said, "The comment was admiring, but the implication also was that he felt he *wasn't* perfect."

Rodgers was so enamored of his new project that he was actually getting up early to write songs for the first time in his life: "The sweetest sounds I'll ever hear / Are still inside my head." With *The Sound of Music* paying the bills, he could afford to take the kind of leap into the unknown that always stimulated him. He had grumbled for years about the fact that the orchestra was in a pit; now he would bring it onstage and give his music equal footing with the dialogue, scenery, and costumes. Most of the musicians were seated on one side of the stage; seven others were placed close to the footlights. *Time* magazine commented, "Some of the time these minstrels wander about; some of the time they huddle around a table like displaced poker players." There were no strings in the orchestra, and that was the musical's message as well, one of Rodgers's dreadful puns. There was even a song about it: "No strings—no strings / Except our own devotion; No other bonds at all." Meantime there were no breaks for scene changes, either. The curtain came down only twice, at the end of the first and second acts, and in between the cast rotated the cleverly constructed panels and moved the props around themselves. When someone remarked on the daring involved, Rodgers beamed with pleasure, "because he likes to think of himself as spiritually an adventurous youth."

Everyone remarked on how happy he seemed. Taylor said they never had a cross word. Ralph Burns, who wrote the orchestrations, said it was his first experience with Rodgers and he was wonderful to work with, "like a little kid. It was a whole new venture for him and he was so happy. He loved what everybody did and was open to new ideas." He was drinking very little and was always ready for work. Kathleen McKeany, who worked as his personal secretary for the out-of-town run, said she never got enough sleep because they always worked late. "I'd get to bed at one a.m. and he would ring me at eight o'clock and say, 'I am ready any time you are to do the mail.' He must only have needed four hours' sleep." Their tryout run at the O'Keefe Center in Toronto was a success, but an earlier run in Detroit had been nightmarish. Richard Kiley, who played the lead, said, "On opening night in Detroit I am kissing Diahann when I see some flurry of movement. People are walking up the aisle. In the theatre this happens; people get ill. But then more and more began to leave. Perhaps a hundred of them left. It was a pretty new thing for people to see an interracial romance." Kathleen McKeany said, "Rodgers used to get hate letters by the bushel calling him a 'nigger lover.' I asked the

Taylors what to do and they advised me to show him a few and throw out the rest."

If he was concerned, Rodgers did not show it, and there were no such reactions when the show opened on Broadway in the spring of 1962. Insiders knew what an act of courage *No Strings* represented, and everyone—friends, acquaintances, cast members, and stars—rallied round. He was deluged with good-luck telegrams. Kurt Kasznar, who played Max in *The Sound of Music,* wrote, "Your music is the only sensual pleasure without vice. Good luck tonight." Betty Comden, Adolph Green, and their respective spouses wrote, "Dear Mr. Music and Mr. Words, best of luck on your first collaboration." Alfred Lunt and Lynn Fontanne wrote, "Thinking of you tonight, about you know what." Julie Andrews and her then-husband, Tony Walton, sent all their love, and there were many thoughtful letters. Writing to thank one such correspondent, he said, "At exactly the moment that abject terror had taken hold of me, I opened and read your letter . . . You probably will never know what it did to sustain me through one of the most difficult evenings of my life." What he did not add was that since he and his family had financed the musical entirely themselves, more than reputation was at stake.

He need not have worried. Edna Ferber sent a note saying that after waiting for half an hour after the show to try to get backstage, she had given up. "To me, the entire play is merely great," she wrote. "What attack! How fresh, how touching. Your music, your lyrics are dimensional and lovely and funny and sad. What a sensational boy you are." Even the polite but not enthusiastic reception his lyrics received could not dampen his euphoria, and the show would go on to have a handsome Broadway run of 580 performances. The whole experience had been invigorating and reassuring. He said, "When Oscar finished his lyrics he was drained. He had to lie down. But when I finish a tune, you can't sit on me. I'm high. I feel fulfilled, full of energy. I'm pleased, I'm proud that I'm capable of an act of creation. Can you think of any better reason for going on?"

Chapter Eighteen

LOOKING STRAIGHT AHEAD

WHEN THEY WERE REHEARSING for *Two by Two,* the musical starring Danny Kaye in 1970, Rodgers and his lyricist, Martin Charnin, took the same limousine up to the workshop in the Bronx where the rehearsals were being held. Charnin said, "I would meet him at the office. The limousine had darkened windows, and we would drive straight up Madison Avenue and keep going north. Gradually the posh Midtown scenery would give way to homeless people sitting in a semi-shambles, beside broken concrete and burned-out buildings.

"In the very first week I remember being struck by the contrast between the extreme luxury of our travel and what was all around us. I said, 'My God, how does one go on and make this drive every day?' And he replied, 'You look straight ahead.' I took that to mean that you should pay no attention to what's going on around you that's ugly. And that's how he behaved."

It was true that Rodgers's ability to forge straight past unpleasant scenes, refusing to be drawn into them, to simply act as if nothing were happening, had been perfected through decades of struggle and had become, in beautiful rooms hung with beautiful paintings and inhabited by beautiful people, a seamless ability not to notice. He seemed to take ugliness as a personal affront. On the other hand, to say that he ignored the evidence of need would be untrue, because he was the most generous of men. Judy Crichton said that Rodgers perpetually "bailed my father out" when he was going through one of his many financial crises. "He was an amazingly generous man, in every possible way, and he never wanted any credit for it.

"My husband and I were very involved in an interracial movement before civil rights. We lived in an interracial community in the fifties, and I knew

Dick was very interested in this. One day I got a call from him. There was a young black singer with a glorious voice at Juilliard, not then married, living in a slum, and he wanted me to find a decent apartment for her. She was supporting herself as a waitress, and she had no money. He supported her through Juilliard, and paid for her apartment, plus a stipend so she would be well dressed. She went on to the Metropolitan Opera, and the night Dick died, I was at the apartment alone with Dorothy, and called this woman and asked her to sing at his funeral. I didn't know at the time that she gave up a lucrative booking in order to do this. I thanked her afterwards and she said, 'How could I not?'" She was Shirley Verrett.

Secretaries in need of loans knew they could ask for help. In fact, that Rodgers was a soft touch was so well known that even the dressers on shows would write hard-luck letters asking for the money for a new car. Things got to such a point that his lawyer had to intervene and tell him he could not make any more loans. Such acts of kindness were true of both the Rodgerses. Hospitalized friends and acquaintances, even people who did not know Dorothy very well, would find flowers or a thoughtfully chosen book at their bedside. To learn that a niece or a grandchild needed tuition fees or a piece of winter clothing was tantamount to having the necessary funds dispatched the next day, and their private correspondence is full of letters of dutiful thanks—Dorothy Rodgers was very strict about that.

For many years Rodgers had been establishing endowments and awards. When he was made a member of the American Academy and Institute of Arts and Letters in 1955, Rodgers established a production award (he endowed it with $1 million) to provide for staged and studio readings of new musicals. He established three scholarships at Juilliard, scholarships for professional training at the American Theatre Wing, and gave commissions to composers. (He and Hammerstein commissioned Aaron Copland's *The Tender Land,* which was performed at the New York City Opera in 1954.) In a world where the mere fact of survival confers distinction, to have prevailed for four decades began to look like a monumental achievement, and Rodgers's staff was spending hours of every day turning aside offers of honorary degrees, retrospective evenings, invitations to speak and lend his name to this or that advisory committee. Most of all, they were rejecting scripts. There was almost a standard letter going out to all those hopefuls wanting Rodgers to collaborate on adaptations of famous works or write music for new ones. Alfred Palca's outline for *The Ballad of Jamie Bowles* was turned down because "I don't think that I am terribly interested in New Orleans on a white or colored basis." He turned down Ray Stark's *Josie* with the comment that he was looking for "something with a little more heart and something slightly less contrived." He turned down *On The Waterfront* because he feared its climax would be too much like that of *West Side Story,* and although he loved *Jacobowsky and the Colonel* by S. N. Behrman, he was terribly worried that "there is so little story movement . . ." He wanted to do Emlyn Williams's *The Corn Is Green* with Patricia Routledge, but nothing came of it. Years of bitter experience in the business, and of writing musicals he really did not want to write, had convinced him that he would do "absolutely nothing unless I'm tremendously enthusiastic." For the fact was, he no longer had to work. That gave him the luxury of doing only what he wanted to do; but then his native fears and hesitations came into play, and there was no longer a Larry Hart in his life to rub his hands in glee and predict the show would run forever, or even a Hammerstein to weigh the matter up judiciously and decide the show was worth the gamble. He wrote to Stuart Ostrow, "A very smart woman who does a lot of work for me said a few minutes ago that I had saved well over a million dollars last week by turning down ideas . . . I tell you . . . this to give you some insight into my reasons for not wanting to get into *The Laughmaker.* I'm sure that someone smarter than I would know how to make a living musical show out of this, but I don't feel that I would ever know enough answers . . . I am simply afraid of it . . ."

There had been, briefly, the possibility of work with Alan Jay Lerner, who had three new ideas. As soon as *No Strings* was safely launched, Lerner approached him about a musical based on the life of the French couturier Coco Chanel. It was an idea that passionately interested Lerner, who eventually did write it with André Previn as a vehicle for Katharine Hepburn (1968), but he was completely unable to interest Rodgers. Lerner then suggested a musical based on Errol Flynn's later years, when, as a dissolute, fading actor, he fell in love with a teenager. That idea looked promising to Rodgers, and they had arrived at the point of casting: Joey Heatherton was to play the girl and Robert Preston the part of Flynn. But the idea petered out when Preston asked how two such famous men of the theatre could have allowed themselves to be seduced by such a sordid story. Rodgers with Hart would have found a way around that objection, but Rodgers post-Hammerstein had become so accustomed to think in terms of the guilelessly inoffensive that, from that moment on, the project was doomed.

They then turned to Lerner's third idea, one centering around his fascination with extrasensory perception. It was certainly inoffensive: the story of a girl from a modest Brooklyn background who can foretell the future and remembers a past life. However, it trembled on the verge of the kind of whimsy and preposterous plot that had bedeviled Lerner's other venture into the otherworldly: *Brigadoon.* One would have thought that Rodgers, so

Richard Rodgers with Alan Jay Lerner, 1961

hedged in by reservations about what would, or would not, make a musical, would have run miles to avoid this one. But perhaps he felt he owed it to his partner to try out the idea. Lerner was certainly enthusiastic enough about it.

All went well at first. While resolutely refusing to say what their new musical was called (its working title was *I Picked a Daisy*), or anything about it, Rodgers and Lerner told the *New York Times* that they had chosen Barbara Harris as their leading lady, that Gower Champion would direct and choreograph, and that Richard Burton was interested in joining the cast. A Broadway opening was planned for the spring of 1963. Rodgers had reckoned without the peculiar roadblock presented by Lerner's neurosis. This most gifted, urbane, and charming of men was not only a victim of a monumental case of writer's block, one that made those of Hart and Hammerstein look positively benign, but was incapable of telling the truth about it. And so Rodgers would be the recipient of infinitely soothing messages from Lerner's various factota which promised the new lyrics by messenger that day, in two hours, that evening, next morning, by lunchtime: promises that he repeatedly and flagrantly broke. Similarly, he would be just about to return Rodgers's phone call (within the hour) and days of silence would go by. Or he would be about to meet with Rodgers and would fail to turn up. When Rodgers would call to ask where he was, Mr. Lerner was in Capri. It was far worse than working with Hart, because if Rodgers could only find him, Hart would scatter around a dozen lyrics in an hour. By contrast, Lerner had no lyrics, which was why he could not be found. Such malevolent indifference to promises made was intolerable. Burton Lane, who finally succeeded in writing the musical, which became *On a Clear Day You Can See Forever,* was blunter about Lerner's shortcomings than Rodgers could bring himself to be. Lane said, "He's a horrible guy. I don't want to go into it." Lerner's bland response was, "I think I've become an absolute monster of fiendish malevolence in Burton's mind. He must enjoy it. It would exhaust me." That comment gave some indication of the size of the problem his collaborators faced. What Rodgers resented most, he said, after making the announcement in the summer of 1963 that the partnership had failed, was that Lerner had wasted a year of his life.

RODGERS HAD TURNED DOWN the idea of making a musical out of Pearl Buck's novel *Imperial Woman* in 1961, with the excuse that "for some peculiar reason, modern America seems to offer me a certain stimulus which I desperately need." Some years after that, he rejected yet another costume musical: "Somehow, period costumes seem acceptable in the form of fantasy but when these factual people start to sing, reality seems to go out of them." It seemed strange, therefore, that one of his pet subjects during that period should be Nefertiti, the fourteenth-century B.C. Egyptian queen who, along with her husband, King Akhenaton, is considered to have established the world's first religion devoted to a single deity. The story was to concern their courtship and marriage and then their fierce struggles with the priesthood to establish their worship of the sun disk Aton. The thought of Egyptian hieroglyphic characters bursting into song did not, perhaps, seem preposterous in this case because Diahann Carroll was going to be onstage. It was no secret that Nefertiti was being written expressly for her, and the compliment was huge, given that Nefertiti, whose beauty is palpable in a famous painted bust of the period, was one of the most extraordinary women who ever lived. The librettist Sidney Michaels was engaged—Rodgers had been very impressed by his musical *Ben Franklin in Paris*—and talks began with Jerome Robbins as a possible director and with Giorgio Tozzi, playing, presumably, Akhenaton.

Diahann Carroll, however, was still smarting from having been passed over in favor of Nancy Kwan for the proposed film of *No Strings*—she blamed Rodgers for not telling her this was about to happen—and submitted extremely demanding terms for her participation in the musical. In addition Rodgers was dissatisfied with Michaels's treatment of the idea, and there the matter rested for a couple of years. Then Rodgers, who had seen and liked *The White House,* a play by A. E. Hotchner, invited him to work on the project, and Hotchner accepted. The writer, best known for his books about his long friendship with Ernest Hemingway, set to work with a will, and all went well at first. But then, Hotchner wrote, Rodgers became forgetful and would accuse him of not showing him scenes they had already reviewed. At some meetings he would seem alert and energetic; at others, listless and talking so quietly he could barely be heard. Finally Hotchner withdrew.

In the autumn of 1962, Rodgers had taken on the role of president and producing director of the Music Theatre of Lincoln Center at the New York State Theater, and revivals, mostly of Rodgers and Hammerstein productions, absorbed a good deal of his time for the next several years. In May of 1963, for instance, his works were everywhere, "on Broadway, off Broadway and in-between," the *New York Times* commented in an editorial. *Oklahoma!* had opened at the New York City Center, with new productions to follow of *Pal Joey* and *The King and I. No Strings,* on Broadway, was about to reach its five hundredth performance and *The Sound of Music* was still playing, although about to close. There was an off-Broadway revival of *The Boys from Syracuse,* using dancing girls, the *Times* commented, who had not been born when it was first performed. "So without any formal celebrations, there is an unexpected Rodgers festival in town."

In 1964 Dorothy, who had begun a new career as a writer, published *My Favorite Things,* a book about interior decor and entertaining that drew heavily for its illustrations on photographs of their New York apartment and Rockmeadow. Hardly had the book appeared than she decided Rockmeadow was becoming too expensive to run, using the excuse that they could no longer find full-time help. Since this was not entirely true, it proved a difficult argument to make to her husband, who loved Rockmeadow and was appalled at the idea that they should sell it and build a new house, but she convinced him. The result was a vast contemporary, all on one floor, completely walled in glass, surrounded by ten beautiful acres not far from Rockmeadow in Fairfield, Connecticut. Dorothy Rodgers convinced herself that it would be much cheaper to run, being full of labor-saving devices, but it grew to such a size (8,000 square feet) that the idea became self-defeating. Since houses—how to design and run them—were her great passion, it is tempting to think that Rockmeadow had to go because she had run out of ideas for it.

At a party for Dorothy Rodgers's new book, *My Favorite Things,* are,
from left, Mary Rodgers Guettel, Richard Rodgers, Henry ("Hank") Guettel,
Dorothy Rodgers, Linda and Daniel Melnick.

The new house on Congress Street certainly absorbed months, if not
years, of concentrated effort. She threw into it all of her passion for detail: the
precise colors of paint, the exact kind of hardware, the perfect floor covering,
even a plan of her own to have each room individually controlled with its
own thermostat. (When an early run determined that the heating and air-
conditioning pipes had been hooked up in reverse, their mother was in "a
white-hot rage," Linda Rodgers Emory said.) Because it was all on one floor,
the house was "most outrageously expensive to run," and so her idea of having a more economical life-style was a failure. This shortcoming was not
mentioned in the book that resulted from the experiment, *The House in My
Head* (1967). Meanwhile, she was having periodic intestinal crises followed
by the usual X-rays with negative results.

Rodgers and Hart's *The Boys from Syracuse* had a tremendously successful
revival in New York in 1963, running for 502 performances, but when the
same show transferred to London, the reviews were negative: ". . . a show

Elizabeth Allen and Sergio Franchi in
Do I Hear a Waltz?, 1965

that drags horribly to its close . . ." The musical had the misfortune to appear on the London stage at the same moment as Stephen Sondheim's *A Funny Thing Happened on the Way to the Forum*—which Alan Brien called "the cleanest dirty musical of the decade"—and was obviously far less clever, witty, and pointed. Brien wrote, "Mr. Abbott's glittering mausoleum of fossilised vulgarity reveals itself as a monumental folly, marooned miles off the track of modern entertainment."

ARTHUR LAURENTS had approached Rodgers and Hammerstein in 1958 with the idea of making a musical out of his play *The Time of the Cuckoo*. This was a small but affecting story about a middle-aged American woman on holiday in Venice who falls in love with an Italian antiques dealer and discovers, too late, that he is married. At the time Hammerstein thought a bit more time needed to elapse before the play, which appeared in 1952 and three years

A tense moment during discussions of *Do I Hear a Waltz?*:
from left, Richard Rodgers, Stephen Sondheim, and
Arthur Laurents

later became the film *Summertime,* with Katharine Hepburn, returned as a musical. Rodgers doubted whether enough beautiful music could be made for what looked like a slender plot.

However, after the Rodgers-Lerner collaboration fell through, Laurents returned to the idea, and this time he convinced Rodgers that his play would make a perfect "small, intimate emotional musical." From the start, attention revolved around just how old the heroine should be. On Broadway, Shirley Booth had made the part her own: a fading, wistful secretary who longs for romance but feels herself unlovable. The man she chooses is neither handsome nor young, and the play's genuine pathos hinges on her need to accept what life has offered rather than something she cannot have. The playwright now says that he was thinking of an older woman as heroine, Mary Martin, for instance, but, from the start, Rodgers wanted someone younger. This may be true but in a letter Laurents wrote to Rodgers at the outset of the project, he said, "In point of fact, Leona is . . . ideally, in her early thirties, not forties; and a woman who has known sex but not love, rather than a frustrated spinster who has not known either." The demands of the musical stage for beau-

Richard Rodgers congratulating his leading lady,
Elizabeth Allen, of *Do I Hear a Waltz?*

tiful people in romantic settings were in direct conflict with the whole point of this naturalistic drama about what could have been a real-life situation.

Another problem had to do with the choice of Stephen Sondheim as lyricist. Sondheim recalled Hammerstein's having said to him that if he ever felt like writing with another composer, Rodgers would welcome it, and Rodgers did indeed approach him after Hammerstein's death, periodically sending him ideas. Sondheim said that Laurents came to him with this idea. "My memory is that he said to me, 'Look, it's an easy job, and with Dick's music, let's face it, it ought to make a lot of money.' And I thought, 'Okay, I'm doing my little obligation to Oscar, I'm going to make a lot of money, and it's an easy job. And I'm working with Arthur.' So those are all pros, and the only thing that I didn't think of," he added, laughing, "was that it was not a good idea. As I started to look at it, I said I thought what the show was about, was a girl who can't sing." But the news was "greeted with a dull thud, and I know why. You can't do that kind of story with just song. You've got to do it as a semi-opera . . . And Dick thought in terms of song. And to him it was impossible to have a leading lady who didn't sing. He didn't have that kind of imagination."

Laurents said, "This was my fault in trying to bring them together . . . After all, Dick knew Steve when Steve was a smart-ass whiz kid and Dick was a legend. Now this was a peer who was on the way up, and he was on the way down. Rodgers was feeling very keenly that he was old-fashioned. And he was."

Laurents also regretted having suggested the Englishman John Dexter as director. "He was brilliant, but what I didn't know was that he hated women. That didn't help. And he and Dick . . . chose this actress, Elizabeth Allen, who had a big voice. She was very tall, sexless, removed, cold as ice." Sondheim agreed that it had been an unfortunate choice. They had been torn between her and Phyllis Newman, "and I'm sorry we didn't pick Phyllis. But that wasn't the problem. It's an unnecessary musical; it's dead in the water. There's no point to it, and I really believe I'm right. If that character can sing, you're in trouble."

Meetings took place in the Rodgers apartment, and Rodgers, Laurents said, kept disappearing into the bathroom. "Very peculiar, I thought. And I have a very lurid imagination, and a movie came into my head, so after a while I . . . went in and locked the door and picked up the top of the toilet tank, and there was a bottle of vodka. Right out of *The Lost Weekend* . . . So then he was this drunk. And when we went out of town . . . in Boston, for example, I can remember that long stairway down to the men's room and Jerry Whyte standing guard at the door while Dick went inside to booze up." Rodgers was producing the show, which was another problem for Laurents, because he had the final say. "There was a song in that show called 'Two by Two,' and John Dexter's assistant, a guy who later made pornos, staged it, the whole company was walking around the stage singing 'Two by Two,' the most monotonous rhythm. It was so boring. It was the first run-through, and after that I went out and bought a coat. The coat didn't fit, either!

"Anyway, the thing was miscast, and then the guy who played the leading man, Sergio Franchi, terribly nice man, was too young; lovely voice, couldn't act. By that time I think Dexter must have lost interest. He certainly gave up on the show by the time we got to New Haven. He had a hustler sent up from New York every night. He stayed in the hotel room smoking a joint while the hustler saw the show. I'm sure John, smoking the joint, had a much better time than the hustler, and wouldn't rehearse, wouldn't do anything. It got to the point we were in Boston and I said, 'John, I'm going to have to speak to Dick,' because he was the producer. So he gave me a wicked smile and said, 'All right, I'll call a rehearsal.' And he did. That night. During intermission."

As for Sondheim, all went well until the reviews began to come in for the tryouts, and Rodgers began to attack him over his lyrics. On one never-to-be-forgotten day, Rodgers castigated Sondheim in front of the whole company. Sondheim stormed off, saying he was "through," but was talked out of it by Laurents and Whyte. The latter "walked me back and forth in the lobby of the theatre, saying, 'You have to understand.' He never said, 'Dick's a drunk'; whatever it was, he talked me down." The problem was that Rodgers "saw that Arthur and I were talking about the show, without him, and he got extremely paranoid . . ." He was very easily hurt. "He always thought people were talking behind his back, and in fact they often were." Laurents added, "Jerry Whyte, by the way, said to me, 'This is not a good score. His music is no good.' He knew it. He was no fool." If the problem from Rodgers's point of view was Sondheim and Laurents, from their perspective the problem was Rodgers. Laurents said, "He would sleep a lot. He'd sit in rehearsals and be snoring. You see, it's funny. He gave the impression of being a rather aloof, cold man. I realized he was half-gone, and as for removing, he was on his way out."

Do I Hear a Waltz? opened at the Forty-sixth Street Theatre in the spring of 1965 and ran for 220 performances.

MARY RODGERS WAS MARRIED for the second time, in 1961, to Henry ("Hank") Guettel, who became general manager of the Music Theatre of Lincoln Center, and their first child, Matthew Rodgers Guettel, was born a year later. Matthew had, they decided in retrospect, childhood asthma, not diagnosed, and numerous allergies, including an allergy to penicillin. She said, "Matthew came into the bedroom one Sunday morning when he was not quite four and died. I mean, he just collapsed on the floor, and I called doctors . . ." By the time anyone arrived it was too late. That was in August of 1966. It was turning out to be a very bad year for Richard Rodgers. Apart from a long and lucrative run in London for *The Sound of Music,* which promised to beat the run of *My Fair Lady,* and revivals of *Annie Get Your Gun* and *Show Boat* at Lincoln Center, nothing was happening in his creative life. *Do I Hear a Waltz?* had closed. He had lost his beloved Rockmeadow, and the sprawling rambler Dorothy had built in its place was still in a state of chaos, with no real indication of how it would look when it was finished.

Then Jerry Whyte, who had become absolutely indispensable to him, had a serious heart attack in June 1966 and was hospitalized for weeks. By July Whyte was recovering and strong enough to complain about the semiweekly blood tests to which he was being subjected. That summer, Dorothy had to have eye surgery. In early October, as she was running back into the new house to give the painter precise instructions for a paint color, she fell on the slippery pavement and broke her knee. "Dorothy, the efficient one, has done the expected: She has fallen apart," Rodgers wrote. He told Jerry Whyte in September, "The house looks wonderful and will be fine if we ever get the mechanics straightened out. The buck-passing sounds like a dress rehearsal in New Haven but I make myself remember that we always managed to get the show opened . . . I still have feelings of depression and bewilderment but I am assured by the experts that this will pass in time . . ."

He was in the office every morning by about ten-thirty looking over the day's business. Duane Garrison Elliott said, "Dorothy Rodgers controlled the finances. These things were done at the apartment. She made it possible for him to do what he did. I recall seeing a checkbook once and it was just spending money. I think she was a very smart businesswoman, but he was the smartest I ever met. He sat at his table and you brought the papers in, and he looked at whatever it was and would promptly state his position and that was that. He also wrote very short letters. He was a very good delegator and very meticulous, so he did not waste a minute." Since, he told her, he spent as much time at his office as at home, he wanted fresh flowers everywhere, including on the piano, although he rarely played it, not liking to be overheard. His office was at the end of a hall, past her desk. They had a kitchen as well, and as he arrived, Whyte would come running down the hall to get his coat and hang it up. ("Whyte, of course, had been in my office reading all the mail," Duane Elliott said.) He and Rodgers would go out to lunch, or order in. "They would order from Reuben's, which made every sandwich in the world except the one thing they wanted, which was always sliced chicken. So they sent turkey instead. Rodgers had the same methodical thing, day in and day out."

Rodgers always gave very expensive Christmas presents, which were planned by Dorothy. "One year I got a marvelous cashmere sweater like a blazer, with brass buttons. Another year it was a white made-to-order dress, which was perfect for someone who had a chauffeur, which I didn't. Another year it was a sable boa. Dorothy Rodgers turned me off Christmas, because she would start planning for the following year the next day. All wrapped up with elaborate bows."

Joe Layton, a brilliant young choreographer turned director, had also joined the Rodgers entourage. He had been recommended by Mary Rodgers, who met him when *Once Upon a Mattress* was in its early stages, and Layton was subsequently hired to stage the musical numbers for *The Sound of Music*. He made his debut as a director with *No Strings*, was part of the ill-fated attempt to make a musical with Alan Jay Lerner, and was the man Rodgers immediately thought of for his next project, in November 1967. That was to be a musical based on George Bernard Shaw's *Androcles and the Lion* for television, with Peter Stone writing the book and Rodgers providing music and lyrics.

Norman Wisdom was hired to play Androcles, Brian Bedford was Lentulus, and Noël Coward was to play Caesar. This seemed like an inspired choice. Receiving the press in his small apartment on East Fifty-fifth street the day before taping was to begin, Coward was in top form. He said that people thought of him as exotic but they were quite wrong. "All my caricatures show me with a long cigarette holder, an ascot and a blazer, none of which I own. If I drink champagne, I become sick at once. My clothes tend to be comfortable but curiously un-faddy. Of course I do like dressing gowns and I'm devoted to caviar, but that's as far as the elegance goes . . ." Coward had been quite ill and, unfortunately, Stone said, could not remember any of his lines, but was so ideally cast that it hardly mattered.

Stone said, "We did it on tape, which was very early in the transition from live television performances. Cutting tape in those days was very complicated. It was not done digitally, as now, but you actually used scissors and had to do one sentence at a time. As for the script, the Shaw board had to approve any changes. What Lerner must have gone through with *My Fair Lady* (based on Shaw's *Pygmalion*) I don't know, but what I went through was terrible. I finally ignored them. Finally. Because there was a line of Noël Coward's when the young gladiators, who are going off to die, make a statement, and Dick wrote them a song, at the end of which Caesar said, 'Thank you, dear boys.' As only [Noël] could! Well, the board wouldn't have it, but we did it anyway.

"The problem with that show was that Dick somehow trusted and liked Joe Layton, and Layton was a problem for this show as well as *Two by Two*. He was very gifted and extremely smart and articulate, but what he always wanted was that a show be conceived by Joe Layton, and he came up with a conception that hurt *Androcles* terribly.

"The conception in *Androcles* was that it was all going to be shot in a single complete tour of the large studio NBC had in Brooklyn, ending with a scene in an arena. He did it in such a way that there were no close-ups. It was all faraway, and somehow it just had no energy. You couldn't cut it, because there was nothing to cut it against. Just these endless long shots, which on television in those days looked like little tiny figures. It was a failure, which was a shame because I thought the show as written was pretty good. First of all, it was a Shaw play, and how wrong can you get? And I thought Dick wrote some pretty good numbers in the Hammerstein mold."

When there was composing to be done, Rodgers would work at home. He would come into the office with his briefcase, tap it with a big smile, and

Old friends reunited: Richard Rodgers and Noël Coward,
playing Caesar in *Androcles and the Lion,* 1967

say he had "done his homework." Duane Elliott said that he always treated her considerately and one of the few times when she saw him angry was while he was having his portrait painted. The artist liked to hear music while he worked and kept the radio running, not knowing that Rodgers, like most musicians, hated being obliged to listen. Finally the portrait was finished, and Rodgers hated that, too. So she told him, "If you really don't like it, there is only one thing to do. Chop it up. Otherwise it will go into a closet and reappear some day." One morning when she arrived, the picture was on the floor, thousands of dollars' worth, cut to pieces. Dorothy Rodgers commissioned a new portrait.

Duane Elliott thought that Rodgers must have had a stroke one day in the office. He was sitting down and suddenly one side of his body jerked. She went to Morris Jacobs, their business manager, and told him that Rodgers was unwell. Jacobs went in to see Rodgers and thought he was fine, but she prevailed upon them to call the doctor. Rodgers was out of the office for a while after that.

Eddie Blum had started as casting director for *Cinderella* and just stayed on. He knew Douglas Watt, a writer for the *New York Sunday News*. Watt went to interview Rodgers at the office in the summer of 1967, just before his sixty-fifth birthday. Rodgers had just completed the score for *Androcles and the Lion* and was in a mood to reminisce, talking about his career, *Carousel,* and "Bali Ha'i," and the differences between the working methods of Hammerstein and Hart. As Watt was leaving, he stopped to chat with Blum, who said of Rodgers, "He's a crotchety bastard. Walks around most of the time like an old man. But give him something to do and the so-and-so straightens up and gets right to it." Blum spoke admiringly of two of the new ballads Rodgers had written for *Androcles,* but it did not help. After Watt reported his remarks, Blum was fired.

That kind of reaction would not have struck his daughters and grandchildren as particularly strange where his work was concerned. Mary Rodgers Guettel said, "My father used to look at me so searchingly to see what I thought—I mean, more searchingly than he ever looked at me any other time . . . And it was never possible to tell him the truth. As he got older and began to do shows that were less good, you could never say to him when he was in the process of writing, or certainly after the show opened . . . 'This isn't the best you have done' or 'the best you could do.'" Her daughter Kim recalled being quizzed by her grandfather about one of his musicals, finding herself less than enthusiastic and then having him snap at her and realizing her mistake. So the next time there was an opening, "I was determined to tell him I loved it no matter what happened. So I really turned on the raves. I practically cried, and when I got back to the hotel my mother wanted to know what all that was about. She said, 'Did you really like it?' I looked at her and said, 'Are you out of your mind?' She replied, 'You really had me fooled.' I knew by then that he didn't want an honest response."

MARY RODGERS GUETTEL and her mother worked on a book together, *A Word to the Wives,* published in 1970, and in the summer of 1969 they decided to take a two-week trip to Russia. Dorothy Rodgers recalled, "Dick wasn't eager to go, nor was he very well at that time." On the last night of their stay in Leningrad, the phone rang at three in the morning. It was Dorothy's son-in-law Daniel Melnick, calling to say that Rodgers was in the hospital. It took two days of flying to get them back to New York, "and an anguishing two days it was. After I had stopped smoking for three years with great effort, I started to smoke again. I went into Mary and said, 'Give me some of your cigarettes.'" Her daughter was less concerned, because the phone call had been reassuring, and she thought it was a ruse on her father's part to get her mother back home, "because there was something very peculiar about the fact that he had serious illnesses twice when she went away." Once they arrived they discovered just how ill he really was. Dorothy Rodgers said that when she walked into the room her husband looked at her and said, "I didn't think I'd ever see you again."

Linda Rodgers Emory said, "My father had come up to spend a weekend with us in Pound Ridge and seemed all right. Then he wasn't feeling well later in the week and I drove back and forth a couple of times. All of a sudden his doctor had him in hospital because he didn't like his blood pressure, or something else, and the next thing I remember was that he had been going to the john in the hospital and the pressure of trying to have a bowel movement was such that he fainted. Heartbeat irregular, things of concern, so they put him in a coronary unit at Lenox Hill. Danny and I came racing in, and Alan Rose, the cardiologist, confused me because he told me my father had had an MI [myocardial infarction] and I said, 'I thought he had a heart attack,' and he said, 'It's the same thing.'

"It was a boiling-hot summer day and there was a terrific thunderstorm and a downpour of rain. I remember I was wearing a very pretty yellow cotton dress that got absolutely soaked as Danny and I ran home. I was trying to decide whether to call my mother and what kind of a story to make up so she wouldn't be terrified, and while we were at home another call came saying there were some more problems and we should go back. I thought if I changed into a different dress my father would know I had been home, so I had better wear the same one, so I went back in my drenched dress. It was the night they landed on the moon—the twenty-second of July, 1969—and the doctors were watching television. They had another monitor feeding a pacemaker into his heart in the same room. So I sat there holding his hand and thinking, this is quite some scene, with the moon and the pacemaker."

TWO BY TWO came about when Martin Charnin, then a young lyricist who had worked with Mary Rodgers on several shows, came to Rodgers with the idea of writing a musical based on a successful play by Clifford Odets, *The Flowering Peach,* to star Danny Kaye. Rodgers wrote, "The story dealt with Noah and the flood, and though written in 1954, covered such contemporary themes as the generation gap and ecology. There was even a parallel between the flood and the atom bomb. We got in touch with Peter Stone, who had just had a tremendous hit with *1776,* and he agreed to join us as librettist." Stone recalls it slightly differently. He believes he and Charnin both went to Rodgers with the idea, "and the next morning Charnin, to his utter horror and amazement, found out that Dick had gone out and gotten the rights. He . . . didn't tell us about it—he just did it. We were a little naive . . . but on the other hand, we didn't realize we were in that kind of danger . . . So that was the first surprise. The second surprise developed slowly. That was that he did not see the show that we saw." To them the play's charm had to do with its lower-middle-class Jewish background—Menasha Skulnik had been a big success as Noah—and Rodgers "didn't want a Jewish show. He had a lot of friends in Connecticut and he wanted something a little more sophisticated. That came as a bit of a surprise. Although I don't understand why the show appealed to him without that," Stone added.

"I learned everything I knew about musicals from Frank Loesser and he told me no show can succeed if everybody's not on the same level. It ended up that not only were Charnin and I writing a different show from Dick but from Danny Kaye and even the director, Joe Layton.

"Joe had two concepts, which were both very, very heavy-handed. The first, the least troublesome, was that God spoke in images, so he had slides of great art, and mixed them up: there was Renaissance, there was Impressionist, and they were flashed on a screen by banks of carousels, and God spoke in these, and Noah answered them.

"The next was really dangerous. The first act took place in a house in the village and the second, on the Ark. Joe's concept was that when Noah convinces everyone that a flood is coming they dismantle the house board by board and carry it off, so in the end there's no house left, and in the beginning of the second act, there is the Ark, built out of all those boards. It seems impossible now. But we rehearsed at the scenic studio in the Bronx where the show was being built, every day from four until midnight, and the cast learned every line together with moving the boards. It was all done by numbers. We were in a shambles when we opened in New Haven. Marty and I revolted and called Dick aside and said, 'Joe has lumbered us. Either the lumber goes or we go! But we will not have both!' Dick called him on the carpet, but the lumber didn't go. It was modified but it was still terrible."

Rodgers was a difficult man to deal with, Stone said, because he was so

Danny Kaye during *Two by Two,* 1970

evasive. "He was the producer of the show and also the composer, and when
you wanted to talk to the composer he had on his producer's hat, and when
you wanted to talk to the producer you got the composer. So you never could
nail him down. I don't know if he approved of us, really. He was not generous
with praise, or trying to make you feel good about things. But in some ways
he was wonderful to work with, because he knew so much about the theatre
and remembered things." Although Stone worked with Rodgers for months,
"I never could figure him out. The image I always had was, how could beauty
come out of this morass of anger? By the time I knew him he was sick, and he
was angry." For a man in his sixties who had had a serious heart attack, his
pursuit of the girls was "bold and amazingly open." He was chasing Tricia
O'Neill, who played Rachel, and Madeline Kahn, who played Goldie. The
joke was that he chased them around the piano, and Kahn used to be "hilarious about it. She made fun of him, and it," Stone said. For his part, Charnin
found Rodgers a difficult person to know. "He was never Richard Rodgers
my pal," he said. "You couldn't really hug him. It was a very tactile time and

he did not invite touching. It was in his nature always to have a space between himself and whoever. I don't know whether he was ever close to anyone."

Danny Kaye, who had not been in a stage musical since Cole Porter's *Let's Face It* in 1941, was remarkably charming at first. However, when the reviews were less glowing than he expected and, in addition, he was passed over for the Tony Awards that year, he became stubborn and resentful. Then, one day, coming down a plank, he fell and broke his ankle. He was persuaded to return to the show in a wheelchair, and then the trouble started. Kaye began freely inventing his own dialogue. "He'd roll down the ramp in his chair and say he was glad the brakes worked, or he would go through the wall and be in bed with the Greek next door," Stone said. "He totally broke down the invisible wall. He started misbehaving with Joan Copeland [playing his wife], tickling her, doing things to her, and trying to goose the girls with his crutches . . . Some of the ad libs were really raunchy but most of them were just terrible." There was nothing to be done, because Kaye was the whole show and it would have closed without him. (It ran for 343 performances.) So they had to endure his bad behavior. Rodgers was so furious he would not go near the theatre. He called the show "moderately successful and not particularly admirable."

He had begun writing an autobiography and did not know what the future would hold. "The office is here and I am not sure what to do with it," he told another friend. Meantime he and Dorothy had sold the apartment in which they had lived for twenty-six years and moved to the Pierre. "We are at the south end of the Park but unless it is a very bad day we see the George Washington Bridge quite clearly." Mary and Hank had two more boys, Adam and Alec, and Mary's oldest, Tod, was nineteen now and sporting a beard and a girlfriend. So far as Rodgers was concerned, all was well, and he did not intend to do another show unless he could find something he really liked, because "it just isn't worth it any more."

Chapter Nineteen

THE KEY TO THE CURTAIN

B Y 1970 RODGERS HAD CELEBRATED his fiftieth anniversary on the stage, was a multimillionaire and one of the most famous musical-theatre composers in Broadway history. No other composer had equaled him, not just for longevity but for size of output and for the enduring nature of his songs, so many of which had withstood the test of time and been rediscovered by successive generations. They were "standards" that "crossed over into the common musical unconscious of America from the mid-1920s on," Jesse Green wrote.

No popular composer had a larger influence on "the form, content and tone of the art of musical comedy—an art that many people, with considerable reason, believe to be America's most characteristic and vital contribution . . . to music," Winthrop Sargeant wrote. In collaboration with Hart and Hammerstein he had produced "an astonishing succession of shows, some of which have altered the traditions of the musical stage, bringing to it new elements of musical and dramatic cohesion and sophistication." Although Rodgers was hardly the sole developer of this distinctly American form, his position was a special one. "He has been a continuous and restless innovator. He has never conformed to a pattern, either in his choice of dramatic subjects or in the melodies he has written to ornament them. His output of shows and show tunes has been greater than any of his contemporaries . . ." The exact number of songs had been put at two thousand; Rodgers himself did not know but thought it was closer to a thousand.

What made a Rodgers melody so quintessentially his own? One noticed, Sargeant continued, a virtual absence of those jazzy, ragtime idioms that Gershwin put to such good use in his own melodies.

Many of his tunes are rapid waltzes or scherzos ("I'm in Love with a Wonderful Guy" and the waltz from *Carousel,* for example); others are polkas ("The Lonely Goatherd" from *The Sound of Music*); and still others ("If I Loved You" from *Carousel*) are so far from the conventions of dance music of any kind, and so meditative in character, that they seem more closely related to the operatic aria than to what is commonly thought of as the American popular idiom. Many attempts have been made to pin down the characteristics of the Rodgers style. It has been said, for instance, that he is addicted to melodies built on major and minor scales. This particular mannerism, typical of the melodies of Tchaikovsky, is, however, by no means universal in Rodgers's work. There are certainly scales to be found here and there, but there are also plenty of tunes built out of leaping arpeggios, such as "Oh, What a Beautiful Mornin'," whose lingering over the notes of both tonic and dominant chords recalls a number of old folk songs . . . But any attempt to reduce his style to a formula is doomed. He is always doing the unexpected, and the variety of his melodic invention . . . is probably greater than that of any other Broadway composer . . . Time and again, you think you can guess what Rodgers is going to do next, only to find him doing something else entirely.

Like the best in this genre, Rodgers's songs "trade in specific and complex emotions, expressed through a prism of artifice that bends them toward irony and abstraction . . . distinguished by the predominance of melody over harmony and rhythm . . . and by, in the best cases, exceptional wit and wrenching loveliness," Green wrote. They breathed a craftsmanship so exquisitely refined that it seemed effortless. "In a ballad like 'If I Loved You,' a lyricist generally has 75 to 100 words in which to tell the main story . . . they must sit properly on the music and move when it does; provide big, open vowel sounds for high notes and avoid unsingable consonant clusters; and of course make sense for the character and the dramatic situation of the libretto. It took Hammerstein several weeks of constant tinkering to get some of his simplest lyrics right, while Rodgers was perfectly capable of dashing off the matching tune while dinner guests finished their coffee."

What Rodgers displayed was a gift more to be valued than speed, versatility, dramatic appropriateness, or even a subliminal understanding of the needs of his times: that of the inevitable melody. This sequence of notes so imprints itself on the ear that one cannot ever forget it, or ever wants to. One could spend one's life listening to these songs, which rise to the surface of memory at the oddest moments, expressing a mood of which one is barely aware. It is a phenomenon that Dennis Potter exploited in *The Singing Detective,* and also Nora Ephron in *Sleepless in Seattle.* That phenomenon was Richard Rodgers's legacy for a whole generation, the stamp he placed upon his age. His was the rarest gift of all, of writing songs that illustrate the pain of longing for "the lost golden spaces of the imagination."

RODGERS WAS NEVER really able to explain the wellsprings of his art, which seem to have been made instinctive after decades of being refined, so that he no longer knew how he did it. He would insist earnestly that he had no artistic pretensions. "I'm a commercial theatre kid. I don't write for posterity," he told Eckert Goodman in 1953. The very idea that inspiration was somehow involved would elicit total scorn.

> That's a bad word for what happens to me when I write. What I do is not as fancy as some people may think. It is simply using the medium to express emotion. If my medium happened to be colors, I would be trying to express what I feel in that medium.
>
> Mine happen to be notes. It's a particularly potent medium, maybe because it's the only purely abstract one. You can make it mean whatever you like. You have a situation in a play, say, where a girl and boy have never met before. They . . . affect each other—superficially, if they are superficial people, or deeply if they are more emotional, or with certain intellectual overtones if they are intellectual.
>
> Your job is to translate this situation and these people into musical terms. This isn't a question of sitting on the top of a hill and waiting for inspiration to strike. It's work. People have said, "You're a genius." I say, "No, it's my job."

What Rodgers alluded to was that the subject he had set most often was romantic love. His titles alone told the story: "The Blue Room," "Little Girl Blue," "My Funny Valentine," "Where or When" "Bewitched, Bothered and Bewildered," "Some Enchanted Evening," "Falling in Love with Love," "My Heart Stood Still," "People Will Say We're in Love": the list goes on and on. In that regard he was simply following the fashion of the times; and the sentiments displayed—that somehow you had met before, that all you needed to do was see a stranger across a crowded room, that the boy and girl would live happily ever after—were adult fairy stories to which even lyricists as sophisticated as Hart gave lip service. It was the subject everyone wrote about, one of the myths, as Leslie Fiedler wrote, that were "projections of certain unconscious impulses otherwise confessed only in our dreams, but which once raised to the level of full consciousness serve as grids of perception through which we screen so-called 'reality.'" Such myths were embedded in the popular culture, its television shows, comic strips, movies, and magazines, so persistently that, to Fiedler, these messages endlessly repeated constituted "in fact a kind of unsuspected secular scriptures . . . Moreover, precisely because we are not aware that we are being indoctrinated as we watch, listen or read in quest of entertainment and escape, we are less apt to resist their implicit messages."

Such songs could be described as the aural equivalent of Norman Rockwell's art. If you looked at these messages, Mark Steyn wrote, anyone who really believed them was suffering from "'IFD Disease': I for 'Idealization (the making of impossible demands upon life)'; F for 'Frustration (as the result of the demands not being met)'; leading to D for 'Demoralization,' and a retreat into schizophrenia." Believing songs like this could "seriously stunt your emotional development," Steyn wrote. It was against the patent unreality of such sentiments that musical theatre would rebel in such shows as Sondheim's *Follies,* in which the whole edifice was shown to be a crumbling sham.

There is no evidence that Rodgers ever seriously examined the kind of musical he continued to write after 1960, which was, in all important respects, the same kind of musical he had written with Hammerstein. That, Cleveland Amory wrote, had "a simple yet all-embracing" message which "is often called, to their rare irritation, 'sweetness and light.' And yet this message, too, in these days of cynicism, nihilism, satire and humorous escape" (Amory was writing in 1959) "is also controversial. Even some of Rodgers and Hammerstein's closest friends are sometimes bothered that they seem to have sold their birthright as New York showmen for a kind of sentimentality which does not . . . square with the fact that they are civilized and sophisticated men.

"'What's wrong with "sweetness and light"?' Rodgers asks. 'It's been around quite a while. Even a cliché, you know, has a right to be true. I'm not interested in cracking out at anything and I'm certainly not interested in kicking sentiment around. I love satire but I couldn't write it.'" Perhaps if he still had Hart in his life, or a younger equivalent, Rodgers would have returned to the sophisticated style that gave such panache to the songs they wrote together. But by 1970 his best work with Hart had been done thirty years before, and the musicals he chose seemed much more under the unconscious influence of Hammerstein than of Hart. He was too shrewd not to know that the musical was changing—*Hair,* after all, had arrived two years before—and that Sondheim and Andrew Lloyd Webber, in their various guises, were transforming it past recognition. But for him, virtue must triumph, order must come from chaos, and omnia vincit amor; it was all he knew.

When he was asked, after *Two by Two,* why he was not resting on his laurels, he said, "Well, damned if I know. I don't have to do it for the bread, but I think I have to do it for myself. I like to work. I like to write . . . But that isn't it. Maybe I am doing it in spite of the fact that I was very ill. A little over a year ago I almost died, with a very bad coronary. With good treatment . . . I got over it completely. Now maybe this is ego talking—you know, 'I'll show them. I'll not only get well, I'll do a show' . . . Maybe it's simply a will to live. And if you have lived in the theatre as long as I have, to quit would be a kind of not living—which doesn't intrigue me very much. I should say not."

AS HE APPROACHED his seventieth birthday in June 1972, Rodgers was looking for another project. He had been introduced to Erich Segal, then a young assistant classics professor at Yale, who had already written *Love Story,* and they started work on a musical. Segal described it as "a story about a boy in a single day of his life who is looking for his father." As etiquette required, the principals complimented each other elaborately and talked optimistically about the date for the Broadway opening, but nothing came of it.

Then Rodgers took up the idea of making a musical from *Arsenic and Old Lace* by Joseph Kesselring, which had been produced by his old friends Lindsay and Crouse in 1941 with Josephine Hull in the role of the dear, demented Abby Brewster, and became an instant classic. Michael Stewart was to write the book, Sheldon Harnick was engaged for the lyrics, and Harold Prince, a producer who had already made a name for himself with a string of successful musicals, was to co-produce.

Sheldon Harnick said, "Mike [Stewart] thought there was a musical in it but in order to get the rights he had to have someone like Richard Rodgers involved. Rodgers was interested. Mike had already written a book, and Rodgers and I read it. Both of us were disturbed by the fact that, as in most farce-comedies, everything was so tightly written that there was almost no room for songs. Although we could find a few openings, overall it didn't seem a musical project. Mike rewrote it and it still didn't work. At that point he conceded that he could not solve the problem, offered to give us everything he had written, and suggested we get another writer. We went to several others who all said the same thing, i.e., that it was not a musical. Rodgers was very stubborn and persistent. He really wanted to do it. He didn't give up until the experience we had with Tom Stoppard. I met Stoppard in Rodgers's office and he professed to be a longtime Rodgers fan. It was a little embarrassing for me because I felt I wasn't there; Stoppard talked almost exclusively to Rodgers. Whatever questions Stoppard asked I would answer, because Rodgers had had so much illness by then that he didn't talk much. But Stoppard didn't look at me.

"Finally Stoppard said, 'Yes, I'm sure there's a musical in this, and when I get back to London I will write a synopsis. Or rather, a treatment. You'll have it in two weeks.'" Stoppard was as good as his word and sent an outline for an antic opening number in which the thirteen gentlemen Abby and her sister have murdered (thanks to their irresistible elderberry wine, with a little arsenic thrown in) would be resurrected to kick up their heels. They would gradually go back into their graves in the cellar, and as they did so the main set, the living room of the house, would assemble around them. Stoppard also envisioned a slap-up finale in which the two aunts would be cavorting on the grounds of Happy Dale, an insane asylum in which their dotty brother Teddy (who thinks he is Theodore Roosevelt) is to be incarcerated. Stoppard liked the idea of thirteen Roosevelts, referring to the corpses, or perhaps Napoleons, a personage he preferred. He rather liked the idea of bringing Hitler and Jean Harlow into it somewhere as well. Harnick said, "Rodgers finally grinned and said, 'I guess not.'"

Rodgers's seventieth birthday salute at the Imperial Theatre, titled "A Rodgers Celebration," in June 1972, came at a difficult time. Early in May Dorothy Rodgers was "hit with a pretty bad coronary thrombosis," Rodgers told Lawrence Bachmann, and went into Lenox Hill Hospital. By the end of May she was out of intensive care, but, he told Morris Jacobs, "she'll have to be in the hospital three to four weeks which is going to be very difficult for her in view of her personality and her dislike of being quiet but she'll just have to put up with it . . ." By October of 1972 she was getting better, well enough to be "playing pretty vigorous croquet." That was reassuring because, as Jerry Whyte wrote, "I know how deeply and emotionally you are affected by her health."

The marriage of their daughter Linda and Dan Melnick had ended and they had divorced in 1971. Linda Rodgers Emory said, "Danny and I were in the midst of a protracted separation agreement that was going nowhere and my lawyer wanted me to take some small objets d'art out of my apartment, and the obvious place to take them for safekeeping was my parents' house in the country. So I went up there one weekend and in effect asked if it was okay with them, and my father said, 'I don't want to get involved.' I recall leaving the living room in tears at that point. My mother found me later and reassured me and said, 'Of course bring the things up,' which I did. But it was just his knee-jerk reaction. Not necessarily personal! It was just 'I don't want anything unpleasant.' Which I can understand now." Her mother's response, taking her side, did not happen all that often. Dorothy Rodgers was most likely to say that her husband was a genius and his children would have to forgive him.

The next idea that came along was from the producer Richard Adler, who wanted to do a musical about the life of Henry VIII. Given Rodgers's cease-less search for upbeat, romantic material, *Rex* seemed a curious choice. Ed Sherin, who directed the musical, agreed. "I thought there was no way to lighten it up, and you'd have to treat it as a drama set to music, like *Sweeney Todd*, but Rodgers wrote his typical sunny-natured, optimistic score . . ." Sheldon Harnick also had serious reservations but allowed himself to be per-suaded. Sherman Yellen, who wrote the book, said, "By the time he'd gotten around to *Rex* the audience for his kind of show was somewhat diminished. [Rodgers] was against the tide and there was, in the case of *Rex,* a mismating of talent. Both Rodgers and Harnick were, au fond, great American optimists and to do the life of Henry VIII you needed an ironist." In other words, sev-eral experienced men of the theatre who could see the problems clearly enough in retrospect were allowing themselves to be persuaded by the idea of a big, colorful musical full of incomparable Rodgers melodies.

Rodgers had been suffering for a couple of years from hoarseness and was periodically advised to rest his voice. In the spring of 1974, as he was working on *Rex,* he complained to Liza Minnelli that he had a case of "galloping laryngitis." Then came a staggering blow. His friend Jerry Whyte had been having persistent heart problems for several years, but it was still a major shock when in March of 1974 he died of a heart attack. To lose such a dear friend was made especially difficult, Duane Garrison Elliott said, given his belief that "when you died you went into a box, and that was it." So she sensed a certain change in his attitude after she received a letter he wrote on the first anniversary of Whyte's death. The letter said, "There has been an empty feeling around our office for the last year. Everyone . . . misses Jerry but for me there is a special emptiness. . . . I still get the feeling that he'll be coming back soon and we'll be able to exchange experiences and tell each other the jokes we have heard. I also have the conviction that we'll meet again some place . . ." Four months after Whyte died, in July of 1974, Rodgers had surgery to remove his cancerous vocal cords. He wrote to Alvin Cooperman, "My professional and personal life is going through some shattering changes . . ."

Sheldon Harnick said, "We started to work and then Rodgers had a laryn-

With Sheldon Harnick, Rodgers's lyricist for *Rex*, 1976

gectomy and I thought, 'There goes the project!' He'd already had a stroke and a heart attack by then. When he underwent the operation none of us knew whether he would survive it. One of the things that endeared Rodgers to me was the way he lived his life. Whatever happened was a given. He didn't complain; he just accepted it. You overcame it and went forward. As soon as the operation was over, and it was physically possible for him to begin speech therapy, he went. I found that very impressive."

Rodgers could have opted for a voice box but decided on the much more difficult solution of esophageal speech, which required learning to gulp air and then belch it back through the oral passages. His attending physician, Dr. Sidney Kreps, said he had had a difficult time learning the technique, "and we were beginning to worry about whether he was ever going to be able to do it. One day he came into my office and the nurse with him said, 'Mr. Rodgers has something very important to show you.' Rodgers paused for a moment, and then he started singing, 'Doe—a deer, a female deer . . .' I am kidding you not. To this day when I think of it my legs get rubbery." William Hammerstein said, "He went into the hospital and when he came out he could only talk in a whisper. He invited me over to lunch at the apartment a few days later and he was telling me he was angry because the day he left the hospital he had ordered a limousine from this company they used, and the limousine didn't show up. And he was out there with Dorothy on the street waiting for this car. Telling me about it, he said, 'He never showed up, the son of a bitch!' Then he added, 'Baby's first words!'"

Harnick said, "I was so sensitive to his predicament, i.e., learning to speak again, that on a number of occasions I pretended to understand what he was saying when I really didn't. When he really got good at it he called me one night and was croaking out his words and I was so touched by the effort that was going into it I almost wept. I was saying how impressed I was because I could hear him so clearly. And he replied, 'This is nothing. I just spoke to Dorothy, and *she's* in California.'"

Harnick continued: "He was no longer the Richard Rodgers of legend who could write something in fifteen minutes. He took his time. But as I started giving him lyrics, it was extraordinary to see the way he was rejuvenated by work. Because of all the blows he'd suffered, this was not a man in good physical shape. When we first talked he asked me how I liked to work. Did I like lyrics first, or the music? I said I had worked both ways. He said he had, too, and I thought he intended to write both ways, but as it turned out, he was incapable of writing the music first. I once spoke to a friend who was both a doctor and psychotherapist, and she asked whether he had ever had a stroke. She said she had found that some of her stroke patients had lost the ability to think abstractly. I thought that might be the reason. Rodgers always needed the lyric in front of him and he wanted it to be complete.

"I had my problems with him. We wrote a song for Anne Boleyn to sing when she knew Henry VIII had fallen out of love with her. After I played it for the producers, Adler called me that evening and said he thought the verse was more beautiful than the chorus and that we should scrap the chorus and extend the verse. I thought it was an interesting idea and he was probably right. When I explained this to Rodgers next day, to my surprise, he said, 'What do you mean?' I said, 'Well, Adler thinks these eight bars have in them the germ of something more beautiful and he wants us to extend that.' And Rodgers said, 'How do you mean?' I kept trying to explain and he kept asking the same question. By this time I was sweating, because he just couldn't get it." Finally, Harnick asked if he had some music paper, and Rodgers "gave me this pop-eyed look he used when he was being humorous, and said, 'Do I have a piece of music paper!'" Then Harnick actually wrote out what was being proposed, "and Rodgers said, 'Oh. Why didn't you say so?' That was when I saw the Rodgers legend in action. He went to the piano and in about twenty minutes he had the song." Harnick said, "At this point Rodgers constantly needed anchors. He gravitated back again and again to tonic chords. He had lost the ability to think freely." Harnick concluded, "I was sorry when our relationship ended because I really came to love him. I loved his gallantry in the face of all these physical blows, I loved his sense of humor and his patience. I loved the fact that he still turned out some good songs . . . He must have been a feeling man, however he concealed it, to write the music he wrote."

Sherman Yellen said, "When I first met him, I couldn't quite understand why he kept going at it. After all, look at what was against him. Failing health. A talent which, if not diminished, spoke to a certain generation . . . But I've arrived at a point in life when it's one physical problem after another and I begin to understand the meaning and value of work. Work as a connection to life. I understand the superstitious feeling that if one stops working, life stops." He continued, "To see this feeble man walking with the aid of a cane, a walking corpse, coming up with a beautiful melody, was really remarkable. And because he kept that, that was the life he held onto, to the end."

By then he was being accompanied everywhere by a nurse, Eileen Gurhy, on whom he was very dependent, "because he felt she was his contact with life. She would keep him from having to face the horrors of hospitals and things like that." And things were not going well with the show, mostly because of their decision to view Henry VIII's life through three of his marriages. Yellen said, "The show might have succeeded had we dealt with the relationship between Elizabeth I and her father. By having Anne Boleyn, the executions and the cruelty, we created something that was neither fish nor fowl. That show needed Sondheim. It needed someone who could take a very harsh view of behavior without ever attempting to justify it. Whereas Dick had come out of a world, working with Hammerstein, in which one was always looking for the redeeming values in human nature."

Ed Sherin said, "A substantial problem about doing a musical is that it's a hydra. You have to please the composer, the choreographer, the musical director, the book writer, and three or four producers. You're talking about eight or nine people. The only way anything creative can be accomplished is if you have, let's say, the power of a Hal Prince, meaning you're going to tell them how it's going to be done. Because the synapse which reveals the way to go is subtle. It's all largely intuitive. Who can do the part, who gave the best audition, and if there's something in that personality that I can kindle. I may be the only one of eight people who sees that. And I may be absolutely right, spot on for the show, but it can't happen, and the person you all agree on is a compromise. I wanted Rodgers there as much as possible because I didn't want to take any steps without his seeing what I was doing." Barbara Andres, who played Henry VIII's first wife, Queen Catherine, said, "Even though people thought Mr. Rodgers was incapacitated because of his laryngitis, he was there constantly" but, she thought, "protected from a lot of the misery going on in that show. There was an enormous unrest in the company, almost an illness."

As rehearsals struggled onwards, Sherin tried to "darken" the music by giving it a flavor of the music of its time, and asked for appropriate orchestration. "A great deal of money was spent on the extra orchestration, and when Rodgers heard it he was very upset. Very. And perhaps rightfully," he said. "But we were both caught in the trap of trying to do something that was ill-fitting from the beginning."

Another problem was the miscasting of the brilliant British actor Nicol Williamson in the role of Henry VIII. Sherin said, "He was extremely difficult, having a tough time with his marriage, his child, and drinking . . . Nicol would participate somewhat languidly in the rehearsals, arriving late and leaving early. He had some contempt for the writing, which was perhaps justified." Sherin recalled a famous moment in the run that took place during a curtain call. As the cast took its bow one of the dancers, Jim Litton, using television parlance, tapped Williamson on the back and said, "It's a wrap." Williamson heard "It's crap," so he swung around and hit Litton in the face. Barbara Andres said, "The wives tried to get Nicol offstage and away from Jimmy, who was on the floor. At first the audience thought it was all part of the curtain call, but they soon realized it was real. There was a terrible feeling in the company against Nicol, the serfs against the king, as it were.

"One day they brought in Hal Prince. We used to call him the phantom of the balcony because he saw every show from the balcony or a box, while Ed was down front and backstage." One of Prince's decisions was to make her character unattractive. Sherin said Andres "was a very attractive woman with a wonderful voice, whom Prince decided to make ugly to justify Henry's womanizing. I didn't like that. I was in favor of revealing what it was about Henry's character that would explain that behavior."

Sherman Yellen said, "My memory of those rehearsals is getting vague, but I remember one day Nicol threw a crown he was wearing, a rather expensive piece of property, across the stage, and Rodgers in his esophageal voice turned to me and said, 'He's every quarter-inch a king.' And then of course there was the trauma of my big mouth. I was sitting in Sardi's after having put up with what I thought was a lot, and having a drink. It was the eve of Passover, right before we were supposed to open in New York, and I had just received very troubling news that I had a polyp on my vocal cords—and

Dick, remember, had started like that—and I was very nervous about that, although fortunately it turned out to be nothing. So I was a little under the weather with the tension of the whole show, and a reporter from one of the tabloids came by and recognized me. He said, 'What's a nice Jewish boy like you doing sitting in Sardi's drinking tonight?' And I said, 'Well, when you're on the road with Nicol Williamson you no longer believe in God.' Wouldn't you know the next day the paper prints that, right before we were supposed to go on . . . Nicol then said he would not go on and I was challenged to make some kind of apology . . . So I wrote out this apology, the kind you do, trying to get yourself off the hook without humbling yourself too much. I couldn't really apologize for what I had said, because in truth it was hellish, an awful experience, and also for Dick as well." The musical ran for 49 performances in the spring of 1976 and then closed, having lost its entire investment.

Mary Rodgers Guettel, Harnick said, had warned him that her father was capable of throwing a set of lyrics across the room, as he had once done with Sondheim, but the Rodgers he found was "nothing like the person she had warned me about. He was totally flexible. I described this to Sondheim once and he marveled and said, 'This is not the same man I worked with.' I found him funny, working very hard. When Hal Prince came in to take over direction he wanted a new opening song for the Jester. It was like a prologue and I truly could not understand the point of the song. Hal tried to explain and finally I thought I understood and took a stab at it. I gave it to Rodgers and he set it.

"I didn't like the setting very much and by this time we were on terms that I thought I could tell him, so I started to say something about it, and his nurse, who was standing behind him, looked at me, made a face, and shook her head. I decided to leave it alone. A pianist with the company played the song (by then, Dick didn't play) and I sang it. We had a roomful of people and at the end of it there was dead silence. And I thought, 'Well, it's really not very good.' Then from the back of the room Dick Rodgers croaks out, 'Well, I like it!' and everyone started laughing.

"The other story is—our conductor, Jay Blackton, was an old, old friend of Rodgers's. If I'm not mistaken they had worked together on *Oklahoma!* Jay was living in California and when he arrived I was called in to meet him. Jay had a very pronounced limp; he dragged one leg behind him. I guess he had had a stroke, too. Rodgers got up from the desk and started to limp towards the center of the room, and Jay is dragging himself towards Rodgers, and these two elderly men are saying to each other, 'Jay, you look great!' 'Dick, you look marvelous!' We had a production meeting in the theatre after one of the performances and Jay had a terrible cold. So he prefaced the meeting by apologizing for his laryngitis and Rodgers piped up, saying, 'You think *you* have laryngitis!' "

Rodgers invited Harnick to work on his next show, *I Remember Mama,* "and I couldn't see it so I said no. But for quite a while I went up to his office once a month and we would have lunch. He'd provide a tuna fish sandwich and half a bottle of wonderful white wine. I'd ask him questions about his career and Larry Hart, and then I drifted away, and the next thing I knew, he was ill . . ."

The increasing physical fragility of Richard Rodgers was unsettling for everyone who saw him. Jonathan S. Reed, an attorney, attended a book signing for Rodgers's autobiography, *Musical Stages,* in Bloomingdale's on Manhattan's East Side in 1975. "I was struck by how small and fragile-looking Rodgers was, especially in comparison with his wife. As I left the book signing, a publicist was taking pictures of the couple (cutting a cake?) and it appeared to me that the healthy, skinny and energetic Mrs. Rodgers, in high heels, towered over her stocky, pale and seemingly arthritic husband." Alec Guettel was amazed at his continuing ability to laugh at himself, even in this predicament. He said, "When he was getting old and sick he could come in shuffling and walking with a cane. I remember he was coming into a hotel lobby one time and an old lady beside him had a four-post walker, and my grandfather said, 'Race you to the elevator!' " Mary Rodgers Guettel said that after he lost his voice he would call her on the phone and wheeze into it, "Guess who!" She continued, "It was so depressing for him when he lost his voice because he could no longer be funny, and that was one of his great joys. By the time you have swallowed all that air and burped it back up again, the moment for the funny quip is long gone."

After *Rex,* no one seriously thought he would want to work again. The producer Alexander Cohen said, "I had presented Liv Ullmann in a revival of Eugene O'Neill's *Anna Christie,* and she was quite startling in that, and we were in Washington with the play. We were at the National Theatre and Marty Charnin and I were guests at a National Press Club event and Charnin said he had a musical and must meet this woman. He was doing a musical about another mama, he said. Liv Ullmann at the time was a forty-year-old immigrant from Norway with a lovely face and a beautiful accent and, of course, the part was a forty-year-old Norwegian immigrant in *I Remember Mama,* the play by John Van Druten. It was tailor-made. I introduced them and then heard the score which Martin had written. I was very direct with him. I said, 'Your lyrics are really very lovely, but the music doesn't work for me. But I am curiously moved by the story. This cries out for Dick Rodgers.'

Richard and Dorothy Rodgers

And Martin said, 'Well, nobody can get Dick Rodgers to work.' At that time one must remember that Dick had suffered two major operations and lost his voice. He was in a weakened condition.

"But I thought to myself, knowing the indomitable spirit of the man, that he probably would be interested, for several reasons, not the least of which was, when the play was originally done [in 1944], it was one of the few plays ever presented by Rodgers and Hammerstein. Secondly, I knew he had mastered his vocal problems. So I said to my wife, 'I'd like to invite Dick and Dorothy to the Four Seasons, and chat.' I wasn't really thinking. If I had been, I'd have chosen some place where there wasn't a staircase to climb. Because aside from his two operations he was walking with a cane and appeared to be—I was never sure of this—partially paralyzed.

"And I suddenly said to myself, 'My God, what have I done?' and I'm running around looking for an elevator, when I spied Dick coming up the stairs with Dorothy. He walked very gracefully to the table in the main room, which is quite a long walk, and sat down, and we filled each other in on what had happened in the past six or eight weeks. We went through dinner and finally I got up my courage, because as well as I knew him, and I'd now been a friend for almost twenty years, I was afraid to ask Dick to write a musical with Charnin, since I knew they'd already worked together on the ill-fated *Two by Two*. So I screwed up my courage and said, 'I'm thinking of presenting *I Remember Mama* as a musical. Would you . . . ?' And he said, 'Yes.' Just like that. I was overwhelmed. We celebrated and had a tiny little bit of champagne.

"So we did this work together and made this classic mistake—we were all enraptured by the fact that Richard was going to write for the theatre and, second, he was going to write for Liv Ullmann. So Liv came to Dick's office and he said, 'You're going to sing something, aren't you?' and she said, 'I couldn't possibly.' He said, 'Well, we're going to do "Happy Birthday,"' and he sat down and played it, and with his lack of any voice he sang it better than she did! And I thought to myself, at the moment when you know something is wrong is the moment when you should call a halt. Because one thing that was absolutely apparent was that Liv's singing didn't work, never worked, was destined never to work, and it was one of those troubled musicals out of town in Philadelphia and I was forced into the position of getting rid of Marty for what I thought was the good of the project." Charnin, who was directing the show as well as acting as lyricist, was replaced by Cy Feuer acting as director and Raymond Jessel as lyricist.

Mary Rodgers Guettel said, "It was a Sunday, because there wasn't any show. There was Daddy, Eileen Gurhy, and me—Hank must have not been there—and in the middle of lunch Mummy began to get one of Daddy's headaches, which, by the way, she aped. When he died she took 'em right on over. She suddenly had a dreadful headache and took to her bed. With Eileen to rub unguents on her, whatever. Shortly after that the phone call came from Alex Cohen saying he would like to see him later that afternoon, and Daddy said, 'I bet I know what that's about. I bet they want to fire Marty Charnin, and since your mother isn't feeling well would you like to sit in on this meeting? Maybe you'll have some suggestions.' So I did. They ignored every suggestion I made. After it was over I heard this television set on very loud in Mummy's room. And I kept thinking, 'How could anyone with a vicious headache want television on so loud?' So I went to see what that was all about. But it wasn't television. It was Mummy up on her elbows screaming like a banshee at my father, who was standing there the color of the fireplace, white, just listening, and then he backed into the hall. I went past him into the room and said, 'What's the matter?' And she started screaming about how angry she was at how he had treated her. What it came down to was that he

Richard Rodgers's last leading lady, Liv Ullmann, star of *I Remember Mama,* 1979

had asked me to be at this meeting instead of her. And I said, 'Mummy, you had this headache. You were sick. What was he—he figured—' And then she launched into this tirade about how she had always been such a wonderful, devoted, faithful wife and this was the thanks she got. I don't remember what the words were, because it was just so angry and bitter. But when I got out of the room Daddy was sort of lurking in the hallway, and I said, like the child of an alcoholic, which of course I was, but thinking, 'I'd better try to make this better,' so I said, 'I think you'd better go in and have a word with her. She's not too happy right now.' And he said, 'When has she ever been?' With such venom.

"While he was in there talking to her I was in the kitchen with Eileen, who was saying, 'You have no idea what she puts him through.' At one point she said—I don't remember whether she said it to me or to Linda and me—'Sometimes I think I'd like to put a tape recorder under her bed so people would know the kinds of things she says and what she's really like.' She was filling me full of how miserable my mother was making my father, while I was listening utterly fascinated. I hadn't heard any of this from anybody. Then Daddy came back and we sat and talked. He told me he was relieved that they had let Marty Charnin go. I know he was more open with me about his relationship with his wife than I ever believed possible, perhaps more than he had ever been with anybody." She continued, "It's interesting that at this moment I can't remember what . . . he said about my mother, but he was obviously very angry, and sick of her complaints and illnesses . . . I never expected to hear him talk like that." Rodgers went on to describe "the frustrations that I had always suspected but had never heard from him. It confirmed what I had always believed, i.e., that this was a hypocritical marriage. Pretending to be something it wasn't. When I finally heard the truth, my feeling was, 'Now what?' It turns out your parents hate each other. Now what do you do with it?"

Her daughter Kim Beaty felt she understood her grandparents. "He had drawn an invisible chalk line around himself and anyone who came inside it was attacked. I also found that people had such different reactions to him. It was either 'What a gent!' or 'What a son of a bitch.' And that's because he could be really nasty, and at the same time so warm, generous, and sweet. He had violent mood swings. Whereas my grandmother tried to be good all the time. All her perfectionism and controlling behavior could be put down to this, and when it didn't work she felt betrayed, and every once in a while she would just lose it. Part of me feels, 'Who doesn't?' and 'Why do we forgive him and not her?'"

Perhaps it was true to say that Rodgers's feelings about his wife were always in flux. There was another incident, which took place three years before, during the Boston tryout of *Rex*. Barbara Andres said, "Dorothy Rodgers gave us a beautiful party in a private ballroom of the Ritz-Carlton in Boston. It was perfectly catered. There were small tables all around the room and I sat with them. She was so gracious. She went to every single table and talked to every single member of the company. I was watching her admiringly when Mr. Rodgers leaned over to me. He said, 'I have loved her since the first minute I saw her.'"

I REMEMBER MAMA opened at the end of May 1979 at the Majestic Theatre and closed on Labor Day after 108 performances. Cohen said, "It could have run longer, but it was foreclosed by the Shuberts, who owned the theatre. They have a habit of foreclosing. This was a bitter experience for me and Dick. Neither of us ever got over it. They closed because they had another booking. They had a revival of *Most Happy Fella* and it lasted a week. One week! Larry Gelbart [one of the authors of *A Funny Thing Happened on the Way to the Forum*] once said, 'If Hitler is alive I hope he's on the road with a musical.' And I always feel that if Hitler is alive, he's really over there in the Shubert office."

After *Rex* closed Rodgers wrote to a friend that he had survived the bad notices and felt "fresh and eager to work again after I have had a little rest. The rest includes going to my place in Connecticut to just sit and look at the budding trees." That letter was written in the spring of 1976, but three years later, in the autumn of 1979, his mood was bleak. A writer approached him about collaborating on a musical about James Cagney, and Rodgers wrote apologetically, "I am afraid I haven't the energy to start discussing a new work." Nina Beaty said, "He felt that *Hair* had changed the direction and his kind of theatre was over."

He was having constant headaches and only came to life when a fan would appear, "people he didn't know who would come up and praise him," she said. "He loved all the nurses, maids, and people in the Pierre Hotel. But the rest of the time he just switched off. He went numb. Well, my grandmother was really in charge. She would decide when dinner would be served and what he would eat and he didn't seem to mind. The running joke was that he didn't even change a light bulb. Eileen would kneel down and tie his shoes! He was so pampered. He was this huge pet."

Judy Crichton agreed. "At the end of his life the role reversal was so horrible. Well, I don't know that Dorothy was ever dependent on Dick, but he became dependent, period. That was terrible. He became a spectator." When all hope of writing a new musical ended, so did his hope for himself. Mary Rodgers Guettel said, "When he got too sick to move he was trapped there. With my mother watching him like a hawk if he snuck an extra glass of wine. We used to watch him do that."

She continued, "I think by the time *I Remember Mama* closed he was horrendously depressed, but he'd been on a downward slope anyway. Nobody knew what caused his headaches. According to the doctor, they did a complete autopsy after his death, looking for a brain tumor, and they never found anything."

A month after *I Remember Mama* closed, Dorothy Rodgers decided to take a trip to Paris, with Eileen Gurhy along as company. Just before they left Rodgers had "a major seizure," with convulsions, his arms flailing about. He went to the hospital for tests and was discharged just as they left, wearing a Holter monitor, a twenty-four-hour cardiogram test. Mary Rodgers Guettel said, "It was Columbus Day, and that was the night I had to take Daddy to some kind of event. We had to go to the Hilton and because I'd been elected to be his escort, I wanted to take the elevator. He wouldn't take the elevator, and I thought, 'He's going to fall all the way back down the escalator,' which was very steep. So I thought, 'I'll let him go first and stand behind him and then if he falls, maybe I can catch him.'"

When the tests came back from the Holter monitor, Dorothy Rodgers and Eileen Gurhy, who had barely arrived in Paris, were contacted and immediately returned. "Clearly he was so ill those last few months," his daughter continued. "There were times when he was hallucinating. Eileen came into his bedroom one night late and he started screaming. My mother came out of her bedroom to see what on earth was going on, and reported that he was yelling, 'Get her out of here!,' pointing to Eileen. Who knows who he thought she was." At the end of his life he was being given a Brompton cocktail, a mixture of morphine, Demerol, and codeine named for the British hospital in which it was first administered, "a super-knockout, heavy barbiturate," said Nina Beaty, whose specialty is hospice work. Perhaps partly as a result of this, Linda Emory said, "He would sit in the room and absent himself from the rest of us. I remember going there for lunch and it gave me a chill. The television set was turned on in his bedroom. So there was the sound of somebody talking and everybody went out of the room and left him there like a baby with the TV set going. And had lunch. And nobody went to check on him."

That Thanksgiving, she continued, "He came to the table for dinner. I remember him coming down the hall with Eileen, with a handkerchief or a washcloth around his forehead because of his terrible headaches. And he sat there at the table with this thing around his head. He looked just awful. And I don't know what prompted me, but I got up and went over to the piano and started playing a piece of Scarlatti."

At Christmas time, Linda was on holiday but returned on Christmas Day because her father had gotten much worse. "He had been increasingly ill since Thanksgiving. And then he just sort of slowed down, and it was pretty obvious that he wasn't going to get any better. He didn't really want to see people and he didn't want them seeing him. Kitty Hart came over one evening on her way to some black-tie event, looking terribly pretty and being gay and adorable. I remember her as a visiting bright light. But for the most part, I just felt so sorry for him."

Richard Rodgers died on December 30, 1979, just three months after his last show closed. The marquees of Broadway theatres went dark for one minute in his memory, just as they had done for Oscar Hammerstein. The funeral at Temple Emanu-El was private, but many prominent New Yorkers were in attendance, including Mayor Edward Koch, Lillian Gish, Helen

Hayes, former Mayor John Lindsay, and Dore Schary, to pay tribute to the man who wrote thirty-nine musicals, numerous film and television scores, and over nine hundred songs. Rabbi Ronald Sobel eulogized him as "a very gentle man" and "a very private person." Rodgers's body was cremated, and there is no grave. No one knows where his ashes are.

No telephone message arrived, F. Scott Fitzgerald wrote of Jay Gatsby's final hours. "I have an idea that Gatsby himself didn't believe it would come, and perhaps he no longer cared. If that was true he must have felt that he had lost the old warm world, paid a high price for living too long with a single dream . . ."

Late in life, Richard Rodgers wrote, "There is a traditional trick that theatre people have played as long as I can remember. A veteran member of a company will order a gullible newcomer to find the key to the curtain. Naturally, the joke is that there is no such thing. I have been in the theatre over fifty years, and I don't think anyone would consider me naïve, but all my life I've been searching for that key. And I'm still looking . . ."

Chronology

1902   June 28: Richard Charles Rodgers born in Arverne, Long Island.

1916   Attends Townsend Harris Hall and DeWitt Clinton High School. First songs: "Dear Old Wigwam" and "Camp-Fire Days."

1917   Writes "Auto Show Girl," first copyrighted song. First score, music and part lyrics: *One Minute Please*, first amateur musical comedy.

1919   Columbia University (1919–21). Amateur musical comedy *Up Stage and Down* and first published songs: "Twinkling Eyes," "Asiatic Angels," "Butterfly Love," "Love Is Not in Vain," and "Love Me by Parcel Post." First professional song with Lorenz Hart: "Any Old Place with You."

1920   *You'd Be Surprised* and *Fly with Me,* amateur musical comedies. *Poor Little Ritz Girl,* first Broadway show.

1921   *Say Mama, You'll Never Know,* and *Say It with Jazz,* amateur musical comedies. Attends institute of Musical Art (later Juilliard) (1921–23).

1922   *The Chinese Lantern,* a play with music, and *Jazz à la Carte,* musical comedy. Rodgers and Hart write "Manhattan" for the never-performed *Winkle Town.*

1923   *If I Were King* and *A Danish Yankee in King Tut's Court,* amateur musicals.

1924   *Temple Bells,* a one-act musical comedy, and *The Prisoner of Zenda,* an amateur musical comedy. *The Melody Man,* a comedy with music by Herbert Richard Lorenz (Herbert Fields, Richard Rodgers, and Lorenz Hart).

1925   *Bad Habits of 1925,* a revue; *The Garrick Gaieties,* a revue; and *Dearest Enemy,* a musical comedy.

1926   *The Fifth Avenue Follies,* a revue; *The Girl Friend,* a musical comedy; *The Garrick Gaieties,* new version, a revue; *Lido Lady,* a musical comedy; *Peggy-Ann,* a musical comedy; and *Betsy,* a musical comedy.

1927   *One Dam Thing After Another,* musical revue, and *A Connecticut Yankee,* musical comedy.

1928 *She's My Baby* and *Present Arms,* musical comedies, and *Chee-Chee,* a musical play.

1929 *Spring Is Here* and *Heads Up!,* musical comedies. *Masters of Melody,* film mini-documentary about Rodgers and Hart and their songs.

1930 Marries Dorothy Belle Feiner in New York. *Simple Simon* and *Ever Green,* musical comedies.

1931 *America's Sweetheart,* musical comedy. Mary Rodgers is born at Lenox Hill Hospital. Benjamin Feiner, Dorothy Rodgers's father, commits suicide. Film: *The Hot Heiress.*

1932 Films: *Love Me Tonight* and *The Phantom President.*

1933 Film: *Hallelujah, I'm a Bum.*

1934 Film: *Hollywood Party.*

1935 Linda Rodgers born. Film: *Mississippi.* Broadway musical comedy: *Jumbo.*

1936 *On Your Toes,* musical comedy, and *Dancing Pirate,* film.

1937 *Babes in Arms* and *I'd Rather Be Right,* musical comedies.

1938 *I Married an Angel* and *The Boys from Syracuse,* musical comedies, and *Fools for Scandal,* film.

1939 *Too Many Girls,* musical comedy, and *Ghost Town,* described as "an American folk ballet."

1940 *Higher and Higher* and *Pal Joey,* musical comedies.

1941 *They Met in Argentina,* film. Rodgers is unbilled producer for *Best Foot Forward.*

1942 *By Jupiter,* musical comedy.

1943 *Oklahoma!* a musical play, with Oscar Hammerstein. Special Pulitzer Prize for Drama. *A Connecticut Yankee* revival, with Lorenz Hart. Lorenz Hart dies.

1944 Rodgers and Hammerstein produce John Van Druten's play *I Remember Mama.*

1945 *State Fair,* film. *Carousel,* a musical play. New York Drama Critics Circle Award for Best Musical. Motion Picture Academy Award, 1945, for best song, "It Might As Well Be Spring."

1946 Rodgers and Hammerstein produce *Annie Get Your Gun,* with music and lyrics by Irving Berlin, and *Happy Birthday,* a comedy by Anita Loos.

1947 *Allegro,* a musical play. Rodgers and Hammerstein produce Norman Krasna's comedy *John Loves Mary* and revive *Show Boat* (touring company).

1948 M-G-M film *Words and Music,* based on the careers of Rodgers and Hart. Dr. William Abraham Rodgers, Richard Rodgers's father, dies. "Rodgers and Hammerstein Night" at Lewisohn Stadium.

1949 *South Pacific,* a musical play. Pulitzer Prize in Drama; Antoinette Perry ("Tony") Award for Best Musical.

1950 Rodgers and Hammerstein produce the plays *The Happy Time* by Samuel Taylor, *The Heart of the Matter* by Graham Greene, and *Burning Bright* by John Steinbeck.

1951 *The King and I.* Tony Awards for best musical, best performance (female), best score, and best book. *An Evening for Richard Rodgers* on NBC-TV.

1952   *Victory at Sea,* television documentary with score by Richard Rodgers. *The Richard Rodgers Story,* CBS-TV.

1953   *Me and Juliet,* musical comedy. Rodgers and Hammerstein Week in New York, August 31–September 6. Rodgers conducts the St. Louis Symphony Orchestra.

1954   May Adelson Feiner, Dorothy Rodgers's mother, dies. Rodgers conducts the New York Philharmonic at Carnegie Hall. General Foods *Salute to Richard Rodgers* on every television network.

1955   *Pipe Dream,* a musical play. Rodgers is operated on for cancer of the jaw. Elected to membership in the American Academy and Institute of Arts and Letters.

1957   *Cinderella,* a television musical. Richard Rodgers conducts the Philadelphia Orchestra.

1958   *Flower Drum Song,* a musical play.

1959   *The Sound of Music,* a musical play; six Tony Awards, including best musical and score.

1960   Oscar Hammerstein dies. Television film: *Winston Churchill—The Valiant Years.* Emmy Award for best score.

1961   Proposed partnership with Alan Jay Lerner announced.

1962   *No Strings,* a musical; Tony Award for best score. *A Tribute to Richard Rodgers* on CBS-TV. Rodgers is named head of Music Theater of Lincoln Center.

1965   *Do I Hear a Waltz?,* a musical.

1967   *Androcles and the Lion,* television musical. *Rodgers and Hart Today* on ABC-TV.

1969   Rodgers has a heart attack.

1970   *Two by Two,* a musical play.

1974   Rodgers undergoes a laryngectomy.

1975   *Rodgers and Hart,* a "musical celebration" at the Helen Hayes Theatre. Rodgers publishes his autobiography, *Musical Stages.*

1976   *Rex,* a musical play. Two-hour network special on CBS-TV: *America Salutes Richard Rodgers.*

1977   Seventy-fifth-birthday celebration.

1978   Kennedy Center salute to Richard Rodgers.

1979   *I Remember Mama,* a musical play. Richard Rodgers dies in New York on December 30.

Notes

Abbreviations

APB   *A Personal Book,* Dorothy Rodgers, 1977.

BO   *American Musical Theatre,* Gerald Bordman, 1992.

COH   Columbia Oral History of Richard Rodgers.

DH   *Thou Swell, Thou Witty,* Dorothy Hart, 1976.

DROH   Radcliffe Oral History of Dorothy Rodgers.

EW   *Richard Rodgers,* David Ewen, 1957.

FI   *From the Bowery to Broadway,* Armond Fields and
       L. Marc Fields, 1993.

FO   *Getting to Know Him,* Hugh Fordin, 1977.

M-C   *Rodgers and Hart,* Samuel Marx and Jan Clayton, 1976.

MCOH   Columbia Oral History of Mary Rodgers Guettel.

MFT   *My Favorite Things,* Dorothy Rodgers, 1964.

MS   *Musical Stages,* Richard Rodgers, 1995.

NO   *Lorenz Hart,* Frederick Nolan, 1994.

SMUOH   Southern Methodist University Oral History of
       Mary Rodgers Guettel.

WI   *American Popular Song,* Alec Wilder, 1972.

Chapter One

BLUE ROOM

3   Chapter title is from "The Blue Room," by Rodgers and Hart.

4   *The tryout of a new show:* It was *Present Arms,* April 18 to 21, 1928.
In mourning for her father: Jacob Levy died in 1928.
"but you'll know!" he wrote: on August 7, 1929.

5   *"... what a way to live! ...":* letter dated July 19, 1929.

6 *"The Young Master of Melody":* headline in the *New York World,* April 29, 1928.

8 *To Florence for leather goods:* APB, p. 46.

   Designed to be knife-pleated: APB, p. 48.

   "This is going to be a big year," he wrote: on July 19, 1929.

   Engaged during the New York run: on November 29, 1929.

9 Simple Simon *[closed]:* on June 14, 1930.

10 *"... still tied up at the North River dock":* MS, p. 135.

   Making $75,000 a year: Jerry Beaty to author.

   Three large Oshkosh trunks: APB, p. 68.

   "... there was a good piano ...": APB, p. 69.

11 *"So it was trying":* DROH, pp. 59–60.

   "of course we were happy": APB, p. 72.

12 *"Have I been impatient ...":* February 13, 1930, from the Ritz-Carlton Hotel.

   "the darling of the Mayfair set": APB, p. 73.

   "... an extraordinary gift for hope ...": The Great Gatsby, F. Scott Fitzgerald, 1953, p. 2.

13 *"a strange, paradoxical creature ...":* Broadway Anecdotes, Peter Hay, 1989, p. 147.

14 *She cried herself to sleep:* DROH, pp. 56–57.

Chapter Two
ONLY MAKE BELIEVE

15 Chapter title is taken from the song "Make Believe" by Jerome Kern and Oscar Hammerstein II.

17 *He would become an Army medical examiner:* in 1941.

   "... this person could be fun": to author.

17 *Given leave to become William Abraham Rodgers:* on July 13, 1892.

   She was living with her parents: EW, p. 42.

18 *"the aristocratic Jewish neighborhood ...":* World of Our Fathers, Irving Howe, 1976, p. 131. The Levy addresses were established by Richard Rodgers in a letter to Semon H. Springer, September 11, 1962.

   "Both were stubborn ...": MS, p. 6.

   "... his unwillingness to compromise": MS, p. 6.

   "... a loud voice ...": MS, p. 7.

   "a deep feeling of tension ...": MS, p. 6.

21 *"There was a star danced ...":* from William Shakespeare, *Much Ado About Nothing.*

   He "didn't hesitate ...": MS, p. 7.

   "... I was going to faint": MS, p. 18.

   "I was tremendously excited ...": radio interview with Geoffroy Millais, BBC-2, September 11, 1968.

22 *Sometimes bribed the usher:* McCall's, May 1964.

   "... I can hear it ...": New York Herald Tribune, April 15, 1945.

   "... I get happier": Saturday Evening Post, March 13, 1965.

   "... a special world ...": to author.

"... *running around and having fights*": radio interview with Geoffroy Millais, BBC-2, September 11, 1968.

"... *break some windows*": *New York Times,* June 29, 1952.

Shot his first rifle: New York Mirror, July 26, 1959.

23 *He was so shy:* letter to author from Alix B. Williamson, April 7, 1998.

Every inch the little soldier: EW, p. 41.

"*One particularly vivid flash . . .*": *This Week,* November 23, 1958.

"*What did you do . . .*": MS, p. 12.

Screaming with pain: MS, p. 13.

"... *eight months of torture . . .*": MS, p. 13.

His first impulse was to blame the patient: to author.

24 "... *cut me savagely . . .*": MS, p. 14.

Young, slim, and attractive: MS, p. 17.

25 "... *heading in the right direction*": MS, p. 17.

The usual gifts: EW, p. 55.

"*Daddy was militant . . .*": to author.

"*I learned more . . . about words . . .*": MCOH, p. 39.

"... *no symphonies or operas . . .*": *World of Our Fathers,* Irving Howe, 1976, p. 170.

"*a classic outsider . . .*": Stephen Holden, *New York Times,* May 19, 1999.

26 *Affiliated with the College of the City of New York:* EW, p. 58.

It was early in 1917: the month was February. Rodgers graduated from P.S. 166 on January 28, 1917.

"*I decided to quit . . .*": MS, p. 21.

"*raise a little hell . . .*": MS, p. 21.

Going to concerts: EW, pp. 59–60.

26 *Did not seem to know what:* from an undated article by Richard Rodgers.

"*pure, uncontrived . . .*": WI, p. 29.

"*His melodies are as smooth . . .*": from an introduction to a Columbia record album of Jerome Kern's music.

27 *That made it American:* WI, p. 32.

28 "... *an iron-bound formula . . .*": *New Haven Register,* August 30, 1970.

Very Good Eddie was the mold: BO, p. 312.

29 "... *clear blue eyes . . .*": MS, p. 21.

Chapter Three

"MY FUNNY VALENTINE"

30 Chapter title is taken from the song of the same name by Richard Rodgers and Lorenz Hart.

31 *Go back to school:* EW, p. 61.

"*Dick, dear here comes your dad . . .*": letter to Richard Rodgers, June 6, 1967.

"... *the line of battle . . .*": from an unpublished section of Richard Rodgers's autobiography, *Musical Stages.*

32 *Played at the Waldorf:* on March 18, 1919.

"... *published them myself*": MS, p. 35.

32 *Not a success: Collier's,* February 18, 1933.

   The early spring of 1919: The date 1918 is incorrect: Richard Rodgers to Buddy
       Bregman, May 11, 1976.

   "... *tremendously stimulating":* radio interview with Arnold Michaelis,
       December 18, 1955.

33 *The massive undulations:* MS, p. 28.

   His wife screamed: MS, p. 28.

   He was too lazy: M-C, p. 14.

   The smiling admonition: M-C, p. 15.

34 "... *rapt, critical silence* . . .": M-C, p. 38.

   "... *would be a hit song":* M-C, p. 38.

   A nervous tic: MS, p. 27.

   "... *his head would wag":* written for *The Rodgers and Hart Songbook,* 1970.

   In May 1919: the date was May 18.

   He "loved carousing": MS, p. 29.

   "... *the working day was over":* MS, p. 29.

   Had to be reintroduced: New York Sun, January 30, 1928.

36 "... *my pivotal musical idea* . . .": *New York Herald Tribune,* May 31, 1925.

38 "... *a line of strategy* . . .": M-C, p. 41.

   "... *the most dazzling eyes* . . .": MS, p. 30.

   Meeting with Lew Fields: Rodgers writes on p. 30 of his autobiography that
       Hart was not there. I have accepted Leavitt's direct testimony that he was;
       see M-C, p. 41.

   "... *their gloved hands* . . .": MS, p. 30.

39 "... *looks like a stooge* . . .": *Cue,* May 1, 1937.

   "... *Larry would start* . . .": M-C, pp. 42–3.

40 *The spring of 1920:* the date was March 6.

   "... *promptly disappeared* . . .": MS, p. 35.

   The mood was strictly farcical: MS, p. 35.

41 "... *booming bass voices* . . .": M-C, p. 46.

   A limited run: March 24–27, 1920.

   "... *a class by himself":* *Columbia Spectator,* May 19, 1920.

43 "... *slept his way* . . .": MS, p. 37.

   Fling the papers away: Philadelphia Public Ledger, February 17, 1929.

   "... *forty stage hands* . . .": *Cue,* May 1, 1937.

44 *Looking for a scapegoat:* FI, p. 387.

   "... *his son's friends* . . .": FI, p. 392.

   "... *unconquering hero":* MS, p. 39.

Chapter Four

"WAR IS WAR"

45 Chapter title is taken from the song of the same name by Richard Rodgers and
       Lorenz Hart.

   "for an aging actor . . .": FI, p. 397.

46 *"hard, brisk tunes":* BO, p. 351.

". . . grace and fancy": H. T. Parker, *Boston Transcript;* EW, pp. 75–6.

". . . never pay you": MS, p. 45.

Rodgers, who was at first self-conscious: MS, p. 47.

". . . actually learning something . . .": MS, p. 47.

"who was to harmony . . .": MS, p. 45.

". . . I'd avoid that 'pig' . . .": MS, p. 45.

47 *". . . scarcely keep from running"*: MS, p. 47.

"just to make sure . . .": MS, p. 46.

". . . a book for a musical . . .": MS, p. 79.

". . . our great composers": EW, p. 78.

48 *"Change your style . . ."*: DH, p. 35.

one of its periodic slumps: BO, p. 362.

49 *Most popular of all:* *Boston Herald,* November 3, 1929.

Opened in December: the date was December 4, 1921.

". . . Worst Business Slump . . .": FI, p. 399.

Wanted a musical in the spring: it opened on March 25, 1923.

50 *The Vagabond King* opened September 21, 1925.

Performed in a Broadway theatre: on March 23, 1924.

51 *". . . an earlier era . . ."*: M-C, p. 49.

Orville Prescott wrote: in *Cue,* May 1, 1937.

". . . your father isn't willing . . .": M-C, p. 49.

52 *". . . I had no talent"*: MS, p. 51.

53 *". . . professional achievement"*: FI, p. 419.

The Melody Man opened May 13, 1924.

". . . ruin even Hamlet": MS, p. 54.

She was still alive: Helen Ford died in 1982.

54 *". . . ourselves and music"*: MS, p. 45.

55 *Both had a hangover:* Baton, December 1924.

Did not think much of the score: BO, p. 39.

56 *". . . never startlingly original . . ."*: NO, p. 60.

". . . I have no clothes . . .": NO, p. 60.

". . . a kind of flop . . .": FI, p. 433.

A pseudo-documentary: in 1928.

57 *". . . their opportunity came . . ."*: *Dance Magazine,* August 1929.

". . . nobody listened . . .": *Cue,* May 1, 1937.

Only had enough money: *Morning Telegraph,* June 12, 1927.

Perennially hopeful: MS, p. 57.

58 *". . . I hated myself . . ."*: MS, p. 57.

"increasingly impatient": EW, p. 86.

". . . I want a job": *New Yorker,* May 28, 1937.

Chapter Five

"WE'LL HAVE MANHATTAN"

59 Chapter title is taken from the song "Manhattan" by Richard Rodgers and Lorenz Hart.

59 *He asked for time:* New Yorker, May 28, 1937.
   Worrying out loud: EW, p. 86.
60 *"... the whole show!":* M-C, p. 70.
62 *Grumbled but finally agreed:* MS, p. 61.
63 *"a plump, pretty girl":* MS, p. 62.
   "exact harmonies ...": MS, p. 62.
   "'... I'd never heard of you ...'": New York World Telegram, September 27, 1954.
   "... always rubbing his hands ...": DH, p. 41.
   "... a thick red belt": MS, p. 64.
64 *"standing and clapping ...":* MS, p. 65.
   "jumping up and down ...": MS, p. 65.
   "by miles the cleverest ...": Life, November 26, 1925.
   "... a certain quality ...": New York Herald Tribune, June 9, 1925.
65 *"... the acute discomfort ...":* New York Sun, June 9, 1925.
   "like a colonel's heels ...": May 27, 1925.
66 *"... just for today":* DH, p. 41.
   Found a publisher: MS, p. 67.
   "... a dawn dip ...": DH, p. 41.
   "... clapped, cheered": MS, p. 67.
   A traveling salesman: MS, p. 67.
67 *Rodgers corrected him:* MS, p. 67.
   Still to come: in 1927.
   Could be offset: The Broadway Musical, Bernard Rosenberg and Ernest Harburg, 1993, p. 14.
   An entrepreneur could build: The City and the Theatre, Mary C. Henderson, 1973, pp. 190–91.
68 *"... trance of color":* New York 1930, Robert A. M. Stern, Gregory Gilmartin, Thomas Mellins, 1987, p. 239.
69 *"... the show people ...":* Winchell: Gossip, Power and the Culture of Celebrity, Neal Gabler, 1995, p. 71.
   A raffish mix: idem, pp. 88–9.
   "When I started ...": New York Journal-American, October 3, 1964.
   "... the incessant query": idem, p. 91.
   "... in love with Betsy": M-C, p. 78.
70 *"... an awful fool?":* Cue, May 1, 1937.
   "... had some cutie ...": M-C, pp. 80–81.
   "... I'm going to quit ...": M-C, p. 81.
   "... a prominent jaw": MS, p. 55.
72 *"... it sounded wrong ...":* M-C, p. 82.
73 *A gallon can of peaches:* NO, p. 70; MS, p. 72.
   "... just so delightful ...": NO, p. 70.
   "... price of admission": EW, p. 99.
   "... he will go far ...": New York Telegram, September 19, 1925.
   "... sweet, tuneful music ...": Operetta: A Theatrical History, Richard Traubner, 1983, p. 309.
   "... the tightly knit melodies ...": BO, p. 404.

74 *Popularity of the songs:* *Dance Magazine,* October 1926.
75 *". . . the prettiest girl . . .":* MS, p. 74.
   He would wait: DROH, p. 28.

Chapter Six

"MY HEART STOOD STILL"

76 Chapter title is taken from the song of the same name by Richard Rodgers and
   Lorenz Hart.
   Dearest Enemy opened: on September 18, 1925.
77 *". . . smelly rehearsal hall . . .":* *New York Herald Tribune,* March 21, 1926.
   ". . . wholly distinctive . . .": WI, p. 169.
78 *". . . the rising half tones":* MS, p. 80.
   ". . . quaint orchestration . . .": March 18, 1926.
   ". . . the crowd dwindled . . .": FI, p. 443.
   ". . . suspend our royalties . . .": MS, p. 81.
   His songs had been recorded: *New York Herald Tribune,* October 31, 1926.
   In the same league: NO, p. 74.
79 *Something was owed:* idem, p. 73.
   ". . . I scribbled off . . .": *New York Herald Tribune,* May 23, 1926.
   The show opened: on May 10, 1926.
80 *". . . applauded everything . . .":* *Judge,* June 5, 1926.
   A comfortable run: it closed on October 9, 1926.
81 *Signed up Rodgers and Hart:* *New York Herald Tribune,* March 7, 1926.
82 *". . . popular news topics . . .":* *New York Times,* October 17, 1926.
   Distant and cold: MS, p. 89.
   Several provincial cities: *New York Times,* October 17, 1926.
   Adverse comment: *Sun Express,* December 5, 1926.
   ". . . effectively and ridiculously": December 5, 1926.
83 *Opened that December:* on December 1, 1926.
   ". . . all silver-lining . . .": *Sunday Times,* December 5, 1926.
   ". . . it never occurred to me . . .": DROH, p. 27.
84 *". . . I can still see . . .":* APB, p. 16.
   ". . . its flowered label . . .": APB, p. 16.
86 *"an uncommunicative man . . .":* APB, p. 15.
   They became engaged: on October 25, 1902.
   Birth of Ben Feiner Jr.: on August 20, 1904.
   Birth of Dorothy Belle Feiner: on May 4, 1909.
87 *Was so constricting:* APB, p. 12.
   "all kinds of beautiful . . .": idem, p. 15.
   ". . . locked in the maid's room . . .": to author.
   ". . . I would be there . . .": DROH, p. 28.
88 *". . . went on a diet . . .":* APB, p. 46.
   ". . . I never heard it": to author.
89 *"very boring places":* DROH, p. 11.
   ". . . a glorious thing . . .": idem, p. 12.

89 *Shopping for college:* APB, p. 48.
90 *". . . we were alone . . .":* APB, p. 50.
   Threw it out: DROH, p. 29.

Chapter Seven
"HE'S A WINNER"

91 *". . . the mere prospect . . .":* December 10, 1926.
   "shamelessly in love": APB, p. 50.
   Just to be near: APB, p. 53.
   "resentful and jealous . . .": idem, p. 53.
92 *". . . swathed in swan-down . . .":* December 10, 1926.
   ". . . finely tuned words . . .": BO, p. 420.
94 *". . . always the hit songs . . .":* FI, p. 456.
   ". . . head of the class . . .": January 10, 1927.
   ". . . captivatingly concise . . .": December 28, 1926.
   ". . . Gilbert and Sullivan": *Saturday Evening Post,* May 19, 1928.
   ". . . absolutely everything . . .": MCOH, p. 411.
   ". . . a huge voice": MS, p. 92.
95 *". . . eating and sleeping . . .":* letter of November 9, 1926.
   "so much applesauce": letter of November 27, 1926.
   ". . . with our arms . . .": letter of December 5, 1926.
96 *". . . You don't understand . . .":* letter of November 9, 1926.
   ". . . I can't help myself . . .": letter of November 27, 1926.
   "couldn't very well . . .": letter of January 27, 1927.
97 *". . . a lovely glow . . .":* letter of January 11, 1926.
98 *"contributed enough . . .":* letter of January 11, 1926.
   "I can stand up!": *New York Daily News,* January 7, 1944.
   Gave them all watches: MCOH, p. 72.
   ". . . left dirty lyrics . . .": to author.
   "pay any price": *New York Amusements,* no date.
   Buying new outfits: *Philadelphia Public Ledger,* March 3, 1929.
   ". . . water the begonias": *New York Herald Tribune,* August 29, 1937.
100 *". . . some five blocks . . .":* *Philadelphia Public Ledger,* March 3, 1929.
   ". . . two guys in Sardi's . . .": to author.
101 *". . . out of the hospital . . .":* radio interview with Arnold Michaelis, December 18, 1955.
   "a sweet, menacing . . .": *Time,* September 26, 1938.
   ". . . picking up new ones": idem.
   Having his mother find out: Great Performances television show, January 6, 1999.
   Sent Garey a necktie: Bruce Pomahac.
101 *". . . also so naïve":* to author.
102 *". . . I never even kissed . . .":* NO, p. 309.
   ". . . I'll kill you": COH, p. 199.
   ". . . punched the director . . .": to author.

"*. . . he hated violently . . .*": to author.

"*You can imagine . . .*": letter, February 1, 1927.

103 "*laugh like Hell!*": letter, February 13, 1927.

"*. . . a happy foursome . . .*": MS, p. 101.

"*. . . missed us by inches . . .*": M-C, p. 106.

"*. . . so emotionally moved . . .*": MS, p. 103.

Mastery of step writing: WI, p. 185.

104 *The opening night:* on May 20, 1927.

"*. . . for five years!*": *Popular Songs,* June 1936. The revue ran from May 19 to December 10, 1927.

105 "*. . . found ourselves paying . . .*": MS, p. 107.

"*wonderfully funny . . .*": MS, p. 106.

A Danish Yankee: in 1923.

Begins to wear thin: New York World, April 11, 1927.

"*And what music!*": on December 3, 1927.

107 "*. . . the show was in . . .*": MS, p. 108.

"*. . . a faster tempo . . .*": *The American Popular Ballad of the Golden Era: 1924–1950,* Allen Forte, 1995, p. 182.

"*. . . complicated and offbeat . . .*": *Showstoppers,* Martin Rubin, 1993, p. 48.

108 "*. . . soigné and unflappable*": MS, p. 111.

After A Connecticut Yankee *opened:* on November 3, 1927.

"*in a hole*": letter, November 11, 1927.

She's My Baby *opened:* on January 3, 1928.

109 *He hoped to see her:* letter, November 5, 1927.

For London and points south: letter, January 7, 1928.

110 *They might exchange:* letter, January 23, 1928.

"*the disadvantages . . .*": letter, December 12, 1927.

"*. . . too high a price . . .*": letter, no date.

"*. . . we should not . . .*": DROH, p. 35.

"*. . . get me away . . .*": DROH, pp. 34–5.

111 "*. . . the tears ran . . .*": APB, p. 62.

She sent another: DROH, p. 35.

Chapter Eight

"WITH A SONG IN MY HEART"

112 Chapter title taken from the song of the same name by Richard Rodgers and Lorenz Hart.

"*. . . throwing pianos . . .*": letter, December 8, 1927.

"*. . . a consuming passion . . .*": letter, January 12, 1928.

Revues were so inept: letter, January 23, 1928.

"*. . . love your life*": letter, January 29, 1928.

113 "*. . . feeling of depression . . .*": letter, January 29, 1928.

114 "*He now believed . . .*": FI, p. 474.

"*. . . Broadway clichés . . .*": FI, p. 475.

"*. . . tricky formations . . .*": FI, p. 476.

114 *". . . juicy little grape . . .":* MS, p. 115.

115 *". . . most beautiful element":* *New York Times,* April 27, 1928.
Never could tell: MS, p. 115.
"nasty collapse . . .": letter, March 30, 1928.
Rodgers was devastated: MS, p. 117.

116 *Another rendition:* letter, March 30, 1928.
The usual tummy-ache: letter, March 30, 1928.
". . . cute little kid": MS, p. 116.
". . . white-faced and trembling . . .": DROH, p. 46.
Out for revenge: MS, p. 116.
". . . a tough guy . . .": MS, p. 46.
Where Helen Morgan sang: FI, p. 473.

117 *He had a confrontation:* FI, p. 473.
Studying sculpture: in 1929.
A fact of life: DROH, pp. 44–45.
Shooting death: *Glasgow Evening News,* October 16, 1930.

118 *". . . a sagging jaw . . .":* MS, p. 116.
". . . like somebody's chauffeur . . .": DROH, p. 46.
Went bright red: DROH, pp. 46–47.
". . . a special favor . . .": MS, p. 117.
". . . name in lights": MS, p. 117.

119 *". . . very nervous-making":* DROH, p. 47.
Wished he had: MS, p. 117.
". . . constantly amused": letter, June 10, 1928.
". . . more than you think": letter, June 10, 1928.

120 *"striving to write . . .":* May 19, 1928.
". . . forgive us all . . .": *Being Bernard Berenson,* Meryle Secrest, 1979, p. 218.

121 *". . . a daring departure . . .":* MS, p. 118.
". . . would be an essential . . .": MS, p. 118.

122 *". . . I never realized . . .":* letter, September 1, 1928.
". . . our only trouble": letter, September 12, 1928.
". . . done something fine . . .": letter, September 7, 1928.
The show opened: on September 25, 1928.

123 *After thirty-one performances:* on October 20, 1928.
". . . hounded and pursued . . .": DH, p. 63.
"Don't grieve for me . . .": idem.
". . . All is forgiven . . .": letter, September 17, 1928.
". . . He was very nice . . .": DROH, p. 44.
Sold-out houses: *Show Boat* opened at the Ziegfeld Theatre in December 1927 and closed in May 1929.

124 *Went home and wrote it:* MS, p. 122.

126 *". . . our future together . . .":* MS, p. 135.
". . . her eye teeth . . .": DROH, p. 37.
". . . didn't look unhappy": MS, p. 135.
"I need a hit . . .": letter, August 14, 1929.

127 *". . . pronounced it corny . . .":* NO, p. 141.

128 *". . . we're happy":* letter, March 15, 1930.

"... *Roman nobility*...": letter, April 2, 1930.

Dick was moaning: APB, p. 65.

Hated losing money: MS, p. 136.

129 *He had a friend:* DROH, pp. 54–55.

"*terribly young*...": APB, pp. 66–67.

130 "... *the guinea hen*...": *Kiss Hollywood Good-By,* Anita Loos, 1974, p. 23.

"... *Dadda loves Mummy*...": letter, June 21, 1930.

131 "... *routine is simple*...": letter, June 21, 1930.

"... *this strange business*...": idem.

"... *best character sketch*...": letter, June 25, 1930.

"... *Larry is working*...": letter, June 24, 1930.

"... *I'd been framed!*...": letter, June 24, 1930.

132 "*What rotten breaks*...": letter, June 25, 1930.

Feiner was ill: letter, June 26, 1930.

"... *work so fast*": letter, June 27, 1930.

"... *is less crazy*...": letter, June 26, 1930.

"... *my head's swimming*": letter, July 1, 1930.

"... *across Wilshire Boulevard*": APB, p. 86.

"... *simply intensified*...": APB, p. 87.

134 "... *you can imagine*...": letter, August 28, 1930.

"... *I've never loved*...": letter, August 23, 1930.

135 "... *the most attractive*...": DROH, pp. 58–59.

Chapter Nine

"WHERE'S THAT RAINBOW?"

136 Chapter title taken from the song of the same name by Richard Rodgers and Lorenz Hart.

"... *he works hard*...": letter, September 3, 1930.

"... *sounds very good*...": letter, September 4, 1930.

137 "... *I'm just stupid*": letter, September 6, 1930.

"... *attitude is morbid*...": letter, September 9, 1930.

"*I came back*...": idem.

"... *Fat chance*...": letter, September 10, 1930.

"... *a cold sweat*...": letter, September 20, 1930.

"... *that will happen*...": letter, September 27, 1930.

Was visibly "untouched": letter, September 27, 1930.

138 "... *I can't explain*...": letter, September 14, 1930.

"... *Greta Garbo*...": letter, September 14, 1930.

"... *it's so cruel*": letter, September 20, 1930.

End of October: October 26, 1930.

"... *I do hope*...": letter, October 4, 1930.

"... *just don't care*...": letter, October 6, 1930.

139 "... *don't let me*...": letter, October 6, 1930.

"... *a rare experience*...": letter, September 11, 1930.

"*joyous and successful*...": letter, September 14, 1930.

139　*". . . much impressed"*: letter, September 20, 1930.
　　". . . best romantic score . . .": letter, September 15, 1930.
140　*". . . myth of the Twenties . . ."*: *New York Times,* September 17, 1999.
　　Got quite "cockeyed": letter, September 25, 1930.
　　". . . less nervous": letter, April 28, 1937.
141　*". . . only knocked over . . ."*: letter, October 4, 1930.
　　"Bankhead got . . . boiled . . .": letter, September 20, 1930.
　　A smooth opening: the date was October 13, 1930.
142　*". . . I'm more depressed . . ."*: letter, September 27, 1930.
　　Opened at the Adelphi: on December 3, 1930.
　　". . . this lovely thing . . .": December 7, 1930.
　　"the Ascot of . . .": December 7, 1930.
　　". . . a merry-go-round . . .": December 7, 1930.
143　*". . . a quiet fire escape . . ."*: *Cinema,* December 1930.
　　". . . the whole proposition . . .": letter, October 2, 1930.
144　*". . . goose bumps"*: APB, p. 92.
　　". . . was wearing shoes . . .": EW, p. 130.
　　". . . Second needs plenty . . .": January 20, 1931.
146　*". . . this is the end"*: *Cinema,* December 1930.
　　America's Sweetheart: opened February 10, 1931.
　　"bright and fluent . . .": *Musical Comedy in America,* Cecil Smith and Glenn
　　　　Litton, 1991, p. 157.
　　"Things had changed . . .": *Collier's,* February 18, 1931.
147　*". . . Even his breath . . ."*: APB, p. 101.
　　". . . his earning capacity . . .": APB, p. 103.
　　"Nervous breakdowns . . .": APB, p. 102.
148　*". . . waiting to be interlocked"*: APB, p. 102.
　　". . . completely absorbed . . .": DROH, p. 124.
　　". . . very, very wrong": APB, p. 105.
　　"Nothing was ever . . .": to author.
149　*". . . a musical sequence . . ."*: MS, p. 150.
150　*". . . stop-watch composing . . ."*: MS, 149.
　　"wholly enchanting . . .": *Illustrated London News.* (Date N/A)
152　*". . . an ideal suite . . ."*: APB, p. 109.
　　". . . We signed the lease . . .": APB, 109.
　　". . . most of his time . . .": DROH, p. 62.
　　". . . home to Mississippi . . .": DROH, p. 63.
153　*". . . peacefully sleeping . . ."*: *Portraits, Real and Imagined,* Ernest Boyd, 1924,
　　　　pp. 217–18.
　　Pouring with rain: DROH, p. 68.
　　". . . your neighbor's teeth . . .": DROH, p. 66.
154　*". . . all air-conditioned"*: DROH, p. 65.
155　*". . . it was open . . ."*: DROH, p. 45.
156　*The servant problem:* DROH, p. 63.
　　". . . chorus boys . . .": APB, p. 111.
　　". . . just in time . . .": APB, pp. 111–112.

156   *"It's Larry or me"*: Daniel Melnick to author.
    ". . . watched Larry win . . .": letter, October 17, 1932.
    ". . . stabilizing influence": letter, June 22, 1933.
157   *". . . emotionally drained"*: MS, p. 155.
    "Mary kept me . . .": letter, May 30, 1933.
    ". . . a family to support . . .": MS, p. 148.
158   *"I think . . . Hoover . . ."*: MS, p. 155.
    ". . . harmonic progressions": WI, p. 192.
    ". . . strike many people . . .": MS, p. 155.
    ". . . bursting with ideas": MS, p. 157.
159   *". . . the happy position . . ."*: MS, p. 158.
    Hart sat down and wrote: MS, p. 161.
    ". . . and everything else": letter, October 28, 1932.
    Talked about pictures: letter, October 31, 1932.
    ". . . were awfully nice . . .": letter, June 15, 1933.
160   *". . . your attractive sex . . ."*: letter, June 14, 1933.
    ". . . as much whisky . . .": letter, June 5, 1933.
    ". . . my only drink . . .": letter, October 28, 1932.
    ". . . best little solo . . .": letter, May 30, 1933.
    "Whatever happened . . .": MS, p. 164.
    Going back to Broadway: idem.

Chapter Ten

"LITTLE GIRL BLUE"

161   Chapter title taken from the song of the same name by Richard Rodgers and
    Lorenz Hart.
    Taken out a loan: APB, p. 107.
    Liquor stains everywhere: MS, p. 168.
    ". . . I never went in . . .": DROH, p. 69.
162   *Never heard again:* EW, p. 142.
163   *Falling for a ballerina:* MS, pp. 170–71.
    ". . . was getting married": MS, p. 171.
    ". . . their uncouth methods . . .": M-C, p. 179.
    ". . . café keeper . . .": M-C, p. 177.
    Postponed five times: MS, p. 173.
    Jumbo opened: on November 16, 1935.
164   *"never parted with a dime . . ."*: MS, p. 173.
165   *". . . 'Whatever for?' "*: DROH, p. 73.
    "There's a girl next door . . .": as quoted, M-C, p. 187.
167   *Their ambitious musical:* MS, p. 173.
    "If you think . . .": *Literary Digest,* November 30, 1935; p. 19.
    Then Gershwin played: DROH, p. 71. *Porgy and Bess* opened on October 10,
    1935.
168   *"I'm so upset . . ."*: letter, July 11, 1937.

169 *"... its usual standard"*: DROH, p. 119.
170 *"... she's very kind..."*: DROH, pp. 119–20. Of this incident, Dorothy Rodgers also wrote, "That is not hearsay, it was said at my house, and very few people ever heard it."
171 *In single file:* DROH, pp. 120–21.
"Poor Woollcott died...": DROH, p. 121.
" '... What are you doing...' ": DROH, pp. 121–22.
172 *"... everybody was happy"*: DROH, pp. 129–30.
Showing off her new coiffure: Life, October 25, 1937.
173 *A big party:* DROH, pp. 130–131.
"... rather unfair": DROH, p. 122.
Old-fashioned charades: DROH, pp. 128–129.
"... I won them all...": letter, May 20, 1937.
My Favorite Things: published in 1964.
"... badly informed...": MFT, p. 233.
175 *"... full of Lucky Strikes..."*: to author.
"... in front of people": idem.
176 *"... being mild-mannered"*: to author.
"... charming dinner parties...": idem.
"... didn't like it much": idem.
Disturbed the surface: idem.
177 *"You fought with words..."*: idem.
"... would have confessed...": idem.
"... an awful person": to author.
"... these grand people": interview with author.
"... I felt accepted...": interview with author.
178 *"... it was painful"*: idem.
"... coldest brown eyes...": idem.
"... making fun of her": idem.
"... never as happy...": interview with author.
179 *"... saw it on celluloid..."*: MCOH, p. 410.
"... wasn't much left over": interview with author.
"... I resented it...": APB, p. 91.
"as though I didn't...": idem.
She stayed home: interview with author.
"... they'll put up with...": idem.
180 *"... generally disagreeable..."*: letter, July 14, 1934.
"... a young attractive man...": letter, July 24, 1937.
"... I will kick the bejeesus...": letter, July 15, 1934.
"... remember what we have": letter, April 25, 1937.

Chapter Eleven
"THE NIGHT BOAT TO ALBANIA"

181 Chapter title taken from the song "Dear Old Syracuse" by Richard Rodgers and Lorenz Hart.

182 *". . . single musical expression":* Time, September 26, 1938.

"*I hate Hollywood":* letter, September 28, 1945.

"*. . . all the money . . .":* Collier's, May 26, 1945.

Impenetrably anonymous: New Yorker, August 13, 1999.

183 "*. . . sing about love":* New Yorker, June 4, 1938.

Remained a success: New Yorker, idem.

"*. . . heavy in its timing . . .":* EW, p. 147.

Made jokes about it: Stephen Sondheim: A Life, Meryle Secrest, 1998, p. 152. At a low moment during the slow evolution of Stephen Sondheim's musical *A Funny Thing Happened on the Way to the Forum,* George Abbott, who was directing, said in complete bafflement: "I dunno. You had better call in George Abbott."

184 *"ballet on Broadway . . .":* Broadway, Brooks Atkinson, 1970, p. 335.

"Looking through the curtain . . .": M-C, p. 187.

On Your Toes *was revived:* in 1954.

"*. . . something of a classic . . .":* EW, p. 150.

186 *"sweetly forlorn":* BO, p. 498.

187 "*. . . would not have minded . . .":* letter, September 3, 1965.

Opened in the spring: April 11, 1936.

"*. . . one smash success . . .":* EW, p. 155.

188 "*. . . a nice profit":* MS, p. 181.

189 Babes in Arms *arrived:* April 14, 1937.

"*. . . for it swings":* WI, p. 205.

"*. . . forbidden to sing it":* WI, idem.

"I've never seen . . .": WI, p. 206.

190 "*. . . in perfect balance":* WI, idem.

Company *appeared in 1970.*

"*. . . musical-comedy lampoon . . .":* MS, p. 183.

192 "*. . . that son of a bitch . . .":* MS, p. 185.

"*. . . inclined to think . . .":* George M. Cohan, Ward Morehouse, 1943, p. 200.

"*. . . One harsh look . . .":* Stage, August 1938.

"*. . . never added up . . .":* BO, p. 506.

193 "*. . . something is wrong":* Stephen Sondheim: A Life, Meryle Secrest, 1998, p. 215.

194 *No more political satires:* letter to Norman Panama, October 31, 1967.

Persuaded Wiman: MS, p. 188.

195 "*. . . marriage is saved":* MS, p. 189.

196 *The only reference:* Josh, Joshua Logan, 1976, p. 120.

Scribbling furiously: idem.

"*. . . there wasn't one word . . .":* NO, p. 244.

"we finally had . . .": MS, p. 188.

After days and nights: The Far Side of Paradise, Arthur Mizener, 1959, pp. 305–6.

About to open: April 14 to 16, 1938.

197 "*. . . The Renaissance closes . . .":* New York Post, January 10, 1938.

"*. . . can't be printed":* idem.

198 "*. . . say he was finished!":* interview with author.

Actually leaving: M-C, p. 199.

198 *"... 'He was drunk...'"*: M-C, p. 220.
    Took everything off: M-C, p. 221.
    He left prematurely: DH, p. 126.
    A blackmail attempt: EW, p. 176.
    "He couldn't help it": radio interview with Arnold Michaelis, December 18, 1955.
199 *"... and carried him..."*: The O'Hara Concern, Matthew J. Bruccoli, 1975, p. 166.
    "... 'No now-singers!'": *Josh,* Joshua Logan, 1976, pp. 124–4.
    "... like anybody else": January 10, 1938.
    "poised, immaculate...": *New Yorker,* June 4, 1938.
    "... actually painful": M-C, p. 213.
    "... Rabbi Wise's funeral...": Shirley Potash to Oscar Hammerstein, April 22, 1949.
200 *"... hard as nails..."*: interview with author.
    "so cool, so calm...": *American Weekly,* March 6, 1955.
    "when he hears...": idem.
    "... sweet and funny...": interview with author.
201 *"... the romance in relationships..."*: interview with author.
    "The book was so sharp...": MS, p. 191.
    "... a mad dog's tooth": act 5, scene 1, lines 68–9.
    "Shakespeare!": MS, p. 191.
203 *Rodgers brought Martin back:* interview with author.
    "'... the night boat to Albania'...": interview with author.
205 *"Rodgers never knew..."*: idem.
    "He's just sent...": Lois Hunt, interview with author.
    "Infidelity is taken...": interview with author.
    "... never going to leave...": interview with author.
206 *"... God has this girlfriend..."*: interview with author.

Chapter Twelve

"NOBODY'S HEART"

207 Chapter title is taken from the song of the same name by Richard Rodgers and Lorenz Hart.
    He missed the opening: on November 23, 1938; DR, p. 126.
    Made the necessary changes: EW, p. 177.
    "... he'd written the verse...": MS, pp. 191–92.
208 *The company went up to New Haven:* November 3 to 5, 1938.
    "How much longer...": MS, p. 192.
    "joyous romp": BO, p. 513.
    "... bad grammar": MS, p. 193.
210 *Opened for tryouts:* March 7 to 9 and March 12 to 30, 1940.
    "... just like it": interview with author.
    "... we have another one...": *New York Sun,* March 27, 1940.

"... *knock you over*": interview with author.

"... *trained seal* ...": MS, p. 195.

212 *"Gigolos were not new* ...": BO, p. 522.

"*Comparison of an early* ...": *The O'Hara Concern*, Matthew J. Bruccoli, 1975, p. 163.

"*I remember being impressed* ...": *Dancing on the Ceiling*, Stephen M. Silverman, 1996, p. 28.

213 *"more common, venal* ...": idem.

"... *street urchin toughness*": BO, p. 523.

214 *"Hart conveys* ...": *Enchanted Evenings*, Geoffrey Block, 1997, p. 109.

215 "... *welcome musical contrast* ...": idem, p. 209.

"*I'm wild again* ...": M-C, p. 245.

Something like three weeks: NO, p. 273.

Righteous indignation: *The O'Hara Concern*, Matthew J. Bruccoli, 1975, p. 163.

216 *"It cost ten thousand* ...": *Mister Abbott*, George Abbott, 1963, p. 195.

A round of bars: NO, p. 277.

"... *a marvelous little fellow* ...": NO, p. 273.

217 *Laughed at the jokes:* NO, pp. 278–79.

"... *a load of dancing* ...": *Time*, January 6, 1941.

"... *stunned silence*": *New York Times*, December 30, 1951.

"... *wouldn't come out*": NO, p. 281.

A masterpiece: Harold Clurman, *New Republic*, January 21, 1952.

"... *it's the only one* ...": London *Sunday Times*, November 5, 1963.

Wearing dark glasses: December 22, 1940.

218 "... *He worshiped him!*": interview with author.

"... *Dick was nodding* ...": interview with author.

"... *down and dirty* ...": interview with author.

219 *Used to put his arm:* interview with author.

"... *a deep, dark secret*": interview with author.

Rodgers's "minder": interview with author.

"... *I didn't know* ...": interview with author.

"... *a mutual responsibility* ...": *New York Times*, May 5, 1940.

220 "... *constructive suggestions*": MS, p. 208.

A new collaborator: M-C, pp. 247–48.

"*We would be so happy* ...": telegram, June 29, 1941.

Was made into a film: in 1959.

"... *Will you think* ...": letter, July 6, 1941.

When Hart could not "function": MS, p. 209.

221 "... *I had him* ...": MS, p. 211.

Would promptly vanish: idem.

"... *chronic alcoholism* ...": Deposition, Surrogate's Court, 1/10/44.

"... *I'm sorry now* ...": interview with Jeffrey Lunden.

222 "... *all I can ever ask* ...": WI, p. 217.

Curled up on the steps, "how humiliated ...": Deposition, Surrogate's Court, 1/10/44.

"... *'Now I know* ...' ": interview with Jeffrey Lunden.

222   *Another success:* it ran from June 3, 1942 to June 12, 1943.
    "I may have been . . .": COH, p. 174.

223   *". . . an extraordinary love affair":* interview with author.
    ". . . a statute of limitations . . .": interview with author.
    A revival of Green Grow the Lilacs*:* from July 15 to July 20, 1940.
    ". . . the first to say . . .": interview with author.

225   *". . . she loved it too":* COH, p. 222.
    The usual explanations: COH, p. 222.
    ". . . that would be the end . . .": COH, p. 217.

226   *"in no condition . . .":* interview with Arnold Michaelis op cit.
    Even discussed the cast: letter, Charles Kalman to Seymour Britchky, October 5, 1976.
    "looking for a lyricist . . .": DH, p. 173.
    ". . . picking the horses . . .": DH, p. 173.
    ". . . a tug of war": idem.
    ". . . Frieda wasn't fooled . . .": DH, p. 171.

227   *". . . absolutely senseless . . .":* Deposition, Surrogate's Court, 1/8/44.
    Being seven and eleven: in 1942.
    "I believe Hart . . .": interview with author.
    ". . . He put up with Larry . . .": interview with author.
    ". . . it'll be playing . . .": COH, pp. 244–45.

228   *". . . a going concern":* MS, p. 230.
    ". . . the only one . . .": interview with author.
    ". . . arching its back . . .": *Buffalo Evening News,* March 24, 1944.
    ". . . a drinking binge . . .": MS, p. 230.
    ". . . he'd leave his coat . . .": COH, pp. 196–197.
    They sat there and drank: interview with Jeffrey Lunden.

229   *Shuffling along:* as told to author by Bert Fink.

230   *". . . is a runt":* *New York Times,* December 10, 1948.
    ". . . horribly inadequate and embarrassing . . .": idem.
    "They had a story . . .": COH, p. 219.

231   *". . . falling down drunk . . .":* NO, p. 310.
    ". . . He had left orders . . .": M-C, p. 264.
    "It was Richard Rodgers . . .": Deposition, Surrogate's Court, 1/10/44.

232   *He was coaxed:* DH, p. 180.
    "He wasn't sober! . . .": idem.
    ". . . staring straight ahead . . .": idem.
    ". . . asked Hart to leave . . .": M-C, p. 265; DH, p. 180.
    "When I looked in . . .": DH, p. 180.
    ". . . Fritz went out looking . . .": *Broadway Anecdotes,* Peter Hay, 1989, p. 339.
    ". . . Larry's heart had stopped . . .": MS, p. 181.

233   *His death was such a waste:* *Great Performances,* January 6, 1999.

234   *"There goes the murderer":* M-C, p. 272.
    He had no control: COH, p. 219.
    Rodgers never mentioned: EW, p. 184.
    "I had interviewed . . .": interview with author.

". . . [Rodgers] had been . . . cruel . . .": interview with author.

". . . you'd better get . . .": interview with author.

Chapter Thirteen

"MANY A NEW DAY"

235 Chapter title taken from the song of the same name by Richard Rodgers and Oscar Hammerstein.

Named for his uncle: DH, p. 180.

A letter written on his behalf: Harry Phillips Jr. spelled out the changes Hart wanted to have made in a letter to the New York Life Insurance company re: policy #10028538 on December 5, 1932.

236 *A novel way of protecting Larry:* COH, pp. 180; MS, p. 205.

Hours in his company: COH, p. 180.

An auction to pay off his debts: Larry Hart, interview with author.

"did not know what he was doing . . .": New York Times, December 29, 1943.

237 *". . . knew exactly what he was doing . . .":* COH, p. 195.

Statements about Hart's behavior compiled from depositions made in Surrogate's Court and a daily record from Dr. Jacques R. Fischl, dated 12/13/44, about the period September 1942–November 1943.

They accepted a settlement: New York Times, July 12, 1947.

238 *Present value of the trust:* Larry Hart, interview with author.

239 *"I'll never forget . . .":* Larry Hart to author. Since Dorothy Hart's death, on April 11, 2000, at the age of ninety-four, Lorenz Hart's trust set up to benefit her and her husband has closed, and the Hart family no longer has any legal control over the Hart estate.

It ran for 477 performances: from February 7, 1923, to March 29, 1924.

Rose-Marie's *run:* from September 2, 1924, to January 16, 1926.

Show Boat's *run:* from December 27, 1927, to May 4, 1929.

Sweet Adeline's *run:* September 3, 1929, to March 22, 1930.

241 *"I've done it before . . .":* Broadway Anecdotes, Peter Hay, 1989, p. 116.

"His own humor . . .": FO, p. xii.

". . . that benign mask?' ": letter, November 18, 1953.

"as tough as . . .": interview with author.

". . . to trip them up . . .": Stephen Sondheim, Meryle Secrest, 1998, p. 37.

"lurched into sarcasm": FO, p. xiii.

". . . scars have formed": Stephen Sondheim, Meryle Secrest, 1998, p. 37.

242 *". . . the extraordinary serenity . . .":* FO, p. xi.

"a rumpled paper bag": SMUOH, p. 3.

". . . twice as much . . .": interview with Jeffrey Lunden.

". . . a great admirer . . .": interview with author.

". . . a dreary plain": Broadway Babies Say Goodnight, Mark Steyn, 1997, pp. 80–81.

243 *Date of Pearl Harbor:* December 7, 1941.

245 *". . . a long step . . ."*: *Musical Comedy in America*, Cecil Smith and Glenn Litton, 1981, p. 198.

". . . musical complacency . . .": WI.

246 *"I should like . . ."*: *New York Herald Tribune*, December 3, 1944.

247 *". . . simple and pure"*: COH, p. 230.

248 *". . . looking at the corn . . ."*: *New York Herald Tribune*, July 8, 1945.

249 *". . . offhand sketches . . ."*: *New Yorker*, April 10, 1943.

"an affecting simplicity": BO, p. 535.

Made of cement: COH, p. 241.

". . . an obvious technique . . .": *New York Herald Tribune*, December 3, 1944.

250 *". . . that lovely sound . . ."*: *Argosy*, April 1944.

". . . most popular song . . .": BO, p. 535.

". . . this would ruin . . .": COH, pp. 235–36.

251 *" 'Let her pray!' "*: interview with Jeffrey Lunden.

". . . provocation and fun": interview with Jeffrey Lunden.

252 *". . . 'Where have you been . . .' "*: interview with Jeffrey Lunden.

"moderately short and squarish . . .": *And Promenade Home*, Agnes De Mille, 1958, p. 235.

253 *". . . we didn't have a show . . ."*: interview with Jeffrey Lunden.

254 *". . . not one single penny . . ."*: COH, p. 226.

She got her money: American Herald, February/March 1993.

". . . the pigeons flew up . . .": interview with Jeffrey Lunden.

255 *A can of tomatoes: The Sound of Their Music*, Frederick Nolan, 1978, p. 26.

". . . whooping and hollering": interview with Jeffrey Lunden.

". . . do up the zipper": interview with Jeffrey Lunden.

". . . this is the only . . .": *American Herald*, February/March, 1993.

". . . a thousand lanterns": idem.

256 *". . . the emotional sweep . . ."*: essay in program for the Royal National Theatre revival of *Oklahoma!*, 7/15/98.

Oklahoma! opened in London on April 29, 1947.

". . . big gold curtains": interview with author.

Princesses Elizabeth and Margaret: Royal National Theatre program for *Oklahoma!*

". . . like fairy princesses": interview with author.

"every word . . .": *Look*, April 2, 1968.

Three plays had longer runs: Business Week, August 11, 1951. *Oklahoma!* closed on May 29, 1948.

257 *Rodgers recalled meeting:* letter from Rita Chambers to J. C. Ogletree, June 18, 1973.

". . . young together": interview with author.

". . . doing a musical": idem.

258 *". . . It wasn't quite true"*: DROH, pp. 107–108.

". . . liked to break the form . . .": interview with author.

259 *". . . this is my instinct . . ."*: idem.

". . . an extra ten minutes . . .": DROH, p. 113.

". . . a pain in the ass . . .": interview with author.

Chapter Fourteen
"ALLEGRO"

261 *Could not find:* APB, p. 164.
262 *"quite elaborate dishes . . .":* APB, p. 167.
"*. . . tuna fish casserole":* interview with author.
263 "*. . . an independent life . . .":* interview with author.
Neither of them said: MS, p. 196.
264 *"I was never able . . .":* MS, p. 210.
"*. . . wallowing in mud":* letter, September 28, 1945.
"*. . . never be able . . .":* DROH, p. 105.
A Connecticut Yankee ran from November 17, 1943, to March 11, 1944, for 135
performances.
265 "*. . . sharpened their epigrams . . .":* interview with author.
266 "*. . . that is sexy":* idem.
"*. . . They were going to kill . . .":* idem.
"*. . . a woman of great principle . . .":* interview with author.
"Do you want me to go . . .": interview with author.
267 "*. . . a tricky proposition":* interview with author.
268 *"never, ever, acknowledged . . .":* interview with author.
Lovemaking was wonderful: interview with author.
"I'm crazy about . . .": letter, April 3, 1945.
"*. . . part of the world . . .":* interview with author.
269 *"Don't hold your breath":* interview with Jeffrey Lunden.
"*. . . my hat and coat?":* interview with author.
"*. . . burst into tears":* idem.
270 *Hart had translated:* NO, p. 36.
271 "*. . . taken from him":* *New York Herald Tribune,* March 26, 1940.
272 "*. . . romantic effectiveness":* idem.
273 "*. . . lessen the horror . . .":* *Saturday Review,* May 5, 1945.
"*. . . we could see no light . . .":* liner notes for Morton Gould recording of
Carousel, undated.
"*. . . Hammerstein decided to go ahead . . .":* interview with author.
Talks were going on earlier: in late 1943.
"we could never have written . . .": *New York Times,* April 10, 1949.
"*. . . completely broken":* *The Magic Curtain,* Lawrence Langner, 1951, p. 391.
274 "*. . . contentment, tranquility . . .":* *Broadway Babies Say Goodnight,* Mark
Steyn, 1997, p. 92.
275 *"but you don't think . . .":* idem.
"*. . . like this freedom":* *New Haven Register,* August 30, 1970.
276 *"psychological realism . . .":* *New York Times,* April 9, 1945.
Polishing stars: Enchanted Evenings, Geoffrey Block, 1997, pp. 161–62.
"a Rotarian atmosphere . . .": *New Republic,* March 1, 1993.
276 "*. . . reservoir of melodies . . .":* *Broadway,* Brooks Atkinson, 1970, p. 340.
277 "*. . . that umbrella":* interview with author.

277 *Closed two years later: Business Week,* August 11, 1951.

"It affects me deeply . . .": MS, p. 243.

They called it Williamson: Rodgers and Hart, inventing a compound of their names, had founded Rodart Music Publishing in association with Max Dreyfus in 1931.

Who passed it on: COH, p. 266.

At the Music Box: on October 19, 1944.

". . . bit of a brat": COH, p. 266.

278 *Ran for 714 performances: Business Week,* August 11, 1951.

Happy Birthday opened on October 31, 1946, and closed on March 13, 1948.

". . . most belligerent cucumber . . .": Josh, Joshua Logan, 1976, p. 235.

"'. . . we'll produce it'": COH, pp. 268–69.

". . . Welfare Island Hospital . . .": COH, p. 269. Jerome Kern died on November 11, 1945, at the age of sixty.

279 *Put the song back:* COH, p. 271.

The musical opened: on May 16, 1946, and ran until February 12, 1949.

Their annual payroll: The Nation's Business, August 1950.

280 *The book was by Hammerstein:* COH, p. 279.

"a vast and woolly . . .": New Yorker, October 18, 1947.

281 *". . . wanted him to like . . .":* interview with author.

282 *"'You put that back . . .'":* interview with author.

Should be ruthless: letter, September 6, 1947.

". . . no monopoly . . .": Saturday Review, November 8, 1947.

". . . It wasn't about . . .": Stephen Sondheim, Meryle Secrest, 1998, pp. 53–54.

283 *". . . very poor notices . . .":* interview with author.

A respectable 315 performances: from October 10, 1947, to July 10, 1948.

A year to break even: Boston Sunday Post, September 7, 1947.

". . . you have nothing": New York Sun, September 5, 1947.

". . . they were both manic": interview with Jeffrey Lunden.

". . . a terrible time . . .": MCOH.

284 *". . . I've had it myself":* interview with author.

". . . the white knight . . .": idem.

285 *". . . my lumbar vertebrae":* MS, p. 243.

". . . Dick had panicked . . .": interview with author.

". . . there were small symptoms . . .": idem.

". . . see your warts": idem.

286 *". . . It was upsetting . . .":* interview with author.

Chapter Fifteen

"SO FAR"

287 Chapter title taken from the song of the same name by Richard Rodgers and Oscar Hammerstein.

"There was no way . . .": New York Times, April 10, 1949.

288 *"Pinza came East . . .":* *Cosmopolitan,* May 1950.
"*. . . doesn't think it's vocal":* idem.

290 *"Never sing it . . .":* *My Heart Belongs,* Mary Martin, 1976, p. 160.
Filled with flowers: idem, pp. 22–23.

291 "*. . . Then I lean down . . .":* interview with author.
"This proves . . .": FO, p. 43.
"*. . . she had poured her voice . . .":* *Spectator,* November 24, 1951.
"*. . . the most fantastic rumors . . .":* letter to Joshua Logan, June 3, 1949.

292 *Sit and do needlepoint:* Canon Louis C. Schueddig to author.
They went nowhere: memo to Joshua Logan, undated, c. 1952.
"a really mean tongue . . .": SMUOH, p. 22.
"*. . . They just never know . . .":* letter, May 8, 1949.
"*. . . cried out in pain . . .":* interview with author.

294 *Actually predates* South Pacific: the film appeared in 1947.
"*. . . no means unachievable":* *American Mercury,* xii, p. 115.

295 *"From this ancient . . .":* to Edward Marcus, October 13, 1959.
"Wish I could be there . . .": to Nita Novy, June 13, 1961.
"I'm only a small . . .": letter to Edward Jablonski, October 30, 1961.
He could be crude: Bruce Pomahac to author.
"I prefer Providence . . .": interview with author.
"Go back and ask . . .": David Raksin to author.

296 *"That was typical . . .":* interview with author.
"*. . . He didn't take . . .":* interview with author.
"warm, relaxed time . . .": *Josh,* Joshua Logan, 1976, p. 282.
"He was so sought . . .": idem.

297 *Deeply shocked his friend:* *Winchell,* Neal Gabler, 1994, pp. 348–49.
"*. . . he died quietly . . .":* untitled manuscript; he died November 17, 1948.
"*. . . the first five years . . .":* *American Weekly,* March 6, 1955.
"*. . . major depression . . .":* *New York Times Magazine,* October 4, 1992.
"she simply isn't . . .": letter dated April 22, 1949.
"*. . . slow and uncertain":* letter to Joshua Logan, May 8, 1949.
"*. . . tedious and painful . . .":* letter dated June 19, 1951.

298 "*. . . nobody ever saw . . .":* interview with author.
"*. . . Crying and twisting . . .":* interview with author.
"*. . . it is just hell . . .":* letter, March 18, 1952.

299 "*. . . end of the friendship":* interview with author.
"*. . . didn't have any trouble . . .":* interview with author.
"It was around Christmas . . .": interview with author.

300 "*. . . it's pronounced Le*vine*":* idem.
"Did you sleep . . .": Lois Hunt to author.
"the fecund act": interview with author.

301 *Nothing really nefarious:* letter, July 3, 1951, in Federal Bureau of Investigation
files, No. 100-382318.
Rodgers and Hammerstein week: from August 31 to September 6, 1953.
A program on all four networks: on March 28, 1954.
A program of his own music: on February 22, 1954.

303 *Ignoring the orchestrator: Los Angeles Herald-Examiner,* May 8, 1966.
"... '*Arrange me a hit*' ...": letter, May 23, 1966.
"... *I find missing* ...": WI, p. 217.

304 "... *the wrong hymnal!*": idem, p. 221.
"... *It was always tasteful* ...": interview with author.
"... *a minor miracle* ...": interview with author.
"*colorful orchestrations* ...": March 30, 1951.
Completely wrong for them: EW, p. 279.

305 "*While Dick has never* ...": idem, p. 281.
"... *appropriate for battleships*": interview with author.
Their futures secure: as described by Dorothy Rodgers in DROH.
"*If you lose ... momentum* ...": interview with author.

306 *A strongly worded letter:* September 24, 1953.
He did not want: idem.
"*completely stepped on* ...": September 29, 1953.
"*Did you get* ...": letter of April 21, 1955.
"*My feeling coincides* ...": April 15, 1955.
"*The very conception* ...": letter of February 25, 1957.
"... *makes me feel creepy* ...": May 24, 1958.

307 "... *giving me a nightmare* ...": April 30, 1953.
"... *so good at concealing* ...": interview with author.
Did not like to work: New York Post, 1963.
Most painful days: FO, pp. 298–99.

309 *Gertrude Lawrence was fifty-two:* she was born on July 4, 1898.

310 *A vocal coach:* MS, p. 273.
"... *jewelled babouches* ...": *Vogue,* August 15, 1951.
"*Western audiences* ...": MS, p. 273.
"... *Siam as seen* ...": idem, p. 274.
A model in reverse: Stephen Sondheim, Meryle Secrest, 1998, pp. 279–80.

311 "... *admiring applause*": *Collier's,* April 7, 1951.

312 "... *the right movement*": interview with author.
"*we all loved it*": idem.

313 "... *whose awakening mind* ...": *New York Post,* March 30, 1951.
"... *terse and vivid* ...": *New York Times,* April 8, 1951.
"... *each to himself*": letter to R. Kaplan, April 9, 1953.
"... *tremendously moving*": *New York Times,* April 8, 1951.
"... *unremittingly wholesome* ...": *New Yorker,* April 7, 1951.
Film of The King and I: in 1956.

314 "... *sending their money* ...": letter to author, October 21, 1997.
Still she complained: New York Herald Tribune, April 1, 1951.
"... *sentimental melodies*": BO, p. 578.
"*a whirling invitation* ...": *Musical Comedy in America,* Cecil Smith and Glenn
   Litton, 1991, p. 209.

315 *Made light of the comments:* MS, p. 275.
Severely shaken: as told to author by Stephen Sondheim.

Chapter Sixteen
"THE MAN I USED TO BE"

316 Chapter title taken from the song of the same name by Richard Rodgers and
    Oscar Hammerstein.
    ". . . as truthfully as possible": undated essay by Richard Rodgers.
318 *"No one had thought . . ."*: *Mr. Abbott*, George Abbott, 1963, p. 247.
319 *A very difficult song:* interview with author.
    Twelve days of tryouts: beginning April 20, 1953.
    The Shubert in Boston: beginning May 6, 1953.
320 *". . . not in good shape"*: MS, p. 283.
    Interjected arbitrarily: interview with author.
    ". . . Can we still go out?": interview with author.
321 *". . . If this be treason . . ."*: letter, April 30, 1953.
    ". . . deeply in love": from an unpublished memoir.
    ". . . not top-drawer . . .": *Mr. Abbott*, George Abbott, 1963, p. 247.
    Two months at capacity: April 7 to May 29, 1954.
    Too sure of themselves: *Mr. Abbott*, George Abbott, 1963, p. 246.
322 *". . . 'I hate that show' . . ."*: letter to author, October 21, 1997.
    A revival of On Your Toes: October 11 to December 4, 1954.
    ". . . too old to cry": letter to Dr. Sol Ginsburg, October 29, 1954.
    ". . . all that criticism": interview with author.
    ". . . dead-fish handshake": interview with author.
323 *Asking for trouble:* MFT, p. 228.
    "make a break . . .": idem.
    The tablecloths were pink: idem, p. 229.
324 *Making notes:* House and Garden, June 1952.
    A full-time gardener: New Yorker, November 18, 1961.
325 *". . . bursting with fat"*: letter, February 10, 1950.
    ". . . nobody could accuse . . .": SMUOH, p. 13.
327 *"In those days . . ."*: It Happened on Broadway, Myrna Katz Frommer and Har-
    vey Frommer, 1998, p. 112.
    ". . . John's literary stamp . . .": idem.
    Rodgers would have nothing to do: idem, p. 113.
    ". . . not just Oscar": interview with author.
328 *". . . not right for Oscar . . ."*: MS, pp. 338–339.
    Pal Joey's characters: MS, p. 339.
    "a mistake I haven't . . .": MS, p. 340.
    ". . . epidemic within a show . . .": MS, p. 339.
329 *Still in his twenties:* in 1928.
    ". . . some immunity . . .": from an untitled manuscript.
    Diagnosed cancer: EW, p. 298.
    ". . . cried and apologized . . .": untitled manuscript.
    ". . . didn't want to die": interview, December 18, 1957.
330 *". . . It was just terror"*: MCOH, pp. 307–308.

330 *"... publicity was minimal":* interview with author.
"... *we were all ... worried ...":* interview with author.
Barely able to speak: EW, p. 299.
331 "... *good, ambitious kids ...":* letter, September 27, 1955.
"... *laughed so hard ...":* interview with author.
"... *universally accepted ...":* MS, p. 287. The musical opened on November
    30, 1955, and ran until June 30, 1956.
"... *a natural wariness ...":* interview with Arnold Michaelis, December 18,
    1957.
"... *What was hard ...":* MCOH, p. 433.
332 "... *keep it that way ...":* letter, August 27, 1954.
Considered disappointing: COH, p. 244.
333 *"You're just like ...":* interview with author.
"So far I haven't ...": letter, January 16, 1956.
334 "... *especially the latter":* January 20, 1956.
The autumn of 1954: September 30, 1954.
She was ideal as Eliza: from an interview with Tony Walton.
"a most peculiar ...": letter, November 8, 1956.
335 South Pacific *revival:* July 8 to August 10, 1957.
Had fallen downstairs: Edna Ferber to Dorothy Rodgers, June 26, 1957.
336 *"Everyone knew ...":* interview with author.
"... *excruciating pain":* letter, November 22, 1985.
"... *much too smart ...":* interview with author.
337 *"I began sleeping ...":* MS, p. 293.
"... *couldn't have anything ...":* interview with author.
338 "... *how miserable ...":* interview with author.
"... *hard on Dick":* letter, August 4, 1957.
"untroubled by problems ...": MS, p. 294.
339 *En route to Hawaii:* letter, August 22, 1957.
Back for a rest: letter, Edna Ferber to Dorothy Rodgers, July 21, 1957.
"... *never felt better ...":* letter, October 18, 1957.

Chapter Seventeen

"THE SKY FALLS DOWN"

340 Chapter title from the song "A Hundred Million Miracles" by Richard Rodgers
    and Oscar Hammerstein.
"... *every joke and gimmick ...":* Gene Kelly: A Biography, *Clive Hirschhorn,
    1974, p. 259.
341 "... *just not funny ...":* letter to author, July 11, 1997.
"... *No one's good ...":* interview with author.
"... *so nobody could see ...":* interview with author.
342 "... *Aren't you proud?":* letter, September 30, 1958.
"... *he must be as worried ...":* letter, October 1, 1958.
343 *"Gene had nothing ...":* letter, October 3, 1958.
"... *we'll have a score ...":* letter, October 4, 1958.

"... *I'd be happier* ...": letter, October 6, 1958.
"... *I've got reasons* ...": idem.
"*Dutch-uncle*" *confidence:* December 27, 1958.
"... *woozy song*": December 13, 1958.

345 "... *said they would wait*": COH, p. 349.
She walked away: Vanity Fair, June 1998, p. 174.
"... *over the mountains* ...": interview with author.

348 "... *an actor's strengths*": interview with author.

349 "... *only in German*": *Theo,* Theodore Bikel, 1994, p. 210.
"... *also human beings*": interview with author.
"... *took a bow*": *Theo,* Theodore Bikel, 1994, p. 210.

350 "... *nobody was speaking!*": interview with author.
"... *We all chorused* ...": idem.
"*Great Leap Backwards*": *New Yorker,* November 28, 1959.
Tripped over stones: London *Sunday Telegraph,* May 21, 1966.

351 *Schnitzel with Noodles: New Yorker,* February 14, 2000.
"... *They were wonderful* ...": interview with author.

352 "... *he never remembered* ...": idem.
"*cried as he watched* ...": FO, p. 352.
How little time: idem.
Would she take over: MCOH, p. 415.

354 *Two years before:* in 1957.
Chilling Sweeney Todd*:* in 1979.
"*boulevard nihilism*": *New Yorker,* June 18, 1993.
"... *nothing I can do* ...": August 15, 1960.

355 "*I was just wondering* ...": MS, p. 303.
"... *first to be told* ...": August 23, 1960.
"... *not to get killed*": *New York Times,* March 11, 1962.
"... *the best doctor* ...": MCOH, p. 60.
Afraid of dying: interview with author.
Too emotionally taxing: letter to Robert W. Sarnoff, December 24, 1971.
"... '*waste land*' *philosophy*": *New Yorker,* June 18, 1993.

356 "*Leave it alone* ...": interview with Arnold Michaelis on *Camera Three.*
"*right and shining words* ...": undated letter.
So moved Rodgers: letter dated April 10, 1962.
How could he forget: letter to James McCollum, October 11, 1961.
"... *What would I do* ...": *New York Times,* March 11, 1962.
"*My recollection is* ...": *New York Post,* June 24, 1962.

357 "... *sufficiently Oriental*": *New York Times,* March 11, 1962.
"*It was my idea* ...": interview with author.

358 "*Don't you do that* ...": interview with author.
"*We never talked* ...": idem.
"*Jerry told me* ...": interview with author.

359 "*absolutely no difficulty* ...": letter, September 5, 1961.
"... *drunken little fag*": *Diahann!* Diahann Carroll with Ross Firestone, 1986,
    p. 109.
Never quite trusted: idem, p. 110.

360 *"The comment was admiring . . ."*: interview with author.
      Actually getting up early: Richmond Times-Dispatch, April 30, 1961.
      "Some of the time . . .": March 26, 1962.
      ". . . an adventurous youth": *New York Herald Tribune,* March 11, 1962.
      ". . . a whole new venture . . .": interview with author.
      ". . . four hours' sleep": interview with author.
361 *". . . throw out the rest"*: idem.
      "Your music is . . .": March 15, 1962.
      ". . . abject terror . . .": March 16, 1962.
      ". . . a sensational boy . . .": undated letter.
      "When Oscar finished . . .": *New York Post,* June 24, 1962.

                              Chapter Eighteen
                       LOOKING STRAIGHT AHEAD

362 *". . . how does one go on . . ."*: interview with author.
      ". . . amazingly generous . . .": interview with author.
363 *". . . 'How could I not?'"*: idem.
      Not make any more loans: letter to Duke McHale, June 5, 1967.
      Thoughtfully chosen book: as told by William Hammerstein.
      "I don't think . . .": letter, April 26, 1961.
      ". . . a little more heart . . .": November 11, 1960.
364 *Turned down* On the Waterfront*:* letter, March 22, 1968.
      "there is so little . . .": March 18, 1965.
      Nothing came of The Corn Is Green*:* letter, April 15, 1968.
      "absolutely nothing . . .": letter to Johnny Green, April 1, 1968.
      "A very smart woman . . .": January 13, 1964.
      Such a sordid story: The Wordsmiths, Stephen Citron, 1995, p. 332.
366 *"He's a horrible guy . . ."*: *New York Post,* January 7, 1966.
      ". . . a certain stimulus . . .": letter, November 6, 1961.
      ". . . period costumes . . .": letter, April 22, 1968.
367 *Demanding terms:* Rodgers to Jerry Whyte, May 6, 1965.
      Hotchner withdrew: Choice People, A. E. Hotchner, 1984, p. 395.
369 *". . . drags horribly . . ."*: London *Daily Telegraph,* November 8, 1963.
      ". . . a monumental folly . . .": London *Sunday Telegraph,* November 8, 1963.
370 *"small, intimate . . ."*: letter, December 7, 1962.
      "In point of fact . . .": idem.
371 *". . . that kind of imagination"*: interview with author.
372 *". . . you're in trouble"*: interview with author.
      ". . . During intermission": idem.
373 *". . . they often were"*: idem.
      "He was no fool": idem.
      ". . . he was half-gone . . .": interview with author.
      "Matthew came into . . .": MCOH, pp. 274–75.
      Semiweekly blood tests: Jerry Whyte to Paul Gallico, July 15, 1966.
374 *". . . She has fallen apart"*: letter to Johnny Green, August 22, 1966.

"The house looks . . .": September 21, 1966.

". . . with elaborate bows": interview with author.

375 *"All my caricatures . . .":* *New York Times,* November 12, 1967.

"We did it on tape . . .": interview with author.

376 *"If you really . . .":* idem.

377 *He was fired: New York Sunday News,* June 25, 1967.

"My father used . . .": MCOH, p. 229.

". . . an honest response": interview with author.

378 *Two days of flying:* DROH, p. 142.

". . . very peculiar . . .": MCOH, p. 307.

"I didn't think . . .": idem.

". . . quite some scene . . .": interview with author.

379 *". . . agreed to join us . . .":* MS, p. 321.

". . . still terrible": interview with author.

381 *". . . ever close to anyone":* idem.

". . . just terrible": idem.

"moderately successful . . .": letter to Shai Holsaert, January 7, 1972.

". . . I am not sure . . .": letter to Peter Zeisler, November 6, 1970.

"It just isn't . . .": letter to Jerry Whyte, January 7, 1972.

Chapter Nineteen

THE KEY TO THE CURTAIN

382 *"crossed over into . . .":* *New York Times Magazine,* June 2, 1996.

". . . America's most characteristic . . .": *New Yorker,* November 18, 1961.

Closer to a thousand: The checklist of Rodgers's published works has a total of 366.

383 *". . . something else entirely":* *New Yorker,* November 18, 1961.

". . . finished their coffee": *New York Times Magazine,* June 2, 1996.

384 *"lost golden spaces . . .":* Michael Beckerman, *New York Times,* December 20, 1998.

". . . 'No, it's my job' ": *American Weekly,* July 22, 1962.

385 *". . . grids of perception . . .":* *Tyranny of the Normal,* Leslie Fiedler, 1996, p. 112.

". . . implicit messages": idem.

". . . retreat into schizophrenia": *Broadway Babies Say Goodnight,* Mark Steyn, 1997, p. 139.

". . . kicking sentiment around . . .": *Holiday,* February 1959.

386 *". . . a kind of not living . . .":* *Drama Guild Quarterly,* 1971.

". . . looking for his father": *Yale Daily News,* May 9, 1967.

387 *A slap-up finale:* letter from Tom Stoppard to Richard Rodgers, September 15, 1972.

"Rodgers finally grinned . . .": interview with author.

". . . a pretty bad coronary . . .": letter, May 18, 1972.

". . . pretty vigorous croquet": letter to Lawrence P. Bachmann, October 2, 1972.

". . . deeply and emotionally . . .": June 26, 1972.

388 *". . . knee-jerk reaction . . .":* interview with author.

388 *"galloping laryngitis"*: letter, April 9, 1974.
"... went into a box ...": interview with author.
"... we'll meet again ...": letter, March 14, 1975.
"... shattering changes ...": March 21, 1975.

389 *"... speech therapy ..."*: interview with author.
"... I am kidding you not ...": interview with author.

390 *"... 'He never showed up ...'"*: interview with author.
"... how impressed I was ...": interview with author.

391 *"... a feeling man ..."*: interview with author.
"... the redeeming values ...": interview with author.

392 *"... what I was doing"*: interview with author.
"... almost an illness": interview with author.
"... perhaps justified": interview with author.
"... down front and backstage": interview with author.
"... explain that behavior": interview with author.

393 *"... an awful experience ..."*: interview with author.
Ran for 49 performances: April 25 to June 5, 1976.

394 *"... a terrible cold ..."*: interview with author.
"I was struck ...": letter to author, December 24, 1998.
"... an old lady ...": interview with author.
"... the funny quip ...": interview with author.

396 *"... good of the project"*: interview with author.
Account of the afternoon Richard Rodgers met with Alexander Cohen is taken
   from two accounts Mary Rodgers Guettel gave to the author and from her
   version in MCOH, p. 423.

398 *"... All her perfectionism ..."*: interview with author.
"... 'I have loved her ...'": interview with author.
Closed on Labor Day: September 2, 1979.

399 *"... the Shubert office"*: interview with author.
"fresh and eager ...": letter to Bob Alexander, April 28, 1976.
"... haven't the energy ...": letter to John McCabe, September 25, 1979.
"... this huge pet": interview with author.
"... the role reversal ...": interview with author.
"... like a hawk ...": interview with author.
"... never found anything": idem.

400 *"... thought she was"*: idem.
"... like a baby ...": interview with author.
"... a piece of Scarlatti": idem.
"... just felt so sorry ...": interview with author.

401 *"... a single dream ..."*: *The Great Gatsby,* F. Scott Fitzgerald, 1953, p. 162.
"I'm still looking ...": MS, p. 327.

Index

Page numbers in *italics* refer to illustrations.

437

Permissions Acknowledgments

Special thanks are due to Mary Rodgers Guettel for permission to make quotations from her Columbia Oral History and her Oral History for Southern Methodist University: used by permission of Mary Rodgers Guettel. All Rights Reserved. Quotations from the Columbia Oral History, the miscellaneous writings and published and unpublished letters of Richard Rodgers, are used by permission of the Rodgers and Hammerstein Organization. The quotation from a letter of Dorothy Rodgers and quotations from her oral history of Radcliffe College are also made by permission of the Rodgers and Hammerstein Organization. Finally, excerpts from Richard Rodgers's autobiography, *Musical Stages,* are used by permission of the Rodgers and Hammerstein Organization, © 1975 by Richard Rodgers. All Rights Reserved.

Grateful acknowledgment is made for permission to quote from the following lyrics: "The Sweetest Sounds" by Richard Rodgers, © 1962 by Richard Rodgers, copyright renewed. Williamson Music owner of publication and allied rights throughout the world. International copyright secured. All rights reserved. Reprinted by permission; "I Cain't Say No," by Richard Rodgers and Oscar Hammerstein II estate, © 1943 by Williamson Music, copyright renewed. International copyright secured. All rights reserved. Reprinted by permission; "When the Children Are Asleep," by Richard Rodgers and Oscar Hammerstein II, © 1945 by Williamson Music, copyright renewed. International copyright secured. All rights reserved. Reprinted by permission; "A Puzzlement," by Richard Rodgers and Oscar Hammerstein II, © 1951 by Richard Rodgers and Oscar Hammerstein II, copyright renewed. Williamson Music owner of publication and allied rights throughout the world. International copyright secured. All rights reserved. Reprinted by permission; "A Cup of Tea," © 1986 by estate of Richard Rodgers and estate of Lorenz Hart, The Family Trust U/W Richard Rodgers and the Family Trust U/W Dorothy F. Rodgers (administered by Williamson Music) and the Estate of Lorenz Hart (administered by WB Music Corp.) owners of publication and allied rights throughout the world. All rights reserved. Used by permission; "The Blue Room," © 1926 (Renewed) Warner Bros. Inc. Rights for the Extended Renewal Term in the United States controlled by the estate of Lorenz Hart (administered by WB Music Corp.) and the Family Trust U/W Richard Rodgers and the Family Trust U/W Dorothy F. Rodgers (administered by Williamson Music). All rights reserved. Used by permission; "Dear Old Syracuse," © 1954, 1963 and 1965 (Copyrights Renewed) Chappell & Co. All rights reserved. Used by permission; "The Third Degree of Love," © 1986 the Trustees of Columbia University in the City of New York (administered by Williamson Music) and the estate of Lorenz Hart (administered by WB Music Corp.). All rights reserved. Used by permission; "Blue Moon," © 1934 (Renewed) Metro-Goldwyn-Mayer Inc. All rights controlled by EMI Robbins Catalog Inc. All rights reserved. Used by permission; "The Girl Friend," © 1926 (Renewed) Warner Bros. Inc. Rights for Extended Renewal Term in U.S. controlled by the estate of Lorenz Hart (administered by WB Music Corp.) and the Family Trust U/W Richard Rodgers and the Family Trust U/W Dorothy F. Rodgers (administered by Williamson Music). All rights reserved. Used by permission; "Give It Back to the Indians," © 1939 (Renewed) Chappell & Co. Rights for the Extended Renewal Term in the U.S. controlled by the estate of Lorenz Hart (administered by WB Music Corp.) and the Family Trust U/W Richard Rodgers and the Family Trust U/W Dorothy F. Rodgers (administered by Williamson Music). All rights reserved. Used by permission; "Gone Are the Days," © 1920 by Richard C. Rodgers. Copyright Renewed. Reprinted by permission of the Trustees of Columbia University in the City of New York (administered by Williamson Music) and the estate of Lorenz Hart (administered by WB Music Corp.). All rights reserved. Used by permission; "Her in My Arms," © 1925 (Renewed), Warner Bros. Inc. Rights for the Extended Renewal Term in the United States controlled by the estate of Lorenz Hart (administered by WB Music Corp.) and the Family Trust U/W Richard Rodgers and the Family Trust U/W Dorothy F. Rodgers (administered by Williamson Music). All rights reserved. Used by permission; "Ladies of the Box Office," © 1986 the estate of Richard Rodgers and the estate of Lorenz Hart. The Family Trust U/W Richard Rodgers and the Family Trust U/W Dorothy F. Rodgers

Grateful acknowledgment is also made to the Joshua Logan estate, for permission to quote from his letter to Oscar Hammerstein; to the Edna Ferber Literary Trust, for permission to quote from her letters to Richard Rodgers; to the Oscar Hammerstein II estate for permission to quote from letters of the late Oscar Hammerstein II; to the co-executors of the will of James Hammerstein for permission to quote from a letter; to Jonathan S. Reed for permission to quote from a letter; and to Bill Hayes for kind permission to quote from his unpublished memoir.

Photographic Credits

Margot F. Conte Collection: 84

Culver Pictures, Inc.: 5, 65, 121, 133, 147, 168, 169, 203, 270

Larry Hart Collection: 36, 187, 193, 216, 233

Zoe Hyde-Thomson Collection: 262, 263, 326

Library of Congress: 54, 118, 129, 145, 170, 172, 188, 240, 261, 279, 302

Museum of the City of New York: 27, 52, 124, 225, 238

New York Public Library at Lincoln Center: 153, 154, 370

Photofest: 37, 125, 140, 149, 151, 155, 157, 174, 185, 186, 189, 191, 195, 211, 213, 224, 229, 231, 243, 246, 265, 272, 319, 328, 346, 348, 369, 376, 380

Harry Ransom Humanities Research Center, the University of Texas at Austin, Theatre Arts Collection: 115

The Rodgers and Hammerstein Organization: 7, 9, 19, 20, 42, 61, 71, 77, 93, 99, 106, 109, 141, 166, 204, 209 (both), 214, 247, 248, 267, 274, 281, 289, 293, 294, 308, 309, 317 (both), 323, 333, 335, 339, 342, 346, 347, 353, 358, 359, 365, 371, 389, 395, 397

A Note on the Type

This book was set in Adobe Garamond. Designed for the Adobe Corporation by Robert Slimbach, the fonts are based on types first cut by Claude Garamond (c. 1480–1561). Garamond was a pupil of Geoffroy Tory and is believed to have followed the Venetian models, although he introduced a number of important differences, and it is to him that we owe the letter we now know as "old style." He gave to his letters a certain elegance and feeling of movement that won their creator an immediate reputation and the patronage of Francis I of France.

Composed by North Market Street Graphics,
Lancaster, Pennsylvania

Printed and bound by Quebecor Printing,
Fairfield, Pennsylvania